Arts & Crafts Churches

DOMINE

Arts & Crafts
CHURCHES

by

Alec Hamilton

LUND
HUMPHRIES

First published in 2020 by Lund Humphries

Lund Humphries
Office 3, Book House
261A City Road
London EC1V 1JX
UK
www.lundhumphries.com

ISBN: 978-1-84822-321-9

Copyedited by Alison Hill
Designed by Oliver Keen
Maps by Stu McLellan
Set in Adobe Garamond Pro
Printed in Slovenia

A Cataloguing-in-Publication record for this book is available from the British Library.

Front cover: St Andrew, Roker: east end
Back cover: Holy Trinity, Bothenhampton: altar front
Frontispiece: St Bartholomew, Brighton: east end

All photographs © the author, except on the following pages:

Geoff Brandwood: 11, 59, 87, 106, 110
Richard Cann: 153
George Cogswell: 232
Martin Crampin: 276, 281
James O Davies: front and back covers; 48, 51, 68, 256, 261, 262
Oliver Dixon (cc-by-sa/2.0): 204
Friends of Friendless Churches: 185, 274
Keith Greenough: 112 (left)
David Morris: 218
Arthur Rope: 209 (left)
John Salmon: frontispiece, 43, 100, 103, 104, 107, 109, 111, 116, 117, 118, 120, 122, 123, 135 (left), 200
Chris Stafford: 84, 93
Christian Tuckell: 147
Mark Watson: 224, 225, 226, 227, 236, 238, 312
Reproduced with permission from St Peter's Church, Blaxhall: 209 (right)
Reproduced by kind permission of St Hilda, Jesmond: 265
© The Hunterian, University of Glasgow: 292

To Mirabelle, Ursula, Charlie, Laurence,
Claire and Charlotte
and Susan

My remarks are the result of many years' observation; and are, I trust, true on the whole, though I do not pretend to say that they are perfectly void of mistake, or that a more nice observer might not make many additions, since subjects of this kind are inexhaustible.

GILBERT WHITE, *The Natural History of Selborne*,
Letter to Daines Barrington XVII (1789)

CONTENTS

ACKNOWLEDGEMENTS

My thanks to the many academics and researchers who were unfailingly encouraging and helpful along the way: first and foremost, my DPhil supervisors Paul Barnwell and Geoffrey Tyack; my examiners Andrew Saint and William Whyte; my kindly mentors Clyde Binfield, Peter Cormack, Alan Crawford, Mary Greensted, Peter Howell, Margaret Richardson, the late Gavin Stamp, Christopher Wakeling and Lynne Walker. And special thanks to Simon Green, for his generous help with the Scotland section.

Thanks also to those kindly scholars who responded with such generosity to my request for further churches to go and look at: James Bettley, Polly Blakesley, Simon Bradley, Paul Britton, Annette Carruthers, Louise Durning, Jennifer Freeman, Richard Halsey, Frank Kelsall, Julian Orbach and Ken Powell.

And to so many other supporters, positive influences and interested observers, including Malcolm Airs, Emma Anderson, Barrie and Wendy Armstrong, Jackie Banerjee, Alan Brooks, Alan Calder, Trevor Cooper, Elizabeth Cumming, Catherine Eyre, Gill Fitzpatrick, Charlotte Gere, Michael Hall, John Hume, Sharman Kadish, Ayla Lepine, Cyndy Manton, the late Charles McKean, Christopher Marsden, the late Neil Moat, John Morgan-Guy, the late Cathy Oakes, David Ottewill, Steve Pilcher, Alan Powers, Clare Price, Arthur Rope, Matthew Saunders, Alison Scott-Baumann, the late Sue Selwyn, Teresa Sladen, Steven Parissien, Phil Thomas, Kate Tiller, Adam Voelcker, Chris Webster and Rosemary Yallop.

To those who offered to take, then took, marvellous additional photographs, my great gratitude: Geoff Brandwood, Martin Crampin, James O Davies, John Salmon, Mark Watson; and to my friends in the Church Crawlers Anonymous Facebook group, in particular Chris Stafford. And to many other webmasters and webmistresses who supplied photographs.

And big bouquets to Rochelle Roberts, Val Rose, Sarah Thorowgood, Anna Norman and Oliver Keen at Lund Humphries, and to Alison Hill.

At the churches I am grateful to all those who opened up their church and met me there, and especially those who took lively interest: at Aberlour, Colin Stewart; at Barrow Hill, Ann Pickard; at Ben Rhydding Methodists, Laurence Turner, Kathleen Pinder, Colin Dews and Roger Davy; at Borth-y-Gest, Carol Cooper and Christine Dinneen; at Brockhampton, Jeremy Clay; at Charterhouse-on-Mendip, Jane Chamberlain; at Cheltenham College, Nicholas Lowton; at Chorleywood, Arderne Gillies; at Colehill, John Goodall; at Cricklewood, Chris Bayfield; at Curbridge, Tim Partridge; at Dockenfield, Maureen Stone, Tony Clayton, Ursula Howard and John Chuter; at Egremont, Wallasey, Alan Fernback; at Great Warley,

Fiona Agassiz; at Gunnerton, John Wylam and Michael Slade; at Hadleigh, Jan Byrne; at Haslemere, Frankie Gaiter; at Hatch End, Clive Pearce; at Haughton, Jill Cronin; at Hutton and Shenfield, Rod Greig; at Inkpen, Gerald Atkinson and Penny Stokes; at Kempley, Chris Bligh and Basil Jarvis; at Leeds Cathedral, Robert Finnigan; at Liscard, Wallasey, Terry Edgar; at Low Marple, Ed McKenna; at Matlock, John Drackley and Adam Bench; at Melsetter, the late Elsie Seatter; at Middleton, Christine Grime; at Onibury, Caroline Magnus; at Oxford House, John Ryan; at Paisley, Wesley Hands and Norman Gilkison; at Pamphill, Vera Ricketts; at Pixham, Alexandra Wedgwood; at Port Seton, Tom Donaldson and Sheila Bulloch; at Sloane Street, Nicholas Wheeler; at Small Heath, Oliver Coss; at Stamford Hill, Charles Card-Reynolds; at Stonebroom, Margaret Jacques, Sally Mason, Kath and Eddie Greenwood, Jennifer James and Graham Ullathorne; at Sudbury, Felicity Scroggie; at Summerstown, Roger Ryan; at Ullet Road, George Craig; at Welbeck, Derek Adlam; at West Woodhay, Lizzie Hayes, James Cole and Rachel Lewis; at Woolmer Green, Tony Rook.

I am especially indebted to eight historians who made special contributions: at Buckley, Malcolm Hislop; at Cross Green, Stephen Savage; at Hoarwithy, the late Philip Anderson; on W.H. Brierley, Edward Waterson; on Peter Macgregor Chalmers, the late Tom Davidson Kelly; on the Pinwills, Helen Wilson; on Richard Bassnett Preston, Ian Lucas; on William Seth-Smith, David Rodger. Thanks also to Torsten Fjastad for the loan of Norman Shaw's Richards Castle letters.

Thanks for help and advice to the many libraries, archives and record offices I haunted and plagued, especially Kate Jones and Kurt Helfrich at RIBA; Mark Smith at Derbyshire Records Office; Ann Laver at Dorking Museum; Cate Metheringham at Berkshire Records Office; Maggie Goodall at SPAB; Sue Killoran at Harris Manchester College; Alma Jenner at Mansfield College; Emma Walsh and Emily Burgoyne at Regent's Park College; Dolgellau Library Services; Dorset History Centre; Gloucestershire Archives; Haslemere Educational Library; Hertfordshire Archives; Liverpool Records Office; and Surrey History Centre.

The greatest thanks are to my wife Susan, who endured the conception, growth and eventual delivery of first the thesis, then the book; who delighted in the visits and encounters; and who mopped the brow, sometimes sternly, always lovingly.

LIST OF ABBREVIATIONS

ACES	Arts & Crafts Exhibition Society
ARIBA	Associate of the RIBA
AWG	Art Workers' Guild
(AWG)	Member of the Art Workers' Guild, with date of election
BL	British Library
BMSA	Birmingham Municipal School of Art
CofE	Church of England
CofS	Church of Scotland
CofW	Church of Wales (CinW after 1921)
Central School	London County Council Central School of Arts and Crafts
DSA	*Dictionary of Scottish Architects*
Episc	Episcopalian (church)
FC	Free Church of Scotland
FoFC	(Church in care of) Friends of Friendless Churches
FRIBA	Fellow of the Royal Institute of British Architects
FSA	Fellow of the Society of Antiquaries
GoH	Guild of Handicraft (Chipping Campden)
HAIA	Home Arts and Industries Association
HCT	(Church in care of) Historic Chapels Trust
HE	Historic England
ICBS	Incorporated Church Building Society
JRIBA	*Journal of the Royal Institute of British Architects*
KSIA	Keswick School of Industrial Arts
LES	Leek Embroidery Society
NAL	National Art Library (at the V&A)
NAWG	Northern Art Workers' Guild
NC	Non-conformist, non-conformity
n.d.	no date given
n.p.	no publisher given; no page number
PCC	Parochial Church Council
PRB	Pre-Raphaelite Brotherhood
Presb	Presbyterian
Prim	Primitive Methodist
RA	Royal Academy
RC	Roman Catholic
REEA	*Recent English Ecclesiastical Architecture* (see Further Reading)
RIBA	Royal Institute of British Architects
RO	Records Office
SGAS	St George's Art Society
SPAB	Society for the Protection of Ancient Buildings
UPC	United Presbyterian Church
URC	United Reformed Church
V&A	Victoria and Albert Museum
VCH	*Victoria County History/ies*

PART I

THE CONTEXT

I

INTRODUCTION

WHAT IS AN 'ARTS & CRAFTS CHURCH'?

'Arts & Crafts church' is not a category with well-defined boundaries – unlike 'Gilbert Scott church', say, or Roman Catholic church, or even Gothic Revival church. Indeed 'Arts & Crafts church' is so elusive and arguable a category that some people – academics especially – deny it can be a category at all. The urge, the need to classify is so very powerful: if one can't define it, how can it exist? Yet the idea won't go away.

This book has its origins in my 2016 doctoral thesis, *The Arts & Crafts in church-building in Britain, 1884–1918*. That research took me to over 600 churches: in pretty well every case, a church where someone – local historian, *Pevsner* editor, Arts & Crafts scholar – had used the phrase 'Arts & Crafts' in writing about the architect, the fittings or a particular object in the building. Sometimes the very phrase 'Arts & Crafts church' was used. Often it was clear the writer was responding to the feel of the place as much as to its history: they rarely tried to explain just what they meant. While there is not much agreement about what *is* an Arts & Crafts church, people seem very clear about what *isn't* one.

So, let me set out here, at the start, the parameters for what I mean by 'Arts & Crafts church'. After all, without parameters, how could I have written this book?

1 It has to be built in or after 1884, the founding date of the Art Workers' Guild (AWG).
2 It has to be designed by a member of the AWG.
3 Or by a member of, or someone who exhibited with, the Arts & Crafts Exhibition Society (ACES), founded in 1888 by Walter Crane. The ACES included many members of the AWG but, unlike the exclusive private AWG 'club', held public exhibitions open to all.
4 Or someone sympathetic to these ideas, but who perhaps lived too far away to attend the meetings, or was not a joiner-in, or who said they despised the Arts & Crafts, but couldn't help themselves from working in a rather similar way; or whose buildings look Arts & Crafts-y even though they had no idea that was what they were doing.
5 And there are some buildings which, while not in themselves Arts & Crafts by these definitions, have interiors furnished or fitted by such people, or in such a way, that they have also to be considered – for it would be absurd or awkward to leave them out: Arts & Crafts was quite a lot about interior decoration, and sometimes a superficial 'looking like' could be the real thing, and sometimes not.
6 And it doesn't have to be a church – it can be any building constructed by any

religion or denomination for the purposes of its liturgy or worship.

7 And, in some cases, it is the client who 'is' (or seems) Arts & Crafts, either in their tastes, or in their political and social attitudes.

8 There are exceptions to all the above.

Of course, this is all at once too precise and yet too vague. 'Arts & Crafts church' is a category highly resistant to categorisation.

FELT MORE THAN REASONED

Those who designed these churches, and those who paid for them, were not driven by logic, reason or clarity of vision, but by individual ideas and personal agendas. These were not always clear-cut or coherent. Why should they be? An 'Arts & Crafts church' is something felt more than reasoned. Architects and clients alike were doing something odd, after all: building a church at a time when believing in God was no longer essential – no longer obligatory, or even the norm; when you could perfectly well believe in your own personal version of Him. Or not believe at all.

It has been suggested to me (by an eminent historian of Victorian architecture) that 'Arts & Crafts churches exist only in the eye of the beholder'. Up to a point, he's right. Yes, when I arrive at a new church, I find I can see it, feel it even, before I can explain it. But I *can* explain it. It is just that one has to be resigned to fluid and provisional boundaries: even my parameters have to be flexible.

In order to clarify all this, the book is divided into two parts. The first part – Chapters 1–4 – sets the scene through an analytical account of the architectural history, and the religious and social contexts. The second part – the Gazetteer – reflects the excitement of exploration of the churches themselves, and is much less academic.

Why all this rigmarole? What's so difficult? There is a book called *Arts & Crafts Architecture*,[1] after all, and any number on *The Arts & Crafts House*. There have been exhibitions and conferences on all sorts of aspects of the Arts & Crafts. There has never been greater interest in the phenomenon or the period. William Morris has become a giant of British culture. Arts & Crafts is everywhere. And yet there has never been a book called *Arts & Crafts Churches*.[2] Why not?

TOO DIFFICULT?

For many architectural historians it simply falls into the 'too difficult' box. The category's arguability means it won't fit: there can't be a definitive typology or *catalogue raisonné*. It doesn't work that way. So, in order to do it justice, this book is, perforce, something else: it considers churches not merely as architecture, or even as works of art, still less as a 'type', but as expressions of how we, the British, changed from church-going Victorians into happily agnostic moderns – humanists and atheists and Jedi and don't-think-much-about-itists: exponents of what Thomas Hardy called 'indifferentism'.[3] And how, when that change was happening, since building a church was still something worth doing – something one might be expected to do – these churches express, willy-nilly, that change. They did not mean to, but they do. This book might have been called, had I been less cautious, *Why Agnostics Went on Building Churches*. Or *How Art Replaced God*. Or even *Losing Our Religion*.

It is simply this: there were churches built after about 1875 and up until about 1925 (bang go the parameters already) that were the work of architects and designers influenced by the various and visionary ideas of William Morris and John Ruskin; who were members of the AWG and/or the ACES; or might have been, or should have been. Their churches were not Gothic Revival, nor High Victorian; they were not exactly 'anti-Victorian' or even 'Post-Victorian'. They were perhaps simply 'No-Longer-Victorian.' As were the people.

These churches were built in a rather unregarded period between two great peaks of British ecclesiastical architectural orthodoxy – the Gothic Revival (a Gilbert Scott church, say), when churches were built because we all believed in God, and it was important to make great machines for worship; and the Modern (a Cachemaille-Day church, perhaps), because we were all now rational beings, and didn't buy the whole God package any more.

Yet 'Arts & Crafts churches' cannot be fully understood in terms of either. Unlike Gothic Revival churches, they looked to the past not for great originals to be perfected, but for echoes and impressions with which to hint and suggest. Nor, despite what Pevsner would have liked, can it be convincingly argued they prefigure Modernism, for they do not look to the future at all: they look back with nostalgia, exaggerating the vernacular, re-creating an idealised England, Scotland or Wales, and with far more interest in decorative detail than in the rigours of purposeful construction.

They were built in a new spirit – co-operative, non-competitive – by architects who wanted to be hands-on, not grandly distant, and with craftsmen they knew and trusted as friends. Their churches were free and personal, rejecting templates and copying. The architects saw them as personal expressions, not merely architectural 'jobs': their approach was romantic, about beauty and truth, and about the loveliness of creation. This may look like sentimentality, but it was not. The architects weren't – with a very few exceptions – pious: they did not make a spiritual investment in these churches. Many of the clients were the same.

A NEW DELIGHT

Beresford Pite characterised the end of Victorian Gothic like this: 'When the lamp went out, there was no residuum, framework or principle, only the inchoate notion of the wild but real beauty of old work, and a new delight in picturesque draughtsmanship.'[4] Inchoate … wild … delight: that spirit lurks behind most of these churches.

As Morris complained of all handicraft, these churches were very often built at the behest of the rich. The rich were not necessarily, as Morris feared, 'swinish', but they were certainly self-indulgent, as people with money feel they can be. They tended to be even more singular than their architects, with personal views of God; peculiar, autocratic notions about liturgy and ceremonial; in some cases, a somewhat secular outlook, even amounting, with hindsight, to irreligious. Unlike the architects, they did not belong to clubs or guilds. They were mavericks – because they could be.

Significantly, they were often women – with their own money, their own ideas, their own determination. These churches were built in the context of the campaigns for women's suffrage. A woman could not be a member of the AWG, but she could make her voice heard at last, build a church, be a member of the ACES and submit work to its exhibitions, have an existence undefined by male permission; be somebody, have ideas. Hierarchies were tottering.

The mix of idealistic architects and individualistically spiritual clients led to sparks of creative friction. The result is buildings that are seductive, original; seemingly simple, yet disarmingly complex; and neither Victorian nor Modern. There is a delicious lack of the clear-cut – it's a big part of their appeal. They ask questions. They demand explanations. And they persistently provide at best equivocal answers.

It is easy to hate the big Victorian churches that loom yet in so many city suburbs – to find them gloomy, dingy, fearful, irrelevant. It is much harder not to enjoy, even love, the friendly, approachable, homely little churches that came after them, and before Modernism decreed churches should be rational, uncluttered boxes. Churches built in the four decades that straddle 1900 are more domestic than ecclesiastical – places of meeting, on a human scale, comfy and cosy. They are not the Houses of a judgemental God, nor dominated by the drama and pain of Crucifixion, but somewhere to meet gentle Jesus, meek and mild, the Good Shepherd.

DOES IT EXIST?

This book is not, I know, definitive – it cannot be. But it *is* comprehensive, in the sense that I have been to see and photograph, and read and researched the churches written about in detail (and many more besides, which, for one reason or another, I have decided not to include – I explain why in 'Other Architects' (p.319)). And I have only felt the desire to write about these buildings because they strike a chord – aesthetic, emotional, spiritual – in a way other buildings (great houses, for example, or Gilbert Scott churches) simply do not. And this is thus a sort of psycho-geography: you can't study what you don't love – nor can you study what you already understand.

So – does the Arts & Crafts church exist? There is the worrying possibility that the very idea is a mirage. May it simply derive from our own confused ideas about what the Arts & Crafts is or was? Even at the time, the Arts & Crafts was porous and fractive. The architects who were AWG, or adhered, however semi-detachedly, to AWG's ethos, were various enough to defy categorisation, and their ideas changed over time. And the 'boundary' between High Gothic and Arts & Crafts is/was shifting and uncertain. The pursuit of beauty animated Bodley's career, but for those who came after him, beauty lay in different places, and not all of them in God. Since there was no longer consensus about who or what God was, churches seemed to be less and less church-like. All one can say of them for sure, sometimes, is that they were built around 1900.

And what of churches that 'look' Arts & Crafts – whether deliberately or unconsciously – but somehow 'aren't'? Towards the end of the period, say 1910, was it possible for an architect to build a church without 'being' Arts & Crafts? Without having some knowledge of the churches already built by Norman Shaw, Sedding, Caröe, Nicholson, Spooner? Or the ideas – perhaps more powerful and visible – of those who were *not* church architects: Ashbee, Gimson, and the two great non-church-building opinion-formers, Baillie Scott and Voysey? It is arguable that, by 1910, whether an architect subscribed to the egalitarian ideas of Morris, or the campaigning of Walter Crane, or the theoretical flights of Professor Lethaby, he was unable, certainly unlikely, to continue in the vein of Gothic Revival without a conscious effort. Arts & Crafts attitudes had arguably become so diluted and normative by 1910 that non-hierarchical, non-precedent-obsessed thinking meant it was hard not to prefer new forms and new approaches: what had been experimental and even revolutionary in 1884 was now rather mainstream, even old-fashioned. There is, as a result, a certain amount of 'Arts-&-Crafts-lookingness' to deal with.

So where do the boundaries lie? If they are porous, why have some churches not been examined? Even the work of some AWG men is here little noticed – Leonard Stokes, Walter Tapper. And what of other (comparatively) prolific church architects who were not members of the AWG – Temple Moore, Ninian Comper, Giles Gilbert Scott, William Seth-Smith? How come their churches are sometimes included, but usually not? And what about George Baines? It is because they are, somehow, something else. One clue can be found in the *British Architect,* 1915:

> There is this to be said for the Gothic phase: that it has left behind it something vital and creditable to our time in the church architecture of Butterfield, Sedding, Pearson, Bentley, Bodley and Geo. Gilbert Scott. Right down to the present time we have all seen how the very spirit of Gothic art has lived in the work of Messrs Paley and Austin, R J Johnson, Basil Champneys, Leonard Stokes, W J Tapper, Sir Aston Webb and Geo. Gilbert Scott [jr] who has proved much more than the inheritance of a great name in his fine work at Liverpool.[5]

For that writer at least, it was only the Gothic that still 'counted' as church architecture: 'the great national inheritance of a Gothic tradition.' He mentions none of the architects – apart from Sedding – who figure largest in this book. The 'not-Gothic' church somehow didn't count. But it is those that didn't count then, that count most now.

WHEN WAS ARTS & CRAFTS?

The phrase first appeared in the 1887 discussions leading to the ACES. However, 1884, the date of the founding of the AWG, which first and best embodied the ethos, makes a more logical start point.

The 1880s was meanwhile the decade in which socialism arrived with dizzying suddenness to become a power in British intellectual circles – in 1883 the Marxist Social Democratic Federation arose from the ashes of the Democratic Federation; in 1884 the Fabian Society was founded; and in 1885 William Morris founded the Socialist League.

For the purposes of this book, anything before 1884 is considered a 'pre-cursor': in churches, Sara Losh at St Mary, Wreay, Cumbria in 1842 seems to be well ahead of the field. Other churches from the 1870s are interesting in what they foreshadow: they teeter on the border between Victorian Gothic and something freer and more individual. There is a suggested list of 'Pre-cursors' on page 316. It did not all start one fine morning, nor finish one dark day.

The end point of the Arts & Crafts is harder to establish: Gavin Stamp put the case for Coventry Cathedral (1956–62) being Arts & Crafts.[6] Yet in 1933 Betjeman identified that 'by 1912 … 'Arty-craftiness' became an expensive joke.'[7] A slightly later moment feels more significant: in 1916 the ACES finally succeeded in having its biennial exhibition held at the Royal Academy – the ACES's high-point, a recognition at last by the Art World that crafts could be allowed into hallowed halls. It was the zenith of Henry Wilson's career, Master of the AWG that year, and a central figure in this book. But the end of the Great War was a more significant moment for churches: it meant new churches were expressing a need to memorialise, rather than new spiritual or liturgical ideas. After 1918 churches necessarily had a new and sombre meaning. Besides – though this has never been demonstrated statistically – there were perhaps now fewer craftsmen to do the complicated craft-work required for church fittings.

Alan Crawford has pointed out that many with Arts & Crafts sympathies went on working right through the 1920s.[8] Indeed there are a number of churches of the 1920s which it would have been difficult to exclude from this book – a lingering diminuendo. Modernism perhaps snuffed out the ideas in architecture in the 1930s – though faint echoes of Arts & Crafts homeliness continued to appear in the details of some post-War housing. In churches, these echoes, when they appear after 1930, can easily be accounted whimsy and self-conscious eccentricity. It is not an exact science.

WHAT IS MEANT BY 'CHURCH'?

In this book 'church' means any building built by a religious organisation for the purpose of conducting whatever rites and ceremonies constitute its liturgy. This then includes Church of England (CofE) churches, Church of (later 'in') Wales churches, Roman Catholic (RC) churches and chapels, the churches of all the Scottish denominations; Nonconformist (NC) churches and chapels, Friends Meeting Houses (even though Quakers lack a formal liturgy), Salvation Army citadels (again, with no formal liturgy), Kingdom Halls, synagogues, mosques and gudwaras amongst others. But it does not include church halls, vicarages, parsonages, RC presbyteries; nor monasteries (except their chapels); nor schools (except their chapels). Private chapels are included, at least partly because some of the key examples, while ostensibly parish churches, are really the product of a single purse, whose owner remained proprietorial. Also considered are exemplar buildings which were churches, but are now closed, or used for other purposes, or demolished (see p.317). Some of these last are a central part of the story, and might have figured more largely in a different kind of survey, but I didn't want to spend time discussing what you can't see.

Originally the research for this book was only interested in *new* churches. But visits increasingly suggested two important strands would be excluded by this: complete and substantial interiors in ancient churches by a member of the AWG or ACES, or by men and women with Arts & Crafts sympathies; and craft-work in churches by individuals who, whilst not themselves architects, or even members of the AWG or ACES, were encouraged by the Arts & Crafts spirit and influenced by Arts & Crafts ideas – 'earnest amateurs'. However, 'restorations' and 'enlargements' of earlier churches, whether done sensitively or not, have on the whole been excluded.

STRUCTURE OF THE BOOK

The book is in two parts.

Chapters 2–4 set the buildings in three intertwined contexts – artistic, religious and social. Without these contextualising chapters, the rest of the book may seem to be a mere spotters' guide, for the remainder is a region-by-region Gazetteer – in the wake of, and grateful to the spirit of the church guides of John Betjeman and Simon Jenkins, and as interested in the 'how' of the building as in the 'what'.

Presenting the churches chronologically would have suggested a single, solid direction of travel, and a coherence of purpose and practice which simply wasn't there. And I could have gone for alphabetical – but region-by-region allows something else to emerge: that 'Arts & Crafts' meant different things, and had different impacts, depending on where you were.

The surviving churches tend to be small enough not to terrify even a dwindling congregation, so they can be maintained – and they do tend to be in good nick. Being only 100 years old, they don't have to be unpicked or explained with a scholarly timeline. They are more or less all 'as built', and mostly without agonies of reordering and re-seating, though many a pulpit has been spirited away, and lectern banished to a corner. Many have just had their centenary, and someone has taken the trouble to write up their history, a copy of which may be found at the back of the church – in which case, please buy it. In some cases, the history is online. Mostly, the churches are loved – because they are lovable. They are so much less 'churchy' than the Gothic Revival monsters of the middle of the century. They do not try to bring us to our knees – which nowadays we tend not to want to be.

By and large, they survive. You can go and visit them, to see for yourself (though many are locked, and some require a certain persistence to get into – you should email incumbents or churchwardens at least three weeks in advance, and I apologise for any inconvenience caused).

These are *our* churches, built by *us* – the people of a Christian country and culture who no longer quite buy the whole deal, or for whom that deal is alien and unfamiliar. People who 'don't believe in God, but ...' Or believe in a different way. Eclectics. Pick-n-mixers.

The question is not so much, then, 'What is an Arts & Crafts church?' but, '*Why* is an Arts & Crafts church?' As well as pleasure in objects and experiences, I try to offer some tentative replies with which wiser (and less wise) heads will doubtless disagree.

My hope is not just to encourage you to admire and appreciate, but to go and look. To think about the ideas, and test them for strength and adequacy. To argue against them. And to find churches I didn't find or even think of. And, like the architects and clients, to think for yourself.

2

ARTS & CRAFTS CHURCHES IN CONTEXT

ARCHITECTURE AS ART

Arts & Crafts is not a set of rules, nor a hermetically sealed pigeon-hole – it is a collection of sentiments, feelings and instincts. Sometimes they cohere into what can look like a credo – in the case of Philip Webb, say, or C.R. Ashbee – or they can simply be a box of tricks into which some architects dip from time to time – as with Lutyens, Charles Nicholson and Giles Gilbert Scott. Around 1900, church architecture was different from what it had been – that's all. But how? And, more to the point, why?

Arts & Crafts never satisfactorily defined itself. Books on the subject tend to start, therefore, by trying to account for its origins. Much the best survey of this kind is by Linda Parry.[9] There is a rather more detailed account of the emergence by Peter Stansky[10] and a more recent, succinct overview by Mary Greensted.[11]

Despite this purposeful scholarship, for many the Arts & Crafts is a look, an aura – the kind of thing Liberty's and Heal's learned to copy and make accessible in fabrics, furniture, metalwork and jewellery: a sort of sophisticated simplicity, which ran on into the 1960s at Habitat, and is still discernible in some aisles at IKEA.

Arts & Crafts can also be understood as a state of mind – to do with sandals and stoneware and a loom in your attic, and left-leaning earnestness: neatly exemplified by Richmal Crompton in the uncorseted women and wildly-bearded men who rented cottages for the summer in William Brown's village, somewhere in deepest Middle England.

In short, despite its wide currency, and its specific application to, and coining for the Arts & Crafts Exhibition Society (ACES), whose first exhibition was in 1888, the phrase 'Arts & Crafts' was, and remains, contested.

A MOVEMENT?

Was it even really a 'movement'? It was called one by surprisingly few people at the time: Walter Crane,[12] C.R. Ashbee,[13] A.H. Mackmurdo[14] and T.J. Cobden-Sanderson.[15] And whilst a few of its adherents saw it as a movement, whether political or aesthetic, most did not think of it in that way at all; some only did in retrospect. Besides, 'movement' suggests a commonality of purpose and direction which belies the reality of diffuseness and individuality. Was it perhaps something far less coherent? What were its core beliefs? Did it have any? Who subscribed to them? Was there consensus? There were certainly shared ideas, inclinations and sensibilities, but Arts & Crafts meant different things to different people, and its meaning changed over time. Was it genuinely new, even revolutionary? Or more to do with rebellion against received wisdom?

Accounts tend to start with the 'founding fathers' – Ruskin and Morris – often also with reference to Pugin, and occasionally even further back to Thomas Carlyle and Robert

Owen. These men – and especially the first two – wrote and lectured copiously, but they were pedagogic pundits, who varied their focus and interests over time, and scarcely stated their views in consistent rigorous formulae. They coined any number of aperçus; in these there is a sense of something fresh, provocative, clever, and bracingly different from what had gone before:

> I believe the right question to ask, respecting all ornament, is simply this: was it done with enjoyment - was the carver happy while he was about it?
> Ruskin, SEVEN LAMPS OF ARCHITECTURE (1849)
>
> Have nothing in your houses that you do not know to be useful or believe to be beautiful.
> Morris, 'The Beauty of Life' (1880)
>
> Art is man's expression of his joy in labour.
> Morris, 'Art under Plutocracy' (1883)

Such visionary statements excited their first audiences, but they were not intended to be definitions. They induce reverence, amounting to awe, even now – a sacerdotal aura which obscures their sentimental imprecision. It is rather more instructive to consider what those who were influenced by Ruskin and Morris (in particular) *did.* They started, and joined, clubs.

First it was the St George's Art Society (SGAS), which begat the Art Workers' Guild (AWG), which begat the Arts & Crafts Exhibition Society (ACES). At the heart of it all was a ferment of artistic young men, chummily debating in smoke-filled London rooms and restaurants.[16] And not just in London – as the Gazetteer explores, these same ideas and sentiments were in the air, in different guises and strengths, in Liverpool, Birmingham (in both of which there were AWGs, respectively 1886 and 1902), Manchester (the Northern AWG), Glasgow (Scottish Society of Art Workers, 1898), Edinburgh (Edinburgh AWG, 1905), Sheffield, Derbyshire, Cardiff and elsewhere. Besides, exhibits came to ACES exhibitions from all over the nation, demonstrating an informal consensus about what could now be art, and that it was not so different from craft – and that it was the *making* that counted, and the spirit of that making.

The phrase 'Arts and Crafts' was never intended to be anything more than a memorable name for publicising that first exhibition: it was proposed by T.J. Cobden-Sanderson during a meeting to discuss what the exhibition was to be called. Walter Crane proposed 'Exhibition of Decorative Arts'.[17] He also suggested 'Applied Arts' and 'The Combined Arts'.[18] Those who agreed to Cobden-Sanderson's compromise had no intention of using it to define their work or their lives, still less had any idea the phrase would ultimately come to mean a period and a style. For some, that would have been anathema. The difficulty they had in coming up with an acceptable 'catch-all' title reveals how very different they were from each other – architects, illustrators, fine art painters, sculptors. They saw no reason to set down rules. It would have been limiting – and difficult. They relished their independence and individuality. They were free.

Besides, it would be a mistake to assume Arts & Crafts was seen as clearly then as it is now. Peter Davey points out that Arts & Crafts 'never produced a manifesto to which all subscribed, nor a very recognisable style, nor a clear ideology.'[19] Peter Cormack, whose book on Arts & Crafts stained glass was published in 2015, has written:

> the Arts & Crafts spirit was a subtle and pervasive force that penetrated deep into the way architects and designer-craftsmen worked throughout the first half of the 20th century. ... And though it might have been more 'radical' when it started in the 1880s and 90s, it really had achieved a very considerable level of acceptance by the 1900s. In so doing it became all about good craftsmanship that wasn't formulaic or too historicist, that reminded you of the past without trying to reconstruct it.[20]

Cormack's useful notion of 'reminding without reconstructing' emphasises the contrast between the Arts & Crafts' trust in instincts, and the rather different focus of the preceding generation of church architects, who wanted to be 'correct' – and indeed of those who came after, who sought to be 'rational'.

WHO WAS ARTS & CRAFTS?

However, since the ACES deliberately set out to spread their ideas and values to the wider public, attitudes that seem in accord with the Arts & Crafts, when expressed by architect non-members, clients or private individuals, are also, in this book at least, allowed to 'be' Arts & Crafts: this therefore includes the diffuse and disparate members of the Bromsgrove Guild (only two of whom were architects), those who taught and were taught at the Birmingham Municipal School of Art (BMSA), and those who taught and studied at the LCC Central School of Arts and Crafts (Central School). And, for the avoidance of doubt, architect members of the later Northern Art Workers' Guild (NAWG) and the earlier Century Guild are also included. (There are comparatively few churches built by members of either.) All of these, and the AWG and ACES, are what are called here 'The Arts & Crafts'.

The AWG was a closed shop. It was not possible to simply join by application or subscription – if you were the 'right stuff', you were invited in and elected. Once 'in', you were free to follow your own star. And you had to be male – women were only admitted in the 1960s. Some AWG architect members took a rather less Arts & Crafts line as their careers blossomed: W.D. Caröe and Lutyens, for example. Some rather came and went: Charles Nicholson and J.F. Bentley. Some were perhaps 'more' 'Arts & Crafts' – Sidney Barnsley; some 'less' – Basil Champneys. Despite membership of the AWG some seemed hardly to 'belong' at all – J.T. Micklethwaite, perhaps. And some were 'of' the Arts & Crafts by the way they worked and behaved, without being members of any guild or club – Godfrey Pinkerton, for example (whose partner was a member of the AWG, but who never himself joined), and Charles Ponting, Percy Currey and H.A. Prothero, who were all happily provincial and weren't known enough in the right circles to be asked to join (and might not have joined even if they had been asked).

If there was no manifesto, there were certainly shibboleths and taboos which, while never subject to an oath, could not well be broken. We can start with Peter Davey's suggestion that 'Arts & Crafts people ... shared Morris's affection for simplicity, truth-to-materials, and the unity of handicraft and design.'[21] To which might be added the following generalisations: distrust of the machine-made; preference for the hand-made; trust in the maker; a preference for local materials and skills; a desire for closeness between designer and maker – ideally, an architect should be both; a distrust of the contract building system, and a disinclination to employ Clerks of Works; an inclination to only take on one job at a time; belief in the dignity of labour; a co-operative spirit; a disdain for 'copying'. And, when it came to churches, a fastidious dislike of the bought-in or off-the-shelf, or anything from church furnishers' catalogues. And, as Andrew Saint has put it: 'a professional ethic of diffidence ... espoused by many (not all) Arts & Crafts architects, artists and designers; ... [who had] no wish to be regarded as a major artistic figure in any conventional sense.'[22]

There was an instinctive revulsion for the environments in which architects had so often been taught: large offices; ubiquitous principals; the suppression of individual initiative; high pressure working at speed; repetition of tasks and motifs; a sort of design slavery. All of that was rejected by the Arts & Crafts.

To whom did this matter? The audience for Street's and Scott's churches was, yes, their peers as well as their clients, but they also had the Ecclesiological Society looking over their shoulders: a level of attention reflecting an interest in churches among the church-going classes as a whole. For the Art & Crafts it was different. Yes, the journals published their work – if they chose to submit it – and commented on it, but they did so architecturally rather than ecclesiologically. The wider world was decreasingly interested in churches: 1911's sturdy survey, *Recent English Ecclesiastical Architecture* was not succeeded by later volumes.

For the architects, a more important audience, and perhaps even more important than one's client, was one's fellows – the Brothers of the AWG. They read the journals, and passed on bouquets and brickbats on new churches in quiet words in their favourite smoke-filled rooms. The Goths had been bustling and competitive: the Arts & Crafts drew together. The resonant relationships between members of the AWG, working in these churches alongside each other in trust and sympathy, was consciously different from what had gone before. The men of the AWG thought along similar, but not identical, lines, and shared a commonality of purpose, and the spirit of egalitarianism. It was convenient, then, that their clients were no longer intent on perfecting churches as they *should* be, but were more interested in how they *wanted* them to be – self-expression, even self-indulgence. Subjection of the self in glorifying an unapproachable God was no longer expected of an architect, nor necessary. It was enough to go about it in the right way: it is not easy to find AWG men critical of each others' church work.

Where the AWG was a closed club, the ACES was outward-facing. It campaigned to have craft work and two-dimensional design accepted by the Art World, specifically the Royal Academy. And you could be female – very many exhibitors were. The ACES's inclination to accept works democratically from all comers, with or without provenance or training, meant it seemed to observers that objects had to 'look the part' in order to be exhibited. Whether this was deliberate, unconscious or a natural outcome of political strictures is hard to say – but certainly by 1900, in church architecture, it is easy to see a sort of 'Arts & Crafts façadism' arise. In particular, it became a visual shorthand by which Nonconformist churches could say, 'we are modern, fashionable, interesting: we have arrived.' (However smart they looked from the street, in their chapel interiors Nonconformists tended to stick to aesthetic and structural precedents.)

'LOOKS LIKE'

It all swiftly elided into 'Artsy-Craftsy' – 'looks like' rather than 'is'. Arts & Crafts, despite itself, rapidly moved from an attitude of mind (and even a political stance) to a style – fashionable because rare and therefore expensive, and appealing therefore to 'early adopters' amongst clients because of its counter-orthodox character. In contrast to the elaborations of High Victorian Gothic, Arts & Crafts was interested in simplicity: mannerisms and devices which commercial firms could easily and cheaply copy.

As the period progressed, Arts & Crafts 'looks' influenced designers who were broadly sympathetic without being in any way committed to the ideals – for example, the Scottish architects W.D. McLennan, Archibald Macpherson and Sydney Mitchell. Scotland had (and has) its own loyalties. And it was easily possible to emulate the look without subscribing to the ideals in any way: the prime examples perhaps the ubiquitous Nonconformist architects George Baines and his son. By 1910 Arts & Crafts had become the language of 'today's' architecture.

As a further complication, it should be noted that Arts & Crafts ideas were in the air elsewhere. The Home Arts and Industries Association (HAIA) was, like the AWG, founded in 1884: 'cottage crafts' and the revival of peasant industries in Scotland and Ireland by aristocratic female landowners is contemporary with, even a little ahead of, the rediscovery by James MacLaren of the Shropshire chair bodger Philip Clissett, and his subsequent beatification as the *echt* rural craftsman (chairs to his design still people the AWG's London meeting room in Queen Square). It is even arguable that William Burges was Arts & Crafts in spirit – and that Sir Gilbert Scott respected his craftsmen every bit as much as did Lethaby.

Even though something broadly similar was happening elsewhere (America, Northern Europe), Arts & Crafts was a deeply British phenomenon – before transatlantic flights, television and the internet, our Little Britain, despite any pretensions to internationalism and a taste for sketching tours of Italy, looked not only inwards but backwards (as it still does). Arts & Crafts had no despotic demagogue like Le Corbusier or Mies van der Rohe, and no mythic gunslinger like Frank Lloyd Wright. Like all British phenomena it was constitutionally self-effacing – 'We are British, so we can't really be all that brilliant, and if we are, it's best not to talk about it.' And it *was* very British – what was going on in Europe and America was different: nationalistic, nation-defining, combative (like the quest to write the Great American Novel). It is worth bearing in mind that, as Gombrich points out, Arts & Crafts is coeval with Van Gogh, Cézanne and Gauguin – which tends to suggest that, artistically, it was small-scale, introverted and marginal. And, despite Pevsner's persuasive arguments, it did not lead to Modernism. Arts & Crafts in Britain, one might go so far as to say England, was ineffectual and fey, and all a bit embarrassing. The petering out of Arts &

Crafts, in the light of all this, is taken by many historians of 20th-century architecture as proof that it did not matter. But look at it another way. Yes, it was a tiny *cul de sac*, perhaps. But it was a luminous *cul de sac*. If an idea doesn't lead anywhere, it tends to be seen as unimportant. But dead ends have a sense of direction just as clear as dogmas do: it is just that, by its adherents' diffidence, the Arts & Crafts did not turn into a dictatorship. That does not mean it failed. It just wasn't inclined to fight.

But it was inclined to argue. Taken simply as architecture, regardless of the democratic *how* of their building, churches built by Arts & Crafts adherents *look* different from Gothic Revival churches. Their architects did not seek to emulate or elaborate on Middle Pointed or any other era or style; they did not wish to be historicist or drily scholarly – but they did want to know what they were doing, and to be seen to know. Their churches tend not to have Gothic stylistic tics like crockets and ogees, nor elaborate external stone decoration: their outsides tend to be comparatively unadorned – there is a preference for restraint, in many cases because of economy. Restraint, however, does not always extend to the interior, where elaborated detail is frequently encountered – the work of craftsmen is often foregrounded, so that a church can seem to be more a collection of objects than a coherent whole.

SCALE AND TASTE

A very common feature of these churches, and in marked contrast to those of preceding decades, is their smallness: they often have an intimate, enclosing quality, almost homely – perhaps not surprising, since the Arts & Crafts was most interested in houses and the right way to live. The churches thus sometimes can seem positively miniaturised: W.D. Caröe delighted in 'toy' churches that somehow look smaller than they are, for example, St Bartholomew, Stamford Hill (1903–4) (p.114). There is a slight corollary sense that large churches like St Andrew, Roker (p.261) and Holy Trinity, Sloane Street (p.102) are too big to be 'really' Arts & Crafts: hence the recourse by Betjeman to the seemingly explanatory phrase, 'Cathedral of the Arts & Crafts'.[23]

It is tempting to link this sense of the domestic and small scale to the role of women as clients. But that is a dangerous – and patronising – analysis. It could equally have been an unconscious expression of the understanding in church hierarchies that the role played by women in church life could no longer be ignored or belittled. Or – a more subtle point – simply that women were increasingly playing a part as artist-makers: there are not only important Arts & Crafts women makers like Mary Lowndes in glass, and the Pinwills in woodwork (p.63), but idiosyncratic 'outsider' architects Sara Losh and Mary Seton Watts, and wife-and-husband teams where the work and ideas were joint – Georgie and Arthur Gaskin in jewellery, Nelson and Edith Dawson in silver, the Powells in ceramics; and among architects, John Dando Sedding and his wife Rose, and Charles and Dinah Spooner. The macho architecture of Gilbert Scott's generation seemed no longer quite to fit. And LGBTQ+ sensibilities – far too contested and intricate for this book – may also be borne in mind: there were gay designers and architects in the Arts & Crafts, not least C.R. Ashbee, F.C. Eden and Walter Tapper, and others not 'out', or equivocal, such as Philip Webb, and some who simply 'never married'.

There was something of a taste for the Byzantine (especially in Birmingham), and for the medieval Italian, though the language was adopted in an impressionistic rather than literal manner. The churches are most often found in the country or outer suburbs because that is where the rich middle classes (who tended to be the clients) could now live. Thus these churches often have the air of escape to the country: people deliberately and visibly swimming against the tide, and doing it, to some extent, out of the spotlight of convention and consensus: 'Out of Town'. Some are, indeed, deep in the country – Brockhampton, Brithdir, Great Warley. Some are in holiday resorts – Teignmouth, Lynton, Boscombe – though not always in holiday mood. Some were conceived as private chapels, though by 1900 there is an uncomfortable sense that they ought to be open to all.

GOD'S DRIFT

The Arts & Crafts coincided with – reflected, did not cause, but sprang from the same sources as – the sense of God's drift from Victorian public figure to Edwardian private man: from a great higher Truth to poetic metaphor. The architects of the AWG were feeling their way towards new ways of working (and living). A church was no longer the ultimate expression of an architect's career. Churches became, instead, an opportunity for applying original artistic ideas to a form still interesting, but no longer crucial.

In some cases, the disparity between artistic architectural adventure and personal religious intention resulted in churches that now seem faintly absurd. They lack the sure-footedness of Gothic Revival churches. If they have confidence, it is in something less exalted than God – lovely things, the picturesque. There is a lack of authority; perhaps because those who wanted the churches built were no longer intent on authority. Their churches do not trumpet the glory of God, but express rather the significance of the self, or the importance of community, and that community's belief in the worth of its own togetherness. This may account for why they often seem to look inward: their sense of enclosure.

Of the 5000 or so religious buildings erected in England, Scotland and Wales between 1884 and 1918, perhaps only 350 can in any sense be understood as 'Arts & Crafts'. Many branches of British Christianity were hardly touched by Arts & Crafts ideas, whether in the building or the design: the Congregationalists of Ashton-under-Lyne competed with the Anglicans not through modish Arts & Crafts décor, but by deliberately using the Anglican architectural language of earlier decades. Some denominations in the period – The Salvation Army and English Methodists, for example – inclined away from church-like buildings altogether, and instead adopted more secular forms. Roman Catholics, active in poor areas of cities, looked first for capacity; then, where money allowed, tended towards classical models, as at Brompton Oratory, South Kensington, London (Herbert Gribble, 1880–4) or St Aloysius, Glasgow (C.J. Ménart, 1910).
In all parts of the country a younger generation of Jews, newly arrived from Europe, tended to re-create the synagogues of their grandfathers (though there are arguable exceptions, at Blackpool, Bournemouth and Leicester).

The Arts & Crafts had its most vivid and explicable expression in the design and making of *things*: pots, plates, jewellery, chairs. This extends to church furnishings too: pulpits, lecterns, fonts, candlesticks – objects that members of congregations donated (or made) in the period. These are noticed here, but only when they form part of an overall scheme, not as standalone pieces. Nor does this book deal with stained glass, unless it is part of the original design concept of the church: glass often comes later, and is to the taste or specification of persons other than the architect or his client.[24]

Nor is this book especially inclined to try to draw hard and fast lines between styles. The men of the Arts & Crafts were rather allergic to 'style' as an idea: they tended to see it as a kind of copying, which they did not care for.

So, what is the difference between Arts & Crafts and Art Nouveau, for example? The pedantic answer is that Art Nouveau can't exist until 1895, which is when the shop of that name first opened in Paris. The slightly more contentious answer is that Art Nouveau is a continental phenomenon, and unashamedly interested in the 'look' of things. Some Arts & Crafts men despised Art Nouveau, especially its sinuosity, which was seen as decadent and foreign, in the eyes of Henry Wilson for one. The same goes for neo-Baroque, Imperial Edwardian, or any one of a dozen other cleverly devised categories. Trying to classify buildings into stylistic boxes at this period (and probably any) is pretty pointless. This is not an orderly world of pigeon-holes. By 1880 the world is almost as full of ideas and images and directions as ours is now – you may see a stylistic influence in a building, but whether the architect meant it or not, who knows? And how does knowing help us understand?

In comparison to the stylistic certitude and aesthetic confidence of Gothic Revival churches, many Arts & Crafts churches seem, by contrast, slight and insubstantial. And there can be self-indulgence and egotism – so many were built for egotists. These seemingly conflicting characteristics perhaps express a reaction – both conscious and unconscious – against all that was embodied in the imposing churches of the previous generation. Now emerges an insistent questioning of old certainties: in some, a spirit of intense personal enquiry, amounting even to new visions of God; in others, a desire to supplant Victorian grandeur with something smaller-scale and intimate. At the heart of these buildings is the impulse to express new truths. For it is through the *in*tangible notions of the Arts & Crafts – its ideas, beliefs and influences – that these churches have to be approached. Arts & Crafts is not just a movement of the mind: in churches, it is of the spirit and the emotions too.[25]

Among clients it is impossible to detect any desire for consensus in what was now wanted in a church. The spirit of exploratory individualism means many of the churches seem to be monuments to things other than God: some seem to glory in their unconventionality. So, what they have in common – what makes them a genre – is their uncomfortable variousness: in plan, elevation, materials, texture, mood, light, space and spiritual depth. The primary evidence is in the buildings themselves, to which correspondence and architectural drawings, where they exist, lend support, but are not wholly trustworthy: what people do reveals more than what they say. But what they *say* they are doing can reveal yet more. It all makes for thrilling debatability.

But, after all that, why were people building churches at all?

3

ARTS & CRAFTS CHURCHES IN CONTEXT

RELIGION

In 1884 Britain was full of churches: in some places, over-full. Yet there was still, in some breasts, the desire to build a church. Why? By the 1880s the broad mass of the people were much less inclined to go to church than they had been in, say, 1851, and rather less inclined to believe in God. Not that they were all atheists – though you could be an atheist in 1900 in a way you could not have been in 1800.

The Victorian age was religious – self-consciously so.[26] At the centre, in England, stood the Church of England – established, rich and powerful. The central position of the CofE was proclaimed in its assertive architecture, the unmistakable manifestation of religious certitude. In the mid-century new Anglican churches were subject to scrutiny by the Ecclesiologists – mandarin arbiters, originally from Cambridge, of the 'correct' and 'incorrect' way a church should be. The Cambridge Camden Society (from which the Ecclesiologists sprang) was able to identify – and condemn – imperfect faith by the height of an altar or the placing of a screen. They wielded power which we find hard to believe – the notion that a church's physical character could make it a better or worse means of worshipping God. And that it mattered.

By 1870 most church interiors in England had been modified to reflect Ecclesiologist expectations.[27] But by the 1880s that orthodoxy was being challenged, as was the Church of England's centrality. The Public Worship Regulation Act of 1874 brought to a head anxieties about the 'threat' of Popery to the CofE – that there were moral and even existential dangers in deviation from liturgical orthodoxy. Ecclesiastical courts had once disciplined erring clergy with admonition and reprimand, but now they could – and did – send clergymen to prison. Nice points of detail in ceremonial or furnishings looked increasingly absurd when brought to court. Worse, the complaints were seen as embarrassingly un-Christian: evidence against priests was often brought by their own parishioners, or people from nearby parishes acting for organised groups of objectors.

The last spasm of this internal Inquisition was the trial in 1888 of the Bishop of Lincoln, the saintly and mild Edward King (1829–1910), accused of 'ritualism' by two of his own parishioners and a solicitor. He was acquitted, and there were no more trials, but there was still anxious debate. The Church – not for the last time – was out of touch. In 1903 Archbishop Randall Davidson (1848–1930) asked for a Royal Commission on Ecclesiastical Discipline. Its 1906 findings were worldly and weary:

> … the law of public worship in the Church of England is too narrow for the religious life of the present generation. It needlessly condemns much which a great section of the

> Church people including many of her most devoted members, value …[28]

The Commission proposed 'reasonable elasticity' in the law: but felt it 'necessary that [the law] should be obeyed'. The Anglo-Catholic commentator W.H. Frere acknowledged in 1906 something which had been less frankly admitted in 1874: 'we must recognise that access to God is to a large extent a markedly individual act. The worshipper is throughout the service in an individual relationship to God.'[29]

Individualism was breaking through. But the Church would not let things lie: in 1908 a committee of five bishops presented a Historical Report (120 pages long) on Ornaments. Then, in the years before the Great War, 'the critical question [in the Church of England] was that of Eucharistic vestments.'[30] The war made vestments utterly irrelevant. In the 1920s attention turned to the Prayer Book, trying to make it – what? – more understandable, more relevant, more true? But once the genie of individualism was out of the bottle, it could not be legislated back in. Parliament declined to approve (or disapprove) the 1928 Prayer Book.

While bishops and intellectual busybodies fretted about vestments and ceremonial, around 1900 few clergy in the parishes could claim much knowledge of liturgy.[31] The Alcuin Club was founded in 1897, to encourage the study of ceremonial and to give guidance on the arrangement of church furniture and ornaments.[32] Their public face was Revd Percy Dearmer (1867–1936), author of *The Parson's Handbook* (1899). He attacked the 'vulgarity' and 'tawdry stupidity' of church aesthetics.[33] He declared – perceptively – that 'art is out of touch with religion.' Dearmer is often cited as a key influence in church architecture and decoration in the period, but treat him with caution: not a scrap of evidence has been found in the research for this book that any non-cleric client or his/her architect had read a word of *The Parson's Handbook*.

The people were getting out of touch with religion too. The historical and moral authority of the Bible was under threat. *The Origin of Species* (1859) had dealt a blow to the Christian creation myth, and made possible rational, scientific questioning of Biblical authority. Post-Darwin, it is almost impossible to believe an intelligent man could change his life's course on such tenuous grounds as Virginia Woolf's father, Leslie Stephen (1832–1904) did: he left holy orders in 1862 on the realisation that the story of Noah's Ark was not literally true.[34]

Further blows were struck by the Higher Biblical Criticism of German scholars like David Strauss (1808–74) who portrayed an 'historical Jesus', whose divine nature he denied; and Heinrich Julius Holtzmann (1832–1910) who worked out the order and structure of the Gospels as historical texts, not divine revelation (1863).

FAITH AND UNBELIEF

The centrality to public life of religious observance and thought in the mid-19th century is unreachably remote now. Unquestioning faith was being countered by technology, science and a Gradgrind insistence on facts. There was no reason to except the Bible from scientific enquiry. Analytical thought made religious certainty untenable – and thus drove those who still believed, or wanted to, towards what became a more emotional engagement with the spiritual, concerned with beauty; the short life on earth rather than the possibility of an eternal Heaven; and new, ethereal ideas about Man's inner nature and personal destiny.

By 1900 the form of a church no longer mattered to establishments, neither ecclesiastical nor architectural. Personal belief was irrelevant in national matters. Churches were no longer part of government policy, as they had been in 1818, when Parliament voted £1,000,000 to build more of them (the Commissioners' churches), nor physical demonstrations of morality, as they had been for Pugin and Gilbert Scott. Nor were they any longer the ultimate statement of architectural status. They mattered now to individuals as personal expressions, and to architects as playgrounds. The decline from importance to unimportance allowed churches to be various and unorthodox.

Nonetheless, there remained an important institution which still mattered in church architecture. The Church Building Society was founded in 1817 – the year before the first of the Commissioners' churches was built, when church-building was government policy in the face of threats from France and fears of revolution and atheism. The Society was for 'promoting public worship by obtaining additional church-room for the middle and lower classes.' It was still active in 1900 – now as the Incorporated Church Building Society (ICBS) – providing funding through grants for new Anglican churches and church enlargements. The ICBS Architects Committee saw, commented on, and approved or disapproved all proposed plans. The value of the grants was small, and declining, and the experienced members of the Architects Committee were increasingly inclined to be helpful to up-and-coming architects decreasingly familiar with liturgical and practical church needs, but the Committee's views were clear, firm and usually decisive. Its members in 1909 included W.D. Caröe, E.S. Prior, Charles Spooner, John Oldrid Scott, Temple Moore, W.H. Bidlake, Aston Webb and G.H. Fellowes Prynne. (All but the last figure in this book.) To them, at least, church building as an expression of religion mattered.

To those who had for seventy years been the Anglican church-building classes – county grandees and wealthy individuals – the *purpose* of a church was no longer self-evident. While 'restoring' the parish church – those few which were yet left unrestored – remained for a time 'the right thing to do', building a *new* church had now to be for a reason. Some wealthy clients clung to outward forms of mid-Victorian certainty, others sought something fresher. For confident urban Nonconformists, new building was a way of demonstrating substance and sense of purpose, home-town success, or respectable equivalence to Anglicans. For dedicated priests toiling in the slums, their church was a physical beacon of practical faith, even if those for whom God cared did not care all that much about Him: Jesus was, through them, now primarily a social worker.

The loosening of central orthodoxy led to – was accompanied by – a 'boom' in new religious denominations. None was overtly anti-Christian, but each expressed a different new perception, or re-statement of Christian values and ideas. The first stirrings were in the 1850s: the Spiritualist Church (founded 1852); the Seventh Day Adventists, first in America (1863), then Britain (1878). The Salvation

Army, founded in 1865, first adopted uniforms in 1878. The Christadelphians first appeared in 1865. The first Pentecostal church was founded in the USA in 1901, and their first building was opened in the UK in 1908, in Bournemouth. Other splinters of Christian belief active in the period included the Universalists (1870s), the Reformed Episcopal Church (1873) and the Church of the Nazarene (1895, with many splits and reunifications). Meanwhile the Greek Orthodox Church established its first place of worship in England in 1872, and the first mosque in England was founded in 1889. (The Mormons – Church of Jesus Christ of Latter-Day Saints – date from the 1830s, and were active in Britain from 1837, but they built no new building here until the 1950s.)

In 1875 two new quasi-Christian sects appeared, both of which grew steadily and prospered: Christian Science and Jehovah's Witnesses. And two entirely new religions with no direct connection to Christianity: the somewhat mystical, universalist Theosophy in 1875, and the more earth-bound, humanist Church of Humanity in 1878. The London Society for Psychical Research was founded in 1882 – in tune with the times, more inclined to see itself as a science than a religion. The Fellowship of the New Life (1883) wished to transform society through clean living, pacifism and vegetarianism – Christian moral values, without God. Others – independently and individualistically – followed similar lines of thought: Mary Ward (Mrs Humphry Ward), a wealthy novelist, established University Hall in 1890: 'an attempt at Christianity without Christ'[35] based on 'the inspiring memory of a great teacher, rather than a system of dogma' (p.113).[36]

The energy and variety is bewildering – an expression of something like excitement in spiritual searching. By 1907, the mix, at least in forward-thinking Letchworth Garden City, had become head-spinningly diverse:

> a morris-dance of many-coloured movements – Buddhism, Theosophy, Christian Science, Female Suffrage, several brands of Socialism and who knows how many varieties of Vegetarianism.[37]

There were even Atheist missions to the working classes.[38]

Meanwhile there were new energies in denominations already well-established. Roman Catholicism quietly moved from the cultural periphery in England to somewhere near its centre. In 1850 St Chad's, Birmingham became the first Roman Catholic cathedral built in England since the Reformation. At the top of society a process of normalisation took place. In 1886 the Roman Catholic Lord Llandaff became Home Secretary; the next year Queen Victoria, fresh from her Jubilee, sent the (RC) Duke of Norfolk to the Vatican to assure the Pope of her 'sincere friendship and unfeigned respect and esteem.'[39] In 1900 Elgar set Cardinal Newman's 1865 *Dream of Gerontius* to music. Newman's hymn *Lead Kindly Light* was read to Queen Victoria on her death-bed.[40] Rome was no longer inimical to Anglican culture, but rather its friendly colleague.

NONCONFORMISTS

For Protestant dissenters, there was rather less establishment acceptance, but no less influence and visibility, especially in the mercantile and industrial cities – Liverpool, Manchester,

Leeds, Birmingham.[41] Church-building energies in the period almost certainly created larger numbers of Nonconformist buildings than Anglican or Catholic, certainly in Birmingham.

Nonconformists were independent-minded: disputes and separations, as well as growth and 'planting', created a constant need for additional places of worship. But they were, on the whole, not so rich as Anglicans: their chapels and churches tended to express sturdy respectability and burning meritocratic zeal more than wealth. There were exceptions – the extravagant Coats Memorial Church, Paisley (1894) for the Baptists, and the ambitious Ullet Road (1896–9) for Liverpool's Unitarians (p.220), for example. They seemed to out-do even the Anglicans in richness of embellishment, and were built on a grand scale.

The largest nonconforming group in England and Wales was the Methodists.[42] The number of Methodist chapels in England in 1818 was 2000; in 1839, 3500; in 1910, 8606. Though Methodists were regarded with some suspicion by the Church of England for their religious ardour, they were not excluded from public office: they were in Parliament from 1780. Methodism was essentially lower middle class: Wesleyans were especially strong among shopkeepers.[43] The Primitive Methodists (Prims), who broke away from the Wesleyans in 1812, were also keen builders: in 1843 there were 1278 Prim chapels; by 1888 there were 4406.[44] They were, in their own view, responding to the growth of population – the rapid emergence of new towns like Middlesbrough and Barrow-in-Furness, and the growing numbers of people in cities. The Prims had some artistic pretensions, notwithstanding their attachment to moral rectitude: 'our chapels have a poetic, as well as a prosaic side; and to many this side will be the more attractive.'[45]

One important characteristic of Methodists in towns and cities was this: by 1900 they were concerned that buildings that looked like churches were driving away potential worshippers, and they tended then towards meeting places that looked distinctly secular. These re-statements of Christian centrality (many were called 'Central Hall') were as confident and ambitious as any church by Gilbert Scott – now, in the 20th century, God's majesty had to be disguised under municipal robes.

Congregationalists, also known as 'Independents', were also energetic. The scale and confidence of many of their churches expressed their strength and civic power. In 1875 there were 2980 Congregational churches in England; in 1880, 3176; in 1900, 3433.[46] They were bustling, full of activities; there was a dedication to hymn-singing and 'a simpler, warmer, more direct style' of preaching.[47] Between 1850 and the end of the century there was a great deal of chapel-restoring and chapel-building.[48] Moody and Sankey's Mission to Birmingham in 1875 gave rise to the 'Pleasant Sunday Afternoon' movement of the 1890s – 'Brief, Bright, Brotherly but still evangelistic.'[49] It was a far cry from both Low and High Anglicanism.

The Unitarians, though a small denomination, were influential beyond their size, partly because of their civic role, especially in Manchester and Liverpool, and partly because of their interest in expressions of their ideas through the churches they built. The Unitarian Historical Society lists records for 398 Unitarian congregations in England; of these 77 built new churches in the period.

Thus, by 1884, England was indeed full of churches. But conventional (and consensual) sermon-enjoying, Sabbath-observing piety was, on the whole, passing away and being replaced by something more personal and elusive. This new relationship with God has been called 'incarnational theology': the notion that God is present, visible and near in the material and secular world all around us.[50] For it is not that *religion* was in retreat, but that regular church-going was in decline: by 1880 Anglican church membership had sunk to its lowest point in the 19th century. Notwithstanding all this, several reasons for church-building remained among Anglicans.

First, and strongest, what might be described as the 'memorial impulse': a church to commemorate a dead relative – often not so much a modest act of piety as a demonstration of personal conspicuous consumption, and more about the patron of the church than the person commemorated. Into this category fall some of the most interesting and assertive churches built for female clients – Brithdir (p.276), Matlock (p.184), Richards Castle (p.147), Barmouth (p.280).

Second, and sometimes allied to the first, the desire to 'mop up' those parish churches which had not been 'restored' in the 1840s–70s, and still provided inadequate or unseemly accommodation for their parishes (though this was no longer being done in a conscious effort to build a church as it 'should' have been).

Third, the desire to proclaim a personal, triumphalist view of religion. New buildings were usually justified by the needs of a spiritually impoverished public, even if no such public were subsequently found as a congregation. In most cases, provision exceeded demand, and optimism outran reality: many urban working-class people never attended any church ever.[51] For many even the idea of any distinctive denominational allegiance was a waste of time.[52] For others, the remains of old superstitious beliefs had been replaced by 'luck'.[53] By 1914, many soldiers believed only in fate.[54]

The other reason was that, if one were rich in 1884 and wanted to 'virtue-signal', the options were few. Some were fusty echoes of the past – founding almshouses was slightly out of fashion; it was not quite yet the era of the named art gallery, though the startlingly rich and pious Alexander Carnegie founded local libraries. A church was still the approved site for an act of public devotion: for the modestly wealthy, a lectern or screen; for the rich, a stained-glass window (church authorities were rather against elaborate monuments by 1880); and for the plutocracy, a new church. Others eschewed the whole business, and preferred racing yachts, mistresses and ballrooms: passingly few Edwardian country houses were built with chapels, but most had billiard rooms.

SCOTLAND

Elsewhere in Britain, the picture was a little different: competition was the driving force.

In Scotland the three mainstream Protestant strands – Church of Scotland (CofS), Free Church of Scotland (FC) and United Presbyterian Church (UPC) – all to some extent regarded themselves as the 'true' church. The rivalry between them meant the number of churches was always greater than demand – which was falling.

The population of Scotland in 1881 was 3,753,573. A CofS survey in 1874 suggested there were 679,488 CofS members and adherents.[55] In 1880 there were 172,982 UPC communicants. There were perhaps 300,000 FCs. There were many other Protestant denominations: the Scottish Episcopal Church, the Reformed Presbyterian Church, the Evangelical Union, Baptists, Congregationalists, Methodists and the United Original Secession, as well as mission halls of the Brethren in mining and fishing villages, and tiny fragments left over from previous and subsequent secessions, such as the Associate Presbytery of Original Seceders, whose governance in 1842 amounted to just two ministers and an elder.

Numbers of adherents, communicants or members did not relate to new churches built. Free Church enthusiasm for church-building following the Disruption of 1843 continued into the last decades of the century, especially in the Highlands, even as populations there shrank as crofters made their way to the cities. In 1892 the Free Presbyterians broke from the FCs: church-building in the Highlands became even more hectic. In Duirnish on Skye, for example, there were five churches for 4,319 people in 1881: in 1901 there were ten churches, but only 3,074 people.

In Scottish cities the dynamics were more muted: the three main Protestant denominations were somewhat averse to new-church-building. There was a preference in the CofS in favour of large central churches with extra clergy: in Govan, Revd John Macleod wanted his new 1884 parish church to be:

> a great church, free to all and open always … the glowing focus and the perennial fountain of active Christian life and manifold good works … with evangelical and fervent preaching.[56]

The Free Church erected some 200 chapels both in town and country – though the courts decided that, notwithstanding the Disruption, the buildings still belonged to the Church of Scotland; which stimulated further the Free Church's determination to build its own churches. And since the government was not willing to grant them funds for new churches, the CofS set about raising its own money for '*quoad sacra*' parishes – a sub-parish within an existing ecclesiastical parish. It looked like retaliation. By the end of the 19th century more than 400 *quoad sacra* parishes had been created.[57]

One realignment is significant in our period. The United Free Church (UFC) was formed in 1900 by the union of the FC (formed at the Disruption of 1843) and the UPC, which itself had been formed in 1847 from the union of two churches which had earlier left the established Church of Scotland: the Secession Church and the Relief Church. A minority did not go into the UFC and continues today as the Free Church of Scotland (colloquially, The Wee Frees). In 1929 the UFC united with the established Church of Scotland, and that name now includes both. Again, a minority did not join that union, and continues today as the United Free Church.

Despite all that, by 1885 it was the Roman Catholics who were the most energetic, with 342,500 baptised persons in 183 'missions' (Scotland was still officially regarded as a mission country by the Vatican until 1878).[58] RCs were the most inclined to build churches in poor areas. The Catholic priest lived in a house next to his church; Protestant ministers were in their manse, often in a separate residential district. In Scotland church-building seems to have almost become a habit. And it was so ingrained, it ignored demographic and social reality – more churches, fewer attendees and a growing impression, therefore, among the faithful, of decline.

WALES

In Wales too it was competition between denominations that stoked the fires. By 1890 'to be a Welshman and a Christian meant more or less the same thing.'[59] There was a sort of theological consensus: apart from the Unitarians, all Welsh Nonconformists were moderate Calvinists, even the Methodists.[60] Though people shared the same Protestant, evangelical and moral convictions, there were nonetheless small points on which they could not agree.[61] 'Denominational sectarianism' meant there was a decision to be made about which chapel one should attend, and which not.[62] Numbers of chapels grew – for example in 1831, there were 230 Baptist churches and 87 branches; in 1861, 576 chapels; in 1881, 742; in 1891, 845; in 1902, 896.[63] The Anglicans (Church of Wales, then Church in Wales) were simply outnumbered. The Royal Commission on the Church of England and Other Religious Bodies in Wales and Monmouthshire published its results in 1910. The year most fully reported in the statistics was 1905.[64] It measured robust growth in church and chapel building (see panel below).

One other Welsh factor is that in some places the coming of the railways brought English tourists, and the tendency was for denominations to build an English-speaking chapel to go alongside their existing Welsh one.[69] The 20th century presented other challenges to Welsh culture: the expansion of the secular state; education no longer in the hands of the chapels; and civic buildings, public institutes and working men's halls built in open competition with them.[70] For the working class in Wales, church and chapel as the source of entertainment and social cohesion were being supplemented and perhaps supplanted by trade unions and social clubs.[71]

Wales	Number of buildings		Church members
	1851	1905	1905
CofW	1,180	1,546 [65]	193,081
Independent/Cong	1,340	1,078 [66]	175,147
Calvinistic Methodist	807	1,411 [67]	170,617
Wesleyan Methodist	499	661	40,811
Primitive Methodist	not given	147	8,306
Baptists	567 *(in 1860)*	1,755 [68]	143,835
RC	21	71	19,870

There was a 'Great Revival' of Christian fervour in Wales in 1904–5. It produced a surge of religious engagement: an extra 80,000 members joined denominations in Wales. But by 1912, three quarters of these new people had drifted away.[72] Baptists, Methodists and Congregationalists all reported a drop in attendance numbers.[73] The taste for moral rectitude and self-restraint which characterised the chapel culture of the early 1800s was now old-fashioned, and no fun. Meanwhile, through films and popular music, Wales was succumbing to English-language culture that was materialistic, immediate and worldly. Through Socialism, even atheism became a possible worldview.

Meanwhile, both before and after the Great War, the growing, comfortable Welsh middle class tended to express their sense of arrival by attending church rather than chapel.[74] Between 1900 and 1908 nearly a third of children born in Wales were baptised as Anglicans.[75] The hold of chapel was breaking. Welsh disestablishment was swiftly implemented in 1920. It seemed by then almost beside the point.

'SECULARISATION'

The decline in the importance of organised religion has been called the 'secularisation' of Britain. But that implies that people became less religious and more secular themselves – for which there seems at best contradictory evidence: working-class men in English cities were never great church attenders and, while attendance at Chapel in Wales may have been normative, what evidence is there that all congregants were committed believers? What is really going on is surely something slightly different – the drifting of church life from centrality might be better called 'irrelevencisation'. Church just didn't matter any more. Parliament would neither approve nor disapprove the Prayer Book – it certainly would not spend money on building churches; the Queen could be graciously friendly towards the Pope – and Catholics could build churches without threatening the fabric of state, for no church had that power now. The very idea of blasphemy came to be ridiculous. In 1908 the courts held that 'if the decencies of controversy are observed, even the fundamentals of religion may be attacked without the writer being guilty of blasphemy.' Religion was no longer what *we* did, but what *I* did. Organised, centralised, established religion declined also, at least in part, because of a larger, tectonic change – what Lyotard calls 'the incredulity towards metanarratives'. People were beginning to be sceptical about one big explanation of everything – God – and so also doubtful of its practical manifestations – bishops, baptism, sin. They were much more inclined to be interested in what was in their own direct experience, albeit fragmentary and anecdotal. Society had moved on: people were thinking for themselves.

4

ARTS & CRAFTS CHURCHES IN CONTEXT

SOCIETY

The Church slipped below the horizon gradually but steadily. The competition was overwhelming. The Devil had all the best tunes and the brightest lights.

The sermon had dominated publishing until the mid-19th century.[76] By 1860 the serial publication of fiction was beginning to change reading habits: illustrated weeklies such as *Once a Week* (launched 1859) and *The Cornhill* (1860) grew in popularity at the expense of the worthier non-illustrated magazines like Dickens's *All the Year Round.* There was a new taste for – and ability to obtain and enjoy – secular reading matter, through circulating libraries, newspapers and journals. Greater literacy led to a rapid growth of 'low' culture somewhat antipathetic to religion – music halls and pubs, and easy-reading journals like *Tit-bits* (1880).

The middle classes had their own new forms of 'high' culture, not in opposition to, but outwith the Church: for example, the Royal College of Music (founded 1883). The Church of England set up new, would-be popular organisations, to stand alongside it as buttresses to its role in social cohesion, for example The Boys' Brigade (1883). Other organisations sprang from church origins – football clubs like Everton (originally St Domingo's) in 1878, and Celtic (founded by a Marist priest in 1888): they soon changed their names to conceal their church origins. Such bodies' existence tended subtly to reinforce the general sense of the Church's social shortcomings.

Around 1900 there emerged what has been called 'the divine right of self-development.'[77] There was a clash between the pleasures (sinful?) of growing prosperity and the Church's virtues of self-denial: as one American bishop put it, 'a certain distrust on the part of our people as to the effect of material prosperity on their morality.'[78] And, towards the end of the period, the churches' growing perception that they were 'irrelevant to the "real" needs of society' and that something else was needed.[79] A monolithic institution, dominating both streetscape and culture, was no longer credible: something approachable, more friendly, less *de haut en bas* was called for. One commentator uses phrases that highlight how what had once been the province of the Church was now separating from it: 'The Gospel of Fun', 'The Sacrament of Sexuality', 'The Social Gospel', 'The Undivided Self'.[80]

The CofE was still there, but what it was for was no longer clear, nor unquestioned. However, even if there were a decline in personal and regular commitment to attendance at (or even adherence to) the Church, people remained interested in the spiritual. Though the working class may have remained indifferent, the middle classes were energetically engaged. The novelist George Gissing put it thus in 1903:

The triumph of Darwin was signalized by the invention of the happy word Agnostic, which had great vogue. But agnosticism, as a fashion, was far too reasonable to endure. There came a rumour of Oriental magic (how the word repeats itself!), and presently everyone who had nothing better to do gossiped about 'esoteric Buddhism' – the saving adjective sounded well in a drawing-room. It did not hold very long, even with the novelists; for the English taste, this esotericism was too exotic. Somebody suggested that the old table-turning and spirit-rapping, which had homely associations, might be reconsidered in a scientific light, and the idea was seized upon. Superstition pranked in the professor's spectacles, it set up a laboratory, and printed grave reports. Day by day its sphere widened. Hypnotism brought matter for the marvel-mongers, and there followed a long procession of words in limping Greek – a little difficult till practice had made perfect. Another fortunate terminologist hit upon the word 'psychical' – the *p* might be sounded or not, according to the taste and fancy of the pronouncer – and the fashionable children of the scientific age were thoroughly at ease.[81]

C.F.G. Masterman's *The Condition of England* (1909) examined new currents in contemporary culture: 'Life, for the general, has become more tolerable than ever before.'[82] The national confidence was tangible: 'England has shaken man's authority and found freedom.'[83] And, patrician though Masterman's tone is, a similar vein of affirmative affluence can be found in middle-class experience too – in Max Beerbohm's Oxbridge fantasy *Zuleika Dobson* (1911), in children's romances like E. Nesbit's *Railway Children* and J.M. Barrie's *Peter Pan* (both 1906), even in H.G. Wells's lower middle-class *Kipps* (1905).

In the CofE those who were building new churches were rarely engaged in theological or liturgical debates: in all the correspondence between Norman Shaw and his client Mrs Foster on her church at Richards Castle, Shropshire (p.147), there is not a single mention of anything remotely theological; at Henry Wilson's church at Brithdir, Gwynedd (p.276), there are differences in points of furnishing between Wilson and his client, but it tends to be her personal ecclesiological prejudices that are at issue, not theology, on which Wilson is silent. Individuality was important even in the kind of clergymen appointed: at St Bartholomew, Ipswich (Charles Spooner, 1895) (p.207) the domineering client – a member of the local brewing dynasty, and the architect's aunt – appointed an obliging High Church nephew as the first incumbent: he was pelted with tomatoes by the unrepentantly Low townsfolk.

THE BITTER CRY

In 1876 Revd C. Maurice Davies wrote about a remarkable new phenomenon – the energetic young Ritualist priest who was distinctly democratic in thinking. His encounter with Fr Stanton of St Alban's, Holborn, was a revelation: at the Eucharist, 'the celebrant had a huge gold cross on the back of his cope, and the acolytes were gorgeous in scarlet cassocks and white surplices.'[84] But Fr Stanton also ran a Working Men's Club, where he smiled indulgently on their 'glass of grog' and games of cards. Here was a man who combined the very Highest Church

Anglicanism with a down-to-earth practicality that endeared him to his flock.

The most exceptional of this breed of radical, intellectual priests was Stewart Headlam, '"the most bohemian priest" in the history of his church.'[85] He founded the Guild of St Matthew in 1877;[86] was a member of the LCC; served for a decade on the council of the Fabian Society; was a friend of Charles Bradlaugh, the atheist MP; and provided bail for Oscar Wilde. Headlam insisted that true socialism was not only 'distinctly Christian' but also involved 'the greatest economic change with the least possible interference with private life and liberty.'[87] The Christian Social Union (CSU), founded in 1889, in sympathy with Headlam's socialist ideas but not his radical methods, published *Lux Mundi,* essays edited by Charles Gore, later Bishop of Birmingham (1905–11). The essays emphasised Christianity as the key to practical solutions of social problems: 'To present Christ in practical life.'[88]

Dedication to working-class neighbourhoods was not exclusive to young High Church priests; the publication of Andrew Mearns's 1d pamphlet *The Bitter Cry of Outcast London* (1883) showed that the concern of clerics for the perfect interpretation of rubrics and doctrine was embarrassingly redundant when:

> The Churches are making the discovery that seething in the very centre of our great cities, concealed by the thinnest crust of civilisation and decency, is a vast mass of moral corruption, of heart-breaking misery and absolute godlessness.[89]

Revd Brooke Lambert, Vicar of Greenwich, in an article in the *Contemporary Review* (1883) anatomised the causes of poverty, attributing at least some of it to capitalism's need to cut costs to meet competitive pressures: cut costs meant cut wages. Lambert championed trade unions, favoured workers' co-operatives, and commended the ideas of Christian Socialism first set out by Charles Kingsley and F.D. Maurice.[90]

THE SETTLEMENTS

In 1884 Canon Samuel Barnett founded Toynbee Hall in Whitechapel as an educational and cultural centre for working men: Barnett declared his debt to the Christian Socialism of Maurice.[91] In 1894 he published an essay commending the idea – first mooted by a radical workman, Frederick Rogers – of bringing the resources of educated men to bear on the lives of the poor, through 'settlements'.[92] His engine to re-connect church and masses was the intellectual world of the old Universities. The Barnetts' work (Samuel's wife Henrietta was as influential as he) exemplifies the pouring of spiritual energy, intellectual engagement and practical idealism into the slums, especially in London, in the last decades of the century: liberal, even socialist; spiritual, but humanely Christian without being assertively religious. In the settlements, young men, often Oxbridge undergraduates, went to live in the slums to do good works and bring some sort of enlightenment. To many young men in the University Settlements, religion and politics were the same thing.

The working man and woman remained largely indifferent: it was increasingly understood that, while people needed buildings, things other than churches were likely to be of greater appeal – at first, things in accord with church work:

meeting rooms, working men's institutes, libraries; then, increasingly the secular: cinemas, fire stations, telephone exchanges and department stores.

The shift was subtle, but inexorable. At the start of George Gissing's 1887 novel *Thyrza* the hero, Walter Egremont, presents his fiancée with a copy of Ruskin's bestseller, *Sesame and Lilies.* Towards the end of the novel Egremont posts his long-standing friend, Mrs Ormonde, a copy of Whitman's *Leaves of Grass*. In the three years between these gifts, Egremont's arc from Ruskin – 'very beautiful and noble' as his fiancée describes it – to Whitman, reflects something of the wider cultural shift. To Egremont Whitman now felt modern and prophetic, while Ruskin looked old and tired. Whitman sang the Body Electric: Ruskin analysed what makes a good bishop and the dutiful domestic duties of women. Ruskin's little book became a popular Sunday School prize: Whitman's was banned in Boston for obscenity.[93] Ruskin ends with a vividly Biblical vision of Christ in a heavenly garden. For Whitman:[94]

> underneath Christ the divine I see,
> The dear love of man for his comrade,
> the attraction of friend to friend.

Whitman's is the human Christ encountered at Haslemere (p.88) and Great Warley (p.202) – a personal friend, a confirmation of the value of earthly life as much as heavenly redemption. But humanism, enlightenment and social democracy in the end cannot inform a church, because God the Father will not be democratised. Once personal spiritual quest drives church-building, a church finds it hard to have persuasive divine immanence. It can be approachable, friendly, lovely, but it cannot quite inspire awe and devotion.

MUTUAL FRIENDS

It was in this context that the Arts & Crafts and religion encountered each other.

C.R. Ashbee, founder of the Guild of Handicraft, stayed at Toynbee Hall for a time; and his close friend, the church architect Charles Spooner, and another mutual friend, Walter Crane, both worked with the Barnetts, in particular at the Whitechapel Gallery. Here, in the 1880s, spiritually curious young Turks of the Arts & Crafts were intermingling with non-liturgical Christians, with the same hunger for honesty and glorious simplicity.

Though church-building was not central to the Settlement Movement, mission halls of varying degrees of simplicity were designed. Pembroke College Mission, Newington (founded 1885) had a multi-purpose room that served as a games club when not being used for worship. In 1892 a new building was built in Barlow Street, Southwark (now St Christopher, Walworth, p.112): the architect was AWG founder E.S. Prior. The overlap between social space and church will also be seen at other churches in this book, notably Pixham (p.89), Charterhouse-on-Mendip (p.57) and Hutton & Shenfield (p.211).

Perhaps the most 'Arts & Crafts' of all the settlements (in its architects, appearance and politics) was Mary Ward's 1890 University Hall, with its 'system of practical conduct, based on faith in God.'[95] The settlement was 'multi-faith', concerned with 'social mission'. Mrs Ward's most successful book was *Robert Elsmere* (1888), the story of a clergyman who loses his faith when he realises he cannot believe in miracles. Mrs Ward herself had had a similar experience. In 1895 her settlement moved into new premises (p.113): the architects were Arnold Smith (1866–1933, AWG 1922) and Cecil Brewer (1871–1918, AWG 1894). They were unable to be wholly atheist: the main meeting room includes a curious structure which seems very much like a chancel screen, and, over a side entrance-way there is affixed what appears to be a huge newspaper cutting, declaring a creed that expresses a spiritual version of Arts & Crafts ideas, thought to be Ward's own text:

> THE IDEA OF THE SETTLEMENT
> A settlement is a colony of members of the upper classes formed in a poor neighbourhood with the double purpose of getting to know the local conditions of life from personal observation, and of helping where help is needed. The settler gives up the comfort of a West End home, and becomes a friend of the poor. He sacrifices to them his hours of leisure, and fills his imagination with pictures of misery and crime, instead of with impressions of beauty and happiness. For a shorter or a longer time the slum becomes his home. Only seldom does he show himself at his Club, at the theatre, in Society. This means the loosening of social and personal ties, in many cases the forgoing of the prospect of an early marriage, and neglect of favourite pursuits. It means a sacrifice of life. It means that love of mankind has thrown existence off its accustomed lines, that habitual forms of conventional thought have been burnt up in the fire of a great passion ....

It is a vision of an Oxbridge undergraduate as a modern Christ – self-sacrificing and humble in the service of his fellow man. But Christ is not mentioned – only the idea that self-sacrifice was intrinsically worthwhile: 'noble', in the word George Gissing constantly uses of good actions going against his expected 20th-century grain of self-interest and cynicism. (Ruskin uses it too.)[96]

By 1900 the 'vagueness and indeterminacy' Jose Harris detects in religious belief was able to take many forms: there was a 'mystical revival', a 'spiritual renaissance', an 'experimental and adventurous generation'.[97] Indeterminacy led to variousness: in Manchester Edgar Wood built churches with equal engagement for all shades of optimistically expansive Nonconformity – the Baptists (1889), Unitarians (1892), Wesleyans (1899) and Christian Scientists (1903–7). New religious expressions might even take the form of an entirely new belief system. And here religion and Arts & Crafts could overtly intertwine: in Haslemere in 1908 Godfrey Blount launched The Country Church of the New Crusade:

> The purpose of this church is to interpret Christianity in a Spiritual and Symbolical manner ... the New Crusade seeks to make worship beautiful and uplifting, by devoting to its use what is noblest and most imaginative in our Art; and on the material side it seeks to restore real country life, that life of agriculture and handicraft, which it believes alone can save our land, and restore it to true welfare and happiness.[98]

The local newspaper's notice of Blount's funeral records that he had 'inherited from Ruskin and Morris strong social principles, and his art may be truly described as a religious art expressive of a new and modern spirit.'[99]

Religion was eliding into social justice, and even, for some, Art. In this nexus of religion, social reform and architecture, were born church buildings unlike anything that had gone before – and which, for beauty, complexity, craftsmanship and emotional spark, are unlike anything that came after.

In 1924 Virginia Woolf proclaimed:

> I will hazard a second assertion, which is more disputable perhaps, to the effect that in or about December 1910, human character changed. I am not saying that one went out, as one might into a garden, and there saw that a rose had flowered, or that a hen had laid an egg. The change was not sudden and definite like that. But a change there was, nevertheless; and, since one must be arbitrary, let us date it about the year 1910. The first signs of it are recorded in the books of Samuel Butler, in *The Way of All Flesh* in particular; the plays of Bernard Shaw continue to record it. In life one can see the change, if I may use a homely illustration, in the character of one's cook … All human relations have shifted – those between masters and servants, husbands and wives, parents and children. And when human relations change there is at the same time a change in religion, conduct, politics, and literature.[100]

If she was right, the Arts & Crafts was part of that change. Raymond Williams thought that 'The temper which the adjective Victorian is useful to describe is virtually finished in the 1880s; the new men who appear in that decade, and who have left their mark, are recognisably different in tone. To the young Englishman in the 1920s, this break was the emergence of the modern spirit.'[101]

These churches, then, are not so much about architecture, as about us – what we used to believe, and what we don't believe now. And how spiritual doubt, scepticism, even disbelief in God on the one hand, and defiant, glorious affirmation of the work of Man on the other, permeates churches built towards the end of Victoria's reign, and into Edward VII's: the years when Thomas Hardy was composing his sombre post-Victorian poem of the death of faith, *God's Funeral* (1908–10), its title later appropriated by A.N. Wilson for his 2000 book on the decline of Christianity in Western Europe. Churches built when religion was still around, but slipping away.

The Arts & Crafts was the long birth-pang of our brave new world of self-actualisation, sexual liberation, fast cars and the entrapments of the World Wide Web. Arts & Crafts churches embody our sad, awkward, wistful turning away from certainties towards unembraceable uncertainty.

PART II

THE GAZETTEER

5
INTRODUCTION TO THE GAZETTEER

This Gazetteer is a guide to churches worth seeking out, and why.

Entries for churches well-known and well-researched are comparatively brief – Brockhampton, Roker, Sloane Street, Queen's Cross, Great Warley, Compton: there are articles and even books to be found on all these (see 'Further Reading' p.325). The Gazetteer is more interested in sending you to see churches less well-known.

Inevitably, you will dip in to see if your own favourite church is included, and what is said about it, and whether you agree. Don't be surprised if there is less about it than you are expecting: here is no attempt to tell everything. If it is missing, you may find out why in 'Exceptions and Exclusions', pp 316–320. Where relevant, there are brief notes on architects, and some craftsmen, of largely local significance.

For each church I give a postcode, which is often of a nearby house or pub. A large number of 'Other Churches' worth seeking out for Arts & Crafts aesthetics, works, ideas and connections, are included at the end of each regional section.

I have eschewed footnotes. Detailed citations were repetitious, and cluttered the church entries: a bibliography of 'Further Reading' (p.325) seemed of more potential value.

Queen's Cross, Glasgow

Uncredited quotations are almost all from local newspapers or ICBS documents.

Using the Gazetteer without first reading Chapters 1–4 may cause you puzzlement.

THE GAZETTEER'S STRUCTURE

After they have asked, 'What is an Arts & Crafts church?' (or have asserted there is no such thing), the next thing people tend to ask is, 'Where is there an Arts & Crafts church near me?' For this reason, the Gazetteer is structured geographically. This may seem illogical – Arts & Crafts had its headquarters in London: its beginnings were in the London offices of Norman Shaw (a Scots émigré), and among those who had worked with John Dando Sedding (at heart a Cornishman, though born in Berkshire) and the Essex-born Oxford architect G.E. Street.

But those who imbibed the spirit came to London from elsewhere: Birmingham, Leicester, Liverpool, Bristol and other points of the compass – and many then went 'back to the land', in Gloucestershire especially.

In some parts of the country – Manchester, Glasgow, Yorkshire – there were stirrings of a similar nature, in some cases influenced by, occasionally independent of, London models: Edgar Wood in Middleton was a wholly independent architectural intelligence working along similar lines; as were Percy Currey in Derbyshire and Charles Ponting in Wiltshire.

The regional treatment here allows this to come through.

Besides, if one is going to look at these buildings – and there is no other way to appreciate them – it makes sense for the churches to be grouped together, as if for a logical campaign, be it a day, weekend or fortnight, and whether travelling by bicycle, car, rail or bus. For this reason, there are maps, with each church in the main text identified (pp 340–346).

Thus the Gazetteer divides the country into 14 regions, with a brief introduction for each, followed by the churches in order of what seems to me significance (I try not to give buildings 'marks out of ten'), with longer articles for the ones most worth trying to see.

WHAT IS NOT INCLUDED?

I have not included churches that have been turned into houses – except where they are nonetheless still worth seeing, discreetly, from the road. These buildings are marked with an **H**. Do not trespass on private property, or make yourself tiresome to the occupants.

Where a church has become offices, or similar, but is nonetheless worth seeing from the outside, I have included it in the 'Other Churches' listings.

I have not included individual Arts & Crafts objects or glass, be they never so beautiful, in a medieval or Victorian Gothic church, since this would (a) make the book too big and (b) defeat my purpose of drawing attention to the interface between Arts & Crafts ideas and church ideas. Some large-scale major interior schemes are included, however, where they alter the character of a church; as are some buildings which are not technically churches.

As to significant churches that no longer exist – an account of Arts & Crafts churches that ignores them would be incomplete. On the other hand, I cannot see any merit in a Gazetteer of demolished and lost churches. Luckily, there are not many: they are listed in 'Demolished or Threatened Churches' (pp 317–318).

I have almost certainly left out some blindingly obvious churches, and I have surely included many churches which are 'not' Arts & Crafts. You can email me with your suggestions, frustrations and special pleading at alechamiltonchurches@outlook.com

OTHER SOURCES

If you want to know more about the structure and contents of any church, or plan a visit, consult the latest *Pevsner*: wholly authoritative, and often now with useful contextualising background as well as exhaustive architectural description (though not always).

An increasingly good place to look online is The Victorian Web – for the earliest churches in the 'Arts & Crafts' period and for one or two later ones, and for a number of the personalities, it draws together the key sources, and gives clear, detailed accounts.

Historic England's online listings are meticulous, but give little or no impression of what you are going to encounter – and very few images. But do look.

And do trawl Google or Bing or DuckDuckGo or Ecosia. Information is being added all the time. Some of it is correct. Don't rely on Wikipedia too much: it is only occasionally informative on individual churches of the period, though it is getting better on individual architects.

A FEW CAVEATS

Open or Closed? I have done my best to indicate whether the main churches are open or not – at least, whether they were when I visited. In most cases, they are locked, and you will have to make your own arrangements to see them. (If enough people do, perhaps they will open more.) Start with Googling, of course, to see if you can find an email address for the incumbent or churchwarden. Keyholders come and go, and the situation at every church changes. In cities, Roman Catholic churches and busy Anglican churches are usually open – but don't rely on it. Country churches may be open or closed – it depends. Church websites do not tell you about whether a church is open or not: you have to do a bit of homework, and phone or – better – email, ideally with a proposed date and time you want to call. (Be wary of pro forma/template enquiry forms – they are not always responded to. Where a church only has a Facebook page, be bold and post a message. But don't expect to be answered very quickly!)

Keys hanging in the porch have died out. It is now rare even to find a notice with a keyholder's telephone number. Congregations are largely elderly, small and falling. Their church is often a worry, not a joy. By the time you get to one of these churches, it may even have been declared redundant, or be for sale. Be prepared. But never say never. When I first visited St Christopher, Haslemere, in 2005, it was facing closure. Now it gets coaches.

Names. These churches may now no longer be called what they were originally called (and are called here). In Scotland, congregations tend to take their names with them when they move from one building to another. In England and Wales, new church denominations – evangelical, charismatic, spiritualist – when they take over a building, call it by a new name; and some churches have become mosques. In all cases, this frequently means the interior has been substantially altered, and only parts of the original interior survive. Often, though, it is worth persevering.

Inconvenience. You are almost certainly an inconvenience. Keyholders, churchwardens and incumbents are invariably kindly and polite. But you – a mere rubbernecking tourist – are not their prime interest or concern. So be polite. If there is a copy of the church history for sale, buy it. (The churches have often just celebrated their centenary.) And buy some postcards too.

Generosity. When you have visited, even if the church is a disappointment to you, make a donation – at least £5, but £10 is better. And don't forget Gift Aid.

Encouragement. Don't take these churches as the definitive collection. There are others. And not just here, but all over Europe – yes, and Ireland – and beyond. This is just the start. But go now – churches are closing and the days are short.

> *Let me only observe, as a specimen of my trouble, that I have sometimes been obliged to run half over London, in order to fix a date correctly; which, when I had accomplished, I well knew would obtain me no praise, though a failure would have been to my discredit.*
>
> JAMES BOSWELL, Advertisement to the 1st Edition of *Life of Johnson*, 1791

SANCTVS
SANCTVS
SANCTVS

6

THE WEST COUNTRY

Cornwall, Devon, Dorset, Somerset, Bath, Bristol

The Arts & Crafts penetrated the far west only faintly. John Dando Sedding (1838–91, AWG 1884), in whose office Ernest Gimson (1864–1919, AWG 1891), Ernest Barnsley (1863–1926, AWG 1906) and Henry Wilson (1864–1934, AWG 1892) at various times learnt their craft, had strong connections with Cornwall, where his elder brother Edmund Sedding (1836–68), born near Okehampton, established his architecture practice in Penzance in 1862. John joined him there briefly (Edmund, never robust, died young). Edmund's son, E.H. Sedding (1863–1921), who practised in Plymouth, designed a small number of churches in Cornwall and two in Devon, both highly original.

In Dorset, Edward Schroeder Prior (1852–1932), one of the co-founders of the AWG, started his innovative and idiosyncratic career, and built his first church at Bothenhampton. Four years later W.D. Caröe (1857–1938, AWG 1890) built a church at Colehill. Caröe was sometimes contemptuous of what he saw as Arts & Crafts' pretensions, and never subscribed to its unwritten manifestoes. Nonetheless Colehill reflects Arts & Crafts ways of working rather vividly. His church at Charterhouse-on-Mendip perhaps more so.

Three important makers of church furnishings were in the West: Harry Hems (1842–1916) in Exeter – ambitious, wide-ranging, commercial (pp.75, 118, 132, 151, 167); Trasks of Norton-sub-Hamdon (pp.66, 192, 226, 263, 277) – the kind of careful, artistic craftsmen approved by Sedding and Wilson; and the Pinwill sisters – brilliant 'talented amateurs' of a kind encouraged by the ACES, who grew to be something greater (p.63).

Holy Trinity, Bothenhampton: interior looking east

BOTHENHAMPTON, Dorset

Holy Trinity | 1887–89
Edward Schroeder Prior
DT6 4BH | Usually open

Prior looms large. He was one of the founder members of the AWG (he trained under Norman Shaw); he invented Prior's 'Early English' glass, produced by blowing the molten glass into a metal box, so it is thicker in some parts than in others, an unevenness appealing to the Arts & Crafts taste for imperfection and the overtly 'hand-made'; he designed of one of the 'Big Four' Arts & Crafts churches, St Andrew, Roker (p.261); was friend and co-worker with William Richard Lethaby (1857–1931, AWG 1884), the Arts & Crafts' principal (perhaps, apart from William Morris, only) theorist; wrote the magisterial *History of Gothic Art in England* (1900), and finally, for twenty years, was Slade Professor of Art at Cambridge.

Bothenhampton was the first of his churches. In May 1885 the *British Architect* called it 'A very pleasing Early English design'. There is rather more to it than that.

Prior was rigorously practical and painstakingly knowledgeable. He had closely analysed Dorset building traditions, materials and how buildings responded to their site. Light was his first concern. There would be a strong northern light in nave and chancel, so only small windows were required – three slender lancets in the nave (one was changed to a double). He cared about heating: 'The church must be warm, therefore thick walls, heavy doors …' As to seating, it had to be generous: Prior knew the worshippers would be 'mostly large farmers'. And, as they were also mainly Low Church, they wanted to both hear and see the preacher. Thus, there are no piers to interfere with the line of vision to the pulpit; and the later, spindly 1895 chancel screen does not intrude. Prior observed that 'a simple village church did not need a large chancel'. He also eschewed a baptistry – just allowing space for parents and godparents round the font.

Wind and rain on this exposed site suggested not slates for the roof, but Yorkshire stone slabs (later replaced). It followed that the supporting timbers should be strong: 'In an exposed situation, subject to heavy gales, the ordinary construction of a church roof with framed wood principals is not a useful one. The trusses vibrate under the weight of the wind, and … the creaking and straining of the timbers may make noise enough to seriously interrupt the church services. To avoid the discomfort, stone arches were used in place of wood principals …' The very idea frightened the Architects Committee of the ICBS: 'The character of the roofing proposed is extraordinary, expensive, & unsafe & not to be recommended according to constitution & decor, though the idea is a suggestive one.' Prior exhaustively countered their anxieties with meticulous argument, numerous precedents and calculations double-checked by his brother, a mathematics don at Cambridge. The ICBS eventually agreed.

'An architect must get to love his building,' Prior wrote, 'and be enthusiastic over it.' He felt deeply that a church 'should be unmistakably what it is … It should be reverential, simple and honest. Ornate treatment [is] out of place here … aim at a graceful effect – not flimsy and not coarse.' The church marches up the hill, giving the altar added prominence, emphasised by the extreme narrowing at the chancel arch.

The altar table was made by A.H. Mason, who later became foreman at Kenton & Co., the furniture business set up by Ernest Gimson, Detmar Blow and W.R. Lethaby in 1890. The gesso frontal (not always to be seen) was designed jointly by Prior and Lethaby, and shown at the second ACES Exhibition in 1889. (It has lately been carefully repaired by the St Andrew's Conservation Trust.) Lethaby was just setting out in practice, and Prior put a number of small jobs his way.

Prior designed the font, communion rail, choir stalls, church chest and the doors. The east window is by Christopher Whall, 1896, using Prior's 'Early English' glass: Lethaby seems to have had a hand in the design. The screen was made by F.W. Grange of Bridport, 1910. The church guidebook (Cyril Kay, 1991) suggests the wood panelling of the pulpit, by E.H. Gilbert of Bridport, conceals a painted decoration 'in an Art Nouveau style' by the young MacDonald Gill, who later decorated for Prior at Roker. It seems to have been an innovation too far, and quietly suppressed. Is it still there?

Holy Trinity, Bothenhampton:
altar frontal by E S Prior and W R Lethaby

COLEHILL, Wimborne, Dorset

St Michael and All Angels | 1892–5
W.D. Caröe
BH21 7AB | Usually locked

St Michael and All Angels was approvingly described by the ICBS as 'picturesque'. In a letter to the vicar, Caröe insisted 'there are several half-timbered churches in the county'. Where they may be is debatable: there are half-timbered *houses* in Cerne Abbas and Sherborne.

In the 120 years since it was consecrated, St Michael's half-timbered look has been emphasised by highly contrasted black wood and white render. Caröe intended something more restrained: his presentation drawings show the wood unstained, or weathered to silver-brown, and the brickwork a mellow, biscuity pink.

Caröe worked first, for a year, in the Liverpool office of Edmund Kirby (1838–1920). Kirby had been assistant to John Douglas (1829–1911) (p.228) until 1867, 'the architect mainly responsible for reviving the "black-and-white" timbered style of the North-West'. Kirby admired Norman Shaw, whom Caröe came to regard later as something of a hero. Shaw's St Michael and All Angels, Bedford Park, 1879 (p.111) was especially influential. The Colehill exterior brings to mind an earlier Shaw building, Cragside (1869–95).

The prime mover in the project was a retired military man, Colonel Paget, Royal Artillery. By 1881 there was a permanent building – 'Trotman's tin tabernacle', named after the incumbent of Wimborne Minster, who during the summer of 1880 held open-air evening services in the area, preaching from a wagon. Paget started an endowment fund to pay for a permanent church. Just as plans were taking

St Michael and All Angels, Colehill: altar and reredos

shape in the summer of 1892, Paget died. St Michael's became his memorial. Walter Bankes of Kingston Lacy gave a piece of land near the tin tabernacle, on what was described locally as 'a very picturesque part of Colehill, covered with pine trees … commanding magnificent views.'

Once the church was built, artistic members of the community emerged to furnish it. Two church Inventories at Dorset History Centre tell the story, recording in many cases the makers, as well as the donors.

The organ case, 1897, reredos frame, 1915, cross and candlesticks were designed by Rowland Clark, a carpenter living in Artists' Row, Portland. He also designed and made the wooden chancel screen, painted green and surmounted by a large oak rood surrounded with filigree carving. The rood was removed in 1978: only the supporting brackets remain, though there appear to be plans to remove them.

The cross and candlesticks in ebony, ivory and mother-of-pearl, were made by Laurence Turner (1864–1957, AWG 1886) whose work is also to be seen at Kempley (p.145), Summerstown (p.116) and Dockenfield (p.90).

The Nativity panels in the reredos were painted by Frederick Beaumont (1861–1950) a society portraitist who lived at Witchampton, near Wimborne, and had a studio in London. He studied at the RA Schools, and won a silver medal in Life Study.

The pulpit and sounding board (1897) 'simply carved in Jacobean style' were carved by Revd Canon William Gildea, as was the altar (1897) and four frontal panels of angels. (The sounding board is no longer there.)

Gildea was a talented craftsman. He carved the altar, reredos woodwork, altar rails and the stem of the lectern at West Lulworth, and the pulpit and lectern at St Nicholas, Chaldon Herring. At Upwey, Dorset, where he was Rector in 1901, the choir stalls, lectern and chancel woodwork were also by him.

At West Lulworth the carved panels on either side of the oak reredos are the work of Hans Mayer, 'the son of Josef Mayer who on three occasions (1870, 1880, 1890) acted "Christus" in the Oberammergau Passion Play'. There is also work by Mayer at Colehill: he carved the statuette of our Saviour in the

St Michael and All Angels, Colehill: porch and tower

east (external) wall. The unlikely connection between Dorset and Oberammergau seems to have come about through a lecture on the Passion Play given at Lulworth in 1894 by a Mr Arthur Evans. The villagers were inspired – perhaps by lantern slides – to start a fund to purchase examples of Oberammergau carving for their own Church.

The Colehill Inventories lists two more items of craftsmanship. First, in the north wall of the nave, a carved oak wall bracket and, chained to it, a carved oak casket containing a volume bound in leather and silk recording the Colehill men who served in the Great War, as well as those killed. The whole was designed and illuminated by the vicar, Revd A.W. Stote, who met the whole cost. The carving was done by H.F. Bowers of Bournemouth. This seems to have been replaced by a free-standing modern display case in the south aisle.

Arthur William Stote (later Canon Stote-Blandy, d.1950) was Vicar of Colehill from 1918. He records the Book 'has occupied the Vicar's spare moments for upwards of fourteen months.' He notes that 'each page has an original painted and illuminated design in gold, silver and colours'. Stote was an artist-craftsman and a Fellow of the Society of Genealogists.

The final item of note in the 1927 Inventory is the 'Statue of St Michael & the Dragon in a recess on the north wall of the nave, carved in walnut wood by G Pucci.' The sculptor signed the piece, but little is otherwise known of him. The statue, now in a niche in the south aisle, is made with great suavity, but looks oddly out of place – exotic and, despite its wings, military rather than angelic.

The church is rather self-consciously artistic. It attracted the disdain of John Newman in the 1972 *Pevsner:* 'a Home-Counties church, ill in place in Dorset, though fitting the sylvan setting'. He adds that 'Goodhart-Rendel calls it "not at all nice".'

Caröe is an awkward figure. In her architectural biography of him, Jennifer Freeman describes him as 'bubbling with a rich fund of ideas' and 'delighted to see his buildings furnished, lived-in and cherished by their occupants'. But he was 'inclined to be high-handed'. Eric Gill, who was in Caröe's office from 1899 to 1903, recalled Caröe's 'almost complete lack of any interest in anything but theatrical effect'. Caröe 'would not have relished description as an "Arts and Crafts" architect: he was inclined to be dismissive of the unworldliness of the group'. He became a member of the AWG in 1890, but rarely played any active part, and resigned in 1910.

As to religion, 'His own inclination was to middle-of-the-road Anglicanism, tempered by a Lutheranism inherited from his father.' The church stands, therefore, in uncertain ground. Caröe did not despise the machine-made, yet there is very little not hand-made in the church, and almost nothing demonstrably shop-bought. Stote, in particular, though he arrived after the church was completed, seems to have had an Arts & Crafts sensibility. The amateur wood-worker Gildea, and Rowland Clark, seem both to have had different versions of a proto-Arts & Crafts outlook. If the details were to be examined apart from the known history, and its being by Caröe, the Arts & Crafts influences might seem more overt. The materials – brick and painted timber – do not seem to accord with local tradition: but the effect is unquestionably rural, amounting to 'quaint' and even, in a domestic Artsy-Craftsy way, 'cosy'.

PAMPHILL, Kingston Lacy, Dorset

St Stephen | 1907
Charles Ponting
BH21 4EG | Often open

St Stephen's is a village church which is really an estate church, without the inconvenience of being too near the big house: its door on the north side was for the use of the Bankes family of Kingston Lacy, who came to the church by carriage from their house, half a mile away, on a private drive. The house had been re-modelled by Sir Charles Barry, 1835–41, for William John Bankes (1786–1855), Egyptologist, collector, interior decorator and friend of Byron. Barry and Bankes first met at Abu Simbel, where Bankes was acquiring a monolith of the Cleopatra's Needle type for shipping back to England. Bankes had the house interior lavishly decorated, and crowded with souvenirs of his travels. He decorated one of his rooms at Cambridge as a Catholic church, and paid boys to sing for him: this is history as dressing-up box, and religion as theatrical amusement. The rather cavalier attitude to the Church may explain why Kingston Lacy never had a chapel. There was certainly none in Barry's design.

The house came to a nephew, Walter Ralph Bankes (1853–1904), in 1869. In 1897, at the age of 44 – and to general surprise – he married Henrietta Jenny Fraser, a society beauty, by whom he had three children. Bankes died in 1904, leaving £5000 for 'the building and endowing or contributing towards building and endowing a Church at Pamphill'. His widow carried out his wish. (The house, Kingston Lacy, was left to the National Trust in 1981.)

The lack of a church does not seem to have bothered Walter Bankes in his lifetime: why then make provision for one in his will? A suggestive circumstance is that on 23 September 1902 the Bankeses' third child, a longed-for son, Henry John Ralph, was christened at Wimborne Minster. Perhaps the church is a late thank-offering for the safe arrival of the son and heir after two daughters, to a mother aged 34. Walter's will is dated 6 April 1903, post-dating Ralph's birth by only six months. There is a local suggestion that Mrs Bankes wanted to have a chapel in the house, but 'the family would not let her: she had to wait for her husband to die.' There is also the suggestion that Walter had been a womaniser: he left £40,000 in his will to his supposed mistress, Elizabeth Marshall of Stockwell.

St Stephen, Pamphill:
angel on the choir stalls

St Stephen, Pamphill: pulpit

The architect was Charles Ponting (1849–1932) (see p.74). He was the leading – possibly only – architect in the region (based in Marlborough, Wiltshire), with a reputation as an able church-builder. He had diocesan status: Surveyor of Ecclesiastical Dilapidations for the Archdeaconry of Wiltshire in 1883, and for the Archdeaconry of Dorset in 1892. Considering the connection with Colehill (for which Bankes had given the land), W.D. Caröe may have recommended Ponting to Mrs Bankes. The two architects would have known each other: Caröe was architect to the Ecclesiastical Commissioners from 1885.

The foundation stone was laid by Henrietta Bankes on 15 February 1906, and the church dedicated on 27 July 1907. The exterior is Studland sandstone and Purbeck stone from the Bankes estates. In a niche above the porch is a statue of St Stephen with his hand on the head of a boy. The *Dorset County Chronicle and Somersetshire Gazette* reported, 'The features of the child cannot be mistaken, as representing those of the little heir to the estates.'

At the rear of the church are the Bankes family pews – grand seats like cathedral canons' stalls, affixed to the west wall. Above them the west window contains armorial bearings of Bankes family members from 1618: ten of them reportedly brought from Wimborne Minster. The congregation bench-ends are carved with the Bankes fleur-de-lys (young Walter Bankes carries a tripartite lily in the niche statue). The woodwork inside – including the roof – is reportedly all oak, grown on the estate.

Information from the Collections Manager at Kingston Lacy lists A. Palmer of Bristol as the carver of the figures over the porch and of the credence table; and Herbert Read of Exeter as carver of the font, memorial stone cross, choir stalls and wall lights. *Academy Architecture* published Ponting's perspective drawings for the church in 1906, with a caption, 'Oak lectern and Stone Font: Herbert Reed [sic], Exeter.' The work is suggestive of Harry Hems, whom Ponting employed at Down Ampney, Gloucestershire (1898–1907). Read had worked for Hems, rising to foreman joiner, and left to set up on his own account in 1888. His son, also Herbert, succeeded him in the business in 1908. The same source states 'Oak Seating and Stalls: Hosking Bros, Newbury'. Hoskings & Sons were contractors for the entire building.

A church-minder, Mrs Vera Ricketts (née Conway), from the village, has recounted her family tradition that some of the carving was by her grandfather Conway and a man called Pullman, both of whom worked on the estate. She added that many of the estate workers were expected, after they finished their day's work, to go to the church to apply their craft skills for no extra payment. This caused understandable resentment.

The font was given by the Estate's farmers. When it arrived, Mrs Bankes found it was cracked: she ordered a new one to be made. The hapless maker was Herbert Read.

The reredos and altar panels were designed by Horace Wilkinson (1866–1957) who trained at Brighton School of Art and South Kensington School of Art before working with a number of stained-glass firms from 1886 to 1901, including Burlison & Grylls and Clayton & Bell. The north and south sanctuary windows and east window were also designed by Wilkinson. The light in the latter, second from the left, is said to show Ralph Bankes sitting on Christ's lap, his sisters looking on. The reredos and panels were made by Carters of Poole, who used 'battered brass' to form the golden wings of the angels, and mother-of-pearl for the halos.

St Stephen's is part 'jewel-box', like Brithdir (p.276), part homely, like Colehill (p.51). It is a country church, and as self-consciously so as Kempley (p.145) or Brockhampton (p.142) – cosy and arty all at the same time. It is a half-way house: half grand, half familiar; half welcoming, half distant. Tradition has it the benefactress used to leave the service before the end, by her private door, so as not to encounter the congregation, her employees.

CHARTERHOUSE-ON-MENDIP
Somerset

St Hugh | 1908–13
W.D. Caröe
BS40 7XR | Open on summer Sundays

Charterhouse began life, perhaps as early as 1890, as a 'Welfare Hall' for Mendip lead miners: it blossomed into a treasury of wood-carving under the tender eye of Prebendary Menzies Lambrick, 'a clergyman of independent means who found rest from onerous parochial duties in the east end of London by frequent visits to the secluded Mendips.'

Lambrick later married, became Rector of Blagdon in 1908, and lived at Cheddar. He was philanthropic – built a library in Breaston, Derbyshire, 1904, in memory of his parents. It seems likely he funded the work at Charterhouse, and perhaps paid for the interior wood-carving too. The relationship between Caröe and Lambrick is unknown: Alban Caröe simply reports his father 'knew him in London'. 'When the structure had been finished, the rejoicing Prebendary added fitting after fitting, each more richly carved than the last.'

Caröe's biographer Jennifer Freeman suggests that here 'more than anywhere else Caröe lifts the concept of a simple, hand-crafted interior to new heights of sophistication … [it] marks a high point in Arts and Crafts consciousness, and celebrates the coalescence of the many ideas that informed it.' But that assumes Caröe designed everything. The question of who did what, in the light of lack of evidence, is moot. Might it even be possible that at least some of this

St Hugh, Charterhouse-on-Mendip: interior looking east

carving was carried out by the miners themselves? No drawings survive, apart from three single-page undated entries in Caröe's notebooks for the roof plan, the sanctuary lamp and a fireplace.

The font cover is in memory of a builder from Rickford, near Blagdon, who died in a railway accident in 1909. The font itself was the gift of Cornish miners who came to work in the Mendips. The baptistry is enclosed with a sort of English altar, with crenelated riddel posts. There is one window by Horace Wilkinson (see p.57).

SHALDON, Teignmouth, Devon

St Peter the Apostle | 1893–4, 1899–1902
E.H. Sedding
TQ14 0EA | Sometimes open

Edmund Harold Sedding (1863–1921), nephew (and pupil) of John Dando Sedding, designed two new-build churches in Devon: both are thought-provoking. The more original is the earlier, at Shaldon. Its unpromisingly sombre bulk catches the eye at the south end of the A379 bridge across the Teign. The over-sized buttresses marching down each side seem like

St Peter, Shaldon: chancel screen

+ Dignus + est + Agnus + Qui + occisus + est + accipere + virtutem +

the angular splayed legs of a threatening reptile, but its deeply recessed west window gives the building more the air of a drowsily basking shark. Entering, then, gives a slightly Jonah-esque sensation – the crepuscular nave recedes into a yet darker chancel. Once eyes are accustomed, the interior engulfs.

The energetic originator of the scheme for a new church was a dynamic vicar, Richard Marsh Marsh-Dunn, who arrived in 1890, and immediately decided the dilapidated medieval parish church should be abandoned. 'The whole church from beginning to finish was erected by his sole efforts … notwithstanding a vast amount of opposition on the part of many in the parish, who looked upon the scheme as quite impossible.'

The church is wide and deep – intended to hold 450. Things are spiky – the rood screen, the nave arcades, the crocketed niches in the apsidal (actually semi-octagonal) east end. The Crown of Thorns may be the intended metaphor, but the impression at first is rather of fish bones. The east end bears the unmistakable stamp of Henry Wilson – the steps beyond the screen framed by heavy green marble with intimidating alabaster angels. Beyond, at the communion rail, more angels, but humbled. The pulpit might have been made for Holy Trinity, Sloane Street – stone buffs may spot local Ashburton, Radford and Petitor stone, as well as Bath in a riot of colour verging on the theatrical. The font is not in the intended baptistry, but there a white marble John the Baptist holds a clam shell.

The inventiveness seems overcome by the materials – heavy, dark, substantial – and all accentuated by light levels that are usually low. Bishop Ryle of Exeter at the consecration in 1902 said he 'would rather see proper remuneration of the clergy than magnificent marble'. The altar (presumably also designed by Wilson) being marble, was illegal (the Rubrics insist on wood) – the Bishop wanted it removed. In the end, a compromise: the altar was replaced by a wooden table, but with the marble front slab attached to it. There was also a worry about the figures on the rood screen – might they be conducive to idolatry? (It was a question being asked frequently of figures on rood screens, whose re-introduction in English churches by Anglo-Catholic priests and devotees in the 1890s was becoming more frequent.) The Bishop decided they were not a threat. From left to right they are St Nicholas, the Virgin Mary, St Peter, St John and St Paul. Peter is under the rood.

The exterior rewards examination. The polychrome effects are not – as with Butterfield – in brick, but achieved by adventurous mixtures of local stone: Devon red sandstone, grey reef limestone from Babbacombe, Ham Hill stone, green Cornish 'soap' stone from the village of Polyphant, plus some stone reclaimed from the demolition of the house that originally stood on the site.

ABBOTSBURY, Newton Abbot, Devon

St Mary, Waverley Road | 1904–8
E.H. Sedding
TQ12 2ND | Locked

At the time of writing, St Mary's is threatened with redundancy: it is often the fate of churches such as this, built in fervour by rich enthusiasts in areas regarded, by them at least, as in need of accommodation for worship, and deserving of something beautiful. But local populations do not always agree, and are not

JOHN DANDO SEDDING

Where Richard Norman Shaw has Andrew Saint's monumental architectural monograph to his name, the other key influence on the young architects of the Arts & Crafts, John Dando Sedding, has not been so fortunate: there is a revelatory thesis by Paul Snell, but no definitive modern monograph.

Many of Sedding's new-build churches are to be found in the West Country – though few are really worth seeking out as structures: **St Elwyn, Hayle**, 1886–8 (TR27 4BS) is typical – imposing but without charm; **All Saints, Falmouth**, 1887–90 (TR11 3PN) is equally grand, with choir stalls and font by Sedding, and other fittings by his nephew, E.H. Sedding. It is Sedding's church woodwork, often by Trasks of Norton-sub-Hamdon, that is almost always the most rewarding of his West Country work, combining vernacular ideas with modern invention.

Five churches stand out: two in Devon, three in Cornwall.

At **All Saints, Holbeton, Devon**, 1884–9 (PL8 1LN), Sedding had his golden opportunity: a free hand in design and money no object – the client was a banker, Henry Mildmay of Barings. The medieval structure was hardly touched, though Sedding elaborated the south porch with new carving – and a courtly new door and gate. New glass includes medallions designed by Heywood Sumner (1853–1940, AWG 1884), who also designed the east window. What old woodwork survives is tactfully distinguished from the exuberant new additions – chancel screen, tower screen, north transept screen; panelling round the walls; and a burgeon of nave bench ends – birds, animals, chrysanthemums, foliage and tracery – culminating in the chancel's squirrels, swan, frogs, lizards, squid, monkey, and an altar of many-coloured marbles. Sedding was proud of this work. He suggested his epitaph might be, 'He made the doors at Holbeton, and was an artist in his way.' The most memorable door is the south porch inner door, with diamond panels; he also designed the west door, and probably the tower and north doors.

SS Peter and Paul, Ermington, Devon, 1889 (PL21 9NJ) starts with a flourish – an entirely original lychgate which some see as Jacobethan, some 'Lutyensesque', others pure Hollywood. The seating in the interior is entirely Sedding's, with bench ends of lilies in pots, and writhing foliage everywhere, as well as parclose screens, lavish chancel seating and a communion rail with broad bands of carving. In the windows, spiders-web glazing. Much of the wood-carving was executed by three of the seven daughters of the vicar, Edmund Pinwill, who came to the village in 1880: Mary, Violet and Esther (see p.63).

Pinwill work is also to be seen at **St Mary Magdalene, Launceston, Cornwall** (PL15 8AU) – the chancel screen. The church restoration was planned by Sedding, but carried out, after Sedding's death, under the eye of first Henry Wilson, then E.H. Sedding. Bench ends seem both ancient and modern. In the south parclose screen, an otter shakes a hapless fish.

At **St Maddern, Madron** (TR20 8SW) there was a wholesale restoration including rebuilding three bays of the south arcade, new window tracery, a new north porch (and heavily rebuilt south porch) and much else – the bench ends in the nave are exceptional. Sedding's report in *The Architect* (1885) says he intends to 'replace seating in the nave with benches, the ends being of oak carved after the examples of the best types in the locality.' At **Sancreed** (TR20 8QS) Sedding put in a new chancel roof, 1881–91, and designed the nativity panel in the reredos, now on the north wall of the chancel.

All Saints, Holbeton: west door surround; altar surround detail

always great church-goers. Newton Abbot is a railway town, whose population grew rapidly around 1900. A medieval chapel of ease was thought to be insufficient. Following an announcement in the *Western Times* in July 1903, that a new church was intended for Highweek (it is actually in Abbotsbury, nearer the town centre), £5000 (of a target £8000) was raised in a few months. There was a design competition, and E.H. Sedding won.

This is not, like his Shaldon, a spiky, spiny, crouching creature, but a confident beast, relaxing on a suburban eminence. There is no polychromy, and no theatrically recessed west window, but still plenty of flying buttresses. The interior is pale, with yellowish ashlared stone. There is spiders-web glazing designed by Sedding. (The east window came from the old chapel of ease.) The electroliers and lectern teeter on the Art Nouveau borderline. The woodwork at first looks heavy, somewhat lumbering – but the detail is refreshingly light-hearted: nestlings in their nest, swallows darting south, a peacock, a squirrel contemplating a pomegranate. Bar two later pieces, it is all by the Pinwill company (see opposite), and all after 1912, by which time it was a well-established business. The first work was the pulpit, paid for by Elizabeth Clarke in memory of her husband, and commissioned from Violet Pinwill.

The Great War dampened funding – Sedding died in 1921 with much of the furnishing yet unmade: his ex-partner Reginald Wheatly became architectural pathfinder to the Pinwills, and carried the work through. At her death in 1922 Elizabeth Clarke left £5000 (of her estate of £239,233) for the adornment of the church. The first project was the chancel screen: restrained, domestic and continental in taste, more *buffet* than screen. Then the altar; north and south screens; Lady Chapel; reredos – it was to have been fully coloured, but in the end was gilded with touches of red and blue in the niches, and a band of pink roses and green foliage under the central Nativity. The overall effect is high Edwardian drama, stiffened by the influence of robust West Country woodcraft. The church seats 700. The hall and narthex date from 1985.

St Mary the Virgin, Abbotsbury: squirrel in screen

THE PINWILLS

The Arts & Crafts grappled with gender equality – women could not be members of the AWG, but the ACES had female members from the start. A sort of civilised compromise can be discerned in the phenomenon of 'Arts & Crafts couples' – Nelson and Edith Dawson, Georgie and Arthur Gaskin, Louise and Alfred Powell, even John Dando and Rose Sedding. But, even now, the assumption tends to be that the man was the more significant partner – even where, as with Georgie Gaskin, the reverse is clearly true.

The multiple development of three congruent 'Arts & Crafts' ideas made the Pinwills' work possible: that women could be accepted and acceptable as makers; that 'self-taught' artistry was every bit as good as 'bought-in' (Devon was a long way for London craftsmen to come); and that what might have been dismissed as naïvety by a previous generation of architects, could now be appreciated as a sort of admirable, unapologetic honesty. The boundary between art as the preserve of the elect of the academy, and art as the expression of personal inspiration – 'anyone can do it' – was being explored, and crossed, almost unnoticed.

Edmund Pinwill (1841–1926) became Vicar of Ermington, Devon, in 1880. He and his wife, Elizabeth, had seven daughters. In 1885 the work of restoring his dilapidated church began, initiated and largely paid for by fundraising by Edmund and his family, but under the aegis of the owner of the estate on which the church stood, the Croesus-rich banker Henry Mildmay, who selected the architect for the work, John Dando Sedding. Sedding was absorbed in the lavish and complex restoration of Mildmay's other – and rather more favourite – church, Holbeton, so, after drawing up initial plans, he handed the job to his nephew, E.H. Sedding, using his preferred and usual wood-carving team of Trasks of Norton-sub-Hamdon.

Elizabeth Pinwill seized her opportunity, and asked Trasks' head woodcarver if he would teach her daughters wood-carving in his spare time. Wood-carving was by no means an unusual or eccentric skill for young ladies to acquire – it was taught at Exeter High School for Girls, and the School of Art Woodcarving in South Kensington, established in 1879, attracted over 100 women to classes over its first six years.

Three of the Pinwills emerge as artistic and talented: Mary (14 in 1885), Ethel (13) and Violet (11). They set up a workshop over the vicarage stables. Meanwhile E.H. Sedding was supervising the work at Ermington – in the 1891 census, he was staying at the vicarage. By 1889 the Pinwills had completed a reredos at Chilthorne Domer, Somerset for him, and the pulpit at Ermington.

The sisters established themselves as a company, using Mary's middle name, and making themselves appear masculine (in the Brontës' Currer Bell tradition) – as Rashleigh, Pinwill & Co.

E.H. Sedding became a prime source of commissions. It wasn't just that they were female – they were outstandingly good. They produced rood screens – restored and/or largely new – at Stratton, Madron and Crantock in Cornwall, and Manaton, Devon. They worked for Fellowes Prynne at Buckland-in-the-Moor – the screen restored by Ethel Pinwill. And for Bligh Bond at Lew Trenchard and Lydford. (There is a complete list of their work at www.pinwillwoodcarving.org.uk curated by Helen Wilson.)

St Mary the Virgin, Abbotsbury: pulpit by Violet Pinwill, 1912

PARKSTONE, Poole, Dorset

St Osmund | 1904–5; 1913–27
G.A.B. Livesay, E.S. Prior, Arthur Grove
BH14 9HY | Locked

A magnificent muddle – not a failure, exactly, but uncomfortably awkward and further confused by now being St Dunstan's Orthodox Christian Church, with consequent liturgical modifications. It has ambition and vision, but something is amiss.

The first design was by local architect George Augustus Bligh Livesay (1867–1916), of which the east end was built from a design based on a Romanesque basilica in Verona: chancel, ambulatory, baldachino, crossing, crypt and part of the north transept. In 1911 he proposed the second phase of the work: nave, aisles and lantern. But he fell foul of the ICBS who found fault with his plans – and he had designed the church smaller than required. Leonard Stokes, President of the RIBA, was called in to advise and sent his friend Prior to inspect – he was then appointed architect jointly with Arthur Grove: they were respectively Honorary and Assistant Secretary of the ACES. Prior mapped out the new scheme: Grove saw to the details. Prior was inclined to the Byzantine rather than Italian. He must have had in mind Westminster Cathedral: the brickwork of the west end is in 'every colour from purple to vivid orange', according to one of Prior's obituaries. The interior has busts of angels on the piers, by Henry Wilson. The altar in the Lady Chapel is by William Bainbridge Reynolds, under a screen by Grove, with a painting by MacDonald Gill. Reynolds also designed the candlesticks and tabernacle in the Incarnation Chapel, 1916; and the lectern, 1926. There are inscriptions by Eric Gill and a Statue of Our Lady by Alec Miller. It is absorbing, but lacks cohesion. The glass – in his 'Early English' method – is all by Prior. It was his last building.

LYNTON, Devon

St Mary | 1891–1906
John Dando Sedding and Henry Wilson
EX35 6HY | Open

Lynton is a fruitful town for Arts & Crafts church seekers. Its Edwardian visitors expected respectable, smart churches to suit their church-going needs. The main developer of the town was George Newnes, publisher of the hugely successful *Tit-bits* (at first an educational periodical for children) from 1881. He also founded the *Strand* magazine, in which Sherlock Holmes first appeared, and *Country Life*. And he provided the town with a cliff railway (to Lynmouth, at the bottom of the cliff), its town hall, 1900, and the rail connection to Barnstaple.

St Osmund, Parkstone: brickwork and rainwater goods

St Mary, Lynton:
north aisle glass by Heywood Sumner

The CofE church, **St Mary**, was comprehensively restored (re-imagined, rather) by Henry Wilson. The original designs of 1891 were by his master, J.D. Sedding, who died before the work was started. Wilson took over, and effectively rebuilt the church. (The tower is 13th century.) The principal attraction is the glazing scheme, some (the west window; lancet in north wall of Lady Chapel, 1907) by Sedding's protégé Christopher Whall (1849–1924, AWG 1889), and the rest influenced by him. Whall's daughter Veronica completed the east window. The aisle windows use leading rather than colour to articulate appropriate seaside motifs – seagulls (designed by Heywood Sumner) and clifftop flowers, but also seasonal fruits, and a menagerie of wild animals from Noah's Ark, all in pale glass that allows the outside to come in. The restoration at Lynton replaced modest medieval and/or Victorianised windows at both east and west ends with daring new schemes. This was no modest, respectful SPAB-approved approach, but a full-blooded revitalisation: Sedding often attracted the alarmed attention of the SPAB. But, unlike the leading lights of the SPAB, Morris and Webb, Sedding was a churchman, with a view of churches not as museums, but as engines for prayer:

> We must clothe modern ideas in modern dress; adorn our design with living fancy … No more museum-inspired work! No more scruples about styles! No more dry-as-dust stock patterns! … No more cast-iron-looking altar cloths, or Syon Cope angels, or stumpy Norfolk-screen saints! No more Tudor roses and pumped-out Christian imagery

suggesting that Christianity is dead and buried! But, instead, we shall have design by living men for living men – something that expresses fresh realisations of sacred facts, personal broodings, skill, joy in Nature …

Wilson was far less churchy than Sedding, but the sentiment behind his carrying through of the rebuild at St Mary's is much the same. Wilson added the chancel, 1905, and fitted out the Lady Chapel, 1904–6. The copper altar frontal is by him, as is the pulpit and the lectern (made by Trasks). 'The church has considerable interest provided firstly by the eclectic and sometimes eccentric detailing, but secondly from the rich assembly of fittings', which are described in the 1989 *Pevsner* as 'one of the best collections of their date in Devon'.

George Newnes's only Lynton church commission was the 1904 **Congregational** church (now United Reform) – Newnes was the son of a Congregational minister. It is designed in a rather playful seaside vein, by an as-yet unknown architect. Just up the road, the **Roman Catholic** church, Most Holy Saviour, is part of a convent of the Poor Clares (now departed), designed in a spare, Italianate manner, 1907, by Leonard Stokes (1858–1925, AWG 1886), completed 1908–10 by his partner George Drysdale (1881–1949, AWG 1921), and consecrated in 1931. The **Methodist** Church, 1910, by La Trobe and Weston of Bristol, is now the Lynton Arts Centre, but some good internal fittings survive, especially geometric stained glass, the communion rails, a fireplace, and a magnificent and unnecessarily exuberant roof.

Other Churches

Cornwall

All Saints, Falmouth | J.D. Sedding | 1887–90 | TR11 3PN
The ICBS saw 'a complete absence of harmony in the design'. Sedding refuted them with panache. Reredos designed by E.H. Sedding, 1908–9, made by Harry Hems.

SS Protus & Hyacinth, Blisland (restoration) | 1894–1930 | PL30 4JB
Tactful restoration and imposing rood screen by F.C. Eden, 1894–6.

St Carantoc, Crantock (restoration) | 1899–1907 | TR8 5RB
Interior by E.H. Sedding, including rapturous rood screen, 1905, by Mary Pinwill.

Newquay Wesleyan (now New Creation Church) | Bell, Withers, Meredith | 1904 | TR7 1BH

Flexbury Park Methodist Church, Bude | John Pethick | 1905 | EX23 8RS
'Although not strictly architecturally literate this curious design is extremely ambitious.' (HE) Closed.

Devon

St Andrew, Sands Rd, Paignton | Fulford, Tait, Harvey | 1892–7 | TQ4 6HA

St Matthew, Chelston, Torquay | Nicholson and Corlette | 1895–1904 | TQ2 6JA
Fittings; includes font cover by Gerald Moira.

St David, Exeter | W.D. Caröe | 1897–1900 | EX4 4HR

Britannia Royal Naval College Chapel, Dartmouth | Aston Webb | 1905 | TQ6 0HJ
Can only be seen as part of a guided tour.

St Paul, Yelverton | Charles Nicholson | 1910–14 | PL20 6AB
Heavy-handed church relieved by Violet Pinwill choir stalls, 1915.

Chapel at Castle Drogo | Edwin Landseer Lutyens | 1911–31 | EX6 6PB

St Sabinus, Woolacombe | W.D. Caröe | 1910, 29 | EX34 7BY
1914 screen; 1916 font; lumbering, idiosyncratic south aisle of green-stained timbers.

Dorset

St Clement, Boscombe, Bournemouth | J.D. Sedding | 1871–3 | BH1 4DZ
Tower by Henry Wilson, 1890–3; crucifixion sculpture by F.W. Pomeroy; glass by Holiday and Whall.

St Michael, Bournemouth | R. Norman Shaw (nave) | 1873–6 | BH2 5QU
20 aisle windows by Henry Holiday, c.1880; west window by Christopher Whall, 1913. Sculpture in War Memorial Chapel by George Frampton.

St Mary, Burton Bradstock (restoration) | 1894–7 | DT6 4QY
South aisle, furnishings, glass by E.S. Prior; dado painted 1897 by parishioners, led by vicar's wife *(see p.11)*.

St Aldhelm, Lytchett Heath | G.R. Crickmay | 1898 | BH19 3LR
Whimsical: Kilpeck-meets-Expressionist corbels at eaves.

Annunciation, (RC) Bournemouth | Giles Gilbert Scott | 1905–6 | BH8 9RW

Emmanuel Hall, Winton, Bournemouth (Pentecostal) | not known | 1908 | BH9 1NW
Interior an intriguing combination of Nonconformist painted panels and Art Deco-ish glass.

Bournemouth Hebrew Congregation Synagogue | Lawson & Reynolds | 1910–11 | BH1 1PW
Usually described as 'Moorish Art Nouveau'. Enlarged 1957–62. Listed – at last – in January 2019.

St Mary, West Fordington, Dorchester | Charles Ponting | 1910–12 | DT1 2HJ
In a clear, cool Comper vein, and with woodwork both suave and savage.

St George, Langham, Gillingham | Charles Ponting | 1921 | SP8 5DP
Thatched. Memorial to son, nephew and son-in-law killed in Great War. Owned by family trust.

Somerset

St Peter, Hornblotton | T.G. Jackson | 1872–4 | BA4 6SB
Sgraffito designed by Jackson, executed by F. Wormleighton and Owen Gibbons, plasterers trained at South Kensington School of Art.

Vicar's Close Chapel, Wells (refurbishment) | J.D. Sedding | 1885–7 | BA5 2UH
Gesso work by Heywood Sumner, 1893, in panels by Henry Wilson.

St Mary, Norton-sub-Hamdon | Henry Wilson | 1894 | TA14 6SU
Restoration after a fire: fittings – font, cover, tower screen, west doors.

Our Lady & St Alphege (RC), Bath | Giles Gilbert Scott | 1927–9 | BA2 3NR
Craftsmanship, simplicity, originality – does this make GGS Arts & Crafts? Here, very close.

THAT·LIVETH
S·MARK
MOSES
S·LUKE

7
THE SOUTH OF ENGLAND
Wiltshire, Hampshire, Oxfordshire

The Arts & Crafts did not find a spiritual hideaway anywhere in this business-like slice of England, dominated by no-nonsense towns and cities – Southampton, Portsmouth, Chippenham, Witney – and imposing, patrician cathedrals – Winchester, Salisbury, Oxford. The area is not quite far enough from London to be an escape (apart from the Isle of Wight, which is far too far), and not quite beautiful enough to be idyllic.

Two exceptions run counter. First, the life and architecture of Wiltshire's Arts & Crafts hero, Charles Ponting, who built a dozen or more churches in the county, all of them of interest – and, though he was never invited to join the AWG or ACES, and indeed turned down opportunities to be FRIBA, he expressed Arts & Crafts spirit with un-pretended charm, youthful invention and considerable historical knowledge.

Second, the chapels of Oxford – not the ones everyone has heard of, like Butterfield's Keble or Gilbert Scott's Exeter, but more recherché locations: Blackfriars, Campion Hall, Mansfield, Harris Manchester, and the startlingly austere Founder's Chapel at St John the Evangelist Mission in East Oxford.

The most intriguing of all was designed by an architect whose reputation now, if any, is for slightly dull, workmanlike cathedral repairs. The church is the product of his youth. It feels exotic and remote, even though it is within earshot of Brize Norton aerodrome and the A40.

St Agatha, Landport: east end

CURBRIDGE, Oxfordshire

St John the Baptist | 1904–6
Charles Nicholson
OX29 7NU | Locked

Curbridge is separated from its much larger neighbour, Witney, by a ferocious bypass: it has allowed this part of Curbridge to retain a rural air, even a sense of slight remoteness. (Recent spread of the town means there is now a roundabout with Curbridge mentioned.)

The separateness reflects a 13th-century Bishop of Winchester's wish to have his Curbridge palace outside the Witney borough boundary. Curbridge villagers worshipped at St Mary's Witney up to 1836: they had their own Curbridge churchwardens and sidesmen, and even a 'Curbridge' door.

St John the Baptist, Curbridge from the south; pulpit, dwarf screen, choir stalls and congregation benches

The first Curbridge chapel (and schoolroom) was on land in the middle of the present churchyard. It was consecrated in 1847, but by 1865 it was considered inadequate. Designs for a replacement were prepared in 1874 by the Oxford architect C.C. Rolfe (see Inkpen, p.132). A new school was built instead. Nothing happened until January 1904, when the Rector of Witney, William Foxley Norris, then 79, decided to give way to a younger man. James Barber Kirby was energetic and go-ahead: he found that Curbridge church was in such poor condition as to be condemned. He organised a committee to raise the money to build afresh, including, according to the *Witney Gazette* (15 December 1906) 'several influential laymen'.

The most significant layman was Thomas William Foreshew, partner in Witney's major brewery, Clinch's. The other major benefactor was one of Norris's curates, Cyril Walford Osborn Jenkyn (1874–1933), known as 'CWOJ', a man of substantial means and of gentlemanly interests: Captain of the bell-ringers at Witney, and Master of the Oxford Diocesan Guild of Bell-ringers in 1910. The old church was demolished. CWOJ officiated at the first service in the new church in December 1906.

The singular look of the interior suggests there must have been a 'client': it could surely not have been created without the inspiration of a sophisticated eye. Kirby refers to the chosen architects as 'Nicholson and Corlette'. But CWOJ in his letters refers only to 'Sir C Nicholson' – suggesting he knew Corlette was the junior (possibly even non-designing) partner. Perhaps CWOJ knew Nicholson personally.

In 1904 Nicholson (1867–1949, AWG 1898) was not long established in his career. He had gone into partnership with Hubert Corlette in 1895, and they had built just two churches: **St Alban, Westcliff-on-Sea**, 1898–1901 (SS0 7JY) and **St Matthew, Chelston, Devon**, 1896 (TQ2 6JA). They had also enlarged **St Matthew, Yiewsley**, 1896–8 (UB7 7QH) by adding a new nave to an existing small church by Gilbert Scott.

Nothing quite prepares one for the interior of Curbridge, a vigorously rustic composition of furniture and furnishings in rich carmine and holly green, with an altar and reredos *seemingly* constructed from recycled panelling, a naively simple altar rail and rustic iron candelabra on the end of several congregational benches, at once elegant and simple.

It all *looks* very 'Arts & Crafts' – even down to the 'pink' painted on the front of the pulpit, the device of Ashbee's Guild of Handicraft. The ceiling has beams, rafters and frieze in red and green, emphasised by black and white checkerwork – all rather reminiscent of Edward the Confessor, Kempley (p.145).

The effect is deeply un-English. Painted congregational seating in warm, domestic colours is to be found in rural churches across northern Europe. Why employ this device in Oxfordshire? Green and red are medieval colours on screens and niches, but it was William Morris who first used bold green paint on domestic furniture – a table in 1856. Norman Shaw's church benches at Bedford Park, 1879–87 are painted green (p.111) and Charles Spooner's at Exton, Hants, 1891–2 (p.76) and Caröe's at Colehill, 1892–5 (p.51), amongst others, were stained green.

Who was the presiding genius? The evidence, albeit circumstantial, suggests it was the aged, retiring Rector, Foxley Norris, and his wife Julia, daughter of Thomas Monro, a patron of J.M.W. Turner. She was an indefatigable parish worker, raising money for ornaments and fittings for the church. He was a scholarly man who took delight in ritual and ornamentation. Together they enriched the interior of Witney parish church with lamps: one set made by Barkentin and Krall, and 14 Clayton & Bell windows.

His son, also William Foxley Norris, was later Dean of Westminster, and KCVO. He wrote on cathedral decoration and church history. And he was a talented artist, who exhibited watercolours. Nicholson was also an accomplished watercolour artist – whether they ever exhibited together is not known.

From the road, St John's draws the eye. The path curves to avoid the footings of the demolished old church – the bend lends fairy-tale allure. The exterior detail is striking. On the south elevation are two close rows each of four small, rather cramped hexagonal windows. They provide light not to the nave, as one might expect, but to the vestry. The asymmetrical porch is surmounted by an offset tower – the chimney for the stove that once heated the building. The chancel step is articulated externally by the bellcote, embellished with a low relief cross and an eyebrow drip-mould over the bell opening.

There is an undeniable Mediterranean air – which is what *Pevsner* says of it. Perhaps it is simply a deliberate distancing from the conventional medieval Gothic of Witney parish church: making a point about the fine distinction between Curbridge with its ancient connection with monastic splendour, and its bigger, materialistic and largely Nonconformist neighbour.

Nicholson made only one other church approaching this cosy domestic idiom – **St George, Minworth**, Warwickshire, 1909 (B76 9BU). His next church, **St Augustine of Hippo, Great Grimsby**, Lincs, 1910–11 (p.195), though it too has painted benches, exhibits larger gestures of grandeur. His next, **St Paul, Yelverton**, Devon, 1911–14 (PL20 6AB), is overblown and somewhat grim: Nicholson was on his way to success and fame, and was eventually to be architect to six cathedrals. His youthful fling with Arts & Crafts did not last beyond the Great War. As to the makers of the benches, altar rails, pulpit, lectern, altar, reredos and candelabra, history is as mute as if they had been medieval men.

THORNEY HILL, Hampshire

All Saints
Detmar Blow 1904–6 and
Phoebe Anna Traquair 1920–2
BH23 8DG | Sometimes open

Church work by Detmar Blow (1867–1939, AWG 1892) is scarce. As a young man he drove the wagon that carried William Morris's coffin to Kelmscott churchyard, bestowing on him a sort of sacred Arts & Crafts aura. His most intense church work is the panelled chapel in Bodley and Garner's late masterpiece Hewell Grange, Tardebigge, Worcestershire (1911), but this is now a prison, hard to visit and illegal to photograph. Blow designed the base of the Ridley monument chapel in **St Mary, Stannington, Northumberland** (NE61 6HQ) with the effigy by W. Reynolds-Stephens (1914). Other than that, he was not much engaged with churches.

The church started life as the chapel of Avon Tyrrell, the great house built for the 3rd Lord Manners by W.R. Lethaby. It is exactly contemporary with St Andrew, Roker (p.261), but where Roker is all stark muscularity, Thorney Hill is urbane and restrained. By 1906 Blow was in partnership with Fernand Billerey (1878–1951), a French architect with a Beaux-Arts training. Together they built a successful country house practice to rival Lutyens's. Not surprising then that Thorney Hill church is an example of the then fashionable neo-Baroque.

Blow's structure is a playful Palladian *humoresque,* all columns and capitals. The real glory is the later mural painting, 1920–2, by Phoebe Anna Traquair (1852–1936), Irish-born but most associated with Edinburgh, and in particular, in an ecclesiastical context, her three sets of ecclesiastical murals there (p.301). The murals at Thorney Hill were her last work, and her most important in England. Its theme is the *Te Deum* in a New Forest setting.

A number of the faces are thought to be family portraits. The chapel was conceived as a family memorial as well as a village church: Lord Manners's daughter Mary Christine died of cholera in India, aged 17, in 1904; her

brother John was killed at Mons in the first few weeks of the Great War; her mother, Lady Constance Manners – a close friend of Traquair's – died in 1920. In the apse mural, Lady Manners is surrounded by her family – Listers, Asquiths and Cecils – but the mural also includes portraits of Traquair's heroes: William Blake, Louis Pasteur, Tennyson and (possibly) Detmar Blow himself.

Eric Gill (1882–1940, AWG 1904) is said to have carved the weeping angels on the doors (which seems unlikely), but he certainly did the lettering behind John Manners's tomb, and in the memorial plaque to Mary Christine. The bronze effigy is by Bertram Mackennal (1863–1931, RA 1922), with angels reportedly by Gill.

Traquair recorded her worry about the mural in a note painted high in the frieze: 'This wall from dome to floor has been designed and painted by me. I fear the wall is damp. Phoebe A Traquair July 1922.' She was right. The mural was restored in 1993–7 and again in 2008. Lead thefts in 2013 and 2018 let water run into the building. There was some damage to the murals, now repaired.

All Saints, Thorney Hill:
east end

LANDPORT, PORTSMOUTH, Hants

St Agatha | 1895, 1901
Joseph H. Ball 1893–5 and Heywood Sumner
PO1 4RL | Often open

The church was part of the Winchester College Mission to Portsmouth. It was originally hemmed in on all sides by working-class housing, now all gone. Its exterior, unscreened, seems austere and forbidding. Inside it was decorated in the Highest Anglo-Catholic taste, whose practical pastoral manifestation was the indefatigable Christian Socialist Fr Robert William Radclyffe Dolling (1851–1902). He had 40 parishioners to Sunday lunch every week: in his view, 'if there is one place that needs an impressive church, it is a slum.'

The glory was the Lady Chapel – mosaics, glass and sgraffito work by Heywood Sumner (1853–1940, AWG 1884): the semi-dome a field of blue starred mosaic; Mary's flowers, the lily, standing between each of the five small windows. In 1964, the Lady Chapel was largely

CHARLES PONTING

Charles Ponting (1849–1932) is not quite unstudied, but he is little regarded. He was a profoundly provincial architect, hardly ever working outside Wiltshire and Dorset, and a member of neither the AWG or ACES. Yet there is something unmistakably Arts & Crafts in his work – though rather tamed and circumspect, it has energy, originality and even playfulness: the Arts & Crafts manner is palpable – instinctive, heart-felt, sincere.

He built a dozen new churches, the most interesting of which are all in his native Wiltshire. By far the most exciting is Christ Church, Shaw, 1905 (SN12 8EH); the most Olde Worlde, St Birinus, Redlynch, 1894–6 (SP5 2HU). St Matthew, Mere, 1882, is now a private house, as is St John, North Wraxall, Ford, 1897. He also designed St Thomas, Southwick, 1899–1904 (BA14 9QG); the Chapel of St Mary's School, Wantage, Berks, 1898–9 (OX12 8DJ), now a dental surgery; St Aldhelm, Sandleheath, Hants, 1907 (SP6 1QW), now a brass band storeroom. He built four churches in Dorset – St Martin, Weymouth, 1908, now a house; St Mary, West Fordington, Dorchester, 1910–

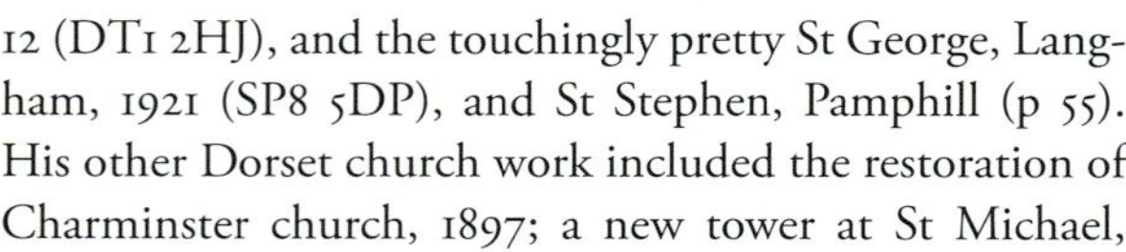

12 (DT1 2HJ), and the touchingly pretty St George, Langham, 1921 (SP8 5DP), and St Stephen, Pamphill (p 55). His other Dorset church work included the restoration of Charminster church, 1897; a new tower at St Michael, Bere Hackett, 1897; a new north aisle at St Andrew, West Stafford, 1897; and the tower at St George, Bourton, 1903–5.

After Pamphill, Ponting built no further churches in Wiltshire. But he did two 'rebuilds': All Saints, Marden, 1885, and St Katharine, Holt, as well as over 30 church repair programmes and enlargements.

He also designed and oversaw the scholarly and elaborate pseudo-medieval woodwork, made by Harry Hems (1897–1907), in the (genuinely) medieval church at All Saints, Down Ampney, Glos. (GL7 5BQ).

Ponting was born at Collingbourne Ducis, Wilts., son of a sub-agent on the Savernake Estate. He trained in the office of the Estate's architect. He was also sent into the estate's masons' yard and into its joinery shop, to acquire craft skills: the perfect Arts & Crafts architectural background – a practical, hands-on knowledge of making. In 1924 he recalled that the restoration of Collingbourne Ducis church by G.E. Street in 1856 came 'at the time of life when such wonderful works made a lasting impression.' He was a dedicated churchman: churchwarden at St Mary, Marlborough 1897–1909.

In 1883 he was appointed Diocesan Surveyor for the Wiltshire part of Salisbury Diocese; part of Bristol Diocese added in 1887, and Dorset in 1892. At the height of his career he was responsible for 237 churches. He was also Surveyor to Marlborough College 1889–1921.

Left: St George, Langham
Right: St Mary, West Fordington, screen

As well as churches he built Almondsbury Institute and Memorial Hospital, Gloucestershire; Dauntsey's Agricultural School, West Lavington; Marlborough Town Hall; and Pewsham House, Calne.

He never became FRIBA, though he was frequently approached to do so. He felt he did not need the backing of a professional body. On the other hand, he did exhibit at the RA – 17 drawings over his career – suggesting he saw architecture as an art more than a profession. And he was a student of Wiltshire church architecture, writing extensively on the subject – at least 120 articles in the *Wiltshire Archaeological and Natural History Society Journal* 1882–1925. He was elected FSA in 1888.

Ponting remained an 'outsider'. In 1905 St Melor, Amesbury was to be restored. A local worthy, Lady Antrobus, took fright: 'Ponting has just been appointed to pull about the chancel.' She claimed he would 'ruin everything', and offered to pay for the more fashionable Detmar Blow to step in. SPAB were called to arms. In the end, Ponting did the work – stripping back the brutal 1852 restoration by Butterfield, lovingly reinstating and repairing the screen and meticulously reassembling the font.

Ponting had it all: craft skills and understanding, a background in local tradition, archaeological expertise, diligence and dogged persistence, and the self-effacing diffidence so typical of the Arts & Crafts.

Top: St Birinus, Redlynch; *Left:* St Aldhelm, Sandleheath; *Right:* Christ Church, Shaw

demolished for a proposed new highway that was subsequently reduced and re-routed to the other side of the church. What remains of it is a blazing remnant of Sumner's sgraffito genius: the arrival of the Magi, high on the left-hand side. Valiant plans are being laid to rebuild the Chapel: its ghostly footprint survives the now long-gone road! Sumner's sgraffito work is also to be seen at Llanfair Kilgeddin (p.281) and All Saints, Ennismore Gardens (p.113).

Notwithstanding the loss of the Lady Chapel, the nave apse, by Sumner, 1901, is a glorious outpouring, dominated by Christ in Majesty atop a rainbow. The small windows have lost

their coloured glass. The nave itself, which survives more or less as built, is grandly austere – Portland stone capitals, 1894–1927, designed by Sumner. Elsewhere in the church: prayer desk by Norman Shaw, *c.*1870; altar, 1908, by Randoll Blacking of Salisbury (1889–1958),

St Agatha, Landport:
sgraffiti by Heywood Sumner

a pupil of Ninian Comper; crucifix, 1927, by Walter Tapper (1861–1935, AWG 1907); war memorial and a reredos, 1926, by Martin Travers (1886–1948, AWG 1921). And much else.

The church stands defiant as a maimed survivor – a victim of violence, municipal stupidity and incompetence. It survived a huge air raid in December 1940 (windows blown out and tiles lost, but fabric by no means destroyed); was closed by the Diocese in 1954 and sold – the furnishings removed to other churches, including the 1894 lectern, subsequently burned in 1960 (or 1970) because of 'woodworm' (!). In 1955 the church was a naval storehouse with partition walls, a mezzanine floor and full-height lorry access (further windows removed). At the part-demolition of 1964 the Admiralty heroically prevented the entire church from being bulldozed, despite the Secretary of State's support for demolition. It took until 1983 for further redevelopment plans to be dropped. St Agatha's was listed Grade II* in 1987, and re-opened by the St Agatha's Trust in 1994. A loving restoration, with the help of Hampshire County Council, has continued since, with some of the original fittings gradually re-acquired – the prayer desk of 1894; the Dolling memorial – and new ones added.

EXTON, Hampshire

SS Peter and Paul | 1891–2
Charles Spooner (interior decorations)
SO32 3NU | Usually open

From the outside, Exton parish church is not very remarkable. The building is small, and looks medieval, but it was largely rebuilt by

a local benefactor in 1847. In 1891, a Vestry meeting resolved that 'certain alterations and improvements be carried out.' Young Spooner's ideas were outlined in a self-confident proposal: 'a scheme of decorating and beautifying' the church; 'all the existing work which it is proposed to remove is quite modern and extremely bad.' He intended to transform what he called a 'somewhat bare and colourless' church which had 'uncomfortable and ugly' seating. He was proposing exciting new aesthetic touches: 'A little rood screen would add to the dignity and artistic effect of the church.'

SS Peter and Paul, Exton: windows in the east end

Inevitably, not everything he cockily proposed was carried out. However, what was, intrigues. Between the two lancet windows at the east end, and into the chancel roof, is stencilled a sinuous Tree of Life, reminiscent of the fabric patterns of William Morris. Spooner designed the east windows with urgent upward movement, burgeoning and ebullient: images of ripe corn and flowers, with a rising fountain of pale waters. There is a robust west screen, rustically medieval, painted (stencilled?) with foliage of almost pagan vigour; the pulpit is also painted with a gentle free-hand scheme of acorns and oak leaves; and a priest's prayer desk, embellished with ripe wheat stalks.

OXFORD CHAPELS

Oxford Colleges are open to visitors at different times and unpredictably. If there is not a 'Closed' notice in the College gateway, politely ask the Porter in the Lodge to see the chapel.

MANSFIELD COLLEGE CHAPEL

(Congregational)

Basil Champneys, 1886–9 | OX1 3TF

The Congregationalists were the first of the non-Anglican denominations to arrive in Oxford when the Anglican monopoly on study at the university was lifted in 1871. Spring Hill College, Birmingham removed to Oxford in 1886. (Mansfield College is named after Spring Hill's original benefactor family.)

Basil Champneys (1842–1935, AWG 1884) was chosen to design the new buildings – his designs preferred to those of the more experienced Alfred Waterhouse. Students did not live in the college, so the buildings round the open-ended 'quad' were hall, libraries, common rooms, lecture rooms, gatehouse (hardly needed) and chapel. The chapel exterior (if classification is desired) is half-way between Decorated and a relaxed Perpendicular. The inside is showily conservative.

Champneys was the son of a clergyman. At Cambridge Basil missed his First, and was put to study architecture under John Prichard (1817–86), diocesan surveyor of Llandaff and partner (1852–63) of John Pollard Seddon (1827–1906), the architect of St Catherine, Hoarwithy, Herefordshire (p.150), whose later partner was John Coates Carter (p.277–80).

Champneys began private practice in 1867. In Oxford he designed the Indian Institute, 1882–96; Somerville library, 1903; new buildings at Merton, 1904–10; the Rhodes Building at Oriel, 1908–11. He had earlier designed St Peter-le-Bailey, New Inn Hall Street, 1872–4, now St Peter's College chapel. His chapel for Linacre College, 1912 – simple to the point of stark – became a library in 2002. He was awarded the RIBA Gold Medal for architecture in 1912, but never joined the RIBA. He was an early member of the Century Guild. Although he was the sixteenth member of the AWG, he resigned in 1896 for reasons unknown.

The college trained URC ordinands until 2007, but its Nonconformist heritage has more or less vanished now – except in the (un-consecrated) chapel, whose windows and statues depict leading Nonconformists – Oliver Cromwell, William Penn, John Milton. The imposing east-end stalls and pulpit survive. Originally, the pulpit was open to preachers of all the Evangelical Free Churches. The chapel is only occasionally now used for services, mainly for dinners and events.

HARRIS MANCHESTER COLLEGE CHAPEL

(Unitarian)

Thomas Worthington, 1891–3 | OX1 3TD

Manchester College, a Presbyterian institution founded in Warrington in 1757, was re-founded in Manchester in 1786 and transferred to Oxford in 1889. It was increasingly Unitarian from about 1809. It became Harris Manchester in 1996 following a large bequest from Lord Harris of Peckham, a successful industrialist.

The architect was Thomas Worthington (1826–1909), the premier Unitarian architect of Manchester, whose best-known building is the Unitarian Church at Ullet Road, Liverpool (p.220).

Harris Manchester College Chapel: Morris & Co Glass

The chapel is unprepossessing from outside: but inside features a spectacular, complete scheme of Morris & Co. glass (1895–9), among the last of Morris's schemes. The designs are by Edward Burne-Jones (1833–1898), apart from Joseph and Mary Magdalene in the chancel window, by Morris. The window iconography is assertively Unitarian: no Holy Ghost/Dove; an emphasis on the Nativity (though no Annunciation – too miraculous); the Virgin Mary is labelled 'Mary the Mother'. The iconography of the liturgical south windows is also crisply Unitarian: six days of creation, with the motto 'Elargissez Dieu' (a quote from Diderot: 'Make your God bigger' or 'Set God free'), the motto of James Losh, grandfather of the donor, and uncle of Sara Losh, architect of the proto-Arts & Crafts church St Mary, Wreay, Cumbria (p.258).

The angels are supposedly modelled on May Morris. There is a verse from *The Rime of the Ancient Mariner.* (Samuel Taylor Coleridge was at one time a Unitarian preacher.) The figures in the liturgical west window –

Religion, Liberty and Truth – were designed specifically for the college by Burne-Jones, 1896. The oak screen, 1896, is by Earps & Hobbs of Manchester. The expressive and energetic bench-ends, 1897, are by Pearson & Brown of Eccles.

PUSEY HOUSE CHAPEL

Temple Moore, 1912–14
Fittings by Ninian Comper | OX1 3LY

Pusey House opened in 1884, primarily as a memorial to Edward Bouverie Pusey (1880–82) of the Oxford Movement, established with a fund of £50,000 to purchase Pusey's books, provide a building for them, and an endowment to pay at least two clergy to act as librarians. It was also to be 'a house of sacred learning', and offer pastoral care to all members of the university.

After the Great War, a pattern of worship emerged: a non-communicating High Mass for all members of the university at 11 a.m., following morning service and breakfast in one's own college. In 2012 Fr Philip Corbett reported, 'The founders thought all college chapels would close because of growing secularism.'

Temple Moore (1856–1920) was approached for designs in 1911, and produced them in 1912. It was his last work. The chapel was completed by autumn 1914; the rest of the complex – library, sacristy, common room, lecture room – was not completed until 1918.

A writer to the *Church Times* (16 October 1914) stated that, of the five chapels built in Oxford in recent times, 'none is so beautiful'. The east window was filled with glass by Ninian Comper in the 1930s. He added the baldachino, 1937, over the altar ('By Comper, need one say? Who else would splash the gold about like that?' *Pevsner*).

What is Arts & Crafts about it? Moore was not a member of the AWG. His son-in-law, Leslie Moore (1883–1957), who inherited the practice in 1920, was perhaps more influenced by Arts & Crafts ideas. (Contrary to some sources, he had no hand in the design of Pusey House chapel.)

Temple Moore built 40 churches. Giles Gilbert Scott thought, 'Temple Moore's work can rank with the finest done in the Gothic revival.' Rather like Pusey, Temple Moore was so convinced of the past's superiority to the present that he sought to re-create it. In 1928 Beresford Pite wrote, 'he summed up and completed the theory of the Gothic revival … We are presented with the work of a genius who reproduced the Middle Ages in our own day.' The architects of the AWG were against the idea of 'reproduction': they despised copying.

Harris Manchester College Chapel: bench end by Pearson and Brown

BLACKFRIARS HALL, CHURCH OF THE HOLY GHOST

Doran Webb, 1921–9 | OX1 3LY

The papacy relaxed its veto on Roman Catholics studying at Oxford in 1895. The Dominicans, who had been in Oxford from 1221 to the Dissolution, returned to Oxford in 1921 and built their small priory just south of Pusey House. The site, originally occupied by three houses, was purchased by an American donor, Mrs Charlotte Jefferson Davies Tytus, fabulously wealthy from the fortune her father left her, made in shirts. The foundation stones were laid by Cardinal Bourne and Cardinal Gasquet on the Feast of the Assumption, 700 years to the day since the first arrival of Dominicans in Oxford. The full community arrived eight years later. The church was consecrated on 20 May 1929.

Edward Doran Webb (1864–1931) was the architect of Birmingham Oratory (1903–9), home of the shrine to that other Oxford giant of religious intellectual engagement, John Henry Newman – Pusey's contemporary, who 'went over' to Rome.

Doran Webb remains largely unstudied. He was not Aston Webb (1849–1930), architect of Admiralty Arch and the V&A. Nor is there any evidence that he was the illegitimate son of Philip Webb. What is known about him amounts to more or less nothing, apart from that he lived in Salisbury and was FSA.

The chapel is 'Gothic, somewhat tired' according to *Pevsner*, or, if you prefer Geoffrey Tyack's view, 'recapturing some of the atmosphere of the lost medieval churches of the preaching orders'. There is an inscription tablet over the entrance, 1937, by Eric Gill. The Stations of the Cross, in a Gill manner, are by Fr Aelred Whitacre OP (1882–1945).

CAMPION HALL CHAPEL,

(Jesuits)

Edwin Lutyens, 1935 | OX1 1QS

In 1896 the Society of Jesus established a hall for six undergraduates at 11 St Giles, adding 13–15 St Giles later, and in 1918 becoming a permanent private hall of the university, re-named Campion Hall after the 16th-century martyr, Edmund Campion. There was only space for 16 undergraduates, and something bigger was needed. Eventually, Fr Martin D'Arcy (1888–1976) became Master, 'the foremost English apologist for Roman Catholicism' and part of the fashionable Roman Catholic *beau monde* that included Evelyn Waugh and Frances, Lady Horner of Mells Manor, one of Edwin Landseer Lutyens's earliest and most faithful patrons. She introduced Lutyens to D'Arcy, who asked for advice about a good young architect for a new building for Campion Hall. 'Why not ask me?' 'But you are far too expensive.' Lutyens said he had no building of his own in Oxford, and that he would like to do one, and would charge a very low fee. Lutyens (1869–1944, AWG 1903) was confirmed as architect in 1934.

Apart from New Delhi, the Cenotaph and the Memorial to the Missing of the Somme at Thiepval, Lutyens is perhaps best known for his plan for a gargantuan Roman Catholic cathedral at Liverpool, of which only part of the crypt was ever built. He always wished to build churches, but rarely had the opportunity. In 1903 he built a small church for the working-class village of Pixham, near Dorking (p.89).

Geoffrey Tyack has described the chapel at Campion Hall as having 'something of the air of a private oratory, removed from the clamour of the outside world … The pervasive presence of the round arch imparts a subtly ultramontane feeling.' The pew ends rest on red bases – no reason. The electric light fittings have red tassels like cardinals' hats – Lutyens's wit could be heavy-handed. He is reported to have started each family Christmas morning with the same crack: 'Have you heard? It's a boy.'

Campion Hall Chapel:
Stations of the Cross by Frank Brangwyn

Rhodes House is normally open on Heritage Open Days. Otherwise you need to contact the college to fix your visit, which should include the gracious Milner Hall and the Library. Sir Herbert Baker (1862–1946, AWG 1914), its architect, came to the AWG late. He had great success as architect to Cecil Rhodes (and wrote a hero-worshipping biography), as well as more widely in South Africa. In later life, he built St Andrew, Ilford, 1924 (IG1 3PE).

For completeness, the chapel at **Lady Margaret Hall** (LMH) must also be included – Giles Gilbert Scott, 1932; and the usually overlooked chapel of **St Hugh's** (H.T. Buckland, 1916) with its Norman Shaw colour scheme and faintly Mackintosh-ish benches.

Elsewhere in the city, the **Founder's Chapel** of St John the Evangelist Mission, Marston Street, 1887 (?), by C.C. Rolfe, (OX4 1JX), now St Stephen's House, is tucked away, inaccessibly high above the neighbouring glories of Bodley's monastic complex. This ascetic space is as austere as a drawing by F.L. Griggs.

The highlight is the Stations of the Cross by Frank Brangwyn (1867–1956), reproduced by lithography on sycamore panels. Brangwyn was almost ludicrously prolific and Arts & Crafts. He was RA, but never joined the AWG. He painted, designed glass, furniture, ceramics, buildings, interiors, was a lithographer, woodcutter and illustrator. He was associated early on with Arthur Heygate Mackmurdo of the Century Guild, and got some tuition from William Morris.

The (unfinished) wall paintings in the side chapel are by Charles Mahoney (1903–68). Stanley Spencer was proposed for the job: he visited the Hall in 1939 and stayed for a month, but declined to produce cartoons.

OTHERS

The most 'Arts & Crafts' building in Oxford is **Rhodes House**. It has no chapel – instead what began life on the plans as a Chapter House, 'a sort of shrine for memorials of statesmen who have had the great vision of the commonwealth of Nations', then a 'Heroön' or hall of fame, and finally a Pantheon-like ante-hall memorialising past Rhodes Scholars. The lack of a chapel demonstrates that, as the founders of Pusey House had feared, secularism would indeed eventually triumph.

Campion Hall Chapel: light fittings by Lutyens;
St Hugh's College chapel looking east

ALDERSHOT, Hampshire

St Joseph (RC) | 1911–13
George Drysdale
GU11 3JB | Locked: ask for key at presbytery

Drysdale (1881–1949, AWG 1921) trained in the École des Beaux-Arts, then was in the offices first of Ernest George, then Leonard Stokes, with whom he later went into partnership. St Joseph was his first church design. A dramatic and provocative church in Birmingham Byzantine, with subtle hints of Henry Wilson and Eric Gill.

St Joseph, Aldershot:
brickwork on south doorway

TEMPLE, CORSLEY, Wilts.

St Mary | 1902–3
William Henry Stanley
BA12 7QW | By arrangement

Paid for with £10,000 from the 1899 will of Mary Barton of Corsley House, in memory of her husband and son. She gave the land too. Her architect was W.H. Stanley (1856–1933) of Trowbridge, county architect of Wiltshire, who built no other church. It is the work of a man of real, perhaps unfulfilled, talent, influenced by Arts & Crafts aesthetics: intimate, thoughtful, restrained, precise, unfussy, harmonious. A doll's house, now in the care of Friends of Friendless Churches.

St Mary, Temple, Corsley:
the nave, north side

Other Churches

Wiltshire

St Mary & St Nicholas, Sandy Lane, Calne | J.M. Hopkins | 1892 | SN15 2QB
Built as a private chapel. Assertively rural: timber with thatch and robust buttresses.

Hampshire

Abbey URC (was Cong), Romsey | Paull and Bonella | 1885–8 | SO51 8EJ

St Agnes, Freshwater Bay, Isle of Wight | Isaac Jones | 1908 | PO40 9FG
Thatched; idiosyncratic screen (1940s?); all studiedly quaint.

Central Baptist Church (Polygon), Southampton | G. & R.P. Baines | 1910 | SO15 2GY
Vigorous example of the Baines manner: a fortissimo *on trombones.*

Ascension, Portsea, Portsmouth | A.E. Cogswell | 1913–17 | PO2 0JG
Spell-binding, enormous reredos designed by John Coates Carter, made by R.L. Boulton & Son, 1921.

St Alban, Copnor, Portsmouth | Charles Nicholson | 1913–14 | PO3 5AL
Nicholson moves away from Arts & Crafts. West end, damaged in war, rebuilt by Dykes Bower, 1956.

St Andrew Garrison Church, Aldershot | Robert Lorimer | 1926–7 | GU11 2BY
No-nonsense Scottish clarity.

Oxfordshire

St Mary the Virgin, Buckland | medieval | SN7 8RL
On the turn from Victorian to Arts & Crafts: glass by Henry Holiday; mosaics by Powells, 1891.

Nativity, Christmas Common | Walter Cave | 1889 | OX49 5HL | **H**

St James, Somerton, Bicester | 1890s | OX25 6NB
Memorial, choir stalls, chancel glazing by Henry Wilson; Christopher Whall windows.

St Helen, Berrick Salome | A.M. Mowbray | 1890 | OX10 6JP
*Restoration by A. Mardon Mowbray 'exceeded real necessity'. (*The Builder*, 1926, pp 786–7)*

Cowley Rd Methodist Church (Wesley Hall), Oxford | Stephen Salter | 1903–4 | OX4 1BN
Reordered and divided 1984.

Christ Church (URC), Henley-on-Thames | Hampden Pratt | 1907 | RG9 1AG

St Gregory & St Augustine (RC), Summertown | Ernest Newton | 1911–12 | OX2 7NS
Originally a private chapel: simple and rich all at the same time.

St Etheldreda, Horley | medieval | OX15 6BJ
Chancel screen and rood loft, 1946, by Laurence Dale (who was articled to Charles Ponting).

8

THE SOUTH EAST OF ENGLAND

Surrey, Sussex, Kent

There was – is – so much Arts & Crafts in Surrey, there is a society devoted to its study: 'The Arts & Crafts Movement in Surrey'. In a 'Golden Triangle' bounded approximately by Farnham, Guildford and Haslemere, the ideas and their exponents flourished. To Surrey came writers like H.G. Wells, Conan Doyle and George Bernard Shaw: he typically was somewhat scornful – 'Our Hindhead and Haslemere population makes an almost oppressive parade of its devotion to art.' His words encapsulate an Arts & Crafts conundrum – was it sincere, or was it merely faking sincerity? True-hearted simplicity, or humble-bragging? And, in churches, then, which is the more important, art or religion?

Sussex was less appealing to would-be rural idealists – though Eric Gill and his circle were at Ditchling from 1907. (Gill's one church is in Norfolk, p.214). Nonetheless, one of the most potent Arts & Crafts interiors of all is in Brighton – Henry Wilson's furnishings for the lofty, breath-taking St Bartholomew's.

Kent was home to A.W.N. Pugin, for whose architectural and perhaps even moral authority John Dando Sedding, for one, had a reverential regard. Pugin died in Ramsgate in 1852. Arts & Crafts never took root in the county, though some church commissions there are suggestive, especially at the Edwardian seaside, and in each case strikingly different from what one might expect. Was it something in the sea air?

The Mortuary Chapel, Compton: ceiling

LOWER KINGSWOOD, Surrey

Wisdom of God | 1891–2
Sidney Barnsley
KT20 7DH | Sometimes open

The Church of the Wisdom of God is a triple prodigy. First, it is the only church built by Sidney Barnsley (1865–1926, AWG 1892) – though in 1925 he adapted a carriage-house into the 'Little Chapel' at Rodborough, Glos. (p.158). Barnsley is better known as one of 'Gimson and the Barnsleys', who made 'wonderful furniture of a commonplace kind' in rural Gloucestershire from 1893. And he played a part in furnishing St Andrew's chapel, Westminster Cathedral (p.106).

Second, Wisdom of God is a deliberate evocation of academically analysed Byzantine architecture, something which had not happened before in Anglican church-building. It pre-dates Westminster Cathedral (1895 onwards) whose form, borrowing from the Byzantine, was a deliberate statement of difference from Anglican architectural precedent. The next Anglican example, Christ Church, Brixton, designed by Arthur Beresford Pite (1861–1934, AWG 1884) does not come until 1897–1903. (But see also Galston, p.310). Wisdom of God is sedulously correct: the ground plan is based on a 4th-century basilican church at Constantinople; there are traceable precedents from four different Byzantine churches in the brickwork.

Third, it is as much a secular showcase as a church: it houses a number of archaeological antiquities collected from exotic parts by its wealthy, learned founder. The church manages somehow to be very English, yet nonetheless oddly foreign. The land is not consecrated, so there are no tombstones. A free-standing wooden campanile stands to one side, based, it seems, on one in Bulgaria. Inside, the exoticism is even greater: dove-coloured marble and golden mosaics.

It was funded by two local millionaires. Sir Henry Bonsor (1848 –1929), brewer, MP, Director of the Bank of England, provided the plot of land. The cultural presiding genius was his friend and lawyer Edwin Freshfield (1832–1918). Bonsor and Freshfield were not outstandingly pious, but they wanted to express their importance in their community, and the importance *of* that community.

Freshfield was an expert on Byzantine church architecture. He part-funded architectural expeditions to Greece by Barnsley (with Robert Weir Schultz) who spent two years drawing and measuring early and often remote Greek churches. Freshfield spent at least two months every year abroad, looking at and acquiring ancient stone capitals, especially Byzantine, from Ephesus, Mesopotamia and elsewhere. Shipping these stones back to England demonstrated his wealth. On his wife's death they were removed from his garden, into the church. Thus, the building is a personal and complex public statement of wealth, culture, leisured interest, academic endeavour, grief, social conscience and correct piety. The church is vividly 'dedicated' to Freshfield: a memorial mosaic to him and his family was installed before his death, at about the time of his wife's, in 1902. Freshfield was very proprietorial: after services he would stand alongside the curate, shaking congregation members' hands.

Barnsley was just starting out on his career, aged 26. He was hands-on, and according to Weir Schultz, 'lived on the spot, and personally

superintended the work in every detail'. He supposedly camped in the churchyard. He was the son of a prosperous Wesleyan Birmingham builder, in touch with the city's intellectual élite. Was he religious? In later life, at Sapperton, he took his family to church on Sundays, sometimes attending twice, and later shocked his son by telling him that they went to 'set a good example in the village'.

Barnsley painted the roof here with his own hands, apparently to a design by Mrs Freshfield – spring flowers and roses. It is not clear whether Barnsley himself made any of the furniture in the church, though he may have designed it.

The contemporary view was appreciative: in 1893 *The Studio* enthused, finding it 'handled with a reticent feeling and sense of proportion beyond praise … nothing jars one's sense of well-ordered harmony. It is emphatically the work of an artist rather than of a "professional man".'

Wisdom of God is not conventional – even its name is unusual for an Anglican church. It is an evocation of a remote, deeply spiritual eastern monastic tradition: withdrawn, mysterious, unknowable. At the same time, a carefully wrought, hand-made monument to individual enterprise: ostentatiously ancient and modern.

Church of the Wisdom of God,
Lower Kingswood: east end

HASLEMERE, Surrey

St Christopher | 1902–4
Charles Spooner
GU27 1DD | Open 150 days a year

In 1900 Haslemere was a rural backwater with deep social problems. Iron foundries once drove the local economy, but they had long since closed: there was unemployment and poverty. The arrival of the railway in 1859 created an influx of smart weekenders: the 'Hilltop Writers Colony' was founded around 1860 – by 1914, more than 60 writers had come to live and work in the area, including Tennyson, George Eliot, Conan Doyle, H.G. Wells and George Bernard Shaw. The newcomers were rich as well as artistic – middle-class *bien-pensants* taking Arts & Crafts ideals into the countryside to revive village crafts.

Haslemere Peasant Arts Society was founded by Godfrey Blount (1859–1937: Winchester and Cambridge) and his wife Ethel Hine in 1898, to further, as he put it, 'the revival of a true country life where handicrafts and the arts of husbandry shall exercise body and mind and express the relation of man to earth and to the fruits of earth.' The Blounts' tenant, Therese La Chard, observed their 'unswerving faith in handweaving' and meals of 'salads and haricot beans eaten with horn spoons'.

Into these artistic waters swam Revd G.H. Aitken, an energetic Scot, trained in the cheerless East End parishes of London. In the 1900 *Parish Magazine* he reported that St Bartholomew's, the parish church, was increasingly inadequate for the town's needs and 'sometimes overfull'. The Wesleyans were building a chapel of their own. Aitken declared, 'there is no higher work on earth to which we can put our hands than this of being Church builders.' In May 1901 a Building Committee was appointed to find an architect. They chose Charles Spooner (1862–1938, AWG 1887), who presented plans in January 1902.

Aitken's sympathies are expressed in the reredos painting in his new church: a storybook group of High Church heroes and heroines paying homage to a mild, beneficent Christ. The group includes Sir Thomas More, John Keble, Gordon of Khartoum, Florence Nightingale, St Francis of Assisi, and ordinary soldiers and children. The painter was Minnie Dibdin Spooner, wife of the architect, and children's book illustrator, author of *Our Island Saints* (1912). Her retable panels show eight further good men and women, including Mary Magdalene and St Stephen. The lettering is by Eric Gill.

St Christopher, Haslemere:
reredos by Minnie Dibdin Spooner

Spooner was unusual among Arts & Crafts architects – a devout churchman. The parish magazine of his home church, St Nicholas, Chiswick, records, 'On most Sundays … he was in his place at the 10 o'clock Mass.' In 1909 he was appointed to the Consulting Architects Committee of the ICBS, the body which examined architects' plans for new church buildings in order to make financial grants. Spooner served until his death in 1938.

The church is full of refined craftwork. The main items of note are the Holy table and sanctuary chair, 1903–4, by Arthur Romney Green (1872–1945), who set up his workshop in the town in 1902; the lectern, 1904, by William Bainbridge Reynolds (1855–1935, AWG 1888); font, prayer desk and altar rails, 1904, designed by Spooner; the banner by Lily Bristow of Haslemere, 'advised by' Ann Macbeth of Glasgow School of Art, 1904–5 (repaired 1933, re-worked 1950); the organ case and pulpit, 1905, designed by Spooner; and the north nave window, 1910, designed by Mary Lowndes (1857–1929).

Aitken reported, 'Mr Spooner is personally superintending the designing of all furniture and fittings down to the smallest.' He summed up the achievement in what could stand as an Arts & Crafts manifesto for a Christian building: 'Helped by Mr Spooner, the Committee resolved from the first that they would not be content to put into our little House of Prayer anything cheap or ordinary. Each piece of furniture as it has come has been specially designed and made, and, with hardly a single exception, all those machine-made articles, which may be seen by the dozen in the catalogues of Church Shops, have been excluded. "Only the best", we have said, "for the Service of God's House".'

PIXHAM, DORKING, Surrey

St Mary the Virgin | 1903
Edwin Landseer Lutyens
RH4 1PT | By arrangement

Lutyens's early essay in social engineering is usually overlooked. Though he was its designer, it was very much the creation, and domain, of Mary Mayo (1834–1933), a larger-than-life figure, the benevolent chatelaine of Pixham. (The dedication – to St Mary the Virgin – was not applied until 1990.)

Miss Mayo (and her mother) arrived in Dorking in 1862. In 1866 the vicar asked her to be a visitor to the poor of Pixham. The arrival of the railway in 1867 brought an influx of workers: Miss Mayo saw the need for a religious centre. In 1880 she had a school built, and lodging for single men, with Bible and confirmation classes. Activities proliferated: Mothers' Meetings, night school, reading, writing and arithmetic, and chess. In 1883 she had a tin tabernacle erected. By 1890 there was an altar.

By 1902 'Miss Mayo is desirous of erecting a more permanent building … furnishing the same in a manner suitable … as a memorial to her late brother.' She was to completely furnish the new church at her own expense – and it memorialises her *two* brothers (both called Theodore). It was to be erected to 'the designs of an Architect of repute to be selected by Mary Mayo'. It is not clear how she knew Lutyens – possibly through Gertrude Jekyll. Pixham is one of only five churches Lutyens completed: the others are the Methodist chapel, Overstrand, Norfolk (1898) (p.213); St Jude's (1909–35) and the Free Church (1911), Hampstead Garden Suburb; and Campion Hall chapel, Oxford (1935) (p.80).

St Mary, Pixham: west façade; chancel

Lutyens (1869–1944, AWG 1903) was not quite yet established as a great man, but certainly well on the way: he had already built more than 40 houses, including Munstead Wood (1893–4) for Gertrude Jekyll. He described Pixham church thus: 'The conception of the building is that it should be made of local and simple materials, and by their use alone it should give evidence of the care, love and reverence of its object.'

The building was, from the first and specifically, dual-purpose – hall and church: 'two rooms from the larger of which an apse or small chancel shall be shut off for the sanctuary ....' Rather prosaically, the division was by a curtain – cheap but effective. The west end elevation to the street proclaims ecclesiastical status with not one but two crosses, the lower sitting awkwardly in a hexagon with a curved top. The tympanum is a symphony of exuberant brickwork.

Here Lutyens was not flattering a rich client, but delivering something simple and clear: and for someone clearly disinclined to be impressed by his reputation or charm, and more interested in practicalities than display. Miss Mayo was determined, forceful and persuasive. She got what she wanted, far from the Imperial pomp Lutyens has become known for.

DOCKENFIELD, FRENSHAM, Surrey

Good Shepherd | 1911
W. Curtis Green
GU10 4HU | By arrangement

The Good Shepherd is so simple, severe and stripped-down, without transepts or aisles, it might be a Nonconformist chapel. But then it would not have its powerful Evangelists' Cross

high on the east end exterior. (It never got its intended tower, which would have made it much more imposing.) The interior, with bare walls lacking decorative gesture, suggests uncomplicated, simple faith. Yet here and there are signs of something richer, culminating in a vividly coloured rood.

The local paper reported, 'For some considerable time it has been felt that a separate church was needed for this part of Frensham parish.' The church was to accommodate 130 worshippers, and capable of enlargement 'in the future as required'. A 14-strong fundraising Committee was appointed: all but three of them lived not in Dockenfield, but were wealthy inhabitants of Frensham. Might their motive have been to keep the folk of agricultural Dockenfield away from their posh church?

The Good Shepherd, Dockenfield

The desire was to start work in spring 1910 for philanthropic reasons: 'because … employment would in this way be found during part of the winter for some of those who would otherwise be out of work.' Besides, 'Church people residing in the district will be delighted to have a pleasant little church in which to worship in the future.' Something else was going on too: the Bible Christians first appeared in Dockenfield in the 1830s. In 1876 they erected a Chapel. They had an energetic and charismatic preacher.

The architect chosen by the Committee was William Curtis Green (1875–1960, AWG 1911). He was local – in 1911 living in a house he designed for himself in Farnham. He had trained under Bidlake at BMSA, and at the RA.

He was in the office of John Belcher (1841–1913, AWG 1884) 1895–7, then on the staff of *The Builder* as an architectural illustrator. He started in architectural practice in 1898. In 1906 he was elected ARIBA. In 1909 he was asked by Lutyens to take over his London office while Lutyens was in New Delhi. In 1910 he went in with the practice of Dunn and Watson, where he was soon in charge.

His aesthetics were impeccably Arts & Crafts. In 1905 he built the Quaker Meeting House in Croydon, and in 1908, alongside it, the Quaker Adult School Hall (p.119). But his best-known work all came after the Great War – the Wolseley Motors showroom in Piccadilly (now a smart restaurant), the Dorchester Hotel, Equity & Law's headquarters in Lincoln's Inn Fields. He built four churches later, all in partnership with his son Christopher and son-in-law Antony Lloyd: St George, Waddon, 1932; St Christopher, Cove, 1934; St Francis, Meir Green, Stoke-on-Trent, 1940; and All Saints, Shirley, Croydon, 1955–6. Romney Green, the woodcarver who made furniture for Spooner's church at Haslemere (p.88), was his brother.

The rood figures were painted by Henry Albert Payne RWS (1868–1940), like Green, trained at BMSA – and amongst those who decorated Madresfield Court (p.167). The carving of the Instruments of the Passion panels high on the walls at the corners of the chancel opening is by H.W. Palliser (1883–1963, AWG 1922), as is the font. The carving on the altar is by Esmond Burton (1886–1984, AWG 1919). The altar painting is by Margaret Thrower, a 21-year-old art student in 1911, of whom no more is known. The cross on the east wall exterior was carved by Henry Lawrence Christie (1872–1941), who went into partnership with Eric Gill in 1906.

The church sits peaceably by its by-road – without its proposed dominant tower, it attracts no great notice – nor any great opprobrium. It combines Instruments of the Passion and a potent rood with a sense of down-to-earth humanity: bare stone, bare wood, clear glass.

COMPTON, Guildford, Surrey

Mortuary Chapel | 1895–8
Mary Seton Watts
GU3 1DN | Usually open

Mary Watts (1849–1938) was an outsider: not an architect, but a trained sculptor and illustrator. She built only this one building. She was the (30 years younger) wife of the startlingly successful artist, George Frederic Watts RA (1817–1904). She told him, 'When I see your pictures, I feel a better person.' She was an original thinker, and unafraid – in a position to express her own ideas about spirituality and building unmediated by a third party, or confined by bourgeois convention.

The principles underlying Compton's design and construction are impeccably Arts & Crafts: local materials (the clay for the bricks dug from her garden), local workers (most had to be trained by her); ironwork by the Compton blacksmith, Clarence Sex; no contract (Watts was her own Clerk of Works), and no machinery. 'Much of the work having been done gratuitously, and all of it with the love that made the work delightful.'

She also rather implied no architect, but it seems the engineering part of construction was under the eye of George Redmayne of

Haslemere. And she did have help: Louis Deuchars, a young art student from Glasgow, was one of three paid artists on the project; Frank Mitchell as pottery kiln man; Thomas Steadman for carving. A fourth, George Andrews, was photographer/factotum.

The exterior is encrusted with terracotta carvings of swirling foliage and enigmatic figures, the panels made by as many as seventy enthusiastic villagers. Inside is dark, lit by four pairs of high, stained-glass lancet windows. It is a chapel of rest; however, it has an altar, and the chapel was consecrated (before the interior decoration was executed). The only seating is a bench inside the circular wall.

The Mortuary Chapel, Compton: terracotta exterior

The interior (1898–1904) is richly decorated with elaborate gesso-work (Walter Crane pointed out it was really stucco!) – writhing branches entwined with flowers, surrounding a series of stern, androgynous angels staring down, and scenes of mythology, coupled with biblical inscriptions: an allegorical language expressing 'values that replace Christianity'. The gesso was applied over several months by Mary Watts herself and a group of Compton women working as her assistants. The faces are painted on flat surfaces, not modelled.

Watts wrote her own guide to explain the symbolism (1904). Lethaby's *Architecture, Mysticism and Myth* (1891) surely had an effect. But she drew more widely. We know what books she used when preparing the designs: they included *Early Christian Symbolism*, *Early*

Christian Monuments of Scotland, Early Christian Art in Ireland, Sculptured Stones of Scotland. She owned a reproduction of *The Book of Kells*, and consulted *The Book of Durham* at the British Museum.

Is the Mortuary Chapel 'Arts & Crafts'? In period, certainly. In 2010 one book canonised it as 'Arts and Crafts Masterpiece'. It is also described as 'one of the handful of buildings which obviously belong to the Art Nouveau movement'. It can even be understood as a church of the Aesthetic Movement. The abundance of ideas and motifs seems overpowering. The subject matter may now seem fey, even kitsch, but the integrity and seriousness are unmistakable. Mary Watts's gender may or may not inform the choice of images. But here is a female client who did not have to battle with the architect, or manage a clerk of works. She was not worried about money. She was on-site at all times. She was not trying to make a name, or impress. She was intent on her own agenda: a project to involve and enliven the people of the village, with a moral and – as it turned out – economic impact.

The result is wholly uncompromising. The chapel is laid out to an overtly Christian plan: a cruciform of four transepts, but pierced by an 'Eternal Circle of Being'. It is notable that, though there are the symbols of the four Evangelists, and Alpha and Omega, and angels, there is no image of Christ anywhere in the chapel.

BRIGHTON, Sussex

St Bartholomew | 1897–1908
Henry Wilson interior
BN1 4GP | Open

Built in 1872–4 for Father Arthur Wagner, who built far too many churches in Brighton. His money came from his family's hats business. Here was a client who was prepared to disregard cost. The architect was a local man, Edmund Scott. Wagner told him to build high – 42 metres to the roof ridge, reputedly the highest parish church roof ridge in England.

The town did not care for it. In 1893 Brighton councillors called it 'a cheese warehouse', 'a monster excrescence', 'uselessly large' and 'painfully ugly and out of place'.

In 1895 a new vicar, Arthur Cocks arrived: '… vast … congregations worshipped at splendid services, augmented from 1896 by a permanent orchestra, and conducted to their seats by a Japanese verger, John Kendo Feudiekitchi, who had once worked in the stables of the Mikado.' Cocks not only wanted the church furnished extravagantly, but wanted to extend it.

In the apse there was to be an enormous mosaic: The Madonna in Glory, about 10 metres high. (But see frontispiece.)

Henry Wilson's work on the interior was spread over 13 years: hammered brass candlesticks, 1897; chalice, 1898; baldachino, 1899–1900; crucifix, now on the Lady altar, 1902, with a silver-plated copper repoussé frontal of the Adoration of the Magi, encircled by symbols of the seven planets in the Assyrian solar system – the Sun a lion, Mars a wolf, Jupiter a thunderbolt, the Moon a stag, Venus an owl, Mercury a serpent, and Saturn a scorpion. Then the pulpit and organ gallery, 1906; baptistry, 1908. In 1911 Fr Cocks went over to Rome, and Wilson's involvement at the church ceased.

BLACKHEATH, Wonersh, Surrey

St Martin | 1892–3
Harrison Townsend
GU4 8RA | Usually open

This crouching, low-roofed church is often said to be based on an Italian wayside church – something medieval in rural Piedmont, perhaps. But this is a far less rustic affair. Its architect, Harrison Townsend (1851–1928, AWG 1888) travelled extensively in Italy, and was knowledgeable about Italian mosaics. The lack of a spire – none was ever proposed – suggests humility: it was originally intended as a mission church, replacing services in a cottage, converted by Townsend into the new church's vestry. It was unpretending – 'a simple and inexpensive building', according to *REEA* – but the oversized brick arch entrance counters this humility with bold assurance. Some see the influence of the American architect Henry Hobson Richardson (1838–86), who had a taste for such muscular arches. Townsend's journalist brother wrote an article on Richardson, which underlines the possibility of influence. The church has a rather secretive air, sideways on to the road, with low-sweeping eaves and a

St Martin, Blackheath:
wall painting by Anna Lea Merritt

bellcote: solipsistic, miniature, seductive and a little mysterious. There are doll-like dormers. On the exterior east end wall – almost impossible to see – Christ in Majesty.

Inside, the exoticism is even greater, and yet more self-consciously picturesque. The walls, pulpit and organ recesses, and chancel arch are lined with alabaster. The screen is gilded, as are the flat bands in the ceiling. The lectern and candle-holders are reportedly from ironstone, quarried locally and smelted at the Royal Mint. There is a memorial window by F. Hamilton Jackson (1848–1923, AWG 1887) behind the pulpit.

The building was largely paid for by Sir William Roberts-Austen (1843–1902), Chemist to the Royal Mint, who came to Blackheath for his health. It was then remote and sparsely populated, but commutable to London by train from 1865. His wife, Lady Florence, was a member of the Royal Society of British Artists, where she exhibited watercolours. The couple were artistic and sociable – their circle included the Wattses of Compton, and Wickham Flower, a rich lawyer and patron of Whistler: his garden at Great Tangley Manor was designed by Gertrude Jekyll. Flower's wife was a friend of Anna Lea Merritt (1844–1930), an American painter who lived at nearby Hurstbourne Tarrant. Lady Florence visited Merritt's studio, where she saw the cartoons for Merritt's murals for the 1893 Chicago World's Fair: she suggested Merritt should decorate the new Blackheath church, which she did, 1894–5, using a process developed by a German chemist, Adolf Keim. Merritt and Roberts-Austen lectured together on the technique at the Royal Society in 1895. The process meant the colours stayed bright – the entire scheme was conserved and cleaned in 2011. The Keim method was, unaccountably, and as far as is known, employed nowhere else in England, though widely used in Germany.

St Martin, Blackheath

Down the hill from the church, opposite the village hall, is a house – Chapel End – which was once Blackheath Congregational Chapel, also by Harrison Townsend, 1901–2.

MIDHURST, Sussex

Chapel of Edward VII Sanatorium | 1907
H. Percy Adams and Charles Holden
GU29 0BJ | Private property

The King Edward VII Sanatorium at Midhurst is now the King Edward VII Estate – a careful and painstaking conversion into luxury apartments and houses by City & Country, who acquired the site in 2009. The Chapel, which stood derelict after the sanatorium was closed in 2006, is, at the time of writing, to become a restaurant. As this is now an estate of private dwellings, access may be limited or not possible, at the discretion of City & Country.

The architect was H. Percy Adams (1865–1930), though much of the work must have been shared with his chief designer, Charles

Holden (1875–1960, AWG 1917). The chapel's primary interest is, perhaps, its geometric white and blue glass by Benjamin Nelson (1875–1922), a close friend and collaborator of Holden, who provided glass for Holden's Bristol Central Library, and the former BMA building in London, now Zimbabwe House. He was influenced by Henry Wilson, who taught metalwork at Central School, and even more so by Christopher Whall, who taught Nelson stained-glass work there.

The building is an open-air chapel. Fresh air was a prime part of treatment for tuberculosis patients in the early 20th century. The chapel is shaped in a shallow V – one 'nave' for women, the other for men, with the chancel at the join. The south sides of both naves were entirely open, protected by a cloister, to 'prevent snow and rain from driving in'. There was an open-air pulpit for fine weather. The interior pulpit, lectern and altar were in teak with Coromandel ebony inlays – exotic and heavy, with an almost African air: the work of Ashbee's Guild of Handicraft, and probably carved by Alec Miller (1879–1961, AWG 1925). Throughout the complex there is ornamental plasterwork and rainwater heads by George Bankart and the Bromsgrove Guild: 'Work pregnant with the modern spirit and yet imbued with true artistic perception and knowledge' according to *The Studio,* January 1907.

FOUR ELMS, Kent

St Paul | 1881
Edwin Hall
TN8 6NE | By arrangement

The architect Edwin Hall (1851–1923) became best known for hospitals – he designed at least twenty. His original intention here (his only church) was for something chaste – decoration only on the pulpit and font, east window and chancel arch. The driving force for the enrichment of the interior seems to have been Lady Beatrice Rachel Henriques, née Faudel-Phillips (1868–1953). She and her husband had a large country house nearby, Normandy Park, and a townhouse in Eaton Square. The Henriques' son was killed at Ypres. Lady Beatrice commissioned a stained-glass window as a memorial. How she knew W.R. Lethaby – by this time, Professor – is not known, but she had him design screen, lectern, reredos and choir stalls. The work all seems to date from 1915–17, well after Lethaby had given up practice in favour of education. The screen was made by the Four Elms joiner, William Winter; the carving by Lethaby's friend and colleague George Jack (1855–1931, AWG 1906). Lethaby also had a hand in the design of the altar cross and candlesticks, made by John Paul Cooper (1869–1933, AWG 1908), who lived locally at Westerham. The lectern, 1929, to Lethaby's design, was carved by Laurence Turner (1864–1957, AWG 1891). The reredos carving was started by Thomas Stirling Lee (1857–1916, AWG 1889) and completed, following Lee's death, by Henry Pegram (1862–1937, AWG 1890). According to an undated newspaper cutting in the church, of around 1930, 'Everything put into it was in splendid taste, and the best obtainable.' The *opus sectile* tablets are by Powells, 1907. Lady Beatrice seems to have been a craftswoman herself – the carving on the frontals chest is reportedly by her, 1912.

Other Churches

Surrey

St Mary, Sunbury-on-Thames | S.S. Teulon | 1856, 1871 | TW16 6RN
Sgraffito murals by Heywood Sumner, 1892; apsidal paintings, and glass by local artist, George Ostrehan, 1892.

St Thomas, Chilworth | William Seth-Smith | 1896 | GU4 8LQ
Started life as Greshambury Institute for the education of local mill workers. Its colourful interior alas painted over.

St Silvan, Staffhurst Wood, Limpsfield | W.H. Harrison | 1898 | RH8 0RR | **H**
Woodland whimsy – brick nogging and quaint roofscape. Partly used as accommodation.

All Saints, Grayswood | Axel Haig | 1901 | GU27 2DJ
Scandinavian-feeling craftwork in wood and metal; paintings. Haig (Swedish) had been a pupil of William Burges.

St Paul, Camberley | W.D. Caröe | 1902, 1907 | GU15 2AJ
Less flamboyant cousin of Colehill – and more at home here.

Englefield Green Methodist Church | William Seth-Smith | 1903 | TW20 0QX
Now Village Centre and Café Rendezvous, with inside modernised.

St Mary of Bethany, Woking | W.D. Caröe | 1907 | GU22 7UH

All Saints, Woodham | W.F. Unsworth | 1908 | GU21 5SH
In a rather conventional church, arty woodwork, including inlayed altar fronts; rood; opus sectile

St John, West Byfleet | W.D. Caröe | 1910–12 | KT14 6EH
Caröe at his most devout. Rich woodwork; font by Nathaniel Hitch.

St Andrew, Oxshott | W.D. Caröe | 1911–12 | KT22 0LE
Whimsy outside, surprisingly stern inside.

St Thomas, The Bourne, Farnham | Henry Sidebotham, Charles Nicholson | 1911 | GU9 8HA

All Saints (RC), Oxted | Leonard Williams | 1913–19 | RH8 0AG

St Mark, Whiteley Village, Burhill | Walter Tapper | 1919 | KT12 4DW
Tapper teetering on the brink of tender Arts & Crafts detailing.

Charterhouse School Chapel, Godalming | Giles Gilbert Scott | 1922–7 | GU8 6AZ
Sombre War Memorial. Private.

St Michael (RC), Ashford | Giles Gilbert Scott | 1928 | TW15 2TN
Imposing and evocative, despite fierce Vatican II re-ordering. Inventive brickwork.

St Paul, Woldingham | Herbert Baker | 1933 | CR3 7EN
Douglas Strachan glass.

Sussex

Christ's Hospital Chapel, Horsham | Aston Webb, Ingress Bell | 1902 | RH13 0LJ
Murals 1912–23 by Frank Brangwyn. Private.

St Peter, Stonegate | G.E.S. Streatfeild | 1904 | TN5 7EW

Wesleyan Church, Midhurst | Gordon & Gunton | 1902–4 | GU29 9DU

South Street Free Church, Eastbourne | Henry Ward | 1903–5 | BN21 4UP

Bexhill-on-Sea – like so many seaside towns, all its churches are of some interest, even more so when taken as a whole:
—**St John's URC** (now youth centre) | Henry Ward | 1897 | TN39 3PD
—**St Stephen** | Henry Ward | 1898–1900 | TN39 4HD
—**St Andrew**, Wickham Avenue (closed) | J.B. Wall | 1900 | TN39 3EP
—**Christchurch Methodist** | H. Harper (?) | 1907 | TN40 2DY
—**All Saints**, Sidley | G.E.S. Streatfeild | 1909–27 | TN39 5HA
—**St Michael & All Angels** | J.B. Mendham | 1929–30 | TN40 2NY
—**St Augustine**, Cooden | Randoll Blacking | 1933–4 | TN39 3AZ
—**St Martha**, Little Common (RC) | Marshall Wood | 1939–40 | TN39 4SL

Kent

Chapel at Poundsbridge, nr Penshurst | Mervyn Macartney | 1888–9 | TN11 8BL
One of only two churches by AWG co-founder Macartney. Pevsner rightly called it 'uneventful'.

Our Lady (RC), Folkestone | Leonard Stokes | 1889 | CT20 1EF
Austere and restrained, with fine woodwork and sprightly stencilling of the roof timbers.

St Saviour, Folkestone | Micklethwaite, Somers Clarke | 1889–1913 | CT19 5PH
Riotous outside, restrained to the point of shyness inside. Window by Christopher Whall.

Christ Church, Dartford | W.D. Caröe | 1904–9 | DA1 3ET
Dramatic, almost wilfully alien, with Byzantine, Mediterranean and perhaps Roman ideas.

Assumption (RC), Northfleet | Giles Gilbert Scott | 1913–16 | DA11 9ES
Stern, monolithic, aloof, but with an interior that is devout and oddly intimate.

St Bartholomew, Herne Bay | W.D. Caröe | 1915–32 | CT6 6EB
Caröe at the seaside, in expansive holiday mood.

St Augustine, Gillingham | Temple Moore | 1915–18 | ME7 5PW
Temple Moore in a slightly Artsy-Craftsy mood – or is he? Rood of 1926.

Our Lady Star of the Sea, Broadstairs | Giles Gilbert Scott | 1929–31; 1961 | CT10 2RH
A surprise. An intimate, embracing, thoughtful church, soothingly tranquil, with no unnecessary gesture.

9
LONDON AND MIDDLESEX

London was where the fire of Arts & Crafts ideas burned most brightly – even though by 1890 its sparks were lighting up every part of the country. Wherever they had come from, young architects found warm friendships, and opportunity. Many trained in the city's great ecclesiastical practices, in particular those of Gilbert Scott and G.E. Street, and in those of two less conservative spirits: G.F. Bodley, the last of the Goths, whose death in 1907 prompted 1911's *Recent English Ecclesiastical Architecture* (*REEA*) – a threnody, as it turned out, for Victorian church building; and John Dando Sedding, who represented, along with Norman Shaw, a transition to something more expressive and individual.

Shaw's assistants and pupils formed the St George's Art Society (SGAS), which swiftly matured into the AWG. In London too were less clubbable spirits: the uncompromising C.F.A. Voysey, and the unbending but charismatically influential Philip Webb.

London was also the birthplace of the Settlement movement – Oxbridge undergraduates and public schoolboys going into the slums to improve the lives of working men, inspired by Christian Socialism and the vision of Canon Samuel Barnett and his wife Henrietta, founders of Toynbee Hall, where Walter Crane socialised with Voysey and Charles Spooner.

The church took the challenges of a booming city seriously – 'London-over-the-Border' was the unofficial name for those parts of north-east London still under the control of St Albans diocese, which manfully tried to provide new churches for unruly sprawls like East Ham. South of the river, Southwark commissioned Greenaway and Newberry, amongst others, to build new churches with the same purpose. The RCs built what remains their most demonstrative church, Westminster Cathedral, in an eye-catching Byzantine mode – most others were cheap and cheerful. The Methodists built Central Halls in the hubbub of Bermondsey, Walthamstow and elsewhere. New denominations with new interpretations of Christian living, from the Salvation Army to the Agapemonites, built according to their many and various lights.

There was grandeur, of course, and snobbery – so some churches were rather against the Arts & Crafts grain, big, muscular and showy: Holy Redeemer Clerkenwell, St Peter Ealing, Bedford Park, Summerstown. But the availability of like-minded fellow artists meant a church could develop, over a few years, into a collection of lovely things.

Holy Trinity, Sloane Street:
the east window

SLOANE STREET, Chelsea

Holy Trinity | 1887–90 and beyond
John Dando Sedding, Henry Wilson et al.
SW1X 9BZ | Open

John Betjeman declared it 'The Cathedral of the Arts & Crafts'. It is big, yes, and wide (wider than St Paul's by 9 inches) but not especially grand. It is stately, and with imposing fittings – the choir stalls and gallery have almost Sistine pretensions. But it does not compare in either volume or gravitas with St Paul's or Westminster, let alone more modest cathedrals like Lichfield or St David's. Yes, it is beautiful – distractingly so – though that is not a requisite of cathedrals. But it has no diocesan function, no cathedra, and was not designed for any special ceremonial liturgy, but simply for the highest of High Church high masses.

This was not a church for rich aesthetes and the cognoscenti, but for the lower middle and working classes of Chelsea: the Rector in 1887 had a mission to the poor, and Lord Cadogan, who gave the money for the building (£20,000), was known for philanthropy. Besides, his architect, Sedding (this was his last church), 'did not plan for the clergy … but for the people'. He wrote, 'Let us who work in the wild scrimmage and hustling-bustle of nineteenth-century life remember that our churches have still their ancient signification … All without is mean and small | All within is vast and tall.' Holy Trinity is a people's church, capacious and with clear sight-lines to the elevated altar. Sedding was churchwarden at the passingly High St Alban, Holborn, and in sympathy with Christian Socialism. He was Master of the AWG 1885 and 1886. A heady mix.

Betjeman's over-claim was perhaps just to make it stand out from the crowd – he was, at the time, after all, trying to save it from demolition, the Church of England's preferred plan for its future in 1971. Hard to believe. We have him, Gavin Stamp and the Victorian Society to thank for its survival. Perhaps the view of another connoisseur carries more weight: William Morris called it the 'best modern interior of a town church'.

From the street, the building does not *look* especially Arts & Crafts – a late Gothic Revival treatment, in Butterfield/Blomfield polychrome brick. Inside, though, a bewildering display – an exhibition almost – of furnishings and decoration by some of the most admired artists with Arts & Crafts connections. For some, this is its failing as a church – the elements do not cohere. But miscellaneous accumulation is surely true of any large medieval town church – the difference here is that the elements came within a decade, not over centuries. It is a restless space, then: almost too many things to admire.

Sedding was conscious that his interior was potentially controversial, even before any of the furnishings were in place. Its plan and eclectic mix of styles would probably have been condemned by the Ecclesiologists. His other London churches – St Augustine, Highgate, 1884–8 (N6 5BH) and Most Holy Redeemer, Clerkenwell, 1886–8 (EC1R 4QE) – also shun the sort of rectitude the Ecclesiologists praised. Sedding asked his friend Christopher Whall, when they visited the site together, cocking his head to one side mischievously, 'Well, is it too naughty?'

Holy Trinity, Sloane Street: the pulpit

NO ENTRY
STAFF ONLY

It all seems entirely unexceptionable now. Sedding's plan was uncluttered: no screen, no rood beam. The wrought-iron chancel gates, to Sedding's design, made by the firm of Henry Longden (1831–1920, AWG 1884), were rather an afterthought, intended to add status, but not to obscure the altar, which they somehow do.

The original idea was to re-use fittings from the 1828 church. Some of the new elements designed by Sedding were in place by 1890 – the electroliers, pulpit (lacking intended brass panels by Alfred Gilbert), the low chancel wall, chancel gates and piers. When Sedding's plans and elevations were published in 1888, fund-raising produced more money (£7000), and lavish additional fittings were possible.

Sedding commissioned the work in a somewhat haphazard manner, not the co-ordinated co-operative way one might imagine. Christopher Whall only received his commission for the clerestory windows when he encountered Sedding scratching about for help with the new scheme. Then, in 1891, Sedding suddenly died and his assistant, Henry Wilson, found himself in charge.

Before admiring its details, it is worth remembering that the interior is not only not as intended, but incomplete. Burne-Jones was to have added a narrative painted frieze round the entire nave. There were to be statues of the apostles by Hamo Thornycroft (1850–1925, AWG 1884) on the nave columns; carvings by Henry Hugh Armstead RA (1828–1905) in the arcade spandrels; and a painted ceiling. The west window, also to be by Morris to Burne-Jones designs, has never been completed. The interior walls were white-washed to mask some of this incompleteness under the eye of F.C. Eden (1864–1944, AWG 1915), supervising architect in the 1920s, who furnished the south chapel, 1921. The east end as designed by Sedding (several times) was never achieved – the 1912 reredos by John Tweed (1869–1933, AWG 1904) fails to command, and the front of the altar is a rather heavy-handed Entombment by Harry Bates (1850–99, AWG 1886). Henry Wilson's later conception for a mighty reredos, shown at the RA in 1894, would have obscured much of the Burne-Jones window. The outer, narrow side aisles, originally envisaged as a processional way with an ambulatory behind the choir, are now colonised by side altars and enlarged vestries.

But what glories remain – a primer in glass, sculpture and metalwork design in London around 1900. The east window was largely (47 out of 48 lights) designed by Burne-Jones – Morris did just one light. The rest of the interior is almost entirely by men of the AWG. The south nave windows are by Christopher Whall (westernmost 1900, eastern 1907), the north by William Blake Richmond (1842–1921, AWG 1884). The clerestory windows are also by Whall – only six of a planned ten were executed. The figures on the organ chamber and the screens of the south chapel, the panels on the choir stalls, and the angels on the dwarf chancel screen are by Frederick William Pomeroy (1856–1924, AWG 1887). The font, designed by Sedding, is by Edward Onslow Ford (1852–1901, AWG 1884); the relief panel in the wall behind is based on a design by Henry Wilson. Much of the metalwork was designed by Wilson, notably the bronze angels at the entrance to the Memorial Chapel (originally part of the altar rails, destroyed in the Blitz); the organ grille,

Holy Trinity, Sloane Street:
way from Lady Chapel, under organ,
to sancturary, designed by Henry Wilson,
made by Nelson Dawson

executed by Nelson Dawson (1859–1941, AWG 1894), as were the copper capitals on the piers in the south aisle. The bronze angel lectern is by Armstead. The railings and gates to the street front are by Wilson.

WESTMINSTER CATHEDRAL

St Andrew's Chapel | 1895–1903
J.F. Bentley; Weir Schultz
SW1P 1QW | Open

The lifting of restrictions on Roman Catholic worship in the 1820s was followed by the re-establishment of a Catholic hierarchy in 1850, and a growing confidence in building new churches. The apogee was Westminster, created under the urbane eye of Cardinal Vaughan, and, at his behest, in Byzantine rather than Gothic style, to set it apart from the Church of England and perhaps to suggest Catholicism's longer history.

He chose John Francis Bentley (1839–1902, AWG 1889) as his architect – a Catholic convert, and pious, and with Holy Rood, Watford (p.134) already to his name. Westminster became his life work. When he died in 1902, the shell of the cathedral was completed, but the interior decoration had barely been started. However, he left hundreds of drawings for it. Bentley was perhaps not an active AWG Brother, nor especially sociable. Other creative minds produced other embellishments – there is much to weigh and ponder: the Stations of the Cross are by Eric Gill.

The cynosure of Arts & Crafts eyes, however, is St Andrew's Chapel, 1910–16, paid for (£10,000) by the Scottish magnate of Welsh coal Lord Bute, with the stipulation it was to be designed by his in-house architect, Robert Weir Schultz (1860–1951, AWG 1891), successor to William Burges as his architectural dragoman since 1891. The designs were approved in 1910 and exhibited – slightly altered – at the RA in 1915. In January 1916 *Country Life* thought, 'here is no mere archaeological exercise, no dead copy of the churches of Rome or Ravenna or the East, but a live piece of design wrought out in valuable materials, with mature knowledge of design and method.' In the *Architectural Review* Curtis Green reported, 'Under the guidance of Mr Weir [Schultz] the most talented craftsmen of the day have wrought in precious materials a suitable lining to one of the little side chapels ... Like all good work, its perfection pervades one slowly.'

St Andrew's Chapel, Westminster Cathedral: stalls by Ernest Gimson

Half a dozen AWG members were involved: Weir Schultz's guiding eye ensured a harmonious result. The screen, in stainless tin, is by William Bainbridge Reynolds. The figure of Christ under the baldachino by Thomas Stirling Lee (1857–1916, AWG 1889). The candlesticks, reliquary, rugs, mats and cushion by Harold Stabler (1872–1945, AWG 1903). The mosaics were applied by Gaetano Meo (see p.246), who had worked with the PRB, to cartoons by George Jack (1855–1931, AWG 1906). The stalls were made by Ernest Gimson (1864–1919, AWG 1891) to designs by Weir Schultz. The kneelers are by Sidney Barnsley.

The colour scheme of the lower part of the walls and the floor feels chilly – especially when compared to other side chapels nearby.

St Anselm, Hatch End: the rood

Perhaps there is simply too much misty grey marble. The fish in the pavement seem frozen, as if on their way to market.

HATCH END

St Anselm | 1894–1906
F.E. Jones; Charles Spooner, Selwyn Image et al.
HA5 4JL | By arrangement

Hatch End seems always to have been a leafy, prosperous backwater. Its Toytown 1911 railway station by Gerald Horsley (1862–1917, AWG 1884) proclaims high artistic aspirations. St Anselm was built 1894–5, and enlarged in 1906 to become a parish church in its own right. The glass-designer Louis Davis (1860–1941, AWG 1891) moved to Pinner by 1896, and lived near the new church. Whether through his enthusiasm, or the artistic inclinations of

Pinner's energetic vicar, Charles Grenside, St Anselm's fixtures and fittings accumulated with an unforced coherence. The interior gives the impression of a co-ordinated effort: in reality the work was done piecemeal and over a prolonged period.

The east and baptistry windows are by Davis (1903, 1905, 1910, 1927, 1932). Selwyn Image (1849–1930, AWG 1887) designed the west window, 1915. Charles Spooner had three separate commissions here: the rood screen, 1901; the Great War Memorial reredos, 1921; and the baptistry screen, 1938.

Spooner's mighty rood screen was commissioned by the vicar's churchwarden, G.T. Skilbeck, a man of boldness and daring. It became mildly notorious, the subject of a court case in the Court of Arches, where there were accusations of papistical 'superstitious reverence'. It is among the largest pieces of figural carving in the Arts & Crafts, elaborate and sensual. The thickly clustered foliage is continental in feel, darkly filling the upper half of the chancel arch, rather un-English in its emotional excess.

The three figures were designed by Spooner's wife, Minnie Dibdin Spooner. She trained at the RA School of Painting (where they may have first met), and had worked as a painter of miniatures. The carving was by Joseph Phillips (b.1866), rather forgotten now, but the leading woodcarver in the Altrincham studio workshop of George Faulkner Armitage. He later worked with E.S. Prior on the lychgate at Brantham, Suffolk; with Charles Ponting on the screen at Iwerne Minster; and again alongside Spooner at Bridgnorth. His best-known work is the sculpture in the Lady Chapel of Liverpool Cathedral.

EALING COMMON

All Saints: 'Spencer Perceval Memorial' | 1903–5
William Alfred Pite
W5 3JJ | By arrangement

Spencer Perceval, the only British Prime Minister to have been assassinated (in 1812), had to wait 87 years for his memorial – paid for by his last surviving daughter, by her will of 1899: she was seven when he was murdered. Funds may have come from her portion of the £50,000 compensation awarded by the Crown to the bereaved family.

W.A. Pite (1860–1949) was largely a municipal architect – hospitals, town halls and at least one settlement for Dr Barnardo. But he also designed churches, including St Peter, Acton Green – very different from All Saints – and, as Pite, Son & Fairweather, some other London churches in the 1930s. He was the brother of the more celebrated Professor Beresford Pite, architect of Christ Church, Brixton. Within a decade, the church had been modified to further commemorate the fallen of the Great War, including the architect's son. Stonework in the chancel arch records their names.

The imposing lectern, the pulpit, the Perceval memorial tablet and the finger plates on the doors are all by Nelson Dawson (1859–1941, AWG 1894), who was a parishioner. He and his wife Edith (1862–1928) designed and made metalwork and enamel at their workshops in Chiswick Mall, in the heart of the Arts & Crafts colony that had grown up near Morris's house, Kelmscott, by

All Saints, Ealing Common: pulpit by Nelson Dawson

HOLY

Hammersmith Bridge. Edith was the driving force, and the more business-like. It is hard to untangle their hands in their work – and why should one wish to? Like many in the Arts & Crafts, they worked as an equal team. The cross on the high altar was designed by G.F. Bodley.

BEDFORD PARK

St Michael and All Angels | 1878–9
R. Norman Shaw
W4 1TT | Open

The building itself is far too early to 'really' be Arts & Crafts, of course, but instructive when considering Shaw's subsequent churches at Leek (p.162) and Ilkley (p.240), and his aesthetic influence on, for example, Lethaby, Horsley and Caröe. Initially it was a much more severe space: no panelling, no font, reredos, pulpit or organ. The colour scheme – green seating, terracotta walls and white ceiling – was all Shaw's (restored 2007). The panelling – dark red in the chancel – came in 1881. The original plain chairs were replaced by Shaw's benches through the 1880s. The lectern is to Shaw's design, 1882.

G.E. Street thought it not very ecclesiastical. To some it seems almost like a church hall. It's a jovial, theatrical, come-as-you-are sort of place: Andrew Saint called it 'a comfortable auditorium where independent, clear-thinking folk can watch the enactment of the Lord's Supper without loss of self-respect.' Bedford Park was free-thinking, enlightened, urbane, clever.

Much of the work, from Shaw's designs, was executed by Maurice Adams (1849–1933), an assistant in Shaw's office, first churchwarden of the church and subsequently Editor of *Building News*. He designed many of the houses in Bedford Park – Shaw was the first architect of the estate – and was responsible for completing the church building itself, including the north aisle, 1887. The font, by Adams, arrived in 1884. Adams also designed the pulpit, 1894; clock, 1900; sanctuary floor and All Souls Chapel, 1909; reredos, 1922. Much of the glass is by Daniel Bell, brother of Alfred Bell of Clayton & Bell.

EALING

St Peter | 1892–3
J.D. Sedding, Henry Wilson
W5 2RU | Open

Sedding won the job in a competition. He had completed the design by 1890. Drawings were published in *The Builder* (1889) – 'a piece of real originality' – and in *The Architect* (1890). But the foundation stone was not laid until 1892, after Sedding's death, so the church was executed by Henry Wilson. Thus, the details are not perhaps as Sedding might have wished them, nor as

Left: St Michael and All Angels, Bedford Park
Right: St Peter, Ealing: the south door by Henry Wilson

THE SETTLEMENT MOVEMENT

The Settlement Movement was heartily Christian in spirit, so there were chapels. Some survive. Some pre-date our period – St Columba, Kingsland Road, Hoxton (James Brooks, 1868–9) for example. However, at most of those settlements post-1880, there is little or nothing to see apart from the exterior: rather few continue as worship spaces.

The tiny chapel of **St Margaret's House**, Old Ford, Bethnal Green (E2 9PL), 1904, designed by Paul Waterhouse (1861–1924, AWG 1913) is pretty well intact and, although used now as an informal cinema, retains its elevated pews (for whom? the staff, the Trustees?) as well as its neat railed sanctuary. The suave golden-glowing panelled chapel, 1891–4, on the third floor at **Oxford House**, Bethnal Green (E2 6HG), by Arthur Blomfield (1829–99), was refurbished in 2019. Its reredos doors are tenderly painted with the Evangelists' devices on the south, and the Scapegoat, Lamb without Blemish and other Biblical symbols on the north. The chapel was intended for the undergraduates to practice their liturgy – hence a short and narrow processional way!

South of the river, the intense small complex of E.S. Prior's **Pembroke College Mission**, now St Christopher, Walworth (SE17 1QR) survives – worship space, meeting rooms, even the undergraduate accommodation, though the Pembroke College link is today more distant. The upper floors were completed by Herbert Passmore, 1908–9.

Norman Shaw designed the **Harrow School Mission**, 1883, in Latimer (now Freston) Road, Notting Dale (W10 6TH). It is now a community club, with youth activities, though the shell of the worship space and its window tracery survive. The chapel at **University House**, Victoria Park, by an unidentified architect, 1889 (E2 9PE) is now flats, though it retains its unmistakable shape – a Gothic brick prow breasting the street. The chapel of **Bethany House of Retreat**, Lloyd Square, Clerkenwell (Ernest Newton, 1891–2) was for a time a sports hall, and is now private, a photographer's studio.

Notable casualties include Christ Church, Oxford's mission, St Frideswide, Poplar (William Clarkson, 1889–92), first Blitzed, then demolished 1947; and All Saints Mission chapel, White Lion Street, Pentonville (R.A. Briggs, 1901–2), demolished. At Gilmore House, Clapham Common, there was a private chapel by Philip Webb, 1894–7, now stripped of all furnishings. **H**

Mary Ward House (opposite) was a Settlement without Christ. The most famous Settlement, Toynbee Hall, had no separate chapel: it was next door to St Jude's, a Commissioners church of 1845, demolished in 1927.

Top: Chapel of St Margaret's House, Old Ford, Bethnal Green: west end
Bottom: Chapel of Oxford House, Bethnal Green: east end

Wilson would have devised. A sense of deferential compromise, oddly, after even 100 years, survives. Much remains unfinished – the choir stalls suggest what might have been.

Wilson's hand can surely be discerned in the plates on the west porch interior doors. The figures of the four Evangelists on the main altar are energetic – even more so the beasts high in the chancel frieze, including giraffe, camel, elephant and bear. The paintings in the Lady Chapel, 1913, are by Henry Brewer (1866–1950). The south chapel, 1913, was designed by E.J. May (1853–1941, AWG 1888).

TAVISTOCK SQUARE

Mary Ward House | 1895–7
Smith and Brewer
WC1H 9SN | Private

The most 'Arts & Crafts' of all the Settlements (in its architects, appearance and politics) was Mary Ward's 1890 University Hall, with its 'system of practical conduct, based on faith in God'. The settlement was 'multi-faith', concerned with 'social mission'. Mrs Ward's most successful book was *Robert Elsmere* (1888), the story of a clergyman who loses his faith when he realises he cannot believe in miracles. Mrs Ward herself had had a similar experience.

In 1895 the settlement moved into new premises, first known as the Passmore Edwards Settlement, after its principal funder. The architects were Arnold Dunbar Smith (1866–1933, AWG 1922) and Cecil Claude Brewer (1871–1918, AWG 1894). There are eggs – Lethaby's symbols of creation – on the porch, whose placing makes the symmetrical street façade jink. The building had – and has – multiple secular functions: community centre, hostel, schoolroom, nursery, library. The interior – modified and remodelled to meet changing needs – retains some Arts & Crafts details, doors, and fireplaces reportedly by Lethaby, Voysey and Dawber, among others. Some parts have been brought back to the original design, and there is reportedly still some of the original furniture.

Smith and Brewer were unable to be wholly atheist: the main meeting room includes a curious structure which seems very much like a chancel screen. And, over a doorway to the side of the building, what appears to be a huge newspaper cutting declares a creed that expresses a spiritual version of *mutatis mutandis* Arts & Crafts ideas, thought to be Ward's own text (see p.40).

KENSINGTON

Russian Orthodox Cathedral,
Ennismore Gdns | 1885–1903
Harrison Townsend, Heywood Sumner
SW7 1NH | Often open

The church, originally All Saints, by Lewis Vulliamy, 1848–9, was rather severe, relieved only by gold stars painted on the blue ceiling of the apse by Owen Jones, Vulliamy's pupil. The whole was enlarged and embellished by Harrison Townsend from 1885, including a new west front, 1891, with a sgraffito and gold mosaic on the tympanum by Heywood Sumner. Townsend designed a font cover, made by Richard Llewelyn Rathbone (1864–1938, AWG 1892), in hand-beaten copper, 1896 (no longer there). His altar front survives, but now hidden behind the iconostasis. He was also responsible for designing intense woodwork, largely still in place.

CARÖE'S PRETTY TOYS

In East London, three Caröe churches – even if not built in an Arts & Crafts way, nor with an Arts & Crafts mindset – have enough of the flavour to suggest he was sometimes in tune with the ideas, and in a way that was not superficial or modish, but reflected a love of good detail and careful effects. These churches have in common one odd characteristic – from the street, they look smaller than they are: 'toy' churches.

St Barnabas and St James, Walthamstow, 1902 (E17 8NN) has crenelated capitals to its piers as if from Camelot, and a high frieze of blind brick quatrefoils (reminiscent of Colehill, p.51). The servers' stalls were made by a sidesman, Mr Gunton, and his sons. Two windows were designed by a member of the choir, 1927. The statue of St Michael is by Alec Miller (1879–1961, AWG 1925) of the Guild of Handicraft. The rood, designed by Caröe, 1921, was carved by Nathaniel Hitch (1845–1938). The church plate includes work by the Guild of Handicraft and the Artificers' Guild.

St Aldhelm, Silver Street, Upper Edmonton, 1903 (N18 1PA) has intricate Byzantine-ish brickwork outside, and inside, piers with a rather Egyptian – or ocean liner – air: the arcades spring sinuously from Moderne not-really-quite-capitals. There is playful strapwork. The stained-glass windows and reredos painting are by Walter Starmer, who also worked at Lutyens's Hampstead Free Church.

St Bartholomew, Stamford Hill, 1903–4 (N15 6AA) is the most toy-like of the three: lots of quirky fenestration; characteristic Caröe latches and handles; zigzag brickwork on the floor; a whimsical 'squint'; a snug, be-pillared crypt-ish chapel and many Caröe sets of vestments.

To which could be added his **St Michael Bassishaw, Hertford Rd, Edmonton**, 1901 (N9 7LE), in the same spirit, though now flats **H**. And, far to the west, **St Michael, Elswood Road, Chiswick**, 1908–9 (W4 3DZ) exhibits some of the same domestic atmosphere, though a little later, and somehow less refined.

Left: St Barnabas and St James, Walthamstow: the rood
Right: St Aldhelm, Silver Street, Upper Edmonton

In the body of the church, the eye is most caught by Sumner's sgrafitti, 1896–1903. There are also Sumner windows: foliage in the clerestory; a richly coloured East window with angels crying aloud the *Te Deum*, praising the Agnus Dei; and child figures in the small west windows, with 'Suffer the little children' in scrolls. Harrison Townsend and Sumner developed the scheme in happy partnership.

CHINGFORD

Our Lady and St Teresa | 1930–1, 1939
Fr John Howell, George W. Martyn
E4 7HP | By arrangement

The church, by its prettiness and enchanted air, seems to turn blushingly from the buses and lorries that clog the road in front. Round the corner is the unexpectedly bucolic Chingford Green. Town and country vie for supremacy: if it weren't for this tension, the church would be less notable, perhaps. The initial drawing appears to have been done by the priest, Fr John Howell. He showed it to a local builder, George Martyn, a recent RC convert. The lych gate commemorates Martyn as 'architect builder benefactor of this church'; he died in 1970. Neither man appears to have designed (or built) any other church.

The rainwater goods are adorned with naturalistic birds and fleurons of acorns and roses; there is a sturdy rustic porch, picturesquely open on all sides, and with an idiosyncratic holy water stoup, and carving by Donald Potter, who studied under Eric Gill. Inside there are more birds and foliage in a plaster frieze in the Bankart taste, high around the walls, and beneath a linen-folded west gallery. Stairs at the west end are enlivened with newels carrying a chubby frog, tortoise, stork/shoebill/curlew and a pair of billing pigeons. Crisp stone angels lounge in

Russian Orthodox Cathedral, Ennismore Gardens: sgraffiti by Heywood Summer

spandrels, and hold heraldic shields, one with a Pelican in her Piety. Large window by Veronica Whall, 1939.

SUMMERSTOWN

St Mary | 1902–20
Godfrey Pinkerton
SW17 0UQ | By arrangement

The original St Mary's was built in 1835. Alas, the local paper reported, 'sufficient care was not taken with the foundations … Finally [in 1894] the church was condemned … and pulled down.' The site was left empty for eight years; meanwhile the parish had become more populous: 'Fields and orchards have given way to streets of houses and traffic of all descriptions has disturbed the old-time quietude.'

A new priest, John Robinson, arrived in 1899. He summoned 'The Permanent Church Building Committee' and emphasised the urgency of building a new church. Five architects were invited to submit plans: the safe and unexciting J.E.K. and J.P. Cutts; a well-established church and municipal architect, Edward William Mountford; the vanishingly obscure Walter E. Hewitt; Messrs Lee and Pain, architects of Her Majesty's Theatre, Haymarket, 1867 and Godfrey Pinkerton (1858–1937). A vote was taken and Pinkerton was appointed – no reason is given. (There may have been a family connection to the vicar, by marriage.)

Pinkerton's oeuvre is small. Yet his obituary in *The Times* felt his 'attainments hardly won him the recognition which he deserved'. He had AWG connections – his FRIBA proposers included John Belcher and Mervyn Macartney (both AWG) – but he never joined. He was in partnership with Henry Martineau Fletcher (1870–1953, AWG 1902) in the early 1900s.

Fletcher was AWG Master in 1930. He worked with the woodcarver Joseph Armitage and the decorative plasterer George Bankart.

The foundation stone was laid in April 1903 by Princess Christian, third daughter of Queen Victoria. The Parish Magazine reported,

Our Lady of Grace and St Teresa of Avila, Chingford: rainwater head

St Mary, Summerstown: painted ceiling; font, probably by Laurence Turner

'HRH's presence … had entirely dispelled the old idea in the minds of Summerstown people, that they were overlooked and neglected by those in a better position in life than themselves.' The Committee was pleased: the next year they voted that the plans and elevations should be framed and hung in the clergy vestry.

Summerstown is rich in colouring and materials, expressing High Anglo-Catholic ambitions in a language which is part classical, part Byzantine. Pinkerton doesn't quite fit the mould of Arts & Crafts architect – he gives no overt sign that he was especially in sympathy with the AWG or ACES. One connection is suggestive: the font was carved by Laurence Turner (1864–1957, AWG 1891) – see also Kempley (p.145), Dockenfield (p.90) and Colehill (p.51). It is possible Turner also carved the pulpit, reading desk, doors and lettering.

In 1925 four life-size paintings in oils on canvas were fixed in the lunettes in the arcades.

They were painted by Constance Grant, commissioned by the new vicar, William Galpin, who succeeded Robinson in 1923. Christopher Webb was asked by a perhaps anxious Southwark DAC to look at her work. Webb (1866–1966) was a glass designer, as was his slightly better-known brother Geoffrey (1879–1954). They were the sons of Aston Webb. He reported, 'the work is obviously influenced by the modern school of painting, of which it is, to my mind, an excellent example.' The ceilings of the sanctuary, chancel and the arches of the aisles represent the Eastern Sky, with moon, stars and clouds; two life-size cherubim with golden trumpets proclaim 'Holy, Holy, Holy'. In 1927 a stained-glass scheme was commissioned for the east window: it was carried out by John Henry Dearle (1859–1932), now in charge of Morris & Co. A War memorial was installed in 1919, ousting the font from the baptistry. It bears striking figures of a warlike Adam striking at the Serpent (?), and of St George.

In 1980 discussions started about demolishing the church, which was (and probably always had been) far too big for its congregation. A new incumbent in 1988 led a revival of both building and congregation, with a restoration programme of pertinacity and quality. The cooperative community spirit of the Arts & Crafts continues: the church was re-wired free of charge by electricians from nearby Wimbledon greyhound track; a churchwarden painted the vestries and the hall inside and out; another member of the congregation removed dangerous gas fittings – all, it seems, without payment.

EARLS COURT

St Cuthbert, Philbeach Gdns | 1884–1914
Hugh Roumieu Gough, Ernest Geldart
SW5 9EB | Open

Until about 2005 there was a sign on the street frontage of the church calling it 'The Arts & Crafts church'. For whatever reason, it seems no longer to be there. Roumieu Gough (1843–1904) was not Arts & Crafts in intention or method – the *Survey of London* calls him 'an experienced church architect of some refinement but little originality'. He was not AWG. He designed the enormous pulpit and the later rood, 1893. The font and cover, designed by Gough, were made by Harry Hems, 1888.

St Cuthbert, Philbeach Gardens: the lectern by Bainbridge Reynolds

QUAKERS

The practical, humane outlook of the Quakers chimed with the democratic, somewhat Left instincts of the AWG. Friends have a natural preference for honesty and simplicity in building, and a dislike of anything that proclaims 'church'. Of all the denominations in this book, the Quakers are the most inclined to see worship space as a kind of home: sufficiently domestic to not be a church at all.

Fred Rowntree (1860–1927, AWG 1907) was a Quaker, related to the confectionery part of the family, but humbler, the child of a Scarborough grocer. He was articled to a local architect in 1876. In 1890 he married into the Grays, biscuit-manufacturers, and moved to Glasgow, where he went into partnership with Malcolm Stark (1854–1935?) – they were almost wholly unsuccessful. For a time, he worked with George Walton (1867–1933, AWG 1902), a York interior designer. In 1900 the Rowntrees moved to Hammersmith, the beating heart of the Arts & Crafts – they lived at 11 Hammersmith Terrace.

Two Quaker buildings by him survive – confusingly, both in Hampstead. One is the **Friends Meeting House, Heath Street**, 1906 (NW3 1DR) – an awkward corner site, long and thin (burgage plot?), which he contrived to make seem uncrowded, setting it back behind a front garden. The other is – technically – **Golders Green Meeting House**, 1913 (NW11 7AB): in reality in Hampstead Garden Suburb, hidden away in an unregarded garden corner, 17 North Square.

South of the river there is further modesty at **Purley Meeting House**, where George Pepler and Ernest Allen built a compact multi-purpose building, 1909, on an impossibly awkward sloping site (CR8 1BE). The Peplers were Quakers, with York connections. George's brother, Hilary Pepler, a printer who later went to Ditchling with Eric Gill, lived at 14 Hammersmith Terrace, so was a neighbour of Fred Rowntree.

The most spectacular Quaker space – big and demonstrative (and not a church!) – is in Croydon: the **Adult School Hall** by Curtis Green (CR0 1JE). In 1905 he built the Croydon Quaker Meeting House: destroyed in the Second World War, and replaced in 1957. However, in 1908 he had built alongside it the barn-like Hall. It is not hard to see its Arts & Crafts virtues: truth to materials in the absence of applied finishes; and the construction expressed frankly – it is clear which parts of the roof structure are load-bearing. Green was not a Quaker himself, but he records his aunt was 'a gifted and eloquent speaker among the Society of Friends'.

Top: Golders Green Meeting House, Hampstead Garden Suburb
Bottom: Adult School Hall, Croydon

In 1887, the vicar, Henry Westall, began to accumulate fittings by some leading Arts & Crafts designers: W. Bainbridge Reynolds (1855–1935, AWG 1888), a member of the congregation (and friend of C.F.A. Voysey), designed much of it – light fittings, 1887; the Wagnerian lectern, 1897; the great clock, 1898; parclose screens, 1895–1904; altar rails, silver front panel to the altar, 1910; Paschal candlestick, Royal Arms, tabernacle on the altar, 1933, among much else. Ernest Geldart (see p.210) designed the restless, imposing reredos in 1899, made by Boultons of Cheltenham, and installed in 1914. Boultons also made the statues over the piers.

St Cuthbert, Philbeach Gardens:
processional cross by Bainbridge Reynolds

Much of the interior stone and wood-carving and mosaics was carried out by parishioners informally organised into Guilds, along what seem to have been intended as medieval, even Arts & Crafts, lines. Innovatively, the Guilds were mixed gender. The stone diaper-work squares on the walls were each made by a member of the congregation, 1890–1909. The roof was painted by 'Mrs Falcon and daughters', 1897; the Lady Chapel ceiling by Julia Allen. One would like to know more of both.

There were classes and workshops in stone- and wood-carving and metalwork, led by local artisan craftsmen. The choir stalls, misericords and aumbry were made by the Guild of St Joseph; the vestments, many designed by Geldart, made by the Guild of St Margaret, 'under the direction of Miss Harvey'; the marble dado and much of the stonework by the Guild of St Peter. The congregation was leisured and comfortable – the ladies had a reputation for lavishly giving their jewellery to fund church activities: it was a sort of enlightened ecclesiastical further education college, half NADFAS, half U3A.

SUDBURY

St Andrew, Harrow Road | 1924–5
W. Charles Waymouth
HA0 2QA | Open

Plans for a church here by J.S. Alder were interrupted by the Great War. Instead William Charles Waymouth (1872–1967), architect of the London Diocesan Home Mission, was commissioned in 1924. The church was consecrated in 1926.

Waymouth is a rather retiring figure. He designed a modest church, St James, New Barnet, and a community hall and a golf clubhouse in Barnet, as well as houses there. But he also designed The Shakespeare Hut for the YMCA in 1916 – 'the grandest YMCA hut ever built' – a hostel for visiting ANZAC troops passing through London. He had an instinct for nostalgia and Olde England – which is what St Andrew's is: a faint, dwindling echo of the dying Arts & Crafts ethos. There is no suggestion it was built in an AWG way, nor was Waymouth AWG himself (though he was FRIBA). But in the detail there is the glimmer of what can be seen more clearly at Hutton (p.211) and Chingford (p.115) – loving attention to detail, pride in the small-scale, a slightly self-mocking nostalgia, modesty in materials and ambition. It is perhaps as 'fake' as the half-timbering of the Liberty's store off Regent Street – but it is sincerely meant, tinged with an Elgarian dying fall.

St Andrew, Sudbury: brickwork on vestry

EDMONTON

St Mary & St John | 1905–6
Charles Henry Bourne Quennell
N18 2DS | By arrangement

Quennell (1872–1935) was the author, with his wife, Marjorie Courtney, of *A History of Everyday Things in England 1066–1499* (1918): the popularising series eventually ran to four volumes. Muthesius ranked Quennell as a furniture designer alongside Henry Wilson: Quennell worked in Wilson's office 1895–8, and was a member of the Junior AWG. This is his only known church, according to his son, 'inspired by Westminster Cathedral, which was

St Mary & St John, Edmonton: north aisle screen

still in an unfinished state and had not yet acquired its present meretricious incrustations'.

It is large: to seat 832 – for the intended model village (*à la* Port Sunlight, perhaps) that was started around it in 1911, but never completed.

The main glazing is clear, but with decorative leading and flashes of colour, by Paul Woodroffe (1875–1954, AWG 1902). A glazed screen also may be by him. There is something Expressionistic about the interior – restless rhythms in the sanctuary niches and windows, narrow side aisles with a gallimaufry of doors, flat arcading, a reinforced concrete ceiling in the aisles (the concrete has given constant trouble). The church is conjoined to its 1911 Mission Hall and Vicarage by passages, forming a sort of cloister. It was surely intended – like Westminster – to be adorned over time: all that came was the rather severe chancel screen, choir stalls (only the wall benches survive), dado panelling and, it would seem, the pulpit. The architect, glazier and works foremen are listed on one of two foundation stones.

RICHMOND

St John the Divine | 1904–5
Arthur Grove et al.
TW9 2NA | By arrangement

The church is essentially a Commissioners' box (Lewis Vulliamy, 1829–36), enlarged and made more suitable for Anglo-Catholic worship by Arthur Grove (1870–1929) from 1904 – with a new chancel and a Lady Chapel. Grove trained under Sedding, then under Henry Wilson. He called upon AWG members and friends to execute the lavish schemes he laid – but there is a sense of incompleteness, and some has been effaced by later changes. Heroically, this early 20th-century work is now being restored, with plans to do more – this account should, with luck, be overtaken by events.

The chancel was painted throughout, 1906–9, to a scheme by Nathaniel Westlake (1833–1921) from Grove's extravagant drawings. Only the ceiling and Christ at the top of the east end survive – the rest was whitewashed over in the 1950s. The reredos triptych is also by Westlake, who also designed the east windows. Westlake was not AWG, though,

St John the Divine, Richmond:
bas-relief thought to be by Henry Wilson

confusingly, his brother Philip, also a painter, was. There is lettering by Eric Gill over the sacristy door, in the reredos frame, and on the Calvary on the east end gable outside. The altar rails and credence table are by Ernest Gimson. The nave windows are by Grove.

In the Lady Chapel the east window is by Christopher Whall, 1909; the south lancet windows by Mabel Esplin (1874–1921). The figures in Grove's reredos were carved by MacDonald Gill (1884–1947, AWG 1910) (see Roker, p.261), brother of Eric. The screen and gates are by W. Bainbridge Reynolds (1855–1935, AWG 1888). The lectern, 1898, by John Carr, came from Bedford Hospital chapel in 2016. In the narthex is a plaster bas-relief of a rather plump Christ child thought to be by Henry Wilson, who also made the tabernacle cover. Grove also designed the Hall, round the corner (now workshops), again with lettering by Eric Gill.

CROFTON PARK

St Hilda | 1905–8
Greenaway and Newberry
SE23 1PL | By arrangement

Pevsner called it 'rather irresponsible Arts & Crafts Gothic'. For Pevsner even 'Arts & Crafts' was perhaps a pejorative here – Gothic going in the wrong direction.

It was the first church by the partnership of Francis Hugh Greenaway (1869–1935), who had been articled to Aston Webb, and John Ernest Newberry (1862–1957) who had trained under John Loughborough Pearson, in whose office he had worked with W.D. Caröe. Greenaway and Newberry (G&N) designed some 26 churches, almost all of them in South London.

St Hilda is big and bold. The font has a Henry Wilson air, but lighter. The altar cross and robust surviving candle stands were made by the Artificers' Guild. There is pretty glass, 1912, by Henry Holiday (1839–1927, AWG 1884); and other glass has intriguing figurative leading, reminiscent of Wilson and Sedding at Lynton (p.64). The choir stalls by Newberry are Artsy-Craftsy.

Something Modern is struggling to be born here, but on a scale which now seems heedlessly optimistic. Subsequent G&N churches are less Arts & Crafts in look and attitude – and possibly, budget – St Hilda was funded by Sarah Martha Packe, rich widow of a Lincolnshire landowner. Nonetheless worth visiting are the medieval **St Nicholas, Plumstead** (SE18 1LR), where G&N added a north aisle, 1907–9, and where there is also an altar table by G&N; **St Andrew, Coulsdon**, 1911–15 (CR5 2DN), with vigorous metalwork, and **St James, Riddlesdown**, 1915 (CR8 2DL) with inventive roof beams in the aisles. Their churches after the Great War are sparer, and more direct: **St Paul, Furzedown**, 1925–6 (SW17 9TH); **St Mary,**

St Hilda, Crofton Park: figurative leading

Sanderstead, 1924–7 (CR2 0NY), whose altar rails have G&N's characteristic black chequer inlay (the west end of the church is by Dykes Bower); and **St Patrick, Wallington**, 1932 (SM6 0RU) with pretty woodwork and subtle brickwork. **St John the Divine, Earlsfield**, 1915 (SW18 4UJ) is a surprise – an absolutely no-frills mission church.

NORTHWOOD

Mount Vernon Hospital Chapel | 1902–4
Frederick Wheeler
HA6 2RN | Closed

This tiny Grade II* listed hospital chapel stands empty and with a deeply uncertain future. Its aesthetic merits are considerable, as an example of a 'Voyseyan' church building (Voysey never built a church). Stylistically, it prefigures some aspects of Art Nouveau – it would not look out of place in a Vienna suburb, or Darmstadt.

Mount Vernon was the country branch of the North London Consumption Hospital. The chapel was the last building to be constructed, to the design of the hospital's architect, Frederick Wheeler (1853–1931). His only other church design is the incomplete, humble, rather workaday St James the Great, Littlehampton. This chapel was clearly his one opportunity for unwonted creativity. It seems to have been funded independently of the hospital, and is full of unnecessarily pretty and costly detail, such as the green-blue enamel medallions on the door hinges.

The chapel was never consecrated. It was used regularly until the 1960s, by which time TB treatments meant there were fewer long-term in-patients. It was used for one marriage. It fell into disuse, and was gradually overgrown with bushes and brambles. The roof leaked, and there was no heating. In 1988 it became a library. The congregation seating was removed, and library shelves inserted all around the walls (concealing a bright apple-green tiled dado, which appears to survive behind them). Then the Gray Cancer Research Laboratory, whose headquarters were in a 1970s building next door (now empty), converted it into a lecture theatre. In 2009 the Gray Laboratory left, and the chapel became a store.

What remains is the chancel screen, the rood – removed from (or not yet present on) the screen in 1905 – in the vestry; and two of the six elaborate electroliers (the others stolen). Fowler's slightly decadent, European dream remains.

Mount Vernon Hospital Chapel, Northwood: the east end

Other Churches

Central London

Chapel of Baptist Church House, Southampton Row | Arthur Keen | 1901–3 | WC1B 4AA
Now L'Oscar Hotel: the chapel, with Laurence Turner plasterwork, survives as a dining room.

St Cyprian, Clarence Gate | Ninian Comper | 1903–48 | NW1 6AX
The Arts & Crafts zeitgeist very occasionally brushed Comper – here in his intense rood and woodwork.

Cadogan Hall, Sloane Terr. (was 1st Church of Christ Scientist) | R.F. Chisholm | 1908 | SW1X 9DQ
More Indian than English, and now so modernised, it has little spiritual feeling: some alluring details, though.

Holy Trinity, Kingsway | Belcher and Joass | 1909–11 | WC2B 6BA
Only the façade remains of this, one of only two churches by John Belcher (AWG 1884).

Annunciation, Bryanston Street, Marble Arch | Walter Tapper | 1912–14 | W1H 7AH
Breath-taking magnificence – Tapper sets off in a Comper direction.

North

St Augustine, Armoury Rd, Highgate | J.D. Sedding, Henry Wilson | 1884–1916 | N6 5QG
Imposing, with stern Henry Wilson façade. Interior disparate, un-encompassable, with some intriguing detail.

Rosslyn Hill Unitarian Church, Hampstead | Thomas Worthington (extension) | 1885 | NW3 1NG
Font and stalls by Ronald P Jones of Liverpool, from Essex Street Church; glass by Henry Holiday, and Morris.

Most Holy Redeemer, Clerkenwell | J.D. Sedding, Henry Wilson | 1887–8, 1892–95 | EC1R 4QE
Sedding in his classical manner, with Wilson's exotic Italianate tower street façade.

Good Shepherd Georgian Orthodox Cathedral, Hackney | Joseph Morris | 1892–5 | N16 6SS
Walter Crane glass. Built as The Ark of the Covenant church of the Agapemonites.

St Luke, Kidderpore Ave., Hampstead | Basil Champneys | 1897–9 | NW3 7SU
Though AWG 1884, Champneys never quite fitted, and resigned 1896. Too conservative? Too ambitious?

Trinity Congregational Chapel, Lauriston Road, Hackney | Morley Horder | 1901 | E9 7LH
'Edwardian Freestyle Tudor'; 'modernist Arts & Crafts elements'; 'gothic battlemented brickwork' (HE)!

St John the Evangelist, Palmers Green | J. Oldrid Scott | 1903–9 | N13 4DA
The interior does not fulfil the fantastical promise of the chequerwork and turreted exterior.

St Stephen, Park Ave., Bush Hill Park, Enfield | J.S. Alder | 1906–7, 1915 | EN 1 2EU
Alder – elsewhere conventional and safe – here tiptoes towards something more sublime.

Baptist Church, Sneyd Rd, Cricklewood | Arthur Keen | 1907–8 | NW2 6AN | **H**
Keen's only new built church – now flats.

St Jude on the Hill, Hampstead | Edwin Landseer Lutyens | 1909–35 | NW11 7AH
Big and declamatory, but the details are lyrical – aisles and ceiling lushly painted by Walter Starmer; metalwork.

St Peter-Le-Poer, Friern Barnet | W.D. Caröe | 1909–10 | N10 1AQ
Muscular glories, truncated: Gormenghast tower. Touching detail in mosaics and woodwork

St Barnabas, Shacklewell, Dalston, Hackney | Charles Reilly | 1909–11 | E8 2EA
Reilly set Liverpool University's Architecture faculty on a fiercely Modernist path. This shell, his monument.

Hampstead Garden Suburb Free Church | Edwin Landseer Lutyens | 1911 | NW11 7AA
Like its twin next door, but without the embellishments.

Paget Memorial Hall (Christian Centre), Islington | A. Beresford Pite | 1911 | N1 0DH
Heady amalgam of High Victorian excess and Edwardian swagger: barley-twist columns and Voysey hearts.

St John's URC (was Presbyterian), Northwood | Fred Rowntree | 1914 | HA6 1DN
Away from Quaker restraint, Rowntree waxes grandiose. Glass; brickwork.

Unitarian Church, Golders Green | Reginald Farrow | 1925 | NW11 8BS
Intimate treasure house: apsidal painting by Ivon Hitchens; Margaret Warren; pulpit by Charles Spooner.

St Anselm, Belmont, Harrow | N. Cachemaille-Day | 1938–41 | HA7 2HP
Constructed using many elements of St Anselm, Davies Street, Mayfair (Balfour & Turner, 1891–6).

East

Woodgrange Baptist Church, Forest Gate | J.W. Chapman | 1881, 1901 | E7 8AA
Artisan woodwork, but, better yet, an Essex gallery of pargeted plaster panels of a mystery plant – goosegrass?

New Testament Assembly Church, Leyton | Morley Horder | 1899 | E11 4HS
Originally 'Fetter Lane Chapel'. Harsh harled exterior: galleried interior recalls its 1660 predecessor.

St John the Evangelist, Seven Kings | J.E.K. and J.P. Cutts | 1902–3, 1906 | IG2 7BB
Glass by Louis Davis; woodwork.

Woodford Green UFC, High Elms | Harrison Townsend | 1903 | IG8 0UP
Lugubriously pedestrian – much simplified from the original vision of the architect of the Whitechapel Gallery.

St Gabriel, Aldersbrook, Wanstead | Charles Spooner | 1914 | E12 5HH
Embroidery-like brickwork. Clear windows flashed with bold splinters of colour. Interior reordered.

St Luke, Great Ilford | E.T. Dunn | 1914–15 | IG1 2HN
Heavily re-ordered; woodwork; regimental badge bosses; one window by W. Reynolds-Stephens.

St Andrew, Ilford | Herbert Baker | 1923–4 | IG1 3PE
One of only two Baker churches in England. Woodwork by Laurence Turner. Karl Parsons glass.

St Paul, East Ham | Charles Spooner | 1933 | E6 2EU
Spooner's last church moves towards Modernism: interior heavily reordered.

South

St Paul, Wimbledon Park | Micklethwaite and Somers Clarke | 1888–9 | SW19 6EW
Victorian excess dwindles elegantly. Pews by Henley Cornford, 1930s, carved by Wimbledon School of Art.

All Saints, South Wimbledon | Micklethwaite and Somers Clarke | 1891–2 | SW19 1BU
Powerful Victorian screen 1894; reredos, chancel ceiling. Arts & Crafts prayer desks by anon. 1902, 1909.

St Swithun, Hither Green | Ernest Newton | 1892–1902 | SE13 6QE
Few of Newton's churches survive. Lethaby may have designed the reredos.

Christ Church, Brixton | Beresford Pite | 1899–1902 | SW9 6BE
Foundation stone designed by Edward Johnston, cut by Eric Gill. Inside all is hectic pillars and bombast.

Methodist Central Hall, Bermondsey | Charles Bell | 1900 | SE1 3UJ
How the Methodists turned away from church-like-ness. Now largely offices, 1968.

United Reform Church, Purley | Hampden Pratt | 1903–4 | CR8 2LN
Somewhat altered, but with energetic woodwork and a wealth of colourful 'Edwardian pub' glass.

St Andrew the Apostle, Catford, East Lewisham | P.A. Robson | 1904 | SE6 1XD
Gargoyles; choir stalls; altar front carving; prayer desks; glass – like a Nonconformist chapel with attitude.

Blackheath and Charlton Baptist Church, Shooters Hill | Dottridge & Walford | 1905 | SE3 8UL
Wonderful archive of the entire building process – drawings, minutes, accounts.

St Barnabas, Southfields, Wandsworth | C. Ford Whitcombe | 1906–8 | SW18 5EP
Side chapel with painted riddell posts; main altar with angels; organ loft stair; quirky glass.

St Michael & All Angels, South Beddington | W.D. Caröe | 1906–7, 1928 | SM6 9RP
Bit of a Caröe jumble. Processional cross; reredos; organ screen.

Chislehurst Cemetery Chapel | Curtis Green | 1908–10 | BR7 6HF

Penge Congregational Church, Penge, Bromley | Morley Horder | 1912 | SE20 7QG
Curiously reminiscent of Leonard Stokes. Morris glass.

All Saints, Campbell Rd, Twickenham | J.S. Alder | 1913–14 | TW2 5BY
Rather stern, creamy-yellow interior, relieved by a beautiful rood and two reredoses.

St John the Divine, High Path, Merton | C.H. Gage | 1914 | SW19 2JY
Naturalistic animals on choir stalls – camel, bulldog, lion, chimp, goat, ram. And in porch too.

St John the Baptist, Belmont, Sutton | Newberry & Fowler | 1914 (+1970) | SM2 6DY

St Saviour, Herne Hill Road, Ruskin Park | Beresford Pite | 1915 | SE5 9AT
Built as the church hall. Mosaic pattern porch and entrance lobby.

West

St Matthew, Yiewsley | Nicholson and Corlette | 1898 | UB7 7QH
New nave added alongside existing small Gilbert Scott church. Ceiling reportedly painted by a narrow-boat man.

Christ Church, Turnham Green | (Scott and Moffatt, 1841–3) *c.*1906 | W4 5DT
Stalls, screen, chancel panelling, pulpit carved by five ladies and one man who attended lessons at local Art School.

All Saints, The Avenue, Hampton | Greenaway & Newberry | 1907–9 | TW12 3RS
Included for its two fine wooden altars with inlay, including mother-of-pearl, almost certainly designed by G&N.

St Michael, Elmwood Road, Chiswick | W.D. Caröe | 1908–9 | W4 3DZ
Brick and tilework; painted candle stands and side chapel ceiling; panelling.

Our Lady of Sorrows (RC), Isleworth | E. Doran Webb | 1910 | TW7 6DL
Classicism with an Arts & Crafts accent.

St Francis of Assisi, Great West Road, Osterley, Isleworth | Ernest Shearman | 1933–5 | TW7 5PD
Shearman's most Arts & Crafts church: roof beams; gallery front; window leading; tracery; aumbry; brickwork.

Holy Cross, Greenford | Albert Richardson | 1939–41 | UB6 9NJ
Massive, muscular barn church – reminiscent of Curtis Green's Quaker Hall at Croydon.

10

THE HOME COUNTIES

Bedfordshire, Berkshire, Buckinghamshire, Hertfordshire, Huntingdonshire

Hurrying along its motorways and characterless ring roads, one is not aware of the narrow lanes and slumbering hamlets that embroider the landscape north and west of London. In some parts, the spirit of Bunyan's contrarian Nonconformity holds sway – Bedfordshire remains remarkably impervious to Anglican orthodoxies. Brick-bound Reading has gone from bustlingly secular to energetically multi-cultural. But the early New Towns – Welwyn and Letchworth – on the cusp between nostalgic ruralism and rational planning, offer churches, chapels and meeting houses that marry idyllic vernacular with something more brusquely Modernist. It has to be admitted that Arts & Crafts taste and ideas did not resonate here among church-builders – Buckinghamshire and Huntingdonshire, even mighty Peterborough, offer no examples worth a detour.

Yet, in some sequestered villages, glimpses of an older, gentler England linger, defying the encroaching metropolitan tedium and ecclesiastical conservatism. All in all, the pickings may be thin, yet nonetheless here are to be found three of the most potent examples in Britain of not-Victorian church interiors: personal, intense, hands-on, self-absorbed, meant.

St Michael and All Angels, Woolmer Green

WOOLMER GREEN, Hertfordshire

St Michael and All Angels | 1898–1900
Robert Weir Schultz
SG3 6LT | Open

St Michael was built to no fanfares: simply a chapel of ease needed for a rural, under-privileged community. It was built through the energies of a conscientious, but not notably artistic priest; and it is the only surviving complete English church by Robert Weir Schultz (1860–1951, AWG 1891), companion of Sidney Barnsley on research travels to Greece 1888–9, and co-author with Ernest Gimson of the exotic St Andrew's Chapel, Westminster Cathedral (p.106).

Unlike either Barnsley's Lower Kingswood (p.86) or St Andrew's Chapel, Woolmer Green shows little influence of the Byzantine. It bears a very slight family likeness to a later Weir Schultz church – the Anglican Cathedral at Khartoum (which still stands). The church at Woolmer Green is essentially 'Herts' – modest, simple, in its own tree-scattered churchyard, as if it had been there for centuries. It was initiated just at the moment when demand for seats in church was going into decline, and was compromised by the concomitant dwindling of interest among those with funds. Its tower was never built, and the furnishings are far more spare than envisaged at the start. Its understated reticence reflects not so much artistic restraint, as a decline in benefactors.

St Michael and All Angels, Woolmer Green: pulpit

The driving force was Arthur Cayley Headlam (1862–1947), Rector of Welwyn from 1896. He was Fellow of All Souls 1885; and afterwards – he left the parish in 1903 – Professor of Dogmatic Theology, and Principal of King's College, London; from 1918, Regius Professor of Divinity at Oxford and finally Bishop of Gloucester 1923–45.

Woolmer Green was a cause he quickly championed. In his Easter 1897 parish letter he wrote, 'The needs of Woolmer Green are really greater than those probably of any other part of the Parish … a district church is clearly required …' The next year he pressed the case again: the population was growing; the schoolroom – the school had 100 pupils – then used for services, was not large enough and, besides, was 'hardly conducive to reverence'. And – worse – if the people of Woolmer Green came to services at Welwyn, there would be no space for them.

Headlam estimated the likely cost between £1000 and £2000. By mid-1898, five subscribers had given £500: £100 from Headlam himself, the rest from local landowners and the two spinster daughters of the previous incumbent, Charles Lee

Wingfield. Lord Lytton, owner of nearby Knebworth, gave the land.

The foundation stone was laid on 16 September 1899, by Lady Lytton. The church was consecrated on 3 November 1900. The children of the school raised £36-4-3d. towards the font. 1901 accounts show a 'special donation' of £107 for the chancel screen; another, £150, for the pavement in the sanctuary; another, £10, the lectern. It was all very straightforward, and went smoothly and satisfactorily.

In 1907 there remained numerous wants: 'Tower, bells, organ, choir stalls, altar rails' and wainscoting for the chancel. The altar rails, to designs by Weir Schultz, came in 1908. The choir stalls were installed the same year. The organ was not installed until 1936. There is now wainscoting in the chancel, but to whose design is unclear – it is not, alas, marble and oak, as originally proposed. There are few dedicatory or commemorative plaques, apart from, on the chancel screen, a memorial to EPH and MDW, the two spinster sisters – the elder, Evelyn, having by now married Headlam.

A newspaper report of the laying of the foundation stone survives, seemingly written by Headlam and Weir Schultz in concert – a summary of all that was important to Arts & Crafts architects, in a religious context: 'The design includes a tower with a small Hertfordshire spire in accordance with local traditions ... The material is throughout the best local brick ... the object of the designer has been to build a simple village church ... strong [with] no unmeaning ornament but a certain amount of rich chasteness in the more important parts.' Two contributors were singled out in a 1901 List of Subscriptions 'for assistance in carting and preparing the ground.' Their sleeves-rolled-up, hands-on approach was valued. Those with a taste for Burges or Butterfield find it bare.

Weir Schultz's Byzantine researches for Lower Kingswood had given him a sure-footedness about sources. His friendships and AWG connections mattered. He knew Lethaby and Barnsley from Norman Shaw's office, and through them, Ernest Barnsley and Ernest Gimson. At Ernest George & Peto, 1886, he met Herbert Baker, Guy Dawber and Lutyens. He also knew another Shaw alumnus, E.S. Prior, whose obituary he wrote in 1932.

The roll-call of craftsmen at Woolmer Green is impeccably AWG: the screen and font carved by Laurence Turner; the choir desks made by Ernest Gimson; the altar rails made to a design by RWS by 'a country smith'. The trowel used by Lady Lytton in laying the foundation stone was made by Henry Wilson, 'a unique work of art. The handle is of beaten silver, and is ornamented with five precious stones.' (Where is it now?) Over the porch, 1913, St Michael slays his dragon – the carving by H.W. Palliser.

St Michael and All Angels, Woolmer Green: chancel screen detail

INKPEN, Berks

St Michael and All Angels | 1896–7
Rebuilt by C.C. Rolfe
RG17 9DS | By arrangement

There is little to suggest, from the outside, that St Michael is anything other than a restrained late Victorian rebuild of a modest medieval church: and externally, so it is. But to understand what is significant outside, one must go inside.

Whether through the local connections of its restoration architect, Clapton Crabbe Rolfe (1845–1907), or the inspiration of its energetic priest and his family, the church contains some beautiful and perplexing devotional art.

Inkpen was effectively a hereditary living. John Butler (*c.*1815–95) was Rector of Inkpen for 57 years. At his death he left his wife all his worldly goods, including the patronage of the living! His reputation was as a huntsman rather than cleric: he left the church in very poor repair. He was succeeded by his son, Henry Dobree Butler (*c.*1861–1933), who at once proposed a scheme of complete restoration. The Butler family provided much of the initial funding: Henry's sister Caroline, his widowed mother, a sister-in-law and others. Should there be a *new* church? Caroline settled the matter by saying she would withdraw her money unless the new church idea was dropped. By the consecration, the Butlers had given £980 of the total cost of £2077-3-7d.

John Butler had four sisters, none of whom married – Harriet, Lucy, Caroline Charlotte and Ada. They kept house for their brother in the Rectory, apart from Harriet, who was attached to St Mary's Convent, Wantage, from which she emerged from time to time to visit her family.

Rolfe was Oxford Diocesan Surveyor, and deeply sympathetic to Butler's High Church views: Andrew Saint comments, 'Throughout his career [he] thought of himself as a Christian architect whose duty it was to carry out in stone and mortar the principles of reformed Catholicism.'

Box pews had survived – these were swept away. Rolfe added a new north aisle, replacing the crumbling old wall and inserting an arcade. On the south side he added a new porch, and created a window with an unusual flying rere-arch. He rebuilt the east wall with new lancets; he made a new oak roof with angels, carved by Harry Hems, who also carved the rood screen. And Rolfe designed an elaborate reredos and set out the new seating. One element gives the church its most atmo-

St Michael and All Angels, Inkpen:
Uriel spandrel painting by Ethel King Martyn

spheric Arts & Crafts appeal: a set of wall paintings by Ethel King Martyn (1873–1946). During the rebuilding work in 1896, a number of traces of 15th-century wall painting were found. It was decided they were too decayed to be restored. Rolfe 'made provision for future wall decoration of the same type, on either side of the chancel, along the south wall and in the spandrils [sic] of the arches.'

It is reported that Martyn painted the first wall paintings in the chancel in 1910. Then, in 1916 and 1921, further images in the spandrels. The painting of Uriel is in memory of Lucy Butler (d.1921), Henry's sister. The painting of the Archangel Raphael is dedicated to Annie Margaret Butler (d.1916), the niece of a Butler aunt. A splash of local character comes from the landscape set on the road to nearby Coombe, with a then-familiar beech tree in the background.

The north aisle now terminates in a chapel, whose reredos is embellished with a glazed terracotta memorial plaque, its creator unknown. The carving on the wooden reredos itself – more like a bedhead than a reredos – is rugged and raw: either the work of a local carver (amateur?) or recycled from something earlier, perhaps 17th century. On the south wall of the nave is a second war memorial, 1921, by Ellen Mary Rope (1855–1934) (see p.209), in green marble and bronze. The spirit of craftsmanship lives on: in 1969 the font cover (designed by G.F. Bodley, 1909) was removed, and replaced in 1972 by one easier to lift off. The base was made by Alec McCurdy of Cold Ash, 13 miles east of Inkpen; and the top was adorned by Ron Lane from Dibden Purlieu, Hampshire, 50 miles south, with carvings of local water creatures – vole, dipper, newt, kingfisher and teal. The lychgate, 1934, is by F.C. Eden.

WEST WOODHAY, Berks

St Laurence | 1882, 1894
A. Blomfield; woodwork by Jessie Cole from 1893
RG20 0BL | Usually open

West Woodhay (*pron.* 'Woody') parish church was built 1882–3 to the design of Arthur Blomfield FRIBA (1829–99): a picturesque combination of knapped flint and Bath stone dressings.

It is not Blomfield's everyday exterior that attracts, but its contents: the interior is largely the work of an under-regarded artist, Jessie Cole, and her sister Edith, the daughters of the big house. In 1880 their father, William Henry Cole (d.1889), bought the West Woodhay estate. He had married Jane, daughter of Alfred Brooks, who had acquired the wine and spirits business reportedly founded by Giacomo Justerini of Bologna: hence Justerini & Brooks. The Coles had five children. The second son became Governor of the Bank of England. (Blomfield became Architect to the

St Laurence, West Woodhay: the parish chest by Jessie Cole

Bank in 1887.) Then came the Coles' three daughters: Jessie (1853–1936), Annie (1856–1938) and Edith (1859–1940). Only Annie married. As upper-middle-class women, they did not – could not – seek fame, nor was it accorded to them. The woodwork at West Woodhay was both designed and made by Jessie Cole: the bench ends in particular combine scholarship and originality, and were made with vigour and commitment. Here is honest handiwork; selflessness; a commitment to things personal rather than manufactured; a preference for the simple over the complex; an interest in beauty and the natural world; a harking-back to the past.

Mary Howard McClintock, Cole's great-niece, records that Jessie Cole (her aunt), 'was architect for the estate and built cottages and the schools, the laundry and men's club, putting into these simple buildings a dignity of good planning, proportions and materials far better than usual ....' Jessie was mathematical and creative. And she had pursued, on her own initiative, the same grounding as male architects: she 'would wander from Brussels to Lucerne and from Lucerne to Florence and Assisi, noting the architectural details with the mind of a professional ....'

Soon after acquiring West Woodhay, William Cole decided he did not wish to have the parish church hard by his house. His new church was not, however, a private chapel: the family sat in the front three benches on the south side, with their own entrance door in the south wall.

The aisle ends of the congregational benches are all carved; as are the panels in front of the two front benches, and at the rear of the bench immediately to the east of the south door – all the work of Jessie Cole. She also 'carved the pulpit, signing her name deep in the wood at the back where no one could see': a typically Arts & Crafts piece of self-effacement – or female modesty? She also made the parish chest, 1906. More conventionally Edith Cole made all the altar frontals. The sisters also provided much of the glass – though they did not design any of it, with perhaps one exception. The windows were designed by Henry Holiday when he was working for Powells, in 1890. The east window is by Morris & Co. to a Burne-Jones design.

Jessie Cole wrote this personal manifesto: 'There is nothing to compare with creating a thing, if you love what you are doing – you can't make anything beautiful unless you *are* in love with it, of course ... I suppose an artist has the happiest life of anyone, though a craftsman comes pretty near him.'

WATFORD, Herts

Holy Rood (RC) | 1889–1900
John Francis Bentley
WD18 0PJ | Usually open

Is Holy Rood Arts & Crafts? It seems rather refined Gothic Revival, but with some Arts & Crafts sensibility. However, the craftsmanship is never quite foregrounded. We know the names of the makers, but they are not AWG. However, Bentley (1839–1902, AWG 1889) was. And he went on to design Westminster Cathedral (p.106).

The church opened for worship in September 1890: sanctuary, nave, transepts and south aisle were complete. Work then began on the tower, baptistry, side chapel and north aisle: the whole was finished by 1900. All the church furnishings are from Bentley designs

CHORLEYWOOD, Herts

Free Church | 1905
Herbert G. Ibberson
WD3 5AP | By arrangement

The Herts./Bucks. border has a tradition of radicalism – the Chartists built the Heronsgate Estate here for Dissenting families migrating

'unequalled elsewhere in his work' according to the Historic England listing: candlesticks and cross, pulpit, 1893, canopied shrines with alabaster statues; altar and tabernacle 1899; bronze lighting pendants; painted ceiling; rood beam; stained glass. The Stations of the Cross are by N.H.J. Westlake, on copper.

Bentley wrote, 'The church when completed will fairly represent an old English church of the Hertfordshire district prior to the Reformation; though it is in no way a copy of any particular church.' So, not copying, but harking back – very Arts & Crafts.

Holy Rood, Watford: rood group
Chorleywood: west window

from the North. The coming of the railway in 1889 encouraged more building – the developer, James Beckley, was a Baptist: he provided the site and most of the funds for a new meeting house. At the time, the leading architect in the area was C.F.A. Voysey, who had built himself a house here – The Orchard – in 1899. But it was not Voysey who was asked, but the less celebrated Herbert Ibberson (1866-1935). His Arts & Crafts background was solid: he had been trained by John Belcher, and had worked under J.D. Sedding. More significantly, he was cousin to the wife of the other key figure in the church initiative, Revd W. C. Bryan, minister at Rickmansworth Baptist Church.

His first scheme was an extravagant blend of Italian Renaissance and Gothic ideas – and huge. It did not proceed. What was built – 'Chorleywood Free Church' since 1948 – was more modest. The exterior has repoussé lead panels in the cupola/turret; a decorative band of vine leaves above the main door with lettering that could be called 'Art Nouveau'; a bas-relief in the architrave; a heart-shaped door-handle back plate.

Inside, something more European and exotic – the elements individually intriguing, and the whole compellingly disjointed. A repoussé copper cross hangs over the east end – Secessionist in tone. There are small square copper panels set in velvet round the pulpit top – the same motif appears in wood over the doors. The walls have plain velvet and Liberty fabric panels at the east end, and sections of green and blue tiles elsewhere. There is blue and green in the windows too – the round west window restrained to the point of Mondrian. In the roof beams, stylised flat birds and foliage – one might almost believe based on a Voysey wallpaper design.

ALBURY, Herts

St Mary | 1909
William Parker (restoration)
RG20 0BL | Usually open

In 1909 medieval St Mary's had its chancel substantially refurbished by a London architect, William J. Parker. The outstanding feature is the oak panelling in the sanctuary, with a lively panel of a ploughman with his oxen team, and a vigorous carved frieze quoting the *Benedicite*. There is carving of a slightly different flavour in the choir stalls, with fainting angels. The altar front has a crown-of-thorns central blazon, with instruments of the Passion in mother-of-pearl. There is more mother-of-pearl on the reredos. The lectern has a rather Burne-Jonesian angel. It is thought Parker was responsible for restoring the medieval screen, to which a new upper section has been added. The identity of the carvers here is not known. There is a three-light east window of the resurrected Christ, 1909, by Gerald Moira (1867–1959, AWG 1898).

St Mary, Albury: *Benedicite* panel

LETCHWORTH, Herts

Howgills Friends Meeting House | 1907
Robert Bennett and Wilson Bidwell
SG6 3JJ | By arrangement

An utterly respectable white-harled residence in a gracious, decent orchard – a visual demonstration of humane, confident Quaker ideas, its simplicity surprisingly urbane. The house was built at the expense of Juliet Reckitt, niece of the Hull starch and laundry blue magnate. It is loosely based on Brigflatts Meeting House (1675) in Yorkshire, celebrated in Basil Bunting's eponymous poem (1975) – but, while the garden elevation and porch are similar, Howgills has grander fenestration on this face, and its L-shaped plan accommodates a library, classroom and caretaker's flat, presenting an imposing twin-gabled front to the street. Inside, the double-height, galleried meeting space is very much in Brigflatts' image, though. The detailing self-consciously copies older Yorkshire models – door furniture, window latches, shutters, mullions. There are carved panels with improving quotations – George Herbert for one – reputedly by Eric Gill. Bennett and Bidwell designed many Letchworth houses in the Parker & Unwin spirit, and the Broadway Cinema, 1935–6.

Howgills Friends Meeting House, Letchworth: stairs to the gallery

SHEFFORD WOODLANDS, Berkshire

St Stephen | 1910–11
A.C. Burmester
RG17 7AS | Key nearby

A Wesleyan chapel of 1837 was magicked into an Anglican church, 1910–11, by Captain A.C. Burmester. He also carved most of the internal woodwork, latterly as a memorial to villagers who died in the Great War, 'in an accomplished Arts and Crafts manner' according to Geoffrey Tyack in the 2010 *Pevsner*.

Burmester came to the area through marriage: his wife inherited the enormous Lovelock Estate, which included the village, in 1905. The county archaeological society visited the church on 2 August 1935: 'a plain unpretending little building having been until a year or two ago a Wesleyan Chapel … The interior … has been completely fitted up with really beautiful amateur oak carving, very largely, if not entirely, the actual handiwork of Capt. Burmester himself ….'

The carving was actually started before the War – panelling in the chancel, dado in the nave, a Tree of Life at the west end. The benches were, it must be assumed, plain until 1914. Grim events caught up with intentions. In the church are memorial plaques to Burmester and his wife: she played an important part in the work, designing for his wood-carving. This conjugal creative partnership adds to the Arts & Crafts aura. Burmester never took holy orders, but his dedication was surely sincere: a committed artistic gentleman craftsman.

St Stephen, Shefford Woodlands:
west end with font and congregation benches

Other Churches

Bedfordshire

St Andrew's Mission Church, Arlesey | A.H. Ryan Tenison | 1899–01 | SG15 6RA | **H**
Once had a rather lovely 'quaint' interior. Now St Andrew's House (offices).

Berkshire

Albert Memorial Chapel, Windsor | Gilbert Scott | SL4 1NJ
Included for Alfred Gilbert's 1892 onyx, marble, aluminium, ivory memorial to Prince Albert Victor. Private.

St Mary the Virgin, Greenham | Henry Woodyer | 1875–6 | RG19 8RZ
Decorations by J.A. Pippet of Hardmans, 1888–91.

St Mary, Winkfield | Henry Woodyer (refashioning) | 1888 | SL5 9DP
Chancel tiles painted by vicar's wife, Mrs Daubeny 1890; screen by J. Oldrid Scott; font by J.F. Bentley.

Chapel of St Mary's School, Wantage | Charles Ponting | 1898–9 | OX12 8DJ
Now a dentist's surgery, but some good furnishings survive – pulpit, wall lamps, glass. Private.

St Mark, Battle, Reading | Montague Wheeler | 1904–5 | RG30 2TA
Now Greek Orthodox. Glass by Joseph Nuttgens and Reginald Hallward (as well as Kempe).

St James, Ruscombe, Twyford | medieval | RG10 9UD
Window embrasures and organ loft painted by Revd Sidney Macartney, vicar 1907–13. He also carved 1912 tower door.

Hertfordshire

St Michael, Waterford | Henry Woodyer | 1871–2 | SG14 2PS
Arts & Crafts glass compendium: Morris, Madox Brown; Strachan, Image, Karl Parsons. Plus Powells mosaics.

St Peter, Ayot St Peter | John Pollard Seddon | 1874–5 | AL6 9BG
A less inventive pre-cursor to Hoarwithy – with startlingly energetic mosaics (Jesse Rust) and painted apse ceiling.

All Saints, Hertford | Austin & Paley | 1895–1905 | SG13 8AY
Away from their native Lancashire, and with more money to spend here, they became very nearly exuberant.

All Saints Pastoral Centre, London Colney | Leonard Stokes | 1899–1901 | AL2 1AF
On the façade, a frieze by Henry Wilson; the chapel (1927 onwards) is by Comper and his son. For redevelopment.

St Martin, Preston, Hitchin | Thomas Carter | 1900 | SG4 7TP
Voysey-ish pebbledash with battered buttresses; simple interior; Whall window.

St Hugh of Lincoln (RC), Letchworth | Charles Spooner | 1907 | SG6 3TP
Dinky Byzantine scheme with lively brickwork; interior wholly stripped. Demoted to church hall.

St Bartholomew, Wigginton | medieval | 1904 | HP23 6DZ
Inlayed choir stalls, hymn board made by Revd H.J.E. Burrell and eight parishioners. Possibly also angel altar rails.

Breachwood Green Baptist Church, Kings Walden | George Baines | 1904 | SG4 8NX
An especially theatrical example of the Baines schtick, with good glass and heart-shaped motif on metalwork.

Congregational Church, Bushey | Morley Horder | 1904–5 | WD23 3DH
Now the Margaret Howard Theatre. Interior stripped.

St Martin, Knebworth | Edwin Landseer Lutyens, then Albert Richardson | 1914, 1963 | SG3 6EY
Something far grander was planned – a foretaste of Liverpool? Richardson completed it in 1963. Hard to love.

Letchworth Free Church | Barry Parker | 1923 | SG6 1NX
More municipal than ecclesiastical. A vivid statement of end of Artsy-Craftsy – we had all come to our senses …

Holy Cross & St Alban, Brickendon | W.F. Haslip | 1931–2 | SG13 8NU
… yet, for some, the nostalgic idyll drowsed on. Prettily barn-like outside and reminiscently cosy inside. Or twee?

II

THE MARCHES

Gloucestershire, Herefordshire, Shropshire

Gloucestershire attracted Arts & Crafts men who wanted to escape London, but not be too far away. Like all artists, they were looking for somewhere cheap – and Gloucestershire, still largely dependent on wool, was not prosperous. William Morris had praised the beauty of Arlington Row at Bibury (still a magnet for coach tours), and had his own Cotswold foothold at Kelmscott Manor, just east of Lechlade, on the infant Thames (which springs at Kemble, near Cirencester).

Ernest Gimson and Sidney Barnsley, later joined by Sidney's brother Ernest, travelled to Cirencester by train (it had a station then) to find a cheap and peaceful base where they could make simple, honest furniture – the very opposite of Victorian over-elaboration. They settled at Pinbury Park, tucked into a west-facing fold of the Cotswolds, and later moved their workshops to Daneway, a mile or so south, and took houses at Sapperton, at the head of the Golden Valley. They made tables and chairs, cabinets and cupboards; and – especially Gimson – church furnishings. Their influence drew in local men, like Alfred Bucknell, the Waterlane blacksmith, the Cambridge-educated Norman Jewson and the Dutch cabinet-maker Peter Waals. Even though Gimson and the Barnsleys trained as architects, only Sidney built churches, and only one of those is in the county. (The other is in Surrey, p.86). Gimson was in charge of the building of Rodmarton Manor, the largest new-build Arts & Crafts house in the Cotswolds (the other contender, Owlpen, is a re-imagined Elizabethan manor without its own chapel). Rodmarton's chapel was completed by Gimson's son-in-law Jewson, who carried on the Rodmarton project after Gimson's death. Gimson and the Barnsleys are buried in Sapperton churchyard, as is Emery Walker, who taught William Morris printing.

In 1902 C.R. Ashbee led his young craftsmen from Essex House in London's East End, where he had made a commercial and social success of his Guild of Handicraft, to Chipping Campden, then a moribund market town with many unoccupied houses.

Christopher Whall had his greatest opportunity here, with a complete scheme of glass for the Lady Chapel at Gloucester Cathedral. The guiding hand was an artistic Dean, whose connections with the Arts & Crafts – so avant-garde for church work, and at that moment, edgily fashionable – were decisive. It was diligently repaired, conserved and cleaned through a Lottery-funded scheme in 2017. There are around twenty Arts & Crafts objects in the Cathedral besides – plate, glass, memorials, a clock.

Rodborough Tabernacle Chapel: the Tri-sigma window – Sincerity, Self-surrender and Service

BROCKHAMPTON, Herefordshire

All Saints | 1901–2
W.R. Lethaby
HR1 4SD | Usually open

All Saints stands, picturesquely, on a rise, five miles from Ross-on-Wye: Peter Blundell-Jones called it 'the image of rural tranquillity, oddly timeless, as though it had always been there.'

For some, it is the epitome of an Arts & Crafts church – so unusual and striking that in 2009 Japanese entrepreneurs used it as the model for a wedding chapel constructed on the 21st floor of an Osaka hotel, at two-thirds size, and with large west doors for the happy couple to emerge from, which Lethaby unaccountably did not think to include. Pevsner was dazzled – he called Brockhampton Expressionist and acknowledged its originality.

It was built for an American heiress – Alice Madeline Jordan (1863–1932): her millionaire father founded the largest department store in Boston, Mass. In 1885 she married Arthur Wellesley Foster (1855–1929), the third son of the Lancashire mill-owning dynasty. When they met – a shipboard romance – he was in holy orders at a church near the new-built Foster seat, Hornby Castle. He had the Lancashire architects Paley & Austin build him a new church for his parish, Tatham Fell.

When it came to deciding where they would live, as Madeline's great-grandson tells it, 'she looked through Debrett's, and chose Herefordshire because there were no duchesses there for her to compete with. She told her parents to buy her Brockhampton.' The 1500-acre Brockhampton Estate included Upper Court, an 18th-century rectory, which was wholly rebuilt for them by Faulkner Armitage of Altrincham, as a full-blown neo-Tudor country house, and renamed Brockhampton Court. Once in Herefordshire, the Fosters lived a leisured, moneyed Edwardian countryhouse life: Arthur was Sheriff of Herefordshire in 1898, and Master of the South Herefordshire Hounds.

Brockhampton's medieval parish church stood hard by the Rectory – tiresomely near, now it was Brockhampton Court. Foster family tradition suggests the church was too small for the combined congregation of villagers and Foster servants. Abandoned, it mouldered as a picturesque ruin for 100 years, until it was turned into a house in 2004.

In 1901 Madeline had her new church, All Saints, built outside the grounds of the Court, a memorial to her parents, at the end of its 400-metre-long drive, and on the other side of the lane, opposite imposing gates. (Brockhampton Court is now a retirement home – there are William De Morgan tiles in some of the rooms. Edward Elgar used to visit and, reportedly, played the organ in the house.) According to her great-grandson in 2011, 'I couldn't say whether she was a great churchgoer. I expect she had the Rolls[-Royce] drive up to the house to take her.' A memorial cross to the Fosters broods in the gloomy south-west corner of the churchyard.

Madeline chose as her architect William Richard Lethaby, from 1896 head of Central School, and its Principal from 1902; and in 1900 appointed first Professor of Design at the Royal College of Art. His reputation rests now far more on his ideas than on his buildings. His 1891 book *Architecture, Mysticism and Myth* became – *faute de mieux* – the unofficial manual of the Arts & Crafts. It caught something of their visionary spirit,

with its blend of eccentric scholarship, a romantic view of ancient history, and breathless flights of theory on symbolism and ritual. Lethaby only practised as an architect for 12 years, and in that time produced just six buildings, including two prodigious houses – Avon Tyrrell near Christchurch and Melsetter on Hoy in Orkney (p.302).

Lethaby originally intended to be on site himself, but was busy with educational work: he delegated the work to A. Randall Wells (1877–1942). Wells was a bit of a handful. Experimenting with mortars, he allowed an arch at Brockhampton to collapse, but didn't think to inform Lethaby or the Fosters. He decided to make the tower 10 feet taller than specified, with near catastrophic results. There were problems with foundations and the west end. Allegedly it drove Lethaby almost to breakdown. Unabashed, Randall Wells went on to build Edward the Confessor, Kempley (p.145). But he never obtained enough votes to be elected AWG.

Like any good Arts & Crafts man, Lethaby wanted to use local men and materials. Alas, they did not come up to scratch. In the end, the woodwork was executed by Lethaby's Central School colleague George Jack (AWG

All Saints, Brockhampton

1906). Lethaby himself designed the font: its entwined vines echo a Syrian tomb illustrated in *Architecture, Mysticism and Myth*. He also designed and carved the pulpit. Lethaby did not like having things drawn out first: he wrote, 'I do not think a builder could or should foresee the exact expressional results of his work: it should be a growth, not a creation.' The metalwork was produced locally – the door hinges are by the Brockhampton blacksmith. The hangings either side of the altar are by Morris & Co., from 1875 designs by Burne-Jones.

The windows are all by Christopher Whall, designer of the Lady Chapel windows at Gloucester Cathedral (p.152). The south transept window commemorates Madeline's brother, who died in 1916. Whall's grandson Bernard sat for the cherubs.

Lethaby's first intention was to have a plain-tiled roof on exposed purlins running from arch to arch. In the end he decided on a full concrete vault, without reinforcement, and shuttered on rough boards. The consequently muted light of the nave encourages the eye away towards the altar at the east end – but the effect is confused by the unexpected intrusion of light streaming down between, from the high windows of the lantern. The poured concrete vault is both a cheap solution and, combined with thatch, a good insulator. The stone arches without capitals are unadorned and rational in a stripped-back mode – yet they also remind of the wooden crucks in Herefordshire cottages

All Saints, Brockhampton: pulpit panel; font, both by W R Lethaby

and medieval barns, and in particular in the church at Upleadon, 12 miles away. (See also Bothenhampton (p.50) and Roker (p.261).)

The impact is both unsettling and sweetly homely – psychedelic chocolate box. Yes, Brockhampton can be seen as epitomising a 20th-century view of a perfect English country church, but it can also be interpreted as a ragbag of eclecticism, a pastiche of Little Olde England and faintly ridiculous.

Pevsner wrote, 'at first sight the tourist might accept the church as gothic' but 'For all I know, it is original.' Though welcoming and numinous, it seems to express a spirit which is not especially religious, let alone Christian. Is it simply too self-conscious and clever? Is it a religious experience, or just vague, fuzzy, hippy spirituality, amounting to no more than feeling groovy?

KEMPLEY, Gloucestershire

Edward the Confessor | 1902–4
A. Randall Wells
GL18 2BU | Often open

Edward the Confessor was built at the instigation and entire expense of an aristocratic aesthete, William Lygon, 7th Earl Beauchamp, of Madresfield, Worcestershire, and lord of the manor of Kempley. It was intended to replace the medieval church, St Mary's – now in the care of the Churches Conservation Trust, with 12th-century wall paintings – but then dilapidated and dangerous, and inconveniently far from the modern village and susceptible to flooding. In April 1902 the Earl told the vicar he would build a new church. It was to have a chapel for the reservation of the Blessed Sacrament, and a rood. He gave the field for the church so that – romantically, as the *Parish Journal* reported – it would 'nestle amongst the trees'.

Beauchamp exhibited as a sculptor at the Paris Exhibition of 1920: a golfer, raising his club to concentrate on his shot, and naked (!). At Kempley he at first acted as his own architect, but he soon ran into difficulties, and invited Randall Wells, then working at Brockhampton, to take over. Wells agreed, as long as he was to be allowed a free hand.

According to his friend Laurence Bradshaw, sculptor of Karl Marx's tomb, Wells 'was always well-dressed … never quite in fashion … very, very cultured … more interested in Homer than contemporary works. He read a bit of Tennyson and quite a bit of Morris.'

When he arrived, the foundations were already in: Beauchamp asked him to design the church to fit upon them as nearly as possible. The Earl had very particular liturgical requirements – there was to be no east window (presumably so as not to detract from the altar); most of the lighting should be from the west end; and the eaves should be kept low. Wells felt a single window would give 'an appearance of affectation' and suggested adding side windows. Beauchamp allowed just two tiny openings on the south side of the chancel.

The work was done without a contractor, as at Brockhampton. A local builder, Mr James, acted as foreman. Forest of Dean red and grey grit (sandstone) was used, from a quarry about seven miles away. The vicar noted in the Parish Journal that it had been decided the walls were to be 'rock-faced', i.e. rusticated outside, and inside worked smooth. The stone was ordered, and building started, when Wells decided the walls should not be rock-faced, but rubble.

James, the builder, danced with wrath: 'That Mr Wells' "rubble" will commend itself to the judgement of sane men, I cannot believe.' On the other hand, rubble was the usual Herefordshire building style. The local man wanted to be modern; the London architect was being self-consciously rural.

Wells prepared only a preliminary sketch, now seemingly lost. He added he 'did not propose to hamper the building with pre-arranged drawings of details.' The modest skills of the local masons meant Wells had to limit ornament to a minimum. There are exceptions. In the porch is a panel of the Virgin Mary, at the east end a Crucifixion, and over the entrance a large relief of Christ, the figure cut by Wells himself. Everything else, though designed by Wells, was carved by local men under the direction of Laurence Turner.

The most audacious architectural coup is the west end. Lawrence Weaver, writing in 1916, was amazed: 'Perhaps the most startling modern note … is given by the straight-lined tracery of the western light. The absence of curve and cusping makes a notable variant on older Gothic practice.' Wells explained it 'had to be as wide and as high as possible if the church was not to be gloomy; this suggested to me the idea of building the west end as a piece of stone trellis work, and then glazing it.' It is known locally as the 'jam tart' window.

Edward the Confessor, Kempley from the west

Wells even went so far as to try to design the natural surroundings: 'The churchyard was to have walls covered with crimson ramblers and wild briars, with bright nasturtiums at the foot … and just inside the wall wild fruit trees, planted orchardwise, crabs, cherry and pear trees. The grass is to be allowed to grow like a meadow, and to be filled with daffodils, forget-me-nots... meadowsweet, daisies ….'

The rood figures were made by the last ship's figurehead-carver in London, David Gibb, a Scotsman, brought up on the Clyde. The seating, prayer desk, rails and altar were designed by Wells, and made in oak by the otherwise unknown Gloucester Joinery Company. The lectern looks like the work of Ernest Gimson but seems to be by Ernest Barnsley. Two tall wooden candlesticks were supplied by Gimson. George Smallman of the nearby hamlet of Fishpool was responsible for the other ironwork.

Edward the Confessor, Kempley: rood beam

RICHARDS CASTLE, Shropshire

All Saints | 1890–2
R. Norman Shaw
SY8 4EG | Often open

All Saints stands massive and forbidding, on a rise not in the village of Richards Castle itself, but at the nearby hamlet of Batchcott, near Moor Park, home of its benefactress, Mrs

All Saints, Richards Castle

Foster. The site was chosen for eminence rather than convenience. Richards Castle's original 12th-century church – St Bartholomew's – despite Mrs Foster's desire to dismantle and even demolish it, still stands, now in the care of the Churches Conservation Trust.

Shaw's design has nothing to do with Shropshire tradition or vernacular building. He did use local materials – stone from quarries on the Moor Park estate, and from north Shropshire: but this was practical, not doctrinaire. The roof tiles were his preferred manufactured tiles from the Midlands. Yet Shaw felt keenly the relationship between building and landscape. He wrote to Mrs Foster, 'the yew hedge…. will (very soon) enclose the whole thing and will draw it all together and all help to make the church itself part of the country – and not (as so many are) like a thing stuck down on a flat deal board.'

The Foster family fortune was enormous. The patriarch, Johnston Foster (1827–80), was an active churchman. He and his brothers were involved in the building or improvement of at least four churches. When Johnston died of a heart attack at Cannes, he left a wife, Hannah Jane Foster (née Stansfeld) (1841–1918) and three daughters, the eldest of whom died in October 1883 aged 18. His widow decided to build a church as a memorial to husband

and daughter: it was originally 'All Saints' Memorial Church'. Thus, there is in it dynastic pride and society worldliness: Mrs Foster wrote to Shaw, 'I am glad that you feel you will be able to work out the plans so as to meet our requirements & yet give us a church, such as we shall look upon with pride & pleasure, & our descendants, for many generations, after us....' But she was also worldly: 'We are anxious to have the [foundation] stone laid [at] the end of March or beginning of April as we propose going to town on 15 April for a couple of months.'

Shaw hated show. Of the choir stalls he wrote:

> I have made them what would be called 'handsome' – but not too elaborate. They ought to be solid and good looking but not showy! ...
>
> We have alas! all grown so fidgety and restless – that simplicity and quietness does not appeal to us as it ought...Let us throw ... marble floor[s] to the winds – or keep [them] for Restaurants and Theatre entrances ...

He used local craftsmen when he could: for the church gates he thought 'The Village Carpenter & Smith is the right man to make these.' Alas, it seems they were never made.

The focus of the interior is the reredos. Shaw chose the young and impoverished Charles Buckeridge (1864–98) as its painter: Shaw's attention was drawn by work Buckeridge had recently done for G.F. Bodley at St Martin's, Scarborough: 'as unlike the modern rubbish you generally see in churches as it well can be ...' But the frame was a strictly commercial job: 'a very excellent firm, Farmer and Brindley'.

The reredos was to be the first instalment, only: 'Of course all the colour is to come ... Dark seats – stalls, pulpit &c & I hope by easy stages, stained glass windows, and wall and roof painting so that the whole church may become very splendid – but never, I hope, gaudy... Everything comes to those who can wait.' But it did not. The Fosters began the process of enrichment: oak panelling in both vestries, a canopy over the pulpit and the porch at the north door. The altar candlesticks were given by Mrs Foster's sister-in-law and the vases by Mrs Foster's sister. But the hoped-for glass and the new font never materialised. The Fosters' interest waned. The surviving daughters married. There were 250 at Evensong in March 1894. But only 50 at a Lent evening service in March 1906, and 33 at Ascension Day in May 1912. In due course Mrs Foster herself moved away.

All Saints, Richards Castle: reredos detail

HOARWITHY, Herefordshire

St Catherine | 1878–1903
J.P. Seddon
HR2 6QH | Open

Alan Brooks in his 2012 *Pevsner* calls it 'the most impressive Victorian church in the county.' The inspector for what was then English Heritage in 1987 was bedazzled, and declared it in the listing, 'Rundbogenstil with Byzantine, French, Venetian, Lombardic, Tuscan and Sicilian Romanesque influences.' Cooler heads see it as essentially Byzantine with elements of the Romanesque. It is certainly unusual and rather exotic.

William Poole (1819–1902), Vicar of Hentland from 1854, possessed large estates in Herefordshire, Radnorshire, Durham, Northumberland and Devon. He used the rents of his North Country property to beautify Hoarwithy church. Poole was an enthusiastic if perhaps unsystematic architectural antiquarian. He chose as his architect John Pollard Seddon FRIBA (1827–1906), a dependable, established practitioner whose practice had produced, by 1874, 31 new churches, mainly in Monmouthshire, Glamorgan and Herefordshire.

A Commissioners' chapel-of-ease was built at Hoarwithy in 1840 (or 1842): 'an ugly brick building with no pretensions to any style of architecture' according to Poole's niece, Madeline Hopton. The church was not pulled down, but its walls (sandstone, not brick) were encased in new sandstone on the same footprint. The walls were enlivened with eye-catching carving, much of it unorthodox and original: drip-mouldings end in stops of curious design – a hand holding a lizard, a fist, a snail. A claustral walk to the south and an apsidal east end were added, and a lofty campanile. Around the west doorway, motifs echo 12th-century Kilpeck (just eight miles west), but with greater regularity and less verve. The major structural elements were complete by 1883. In some cases stonework remains yet unfinished.

St Catherine, Hoarwithy: capital in the sanctuary

Inside, it is almost gaudy in every detail: this could be the church of an epicure, a sybarite – but we know it is not. Poole was rather against enjoyment: he didn't care for jewellery, drinking or sex; he inveighed against *Quo Vadis*, a play at the Adelphi Theatre – he denounced it as 'sacred texts employed as mere ingredients in a sexual hodgepodge'.

The east-end apse is overseen by a mosaic of Christ Pantocrator, designed by Ada Currey for James Powell & Sons (she worked there

1890–1901) and installed in 1893. The chancel is dominated by columns in grey marble, veined with red, resting on bases of Egyptian porphyry. The altar is white marble inlaid with lapis lazuli, and the central cross is of tiger's-eye (chrysolite). The pulpit is of white marble with panels of red and green.

The choir stalls strike, in this company, a somewhat rumbustious note. Those against the south wall were carved from seasoned oak from Poole's Ledbury estate by Harry Hems of Exeter in 1883, to designs by Seddon. The prayer desk, also by Hems after Seddon, is 1884. The figures represent local saints – Weonard, David, Cynog and Tysilio. The panels on the stall ends, and on the prayer desk, depict scenes in the life of Saint Dubricius, patron of the mother church at Hentland: his birth; exorcising a devil in the form of a bat; miraculously producing cider from an empty cask. Those on the north came later, and seemingly from elsewhere, awkwardly adapted to fit. Madeline Hopton recorded, 'the walls were to have been decorated in harmony with the roof, of which the ceiling, king posts and tie beams have been decorated by Mr George Fox, who had a scheme for the walls which was what my uncle intended to carry out, had he lived, as funds became available.'

The west-end glass, designed by Seddon 1890–6, in very pale colours, reflects Poole's liking for something he saw at Bordeaux cathedral. The topmost light is an 1879 design by Burne-Jones for Morris. The windows in the apse are a memorial to Poole, designed after the clergyman's death by Seddon, by then an old man, in 1903.

It was Poole who was most 'Arts & Crafts' in spirit – nothing was shop-bought (a later brass lectern was a gift); all fine quality work; individual, personal and nothing but the best for his flock. Poole had the village reading room built – just to the right as you climb the steps to the church.

St Catherine, Hoarwithy: from the east

SELSLEY, Gloucestershire

All Saints | 1860–2
G.F. Bodley
GL5 5LE | Usually open

This, the last of the great Cotswold wool churches, was built under the patronage of Sir Samuel Stephens Marling, who owned mills in the valley below. The glass is the work of the Pre-Raphaelite Brotherhood (PRB): Bodley commissioned the up-and-coming William Morris to provide a complete scheme. There is glass designed by Dante Gabriel Rossetti and Ford Madox Brown, as well as Morris's friends, Philip Webb and Edward Burne-Jones. One window is by Morris.

The men of the AWG admired Morris, respected him – even persuaded him to be Master a few years before his death. But he was too big for them. And, while his ideas permeate the Arts & Crafts, it is perhaps best to see him as a presiding spirit rather than a founding father. Bodley, who had trained under Gilbert Scott, got to know the PRB in 1858. His promise to Morris of more stained-glass and decorative commissions contributed to the establishment of Morris, Marshall, Faulkner & Co. (1861–1875), 'Fine Art Workmen in Painting, Carving, Furniture and the Metals', and succeeded by Morris & Co. (1875–1940).

The rose window above the west door depicts scenes from the Creation with a richly coloured Adam and Eve by Morris.

GLOUCESTER CATHEDRAL

Lady Chapel | 1898–1929
Christopher Whall, then Veronica Whall
GL1 2LX | Open

Gloucester Cathedral's Lady Chapel was built just before the Dissolution. By the 19th century it was boarded up and disused. In the 1890s, as part of a restoration programme, it came back to life. The restoration was a sensitive matter: Morris's SPAB criticised the proposals of the Cathedral architect, Frederick Waller. The shrewd Dean, H.D.M. Spence, wanted a low-cost solution, and to avoid debate: he appointed St John Hope, Secretary of the Society of Antiquaries, to sit on his committee. Hope had strong Arts & Crafts connections: his choice fell on Christopher Whall, who had established his reputation with windows at Stamford, commissioned by John Dando Sedding.

Whall was the son of an Anglican clergyman, but became a Roman Catholic. He saw his work as a spiritual vocation. At Gloucester he drew inspiration from the mass of broken medieval glass in the Chapel's east window. He devised a scheme using white glass, and pale tints of greenish-grey, against which his rich colours glow like jewels. Each light depicts a British saint – Northern and Celtic on the north, Southern to the south. Whall's cleaning lady was the model for St Helena. Each of the lower, small lights shows an episode from the life of the saint above. One window in the Chapel is not by Whall. In the south-east corner, Dean Spence allowed a memorial window to the Lee family, owners of the Tootal tie business.

This was an ultra-modern conception in 1898 – portraits derived from photographs! Whall's drawing for this window survives – ready for use should any accident befall this cuckoo in the nest.

Whall's daughter Veronica became his assistant and carried on the workshop after her father's death. Her windows are above the south chantry (Musicians' Chapel), including a portrait of her father as, appropriately, St Christopher.

There is more Whall glass in the Chapter House.

Gloucester Cathedral Lady Chapel:
Fall of Man by Christopher Whall

ONIBURY, Shropshire

St Michael | 1902–3
Interior by William Weir
SY7 9AP | Usually open

William Weir (1865–1950) was the most conscientious, and the busiest, architect working for William Morris's SPAB. There are 66 church jobs to Weir's name in the files of the ICBS. He trained with Leonard Stokes and gave occasional help to Philip Webb until Webb's retirement in 1900. He was a close friend of George Jack, and worked at different times with Ernest Gimson, Alfred Powell and Norman Jewson. He never employed a professional assistant, and tended to employ direct labour, personally supervising all the work on site. He carefully and unobtrusively repaired the medieval fabric: some sources have credited the work to Detmar Blow, but he seems to have supervised the work, under Weir.

All the work was paid for (£922) by Herbert J. Allcroft, son of glove-manufacturing millionaire John Derby Allcroft, who was an evangelical Christian, and built three London churches, as well as purchasing nearby Stokesay Castle and building Stokesay Court (Thomas Harris, 1889). Weir was appointed through a local SPAB member, who was concerned in 1892 that Allcroft was intending to demolish the church: Allcroft was described as 'extremely pig-headed'. The indefatigable SPAB Secretary Thackeray Turner wrote to him: 'there ought not (under a skilful architect) be much difficulty in rendering the church fit for present wants'.

The threat was averted by Allcroft's death in 1893. His heir, Herbert Allcroft, had a keen sense of history, but little interest in liturgy, or, reportedly, church-going. In 1902 Turner wrote to him, and received a positive reply: 'We shall be only too glad to do what we can for Onibury church.' Weir was a success: 'Mr Allcroft is pleased with the result.'

It is curious that, while Weir's restoration of the fabric was tactful and self-effacing in true SPAB manner, the furnishings, and especially the light-fittings like medieval beacon fire-baskets, seem unwontedly theatrical.

St Michael, Onibury looking west

CHELTENHAM COLLEGE CHAPEL
Gloucestershire

1893–1907
Henry A. Prothero
GL53 7AD | Private: open rarely, e.g. Heritage Open Days

Cheltenham College Chapel is tall and imposing, as if to impress upon schoolboys the gravity of religion, and the great head-masterliness of God.

Its architect, Henry Prothero (*c*.1846–1908), laid no claim to be part of the Arts & Crafts and was not a member of the AWG. Without any plan to be so, under his hand the interior became an unwitting showcase of crafts-manship, reflecting changes in taste and even in notions of the religious in the decades after 1900. Much of the work in the chapel is by Cheltenham's two leading commercial decorative furnishers, R.L. Boulton & Sons, and H.H. Martyn & Co. Ltd. While the work of the co-operative Bromsgrove Guild is 'allowed' to be Arts & Crafts, the more commercial Boultons and Martyns are somehow not. It is not really clear why.

On consecration day 1896 it was an empty box: no reredos, altar rails, stalls; only one bay (of eight) of seating completed; no stained-glass windows and no organ case. The first major fixture to be installed was the east window (Heaton, Butler & Bayne), 1901. The reredos came next, 1902–3, made by Boultons, to a design by Prothero. It was to be a celebration of Britain's greatness in the story of Christianity, with figures in groups such as 'Great Churchmen who were also Statesmen' and 'Great Christian Writers, Translators and Liturgists'. But its timing meant it became a memorial to the 55 Old Cheltonians who fell in the South African War, 1899–1902. On the original design for the reredos, the central cross was 'bare and bleak'. The crucified Christ was added during the work, perhaps reflecting a kindlier religious impulse.

The outstanding Crafts pieces are three. First: the Myers monument by H.H. Martyn & Co. on the north wall, 1907 – a burgeoning wild rose Tree of Life against the panelling, in sycamore, with brambles and birds. The part over the door was made by Harry Breckin, who later worked for Fellowes Prynne. The rest is by Harry Dean, whose carving has been rated as good as that of Grinling Gibbons. He reportedly borrowed a book from his employer's daughter for reference: *Wee Tim'rous Beasties*, a book of wildlife photographs.

Cheltenham College Chapel: the Myers monument

Second: the lunettes painted between the carved frieze above the stalls and the stone arcade; Old and New Testament scenes, the facing pairs echoing each other's theme, and each a memorial to an Old Cheltonian. All but one were painted by James Eadie Reid (1868–1928), a Scot who joined Ashbee's Guild of Handicraft, worked with William Richmond on frescoes and glass, and became the North East's leading stained-glass designer (see p.265). Eadie Reid also made the memorial in mosaic to Prothero, 1908–9, in the narthex. 'The Angel appearing to Hagar' lunette is by John Dixon Batten (1860–1932, AWG 1892).

Third: two windows on the south side of the chapel – The Window of the Merciful and The Window of the Pure in Heart – designed by Louis Davis (1861–1941, AWG 1891), and made from his cartoons by James Powell & Son. Davis started out as an illustrator, then learnt glass design and making from Christopher Whall.

NORTH CERNEY, Gloucestershire

All Saints | 1913–20s
F.C. Eden (interior)
GL7 7BX | Open

The 1999 *Pevsner* calls All Saints 'for many the most attractive of Cotswold village churches, largely thanks to William Iveson Croome (1891–1967) of Cerney House, whose benefactions from 1913 onwards filled the church with exquisite furnishings.' Croome was an inveterate recorder and historian, and a leading light of Gloucestershire local history who played an important national role in church architectural conservation. According to Anthony Symondson, SJ, who knew him, he 'was one of the last of a rare breed of late-Victorian and Edwardian country gentlemen who, being men of taste and scholars in their own right, often bachelors, placed their knowledge and energy at the service of the Church.' The other driving force in the re-furnishing of the church was the incumbent, E.W. Martin O. de la Hey (1866–1936), a keen amateur archaeologist and connoisseur of renaissance art.

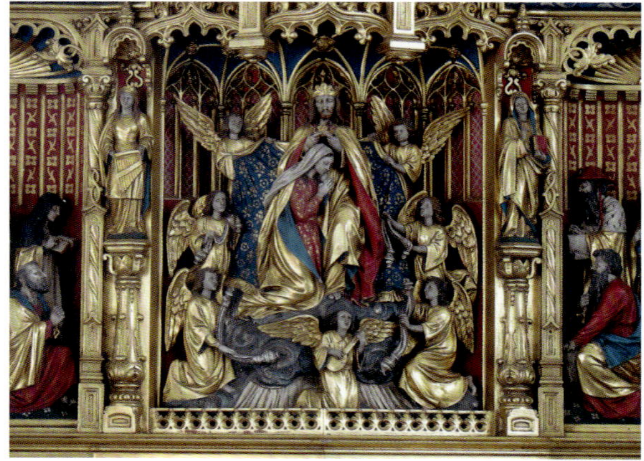

The first work was probably in the north chapel. Croome noted, 'In 1912 the glass of both the North and the East windows was sent up to F C Eden.' The next year Eden was similarly engaged on the east window in the south transept, where by now Croome's first major works were starting. The Croome family had somehow inherited powers over the south transept chantry chapel: 'Ever since my father's death in 1895, my mother had planned to restore the chapel … but for financial reasons it proved impractical until I came of age, when we undertook the work together as a memorial to him.' The most striking feature of the chapel is the screen, designed by Eden and carved by

All Saints, North Cerney: reredos detail

All Saints, North Cerney: the rood loft

his AWG colleague, Laurence Turner. (St George was added in 1920.) Eden's next major structural job in the church was to convert the space beneath the organ loft into a sacristy, 1915 – Croome being both client and sacristan. In 1917, Eden made a small window to the gallery as his memorial to local glazier Percy Joyce, who was killed in the Great War. Eden made another small window in the vestry in 1918.

Next was the design, making and installation of the high altar reredos, 1924, in memory of Croome's clergyman uncle and his wife. Then the porch gates, around 1925. In 1928 Eden designed a new oak frame for a dossal in the north transept. In 1929 came the imposing, elaborate rood loft designed by Eden, and carved by local man William Smith. The Virgin Mary and St John were carved by Alfonso Noflaner of Soho; the Christ is Italian, of about 1600, purchased in Florence on one of Croome's Italian forays. The cross was decorated with colour and gold by W. Court of the Post Office, Woodmancote, Glos., an almost Hardyesque figure: Croome recorded, 'He had been a framer, carver and decorator in London. He is a sidesman at the church now (1950) and for many years past.'

The names of all the craftsmen – some local, some London, some continental – were faithfully recorded by Croome: their short biographies are sometimes to be found on a photocopied sheet in the church.

CHALFORD, Gloucestershire

Christ Church | 1926–36
Interior by Norman Jewson, Peter Waals
GL6 8PP | Rarely open

In 1924 a new vicar set about transforming the undistinguished interior of his church. Norman Jewson, Ernest Gimson's assistant and Ernest Barnsley's son-in-law, was his guiding hand. He worked with Peter Waals,

Christ Church, Chalford: lectern by Norman Jewson

Gimson's foreman since 1902, who, after Gimson's death in 1919, moved his workshop to within yards of the church. Most of Gimson's craftsmen moved with him. The organ gallery was made by Waals, 1927; the chancel screen, 1932, designed by Jewson, made by Waals. The figures of the Virgin and St John, 1934, were added to the screen, carved by William Simmonds (1876–1965, AWG 1923). The crucifixion itself, 1910, is from Oberammergau. The lectern, 1933, pulpit, 1934, and font, 1937, were designed by Jewson; the fishes carved on the outside were by Simmonds; the font cover was made by Owen Scrubey (1905–1988), who had worked with Gimson at Rodmarton Manor. The silver-plated copper dove was made by the Waterlane blacksmith, Norman Bucknell. The communion rail, 1946, is by Jewson. The panelling and chairs are by Sidney Barnsley's son, Edward. There are four large stained-glass windows, 1951–4 by Edward Payne. The spirit of Arts & Crafts was living on, muted but intense.

Christ Church, Chalford: choir stalls

RODBOROUGH, Gloucestershire

Tabernacle Chapel | 1925
Sidney Barnsley
GL5 3UJ | Open sometimes: see website

Revd Charles Watson asked Sidney Barnsley to turn his coach-house into a chapel for the numerous and lively young people of the Nonconformist Tabernacle across the road: the 'Tri-sigma' Afternoon Guild – Sincerity, Self-surrender and Service. Local businessman Reginald Tyrrell paid. Furniture made at Chalford by Peter Waals; lamps by Norman Bucknell; windows by Henry and Edward Payne of Box.

Rodborough Tabernacle Chapel looking west

Other Churches

Gloucestershire

St John, Charfield | W. Wood Bethell | 1881–2 | GL12 8TG
Eccentric. 'A well detailed and intact small church with "Arts and Crafts" details.' (HE listing)

St Catharine (RC), Chipping Campden | William Lunn | 1891 | GL55 6DZ
Glass by Paul Woodroffe. Pulpit and organ case by F.L. Griggs. Rood by Alec Miller.

All Saints, Down Ampney | medieval fabric | GL7 5BQ
Woodwork by Charles Ponting, carved by Herbert Read 1897–1907: a parents' thank-offering for a girl after five sons.

St Nicholas, Saintbury | medieval fabric | WR12 7PX
North chapel screen by Ernest Gimson, 1904; chandelier by C.R. Ashbee, 1911; North chapel reredos by Alec Miller, 1925; Guild of Handicraft candlesticks.

St Katharine, Wormington | medieval fabric | WR12 7NL
Pulpit, pews by Sidney Barnsley 1926–31; altar rails by Norman Jewson 1926–31; Morris window.

Chapel at Rodmarton Manor | Norman Jewson | 1928–9 | GL7 6PF
Can only be seen as part of a guided tour of the house.

St Mary, Brownshill | W.D. Caröe | 1937 | GL6 8SW
Glass by Douglas Strachan.

Herefordshire

Good Shepherd, Upper Colwall | Hill Parker & Son | 1909–10 | WR13 6PL | **H**

Shropshire

Epiphany Chapel, Peplow | R. Norman Shaw | 1877–9 | TF9 3JR
'Epiphany' mural by Douglas Strachan.

St Mary, Burford | medieval fabric | 1889–90 | WR15 8HG
Fittings designed by Aston Webb: some made by W. Aumonier (AWG 1885) and Starkie Gardner.

All Saints, Little Stretton | unknown | 1903 | SY6 6RD
'Tin tabernacle', later thatched: startlingly simple.

12

THE WEST MIDLANDS

Birmingham, Warwickshire, Worcestershire, Staffordshire

As if to demonstrate its importance in Arts & Crafts history, Birmingham – unlike any other British city – is served by three prodigious source books that each throw light on the churches built there around 1900.

Alan Crawford's *By Hammer and Hand: The Arts & Crafts Movement in Birmingham* (1984), Andy Foster's 'Pevsner' *Birmingham* (2005), and even more compendiously, Phillada Ballard (ed.)'s *Birmingham's Victorian and Edwardian Architects* (2009). However, none quite explains what is particular and singular about the Arts & Crafts in Birmingham, nor why the churches, despite their originality and invention, lack the *frisson* found elsewhere. For Birmingham solidity and substance are more its metier than adventure and idiosyncrasy.

Birmingham architects *always* saw themselves as architects, not artists. Any city with a 'Jewellery Quarter' must be inclined to take aesthetics seriously: art and commerce were not at odds. In Birmingham religion mattered, for it was often tied up with civic achievement, and denominations expressed their vigour and significance in buildings.

Something like a local language developed, with, in church architecture, strong Byzantine accents. W.H. Bidlake is the dominant figure, but he does not stand alone – W.R. Lethaby, a natural maker of friendships, was the key influencer and maker of connections.

Birmingham remains a pugnacious city, proud of its sense of self: the superficial is rare to find in church building here – on the contrary, churches and chapels are serious to the point of stern. A self-made city has little time for airy idealism.

At the Birmingham Municipal School of Art (BMSA), under the inspired leadership of Edward Taylor (1838–1911), the teaching was by practical artists like Arthur Gaskin, Mary Newill (needlework), Benjamin Creswick (sculpture), Henry Payne (glass), Bernard Sleigh (wood engraving) and Bidlake (architecture). As a loose alliance of like-minded practitioners, they came to be called, confusingly, 'The Birmingham School'. Alongside, and in some cases with the same *dramatis personae*, came the Birmingham Guild, which morphed from an institute offering craft skills classes, to a small firm with a Ruskinian philanthropic outlook.

As to Warwickshire, modern Birmingham has swallowed swathes of it, leaving the county with few Arts & Crafts churches to boast of. But in Worcestershire, at Dodford, after the faltering of the village's Chartist settlement, a new church spoke in a soothingly compensatory nostalgic rural note.

In Staffordshire, art and money came together: first at Leek, then later in the Five Towns. The county is thus an accidental showcase of Arts & Crafts church architecture.

All Saints, Compton, Leek

LEEK, Staffs

All Saints, Compton | 1885–7
R. Norman Shaw
ST13 5LN | Open

If there must be a first, an *ur*-Arts & Crafts church – can any such thing really be singled out? – Leek is perhaps the prime candidate. Yes, there is the much earlier St Mary, Wreay (p.258), and a case could be made for many others in the 1870s that foreshadow the flavour and intensity (see p.316, 'Pre-cursor Churches').

Leek ticks a number of boxes. It was designed by Richard Norman Shaw, from whose office came the founders of the St George's Art Society – forerunner of the AWG; much of the decorative interior work is by two of those founders, who went on to have architectural careers of their own; yet more was done by local craftsmen and women; the work was done in a free and co-operative spirit, and that spirit carried on for many years; the textiles were produced by a group of women who, as well as reviving the skills of medieval church embroidery, represent something of that glimmer of female emancipation in the Arts & Crafts – if not of authority, then at least of recognition; there was no Clerk of Works – the builder (who left a detailed diary of this, the most significant work of his life) was trusted to deal with the details, and Shaw stretched his skills to the utmost; and the stone is local – Kniveden, Roach gritstone, Hollington and Ladderedge sandstones.

Leek in the 1870s was running short of church accommodation. St Edward's, the parish church, had galleries added in the 1830s, and its chancel arch enlarged to improve visibility by G.E. Street, 1867. St Luke's was built 1848–54; Christ Church 1863, enlarged twice in the 1870s. But still it was not enough.

The site for a new church – All Saints – was given in 1882 by Joseph Challinor, a prosperous solicitor, who also gave £3500 towards the £10,000 estimated building cost. Another major contributor was Hugh Sleigh, ribbon weaver and warehouseman, who had employed Norman Shaw to rebuild the nearby church at Meerbrook (1868–73). Another key member of the Leek silk trade was Thomas Wardle, dyer and churchwarden at Cheddleton, a few miles south of Leek, which he had had 'restored' by Gilbert Scott. Thomas's wife, Elizabeth, was a founder member of the Leek Embroidery Society (LES), which specialised in church

All Saints, Compton, Leek: the Lady Chapel, south wall

textiles. William Morris spent two years working with Thomas Wardle at his dye works to perfect organic dyes for silk. Morris's practical ideas, and his craft skills, resonated with Wardle.

Norman Shaw had been in G.E. Street's office when Street was building All Saints, Denstone, Staffs., 1860–2. He was also influenced by the church ideas of G.F. Bodley, in particular his St Augustine, Pendlebury, Manchester, 1871–4. But, first and foremost, Shaw was an original thinker – at St Margaret's Ilkley (p.240) he wrote in 1876, 'I am sick of the everlasting modern church with its orthodox roof and its feeble spire … let us have the walls as … thick as we can afford, and no very extravagant height.'

Shaw delegated much of the oversight of the work to his assistant W.R. Lethaby, whom he had 'spotted' as a talented draughtsman in 1879. Lethaby designed and made the font and the pulpit. Another Shaw assistant, Gerald Horsley (1862–1917, AWG 1884) (his family knew the Sleighs), decorated the chancel. He also designed the south-east aisle window. The main east Jesse window, 1923, is a late work by the Morris company to designs by Burne-Jones. There are Burne-Jones windows in the porch and other Morris & Co. windows in the nave. The enormous reredos was designed by Lethaby and the painting is by F. Hamilton Jackson (1848–1923, AWG 1887).

The great glory of the church is the Lady Chapel: the east wall was painted by Horsley in a slightly tentative Pre-Raphaelite vein. The rest of the walls were painted 20 years later, 1913–6, by a Leek man, John Edgar Platt (1886–1967, AWG 1929). Heron, magpie, mallard and swallows flock to St Francis – a pigeon and peacock have got there first; in the spandrels Adam, Eve and a pneumatic Serpent; and an Ark on broiling waters. Platt also designed some of the nave glass; and the panel over the organ case, with scenes from the *Benedicite*. He went on to head the art colleges successively of Harrogate, Derby and Leicester. The Lady Chapel east window is by Burne-Jones, 1887.

The textiles of the church are almost entirely the work of the LES – Morris's vegetable dyes have resisted fading to a wonderful degree. The designs were largely by Shaw and Horsley, but there are some also by J.D. Sedding, and Morris. In the north aisle is a framed panel by Beatrice Warren, wife of the then Vicar of Longsdon, Staffs: Gerald Horsley later designed the new church there, St Chad (p.175).

All Saints, Compton, Leek: pulpit

BYZANTINE BIRMINGHAM

The most interesting churches of the period in Birmingham – less famous than Bidlake's – are in a different vein: Byzantine, the same visual language employed by Sidney Barnsley (born in Birmingham – his family's building business was the contractor for some) at Lower Kingswood (p.86) and Rowand Anderson at Galston (p.310). They are Byzantine to highly variable degrees.

St Benedict, Bordesley by Nicol and Nicol, 1905–9 (B10 9AY) is an uncompromising dark brick powerhouse, with, inside, an apse painted in warm, glowing tones by Henry Holiday, 1912–19, with mosaic-backed saints. Joseph Lancaster Ball's **St Gregory the Great, Small Heath**, 1910–13 and Holland Hobbiss 1926–8 (B10 0JD), now Bethel United Church of Jesus Christ Apostolic, has exotic brickwork and a playfully complicated roofline, then, inside, potent polished granite piers with elaborate capitals, and unexpected 'folk' paintwork (stencilling?) on the aisle beams. Arthur Dixon's **St Basil, Deritend**, 1911 (B9 4DY) is now a youth support centre, but its chancel is preserved, with a modest, rather countrified chancel screen, mosaic apsidal ceiling and marble panelling.

St Andrew, Barnt Green – Arthur Dixon, 1909–26 (B45 8NR) – has crisp brickwork, and, inside, intense coloured geometric glazing by Richard Stubington, who studied with, then in 1909 succeeded, Henry Payne as glass tutor at BMSA; a stencilled open-work screen, and innovative stripped-down font. **St Edmund Boys Home Chapel, Digbeth** by Mansell & Mansell, 1913 (B12 0LD) with its campanile based on S. Giorgio in Velabro in Rome, was derelict in 2014, but now appears to be offices. **St Germain, Edgbaston** by Edwin Francis Reynolds, 1915–7 (B16 9TD), has utterly original brick detailing, bas-reliefs and rainwater goods, and much of its internal furnishings survive – beams painted with rural motifs; stalls with marquetry inlay; marble panels on altars and

walls; a painted reredos. Another Reynolds church, **St Mary, Pype Hayes**, 1929–30 (B24 0TB) is somewhat stern, but with intricate leading in the windows, refined plasterwork and an unexpectedly fragile-looking sandstone chancel screen. (It is noticeable that Birmingham windows in these churches are not only small and round-headed, but heavily leaded – as if to keep out hot Mediterranean sun, usually lacking in Birmingham.) Holland Hobbiss's **Queen's College Chapel, Edgbaston**, 1938–47 (B15 2QH) has its every inscription in Greek!

The Byzantine connection is intriguing. It was most likely through W.R. Lethaby, who was a close friend of J.L. Ball, who seems to have carried out the work at Lethaby's Eagle Insurance Buildings, Colmore Circus. Reynolds, who had worked with Bidlake, was greatly influenced by Lethaby, and had notes to hand of a 1918 Lethaby lecture. In addition, Lethaby's staff at Central School included Robert Catterson Smith, who went on to teach at Birmingham. The rood figures at St Basil, Deritend are by George Jack.

St Basil, Deritend: the chancel screen
St Gregory the Great, Small Heath: brickwork

Leek's parish church, St Edward's, has a Burne-Jones window of 1902; frontals and falls by LES to designs by Norman Shaw (the red array); and a Leek man John Scarratt Rigby (1833–1914) (green array), who also designed the white array from drawings by Gerald Horsley, and Lizzie Allen of the LES – they were not only embroiderers but designers. Other examples of LES work and Arts & Crafts design are to be found in half a dozen other churches nearby, listed in a Church Trail leaflet of 2016.

DODFORD, Worcestershire

Holy Trinity and St Mary | 1906–8
Arthur Bartlett and the Bromsgrove Guild
B61 9DF | By arrangement

Dodford village was the last gasp of Chartism, founded as a co-operative settlement of smallholders in 1848. Each household had four acres. Unexpectedly, strawberries proved the most viable produce. Although the company was wound up in 1851, adherents were still on the land in 1900. The National Trust owns one of the surviving cottages, Rosedene.

The founder of the Chartist Land Company would not allow a church (or a pub) on the Dodford estate. Soon after the Company was wound up, Dodford had both: the Dodford Inn, and a mission hall or chapel from 1863, later the Memorial Hall (until 1977). A curate at Bromsgrove, Walter Whinfield, conducted the services. When he inherited large legacies in 1902 and 1906 – over £1,500,000 in today's money – he funded the building of a substantial stone church.

He commissioned Arthur Bartlett (1867–1933), a London architect who had trained under either Arthur or Reginald Blomfield (sources differ). The connection with Dodford may have been through Bartlett's wife, who was the sister of Mrs Hendy, wife of the headmaster of Bromsgrove School. The Bartletts, Hendys and Whinfield were part of the social circle of Walter Gilbert (1871–1946), the entrepreneurial co-founder in 1898 of the Bromsgrove Guild with William Whitehouse and the architects' practice Crouch and Butler. Gilbert had trained at BMSA, then travelled widely in Europe to deepen his craft knowledge. He was drawing master at Bromsgrove School in the 1890s, and Head of Bromsgrove Art School from 1898.

He wrote, 'The members of the Guild are individuals who have advanced beyond the limits of "professionalism", that they might adopt the more prolific method of thinking and working in their media. These men and women, while they stand pledged to co-operation and mutual support, have individual studios and workshops altogether independent.' In short, it was a marketing device, branding individual traders as a single coherent Arts & Crafts whole. Gilbert acted as agent, promoting the Guild, seeking work and organising it among a number of small workshops. It is not always possible to work out who did what. The word 'Bromsgrove' is itself somewhat misleading. To meet demand, Gilbert sought craft talent from all over Europe – and makers were willing to come to Britain (and, yes, some settled in Bromsgrove) since wages here were better, and work more plentiful. By 1902 representatives of the Guild were based in London, Glasgow, Edinburgh, Liverpool and Newcastle, and there were workshops, confusingly, in Birmingham.

Dodford seems to have been Bartlett's only church. He passes from British church architectural history by emigrating to the USA in 1909, just after he became FRIBA, then to Canada 1911–14. He returned to England and became architect to the War Graves Commission 1918–20.

The church exterior has its delights – a half-timbered cloister, an outdoor pulpit, and rainwater goods decorated with fish and lilies. The interior is almost entirely by the Bromsgrove Guild. Celestino Pancheri, a carver from northern Italy, who had fled to Paris to escape conscription into the Austrian army, answered an advertisement for craftsmen placed by Gilbert in *Paris Soir* in 1908: he carved the Dodford altar rails and gallery balustrade panels with its musical instruments, as well as Worcestershire fruits on the wall plate. He may also have made some of the congregation benches with bench ends based on the *Benedicite*. The plaster panels in the roof arches are by the Guild: Charles Bonnet from Barcelona, and Leopold Weisz from Hungary (who was later drowned on the *Titanic*). The circular stained-glass window in the transept was made in the Bromsgrove studios of Archibald John Davies (1877–1953). The lectern and the bulk of the congregation benches were made in Worcester by Richard Haughton. The pulpit and choir stalls are by members of the Guild to designs by Bartlett. The rood, in hammered copper, silver and enamels, was designed and made by Amy Walford (1851–1926), who taught metalwork at Bromsgrove Art School and succeeded Gilbert as its Head. The rood beam itself was made by the Cheltenham decorative furnishers, H.H. Martyn & Co., who also made the benches in the transept. (Walter

Holy Trinity and St Mary, Dodford: carved panels on the nave arches; the rood by Amy Walford

Gilbert was later appointed Art Managing Director at Martyns.) A statue of the Good Shepherd stands in the exterior west end gable. It was cast, from a design by Louis Weingartner (who later went to Martyns), by Harry Hems.

In a way it doesn't matter who did what – the entire interior is the work of a co-operative body with a common aesthetic. The Bromsgrove Guild were craftsmen who operated in a business-like manner – though sometimes it is hard to discern the difference between the Guild and the less well-regarded 'commercial' firms like H.H. Martyn and Boultons, or indeed why Henry Wilson's favourite wood-carvers Trasks are somehow 'OK' while Harry Hems is not.

The craftsmanship tradition continued at Dodford. In 1951 Celestino Pancheri's son Robert extended the altar rails; in 1972, he made the sanctuary reredos. The handrails were made by John Gale, one of the last metalwork apprentices to be taught by the Bromsgrove Guild. The aumbry, book cupboard and noticeboard are by Michael Barrow, churchwarden, in the 1990s.

MADRESFIELD COURT, Malvern, Worcestershire

The Chapel | 1902–23
Interior by the Birmingham School
WR13 5AJ | Booked tours

In 1863–5 Frederick Lygon, 6th Earl Beauchamp (1830–1891) employed Philip Charles Hardwick (architect of old Euston station, and what is now Rendcomb College, Gloucestershire) to transform the ancient family seat at Madresfield Court into a romantically moated Elizabethan manor house – reputedly with 136 rooms. A chapel was created from two bedrooms, 'The King's Rooms', where Charles II is supposed to have stayed during the Battle of Worcester. It was fitted out in correct but slightly stodgy Gothic. In 1902 the chapel was wholly refitted and decorated for Lettice Grosvenor, Countess Beauchamp, sister of the Duke of Westminster, as her wedding present to her husband, the 7th Earl, who later had Edward the Confessor, Kempley built (p.145).

The artists employed for the work are usually described as the Birmingham School (or Group), though some also worked with the Bromsgrove Guild. They included BMSA tutors Charles Gere (1869–1957), who painted the reredos and doors for the altarpiece designed by William Bidlake (1861–1938), the project's presiding architectural muse; and Henry Payne (1868–1940) who designed the altar frontal, worked by the daughters of the Madresfield Rector. Payne also painted the egg tempera wall frescoes, with the assistance of three young artists including Harry Rushbury, later Sir Henry Rushbury RA. They show Lord and Lady Beauchamp (she in her wedding dress) either side of the altar, with their family on the side walls – new children were added as they arrived, up until 1923. Payne also designed the windows, and the lavish decoration on the gallery and organ case. The glass quarries under the gallery are by another Birmingham School man, Bertram Lamplugh (?1890–?1964), who designed windows at St Aidan, Small Heath (see p.172), St Alphege, Solihull and St Mary, Langley, Warwickshire.

The altar cross in silver and enamel was designed by Georgie Gaskin (1866–1934), and made by her husband, Arthur (1862–1928), who

JOHN SYDNEY BROCKLESBY

In Staffordshire in the 1920s, John Sydney Brocklesby (1879–1955) built two RC churches – **Sacred Heart, Tunstall**, 1922–3 (ST6 6EE), quickly followed by **St Joseph, Burslem**, 1925 (ST6 4BB).

At Burslem, the interior was designed and worked by Gordon Forsyth (1879–1952), head of the Burslem art school, with his pupils as designers, makers and labourers in painting, mosaic and other decorative work: his daughter, Moira, provided the glass.

Here was the spirit of the Arts & Crafts gone out into the world – unfunded by any bourgeoisie, expressing the educational aspirations of the Potteries, already stumbling in recession and under-capitalisation, and with young people desperately in need of new opportunities.

At Tunstall, the congregation was better-off, so the church is more conventional, yet full of careful artistic detail and craftsmanship. Brocklesby was an Arts & Crafts 'believer': he did not like using a Clerk of Works, and his workmen were allowed considerable latitude in the exercise of their crafts. He was also un-businesslike, and many of his church commissions ended in dispute and/or losses. He meticulously recorded the names of his workers – at **St Oswald, Ashton-in-Makerfield**, 1925–30, they included P. Howe, 'Main Sculptor' and N. Pimblett, 'Head Fixer', as well as four other masons. There is glass here by Harry Clarke (1889–1931).

Brocklesby also built **St Andrew, Langley Mill, Derbyshire**, 1911–13; **St Peter, Belper, Derbyshire**, 1919; **Jesus and Mary, Swadlincote, Staffs.**, 1920–21; **St Francis of Assisi, Long Eaton, Derbyshire**, 1920–29; **St George, Derby**, 1920–2 and **St Augustine, Nottingham**, 1923 – the last two in a distinctly French Romanesque vein. St George and All Soldier Saints, Old Normanton, Derby, 1907 was largely rebuilt by another hand in 1925.

Left: Sacred Heart, Tunstall. *Right*: St Joseph, Burslem

also made the candlesticks and sanctuary lamps, 1903. They had to be cast in France, because, as Gaskin explained to Beauchamp, it was impossible to obtain good-quality metal casting in Britain. The set cost £180, at a time when the average workman's wage was £1.80 a week.

It was not just about money. Payne wrote in a letter to Beauchamp, 'Work is not to be measured by the amount splashed on the wall, but by the value and quality of it when done ... I would far rather abandon the work altogether than to be subjected to ... minute and unjustifiable supervision. I am responsible to no-one but myself for the number of thorns and lily leaves executed *per diem*.'

The Chapel at Madresfield Court: the east end

The 7th Earl was enthusiastically evangelical in his university days, but became increasingly Anglo-Catholic with age. The painted decorations of Madresfield Chapel underline his High inclinations: on the east wall, Christ is reverenced by six medieval angels swinging thuribles, with a choir of Pre-Raphaelite angels at his back. It seems unlikely that Earl Beauchamp was an advocate of the ideas of the more extreme members of the AWG – socialism, or even communism. It is more credible that his wife commissioned the work in the chapel in the spirit of a benevolent patrician: sophisticated, with exquisite good

taste, and rich. She was also, and perhaps pointedly, destroying the only-40-years-old work of her father-in-law: the young Beauchamps wanted to be modern.

The house is often assumed to be Brideshead in Evelyn Waugh's novel *Brideshead Revisited.* Waugh had first known Beauchamp when they were at Oxford together, and he became a frequent guest in the 1920s at the house, which he thought 'the only place in England where one could go and play unsupervised'. He wrote most of *Black Mischief* there. Waugh describes the Brideshead chapel thus:

> The whole interior had been gutted, elaborately refurnished and redecorated in the arts-and-crafts style of the last decade of the nineteenth century. Angels in printed cotton smocks, rambler-roses, flower-spangled meadows, frisking lambs, texts in Celtic script, saints in armour, covered the walls in an intricate pattern of clear, bright colours… The sanctuary lamps and all the metal furniture were of bronze, hand-beaten to the patina of pock-marked skin; the altar steps had a carpet of grass-green, strewn with white and gold daisies.

Waugh's sneer (perhaps Charles Ryder's) – and there aren't any frisking lambs – pinpoints the awkward friction between sincerity and fakery

The Chapel at Madresfield Court: the west screen

just below the surface of Arts & Crafts. Is it all delightful, or twee? Or just unworldly artists doing their best to be honest while unwittingly, as William Morris feared, ministering to the swinish luxury of the rich? As Peter Betjeman points out in *Talking Shop: The Language of Craft in an Age of Consumption* (2011), at the end of *Brideshead* Charles Ryder's attitude is transformed:

> the beaten copper lamp is also the vessel of historical continuity experienced as a comfort, a felt connection, a past that unfolds diachronically rather than just starkly imitating ... Everything was 'as fresh and bright as ever' and not just because it is a recent, faux recreation; the place grew to 'ripeness'.

SPARKBROOK, Birmingham

St Agatha | 1899–1901
W.H. Bidlake
B11 1QT | By arrangement

St Agatha is the most famous church by William Henry Bidlake (1861–1938) – largely, perhaps, because its presence is so imposing in its long, straight arterial roadscape. There is fine stone carving, in particular of St Agatha above the west door. The tower that rises above is 36.6 metres tall. The east end was demolished by bombing in 1940 – and rebuilt to Bidlake's design. A fire (arson) in 1959 consumed the roof – again, restored to Bidlake's designs – but also destroyed all of the furnishings designed by him, apart from the pulpit. The interior is now rather stark. The church plate by Omar Ramsden (1873–1939, AWG 1904) is kept elsewhere.

St Agatha's was not experimental, has not an ounce of the quaint or picturesque, little interest in prettiness, nor is it fey or eccentric. One measure of its conventionality was that Bidlake won the commission in a competition, beating John Douglas, Mervyn Macartney and Temple Moore. The judge was the unexciting Arthur Blomfield. St Agatha's is an extension of Gothic Revival, not a rejection of it.

Bidlake was well able to be warmer and more aesthetically expressive. The Arts & Crafts aesthetic in him is in evidence most at **St Andrew, Handsworth**, 1907–8 (B21 9RE) with sedulous and beautiful woodwork, especially in the choir stalls; a reredos by Martyns of Cheltenham (now in a side chapel) with tender spirit fresco by F.N. Davies (of whom one ought to know more); spandrels in the chancel arcade unusually filled with deep

St Agatha, Sparkbrook:
stone carving above the west door

bas-relief carving; and understated foliate leading in some of the windows.

At **Latimer Memorial Church, Winson Green**, 1904 (B18 4PT), now Seventh Day Adventist, a tantalising fragment of a proposed lavish internal decorative scheme of cheerful Burne-Jones angels could in 2014 still be discerned in the spandrels at the easternmost end of the south nave arcade; and there are imposing doors and inventive glazing. The neat and reliquary-like **Handsworth Mortuary Chapel**, 1909–10 (B21 8JT), and **Emmanuel, Wylde Green, Sutton Coldfield**, 1909, 1923 (B72 1YG) serve to remind that Bidlake was a Goth at heart – lierne vaults with foliate bosses, and green men peeping from a frieze. Of his other major churches – worth at least seeing from outside – **St Oswald of Worcester, Small Heath**, 1893, is now a nursery for the Muslim community; **Emmanuel, Sparkbrook**, 1901, a care home; the robustly Romanesque **Sparkhill United Church**, 1932, became an Indian restaurant.

While St Agatha and St Andrew *seem* Arts & Crafts – stylistically reticent, disciplined, interested in using good materials, in originality and craftsmanship – this is arguing from the characteristics we discern in the completed work, rather than from knowing Bidlake's attitudes and working practices. There ought to be convenient parallels to be drawn between the BMSA and the comparable London institution, the Central School. But there is scant evidence that the way Bidlake worked was in any way comparable with how Sidney Barnsley, Randall Wells or Charles Spooner worked. He was the exact contemporary of those adventurous dreamers, but he was a cannier architect. He is usually regarded as the 'best' or 'leading' Birmingham architect of the Arts & Crafts era, but it is somehow missing the point to see him only as Arts & Crafts.

SMALL HEATH, Birmingham

All Saints (was St Aidan) | 1894–6
T.F. Proud
B10 0PR | Open

All Saints is imposing, craftsmanly and devoutly High. It started as if a Toynbee Hall-inspired Oxbridge mission to a 'wholly working-class parish'. Revd John Agar-Ellis (Trinity College, Cambridge) was the son of a diplomat. He and his sister purchased a site for their church in 1891 – a gardener's cottage – for £1925 (possibly their own money), and erected a corrugated iron church in the garden. There was a sewing class, men's club with speakers and, as the 1921 parish history puts it, 'on winter evenings the founder might be seen playing his violin as his sister taught the steps of the waltz, polka and quadrille to young Sunday School teachers.'

This unconventional pair attracted affectionate devotion: 'he worked like a merry lad at a cricket match'. In 1893 there were accusations of Ritualism, reflected in Agar-Ellis's attitude to his new brick church, 1894–6, a powerful mixture of High and Low – one step up from nave to chancel, but nine from chancel to Altar: 'Our people shall see God's altar above the head of the tallest choirman.' There was a rood beam, 1912, and a Lady Chapel. Local craftsmen did much of the work – the oak pulpit was made by a member of the choir. Agar-Ellis himself carved the panels, as well

All Saints, Small Heath: reredos detail

as the oak altar, reredos and gradine. Vestry minutes in 1893 show £2616 had been raised, representing offerings from 800 persons. The Bishop praised 'the spirit of comradeship and co-operation which the founder infused into the work'. In 1907 the Parish Year Book recorded activities including The Coral League, Girls Friendly Society, Guild of the Good Shepherd, The Band of Perseverance, the Sick and Dividend Society, and Boys Club. It is an East End mission come to south-east Birmingham.

BOURNVILLE, Birmingham

Friends Meeting House | 1905
William Alexander Harvey
B30 1JT | By arrangement

Bournville was developed by George Cadbury (1839–1922), a Quaker, son of a successful tea and coffee dealer who tinkered to good effect with new-fangled cocoa drinks. George's social conscience suggested his workers might be happier away from slums, and with facilities for leisure: 'pleasant and wholesome sights, sounds and conditions'. They should be paid properly too, and with a pension at 60.

Friends Meeting House, Bournville

George and his brother Richard acquired 14½ acres of meadow and woods, with a trout stream (the Bourn), a railway and a canal: their idealism was deeply practical. The chocolate factory was started on the site in 1879. In 1880 120 acres were added, for housing – at first for the management. Soon the land holding was 842 acres, and there were houses for workers, though in practice anyone could acquire them. The first 143 houses were on 999-year leases – which proved rather too good investments: the leases were often sold on. Subsequent houses were let on weekly tenancies, the rents going into a maintenance fund. Cadbury recruited William Alexander Harvey (1874–1951) as his architect: Harvey was 20, and not long out of BMSA. The majority of Bournville's houses are by him.

Though Cadbury was a Quaker, he espoused freedom of religion for others. The first religious building was a Friends Meeting House. Unusually for a Quaker place of worship, it has an organ, which George's wife Elizabeth played: the intention was to encourage Quaker worship to be more expressive, more joyful.

The design of the Meeting House is said to be based on Edgar Wood's First Church of Christ Scientist, Victoria Park (p.231). There is a certain similarity in the positioning of the tower, but the internal arrangements are wholly different – and the 'wings' of meeting rooms and kitchen came later here. The hall seems unnecessarily large for a quiet gathering of Friends – but it was intended as a community space and for concerts.

A hundred metres south is Harvey's Anglican church, **St Francis of Assisi** – the Hall, 1913, the church itself, 1924–5 (B30 2AA). The lectern was made by a local man, Francis Ames, who cast it in his garden, 1920. Not far away is the **Church of Christ**, Beaumont Road (now URC), by E. Berks Norris, a member of the congregation, 1914 (B30 2EB), 'a compact, commodious and beautiful building' with jazzy geometric glass and plasterwork.

LONGSDON, Staffs

St Chad | 1903–5
Gerald Horsley
ST9 9QF | By arrangement

HANLEY, Stoke, Staffs

All Saints | 1910–13
Gerald Horsley
ST1 3HU | By arrangement

Gerald Horsley (1862–1917, AWG 1884) was one of the founders of the SGAS. He was Norman Shaw's Assistant, and painted the walls at All Saints, Leek for Shaw (p.162). Horsley built just two churches, and both are in Staffordshire, just eight miles apart. **St Chad, Longsdon** is a pretty stone church with a curiously squat, outsize tower. It stands confidently on a slight eminence, and back from the road. The church is a filial act of piety in memory of intended beneficence, according to the foundation stone, 'built by the Sons of John Robinson late of Westwood Hall, Leek carrying out herein what he had himself intended to do'. Did the funds come from the estate? Horsley's drawings for the church featured in *Academy Architecture* three times: 1904 (from the west), 1905 (from the east) and 1906 (the interior, looking east), captioned, 'Suggested Decoration in Tempera Painting' – perhaps Horsley was hoping to do the work

All Saints, Hanley; outdoor pulpit;
St Chad, Longsdon: carving on the tower

himself. It did not happen: the interior is somewhat bare. The eye is caught by the chancel gates, the austerely unfussy benches (not unlike Kempley, p.145), and the exuberantly elaborate hinges on the organ. Altar frontals by Beatrice Warren of LES, wife of the first vicar. The east window is by Comper.

All Saints, Hanley more than fills its modest site – the unbuilt north aisle would have made it even bigger. There is loving stone-carving at the west end, and an open-air pulpit (the access has been bricked up). Inside, the bricks are stark cream, relieved by red brickwork crosses and sandstone quoins. The pulpit is powerfully austere. There is a War Memorial window by James Eadie Reid (1868–1928) who also painted the altar triptych reredos, with servicemen, land girls and nurses.

In 2010 All Saints was on the point of closure – a tiny congregation, broken heating system, major and intractable roof and down-pipe problems – it was on the Buildings at Risk register by 2012. The vicar, Revd Geoffrey Eze, applied to the Heritage Lottery Fund – and was successful: since 2017 there has been a new chancel roof, new rainwater goods and lead flashings. All Saints reopened Easter 2018.

MALVERN LINK, Worcestershire

The Ascension | 1903
Walter Tapper
WR14 1JW | By arrangement

Walter Tapper's first church, and his first job as an architect working on his own account after leaving Bodley and Garner, with whom he had worked for 18 years. Tapper (1861–1935, AWG 1907) is not usually considered 'Arts & Crafts' – he seems to come from another, more fastidious ecclesiastical design strand that includes Temple Moore and Ninian Comper. His churches are perhaps more conservative than is suggested by Arts & Crafts adventures. But his instincts were true: his *Times* obituary emphasised he had 'bemoaned mass production and the resultant loss of the "subtleties of the handicrafts".' The *Birmingham Gazette* added, 'Throughout his working life, even into his seventies, Tapper would climb on high roofs and scaffolds to inspect the detail of workmanship, and bestow generous praise on good craftsmen.' Philip Webb and Tapper were great friends. But whereas Webb was an atheist, Tapper was deeply religious.

At The Ascension all is calm and clear. The font has the feel of Lethaby; the chancel screen

The Ascension, Malvern Link: stencilling on the screen

suggests Comper – it is by Bainbridge Reynolds. The reredos is by Sister Catherine Ruth of the Community at All Saints, Margaret Street. There is a rood from Oberammergau, and Gimson-ish candle-stands. The gold stencilling is spare and almost crude, as if extravagance ought to be hand-made and slightly defective, in the Ruskin way. The altar frontal was provided by Watts & Co., for whom Mrs Tapper had worked before their marriage. The tester over the pulpit was made by a parishioner, Frank Barnett, 1989; the banners by Gaynor and David Felgate of the parish, 1990. The relief on the west tower is by Harry Hems.

History has not been kind to Tapper's churches. His largest and most characteristic, St Erkenwald, Southend, 1905–10, was demolished in 1992, following a fire. St Stephen, Grimsby, 1911–14, was demolished in 1974. St Oswald, Deepdale, Preston, 1934, was demolished around 1993. The chapel at Mirfield, 1908, has been mightily restored and reordered, 2009–12. **St Mary, Low Harrogate**, 1904 (HG2 0PN) closed in 2007, but has been born again as a Fresh Expressions church, Kairos, which has altered the interior.

St Oswald, Lythe, 1910–11 (YO21 3RW) is a tactful rebuilding of a medieval monster. At **St Michael, Little Coates, Grimsby**, 1915 (DN34 4ND) he added a tower, chancel and a new nave, which gives the church a lopsided feel – much of the furnishings have been moved or removed.

Other than Malvern, his great survivors are **St Mark, Whiteley Village, Burhill, Surrey**, 1919 (KT12 4DW) and the **Church of the Annunciation, Marble Arch**, 1912 (W1H 7AH), magnificent, where he has reverted to the ideas and aesthetics of Bodley.

At **Our Lady & St Thomas, Gorton**, 1926–7, now Mount Olivet Apostolic Church (M18 7QS) he took another direction entirely.

FOUR OAKS, Sutton Coldfield

Wesleyan Church | 1902–3
Crouch and Butler
B74 2UU | By arrangement

Methodism stirred in Four Oaks as early as 1765, in the home of Edward Hand: he and his family were ruthlessly persecuted, and finally evicted. In 1799 the Methodists, bolder, built their first chapel. A hundred years later the quiet lanes of Four Oaks were being developed for commuter housing. The Methodists – now prosperous and powerful – bought land and raised £10,000 to build the new church. The first stone was laid in October 1902; the church was opened just under a year later. Subsequently a further £4000 added transepts and tower, vestry and schoolrooms by 1910. There was a caretaker's cottage and manse by 1913.

Wesleyan Church, Four Oaks, Sutton Coldfield: pulpit

Joseph Crouch (1859–1936) and Edmund Butler (1862–1936) went into partnership in 1885 or 1886. (They were joined by Rupert Savage (1871–1956) in 1911.) Their practice was largely house, schools, municipal buildings and factories. Between 1887 and 1929 Crouch designed 19 NC chapels. Many of them, and early on, were simple preaching boxes. Later he went for more impressive effects with Gothic columns and arcades, and often with a gallery. Four Oaks has a daring central tower at the crossing. Pevsner saw Voysey's influence in the manse. The main influence in the church is respectability and solidity, with artistic touches of good taste in the pulpit, glass and roof timbers.

St James, Mere Green, Sutton, Coldfield: east end detail

MERE GREEN, Sutton Coldfield

St James | 1906–8
Charles Edward Bateman (east end)
B75 5BW | By arrangement

Mere Green is Bateman country. He built several substantial arty houses here. But Bateman (1863–1947) did not quite build a church. St James is two half-churches unsatisfactorily bolted together. Bateman's east end is giddily theatrical; Daniel Rollinson Hill's west end, survivor of his 1834 Gothick church, is brittle and dry. Frustrating confrontation or entertaining juxtaposition?

Around 1900 the prosperous incomers to Sutton Coldfield, with houses on what had been the Four Oaks Hall estate – the house was demolished in 1898 – demanded something grander. The old chancel and transepts were swept away, and a more lavish east end took their place, with a new Lady Chapel, organ loft and vestries. The Great War drew a firm line under the project, which stands in embarrassed disarray to demonstrate that hope springs eternal, and the best laid plans … In 1990, the exterior of the 1835 church was painted pink in an attempt to harmonise with the red Hollington sandstone of Bateman's chancel.

Bateman did not build any other church, though he submitted a design for St Agatha, Sparkbrook, and had church designs published in *The Builder* in 1906. However, he designed screens and colourful decorations, most notably at **Holy Trinity, Sutton Coldfield** (B72 1TF) – the nave in 1914 and the Lady Chapel in 1929.

TITTENSOR, Staffs

St Luke | 1880–2
Thomas Roberts
ST12 9HE | Open

St Luke is a bit too early to be the genuine article – but it shows there was something in the air. Its architect was a member of no Guild – plain Thomas Roberts, estate architect to the Duke of Sutherland on his Trentham Estate. The Duchess, Millicent, Countess of Cromartie, appears to have been the driving force. The affable playboy Prince of Wales, later Edward VII, was at the laying of the foundation stone.

The church compares with a number of rural churches in a free vernacular spirit such as John Douglas's **St Michael, Altcar, Lancs**, 1878–9 (L37 5AA), and Edmund Kirby's **St John's, High Legh, Knutsford, Cheshire**, 1893 (WA16 6ND) – but if anything, is more fanciful. The porch has proud wooden pegs. There is prettily leaded glass and neat woodwork.

SLINDON, Staffs

St Chad | 1894–5
Basil Champneys
ST16 2HP | By arrangement

Basil Champneys (1842–1935) was a very early member of the AWG (1884). He would not join the RIBA – but he never quite seems Arts & Crafts. In 1912 he won the RIBA Gold Medal – his loyalties were divided, if not conflicted.

His father was Dean of Lichfield, and Basil went up to Trinity, Cambridge, to read Greats. But he turned to architecture not the Church (see Oxford, p.78). In 1880 he designed **St**

George, Glascote, Staffs. (B77 2AT) in rather uncompromising brick. In the 1880s he worked at **St Editha, Tamworth** and **St Bartholomew, Wednesbury**. He designed the reredos at **All Saints, Alrewas, Staffs.** (DE13 7BT) in 1892. But he was busiest in Oxford, especially with Mansfield College. St Chad lies on a sort of aesthetic fault line between sedulous Gothic

Left: St Luke, Tittensor
Right: St Chad, Slindon

and something livelier – not quite the Queen Anne style, later pursued energetically by Champneys.

He was pugnacious and unafraid. At the John Rylands Library Champneys worked with Charles Eamer Kempe (1837–1907) for the glass, and Robert Bridgeman (1844–1918) as sculptor/building contractor: Champneys didn't think much of either. He described Kempe's glass at John Rylands as 'of a crude type with sprays of fruit and foliage of a kind usually associated with villa residences pretending to be artistic'. Bridgeman's figure sculpture for the library he thought 'tame and inartistic' – he preferred rival designs submitted by George Frampton (AWG). Yet Champneys worked with both Kempe and Bridgeman at Slindon, and to good effect. The grotesques and gargoyles are lively and inventive. The reredos is 1902.

Other Churches

Birmingham

St Alban, Highgate | J.L. Pearson | 1879–81 | B12 0YF
Henry Payne glass; tempera reredos with copper surround by Kate and Myra Bunce, 1919.

Lozells (Methodist) Community Hall (Centre) | Crouch and Butler | 1893 | B19 2AH

Birmingham Oratory | E. Doran Webb | 1903–9 | B16 8UE
An experience, but is it Arts & Crafts?

Four Ways Baptist Church, Cradley Heath | A.T. Butler & Bailey | 1904 | B64 6EL

St George, Minworth, Sutton Coldfield | Charles Nicholson | 1909 | B76 9BU
Modest. Less adventurous that Curbridge, and has been re-ordered.

St Giles, Rowley Regis | A.L. Dixon, Holland Hobbiss | 1923 | B65 9EP
Lychgate; pulpit and stairs; candlesticks; font; bench ends with primitive vigour.

Christ Church, Burney Lane | Holland Hobbiss | 1933 | B8 2AS
Stone-carving lingeringly suggesting Aesthetic Movement and Art Nouveau in a Modernist setting.

St Michael, Tettenhall, Wolverhampton | Bernard Miller | 1952–5 | WV6 9AJ
Rebuild of fire-damaged nave and chancel in a hybrid Moderno-Arts & Crafts idiom.

Warwickshire

Holy Trinity & St Thomas Beckett, Ettington | C. Ford Whitcombe | 1902–3 | CV37 7TH
Whitcombe's surviving churches feel Arts & Crafts. He moved to New Zealand in 1909. Whall window, 1906.

Baptist Chapel, Rugby | G. & R.P. Baines | 1905–6 | CV21 2PJ
A serious and substantial example of the Baines genre.

St Peter, Galley Common | Morley Horder | 1909 | CV10 9NG
Unpromising exterior to conceal reconstruction. Interior refreshingly sparse: arcades, timber roof.

Worcestershire

Good Shepherd, Hook Common, Upton-on-Severn | George Rowe Clarke | 1870 | WR8 0AX
Henry Payne glass.

St George, Barbourne, Worcester | Aston Webb | 1893–5 | WR1 1HX
Dainty, trig and trim: painted ceilings, organ case; brickwork.

All Saints, The Wyche, Malvern | A. Troyte Griffith | 1902–3 | WR14 4PA
Griffith is VII in Elgar's Enigma Variations, *'Troyte'. He designed the romantic reredos, painted by Henry Payne.*

Christ Church, Broadheath, Worcester | C. Ford Whitcombe | 1903–4 | WR2 6QY
Rich naturalistic carving of vines on altar rails, reredos; fanciful staircase railings; font by Haughton of Worcester.

St Martin with St Peter, Worcester | G. Fellowes Prynne | 1909–11 | WR5 2ED
Seemingly Bromsgrove Guild were involved – look at those light fittings, and the east end exterior carving.

Hewell Grange Chapel, Tardebigge | Detmar Blow | 1911 | B97 6QJ
Now a prison chapel. Blow's church interior is hard to visit and illegal to photograph.

Sacred Heart & St Catherine (RC), Droitwich | F.B. Peacock | 1919–21 | WR9 8AZ

St Catherine, Blackwell, Lickey | Herbert Luck North | 1939–41 | B60 1BN
North, whose earlier Welsh churches have hardly survived, is here assertively Modernist.

Staffordshire

St Luke, Leek | F. and H. Francis | 1848, 1873 | ST13 6JS
Screen by ?Shaw and Lethaby; reredos by Sedding; glass by Henry Holiday; LES designs by Shaw and Sedding.

St Matthew, Meerbrook | Norman Shaw | 1868, 1873 | ST13 8SJ
An earlier, less costly version of ideas later explored more fully at Compton, Leek.

St Chad, Hopwas | John Douglas | 1881 | B78 3AL
One of Douglas's most confident and countryfied churches, far from Cheshire.

St Mary, Stretton, Burton on Trent | Micklethwaite, Somers Clarke | 1895–7 | DE13 0HD

St Leonard, Ipstones | Gerald Horsley (chancel) | 1902–3 | ST10 2LF
Screen by Gerald Horsley 1912–13; paintings by James Eadie Reid, 1917.

Woodall Memorial Congregational (now URC), Burslem | Absalom Reade Wood | 1905 | ST6 1DW

All Saints, Burton on Trent | Naylor & Sale of Derby | 1905 | DE14 3DD

St Mary, Canwell | Temple Moore | 1910 | B75 5SL
Temple Moore occasionally dallies with pretty detail, as here.

Holy Trinity, Eccleshall | medieval | ST21 6BY
W.D. Caröe's memorial side chapel and organ case, 1927: extravagant Mediterranean complexity.

13

THE EAST MIDLANDS

Derbyshire, Leicestershire, Lincolnshire, Northamptonshire, Nottinghamshire, Rutland

Leicester's pre-eminent Arts & Crafts son, Ernest Gimson, never built a church, not even in his home county, nor, despite designing furniture for several elsewhere, does he seem to have furnished one in Leicestershire – not surprising, perhaps, given his sternly secular upbringing: he first came to the notice of William Morris when the great man gave a lecture to the Leicester Secular Society on 'Art and Socialism' in 1883, when Gimson was just 19.

Here the Arts & Crafts took different shape. In Nottinghamshire working men – mainly miners – turned their willing hands to wood-craft in the service of their church, still not, to their mind, a naïve thing to do. In Leicestershire and Northamptonshire the dogged spirit of un-fancy Nonconformity was expressed in the delights of new design ideas. Elsewhere moneyed Anglicans turned their minds to creating a highly personal expression of religious commitment – most thrillingly at Matlock Dale and Welbeck Abbey.

The outstanding Derbyshire figure is Percy Heylyn Currey (1864–1942), whose ecclesiastical architectural achievements have yet to be much celebrated, even in his native county. His skill, imagination and importance cannot remain long unrecognised. Also in Derbyshire began the architectural career of a less obscure figure – Raymond Unwin's first church is at Barrow Hill, just a short walk from the famous railway Round House.

Less exaltedly, in Nottinghamshire, Arthur Brewill and Basil Baily, in partnership 1894–1922, performed much the same function as George Baines and his son did elsewhere – artistically engaging chapels for forward-thinking yet no-nonsense Nonconformists (and some Anglicans), but here in solid, respectable stone rather than in the Baineses' showy brick, flint and terracotta. They are listed in the 'Other churches' at the end of the chapter.

St John the Baptist, Matlock Dale

MATLOCK DALE, Derbyshire

St John the Baptist | 1897
Guy Dawber
DE4 3PQ | Phone first

Owned by Friends of Friendless Churches. To gain access, you must telephone them in advance, to be put in contact with the keyholder: 020 7236 3934. Parking is extremely difficult.

The chapel stands high on the side of a steep, narrow valley, to the north of the once-fashionable spa of Matlock Bath. It is almost ostentatiously withdrawn, romantically turreted as if on a Bavarian mountain, perched on a massy wall, at whose base a horse trough is fed by a natural spring. Ferns and ivy cluster round – even on a sunny day, it is cool.

The chapel was built for Louisa Sophia Harris (1851– 1908) (née Leacroft), in memory of her aunt and uncle, with whom she had lived since a teenager, at 'The Rocks', a house hard by the chapel, which she inherited from them. It has been suggested Mrs Harris built the church – effectively her private chapel – because she did not feel able to express her Anglo-Catholic sentiments at Matlock's medieval parish church, St Giles. But there is no evidence that St Giles was Low or antipathetic to Anglo-Catholicism: its churchmanship seems simply to have been liturgically unadventurous. Besides, if Mrs Harris were very 'High', where in her chapel are the statue of the Virgin Mary, or the dedicatory saint, or tall candlesticks clustering the altar and elaborate reredos?

Perhaps she simply did not wish to travel the 1¼ miles from her new home to the parish church. Or perhaps she wanted to set herself apart from the many other Leacrofts living in the town. In a parish church already well-endowed with monuments to her family, she would have found it hard to make an impression with a new one.

In St John's there is one monument of significance: a small, undated tablet under the westernmost south window, hard to see against the light, reads: 'IN MOST LOVING MEMORY OF | VIDA † | L.S.H.' Vida was not a person, however, but Mrs Harris's dog. It is not quite in accordance with canon law to commemorate an animal in a church. However, in an unconsecrated chapel (as this remains), she could (more or less) put up whatever she pleased. Aside from Vida, and Louisa's aunt and uncle, the only other

St John the Baptist, Matlock Dale: choir stalls detail

memorials are to herself and her husband, who pre-deceased her. No clergyman, no faithful servant, no friend.

Mrs Harris appointed a young-ish architect to design her church, Guy Dawber (1861– 1938, AWG 1897), then aged 36. He achieved later eminence as President of the RIBA, 1925–7, and as first President of the Council for the Preservation of Rural England, 1926. Matlock, his fifth new-build project, featured in the *Builder's Journal* series 'Men who build' in April 1901:

> Care was taken in designing this delightful little chapel to make it appear to grow naturally out of the wall below and to get the effect of clinging to the side of the hill.

St John the Baptist, Matlock Dale: reredos detail

> The result was most successful .... The coloured east window is by Mr Louis Davis, the figures round the pulpit by Mr Cecil Fabian, the plaster ceiling by Mr George Bankart, the decorations and painted altar-piece by Mr John Cooke.

Louis Davis (1860– 1941, AWG 1891) trained under Christopher Whall, and helped complete one of Whall's first major window commissions, at St Mary's, Stamford, 1893. The theme of the east window here is 'water': left to right – baptism, 'the waters of Death', communion, the Water of Life (with an angel dressed as John the Baptist). *The Builder* also noted: 'the ceiling ... treated with wide bands of modelled plaster ... now being decorated in colour by Mr Louis Davis'.

George Bankart (1866–1929, AWG 1900) often worked with Dawber. Bankart wrote

The Art of the Plasterer (1908), still the standard work. He revived decorative lead-work and later joined the Bromsgrove Guild.

Cecil Fabian (1873–1911) was the son of a Winchester ironmonger. He died poor, and remains unknown: his wealth at death is recorded as £5 0s. 0d. The figures he carved are now, alas, lost.

John Percy Cooke (fl.1892–1939, AWG 1899) later painted a triple-portrait of the first officers of the AWG, which hangs in the Guild's meeting room in Queen Square, London. Decorative panels seem a rather workaday job for a fine artist – but perhaps Cooke had Arts & Crafts diffidence and lack of pride. He was lodging in Matlock at the time. There is another possibility – that John Cooke was someone else altogether, a house painter and joiner of that name, of Wirksworth, three miles south of Matlock. (Or there were two John Cookes working on the job.) The Wirksworth man had three sons – a cabinet-maker, a painter and a carver. These are more likely, if less exalted, interior decorators, and perhaps responsible too for the woodwork: the furnishings, including choir stalls with Voysey-esque heart holes, are by unknown (as yet) hands. As are the sinuously leaded plain glass windows and the pulpit. And whence the rood figures – from Oberammergau, perhaps? The current decorative scheme is later: in 1929, the church was closed on two Sundays in December, 'for Painting and Re-decoration under the Direction of Mr E Guy Dawber ARA, Architect of the Church'. All has been lately restored and conserved.

It's a sort of epitome of 'Arts & Crafts church' – cosy, pretty, delicate, slightly whimsical, fairytale, neat and very unlike the big church in the town.

STONEBROOM, Derbyshire

St Peter | 1900–02
Percy Currey
DE55 6JY | By arrangement

Stonebroom is – was – a colliery village. Shaft 5 at Morton Pit was sunk nearby in 1865, and quickly attracted men to what had been, in 1841, a village of just five farms. The colliery was owned by the powerful Clay Cross Coal and Iron Company, which had supplied George Stephenson – its founder – with coal for some of his first locomotives. In 1880 a corrugated iron church was assembled on land near the colliers' houses.

In May 1895 Reginald Currey arrived as Priest-in-Charge: he stayed just four months. Coincidentally he was the elder brother of the architect. The *Derbyshire Times* reported his successor 'set himself the task of raising a Parsonage, which was accomplished at a cost of about £1000.' He then – rather belatedly – felt 'a church of a worthy character' should

St Peter, Stonebroom from the south

PERCY HEYLYN CURREY

The name of Percy Currey rings few bells, even in his native Derbyshire. It's a shame, when his churches are so interesting – it is hard, perhaps, for churches built so recently by a local man to be seen as anything out of the ordinary. But they are. As a group they embody those intangible characteristics of temperament – sincerity, simplicity, clarity and warmth – which epitomise Arts & Crafts ideas expressed in churches. He was a rather shy, bookish man who never belonged to the AWG nor, as far as is known, exhibited with the ACES.

Currey designed five churches in Derbyshire: **St Stephen, Borrowash**, 1889–92 (DE72 3JX), abruptly self-effacing in unapologetic brick; **St John, Ilkeston**, 1893–4 (DE7 5AJ), big-boned and confident; **St Bartholomew, Hallam Fields**, 1895 (DE7 4AZ), now offices; **St Peter, Stonebroom**, 1900–2 (opposite); **Christ Church, Holloway**, 1900–3 (p.191), which became a striking and moving War Memorial, with Louis Davis east window and carving by Laurence Turner; the tower of St Thomas, Somercotes (1902), and a chapel for Derby School (1891). He also built **St Mary, Westwood, Notts**, 1899 (p.195).

In 1902 Currey went into partnership with Charles Thompson: together they built the rather awe-inspiring, forbidding **St Osmund, Osmaston**, 1904 (DE24 8UW); the modest **Holy Trinity, Fernilee, Whaley Bridge**, 1904–5 (SK23 7HX); **St Mary the Virgin, Buxton**, 1914–5 (p.189); then **St Bartholomew, Derby**, 1920 (DE24 8FH); the crisp and simple **All Saints, Totley** (now in Yorkshire), 1924 (S17 4AA) and the frankly Modernist **St Stephen, Sinfin**, 1935 (DE24 9GP). They also built the chapel at Derby Diocesan Training College, 1913–14, and refitted **St Chad, Church Wilne**, 1917–23 (DE72 3QH) after a disastrous fire. Totley, Church Wilne and Buxton have rather idiosyncratic, open, chancel screens, with exuberantly carved wooden fleurons/bosses.

Their other buildings were houses (many for Currey's relatives), schools, parish institutes, shops, a mill, and church restorations.

Currey came of solid professional stock. His father was solicitor to the Duke of Devonshire. His uncle was architect to the Devonshire estates, based in London. The Curreys were CofE – two (possibly three) of Percy's brothers became priests; and he married into a pre-eminent CofE Matlock family, the Leacrofts. (But he was not asked by his relative, Mrs Harris, to build her chapel at Matlock Dale, p.184. Why not?)

He was articled to Frederick Robinson of Derby, then went as an Improver to Arthur Blomfield. He was Derby Diocesan Surveyor in 1895. In 1907 he was elected FRIBA: a smooth and apparently painless rise to be gently established as Derbyshire's foremost church architect. The only public activity he seems to have enjoyed was first as member, then, from 1901, Secretary of the Derbyshire Archaeological and Natural History Society. His lengthy list of articles in its *Journal* indicates his interests were archaeological, and medieval churches in particular. He wrote little (or nothing) about his own buildings. His politics and working methods were not noticeably Arts & Crafts, but his aesthetics grew in that direction bit by bit. At St Mary the Virgin, Buxton (p.189), just before the Great War, something new happens: with the simple addition of eyebrow dormers, there seems to be an entirely different visual language for a church – at once modern and curvaceously welcoming.

St Osmund, Osmaston: north door
St Thomas, Somercotes: window in porch

be built, and in 1896 initiated a scheme to raise funds. He was supported by John Jackson, JP (1844–1899) of Stubben Edge, Ashover, the principal partner in the Clay Cross Company, who gave a two-day Bazaar to set things in motion. No sooner had the fundraising begun, than Jackson died: it was decided to dedicate the new church to his memory. The foundation stone was laid on 7 July 1900, by his widow.

There was never a very large congregation: the miners and their families, for whom it was built, tended to spend Sunday elsewhere. Initially attendance at the Iron Church was good – 20 October 1892, morning service: 160 ('full' according to the register). But numbers went into steady decline. By 1899 they were tiny – 6 January 1899, 8 am: 'only one came'; 11 May 1899 – 8 am: 'No one came'. In the parish magazine the vicar wailed, 'If ever I have been discouraged and tempted to give up working towards the idea of a Parish church, it has been by the sight of an empty church on Sunday mornings.' In 1912 it was noted that 'eight communicants leave the parish this week: 5 for Canada …' Yet in 1913 new choir seats were erected and a new oak bishop's chair installed. Choir outings (to Yarmouth in 1900) were well supported. But the attractions of the three Nonconformist churches were greater.

Stonebroom United Methodist church (later Bethel) and Primitive Methodist church (Zion) both opened in 1867. A Baptist church opened in 1877. Miners for the local pits came

St Mary the Virgin, Buxton from the north-west

from places like Staffordshire, and brought Nonconformist beliefs with them. The CofE was nervous: The Bishop of Southwell wrote that 'the mass of people, ignorant and unshepherded, are tempted to drift into the ranks of the indifferent or hostile.'

On the inside, St Peter has some of Kempley's self-conscious vernacular awkwardness: nothing is overtly 'arty', but all looks as if it *might* be hand-made and personal. All the work in the nave can be taken to be by the builders, Soults of Ripley – some of whose men may have been from Stonebroom. In the chancel, it is frankly unclear who did what. The churchwardens' accounts note 7/6d to 'Randall for oak table'. There are still Randles in the village. Insistent tradition has many of the furnishings made in colliery workshops by village men. The chancel railings seem to have been made by the Stonebroom blacksmith, who may or may not have also been the Morton Pit blacksmith. The nave roof has the robustness of pit props (the chancel is a more delicate barrel); there is a matter-of-fact solidity in the brickwork, and clever bricklaying to form the Gothic embrasures, such as might have been used in the making of brick arches in steam locomotive fire-boxes.

Furnishings came bit by bit, and with no great fanfare or fame: choir seats in 1913, clock and bell in 1922, panelling in the chancel 1934, oak reredos in 1937 (the reredos was removed in 1968, along with riddell posts), east window 1953, communion rail 1956, sanctuary lamp and aumbry 1961, new lectern 1968.

Here is a church that looks the part – expressing the spirit of the Arts & Crafts, without being self-consciously 'Arts & Crafts'. Had the church been grander, would the people of Stonebroom have loved it more? Would it have lasted 100 years – as the Nonconformist chapels have not?

BUXTON, Derbyshire

St Mary the Virgin | 1914–17
Percy Currey
SK17 6LN | By arrangement

The first church on the site was a wooden mission, 1897, paid for by the Mirrlees family, engineers of Stockport. Currey was appointed architect in 1914 – possibly helped by his brother having been curate to the mission. The foundation stone is dated 28 May 1915. The Great War meant the construction was slow – it has been suggested the workforce

St Mary the Virgin, Buxton: chancel screen detail

at one point consisted of an old man, a boy and a horse.

Eyebrow dormers immediately suggest a slightly unorthodox approach – pretty, even joyful. They are glazed sparingly – large stone blocks interrupted by tiny square lights. The roof is in yellowish slate from Cornwall – and steep, as if to meet the Alpine snows Buxton attracts in winter. The creamy yellow gritstone of the walls is from a Buxton quarry, now a caravan park.

The interior is dominated by understated, aesthetically restrained woodwork, in particular the chancel screen, whose passionate pierced panels and emphatic fleurons are an austere echo of some of the visual ideas carried out far more lavishly at Great Warley (p.202). The lower part was installed first as a dwarf screen, and the slender arrow-head-profiled 'mullions' came later – a drawing in the vestry, dated 1914, confirms full height was always the intention. The powerful lectern is clearly by the same hand. The pulpit, dated 1913, is more restrained. The dark rood beam, oddly, is different in texture and colour, assertively finished with the kind of ostentatious hammering one might see on a Liberty's copper jug. The stone angels on either side of the chancel arch were reportedly carved by the Hunstones of Tideswell: Advent Hunstone and his brother and nephews. Their work is to be seen in many Derbyshire churches. There are hungry, fluttering birds (starlings?) on the wooden organ screen (the organ came from elsewhere), and an angel with outstretched wings high above – but who was the carver? The screens behind the altar seem to be later, and show that an ambulatory was the intention. The choir stalls, more severe, are 1937.

Currey took a detailed, informed interest in the liturgical impact of the layout: 'It always looks much better and is also better musically to have a fair space between the Choir and the Congregation,' he wrote to his client, Canon Charles Scott-Moncrieff, in April 1914. Appearance is all: 'I rather think that if the steps are put beyond the Chancel arch, as suggested, it will look better not to carry them right across, but to have a low screen wall, with the steps in the centre.' Unusually, he had a pleasant experience here: 'I wish that all the Committees with which we have to deal were as intelligent as yours seems to be. I had to meet one a few weeks ago, every member of which seemed to think it his duty to oppose every suggestion made by either the Vicar or myself, though none of them had any reasonable proposals to put in their place.' *Plus ça change.*

BARROW HILL, Derbyshire

St Andrew | 1893–5
Raymond Unwin and Barry Parker
S43 2NL | Closed

Raymond Unwin (1863–1940) was born in Yorkshire, but brought up in Oxford: his father was a don at Balliol. Aged 21, Raymond was apprenticed to the Staveley Iron & Coal Company, Chesterfield, as an engineering draughtsman. In 1893 Staveleys had him design pithead buildings, cottages and a church – St Andrew's – for their workers at Barrow Hill. He designed a simple box with a rather French-looking west end: the harling with revealed brick embrasures is as designed, though the west end was greatly increased in height and bulk in 1936 to house an organ.

Most of the interior fittings – pulpit, lectern, font, choir stalls – were added by

Richard Barry Parker (1867–1947), Unwin's cousin, in 1895. Unwin married Parker's sister, Ethel that year. In 1896 the cousins/brothers-in-law formed an architectural partnership in Buxton. Parker was brought up in Ashover. He went to South Kensington Schools for a short period in 1887, and was then articled to George Faulkner Armitage of Altrincham (1849–1937), who specialised in church interiors. Parker designed a mosaic reredos for the church, but the building committee did not care for the design, so it was modified. Unwin assembled it from Parker's revised design, and gave it as his personal gift.

Both men were members of the Northern Art Workers' Guild, where they came into contact with the Manchester architect Edgar Wood (1860–1935) and his circle.

HOLLOWAY, Derbyshire

Christ Church | 1900–03
Percy Currey
DE4 5JP | Open

The east window is by Louis Davis. Currey designed the rather Baroque pulpit and wholly conventional lectern, and probably also the font cover and credence table. The hymn board seems also to be in sympathy. The tower was added in 1911. After the Great War, the names of the fallen of the parish were carved in a frieze on the nave walls with blazing gold lettering on a scarlet ground, making this sombre, serious church yet more resonant.

Christ Church, Holloway: east window

WORKSOP, Notts

Welbeck Abbey Chapel | 1889–97
John Dando Sedding and Henry Wilson
S80 3LZ | Private
At the time of writing it is not possible to visit.

In 1889 John Dando Sedding was commissioned by the 6th Duke of Portland to create a chapel and library in the footprint of the indoor Riding School, 1622, at his sprawling Welbeck Abbey estate. Sedding's design for the altar frontal was shown at the 1890 ACES exhibition. Sedding died in 1891: at the 1893 ACES exhibition Henry Wilson, his assistant and now successor, showed the finished piece in repoussé silver, together with an altar cross and lectern, made by Henry Longden & Co.

Welbeck Abbey Chapel: choir stalls bench ends

The chapel is, structurally, Sedding's – tunnel vault, alabaster columns. But the detail is all Wilson: plasterwork arches with bands of foliage, saints and apostles; altar rail in green marble and brass; oak stalls, by his favourite maker, Trasks, throughout – the stalls depict the *Benedicite*, always a popular theme for the Arts & Crafts. The simple, square windows are by Christopher Whall.

The lectern – really no more than a pulpit bookstand – is a silver bird with an enamel plaque on its breast: the yellow rays of the sun reaching the green globe. Wilson's biographer Cyndy Manton points out this is like the 'solar bird' Lethaby describes at the Sun Temple of Baalbek. Its crown is studded with opals. Its wings carry a circlet embossed with the signs of the zodiac. Here too are 'Lethaby' eggs – symbols of creation – suspended from the hanging lamps. In the baptistry an intense font, 1893, carved by F.W. Pomeroy and lined by Henry Longden, with pearl mosaics by T. Raffles Davison (1853–1937), best known as an architectural illustrator; and semi-precious stones forming astrological symbols by Wilson's brother, Patten Wilson (1869–1934). The font cover, designed by Henry Wilson, was made by Longdens. The gates, designed by Wilson, are by Pomeroy.

The grandiose double doors to the chapel prefigure Wilson's later work at St Mary's Nottingham and at St John the Divine, New York – visionary and original. The drawings were submitted in spring 1909. Wilson would not be hurried; the panels were to be cast in Paris. The whole was completed in 1912. Over the doors, a Deposition in memory of the Duke's brother, who died in 1903. In a corner lurks another lectern – huge, unwieldy, dark, dated 1896.

SAPCOTE, Leics

Methodist Church | 1902–5
Fred Tuckey
LE9 4JE | By arrangement

In 1786 Wesley preached at Hinckley; in 1794 there were itinerant Methodist preachers in Sapcote – the cottage where the congregation worshipped was burned down by objectors. Undaunted, they built their first chapel in 1805, and added a gallery in 1825. There was a school by 1842. Around 1900, neither was big enough.

Sapcote Methodist Church was built by its congregation – men from Sapcote quarry, whose tough dark granite was supplied by the quarry managers (both Methodists): all they needed for building was provided, free of charge, in return for the men's unpaid overtime. The rough-hewn stone was shaped by chapel men – sett-makers and kerb-dressers – and brought free by wagon to the site by Methodist farmers. The front of the building used the best squared-up stone, the size of street cobbles, or more properly 'setts'. The rest of the building less regularly shaped stone.

The name of the architect is not recorded, though the assistant architect was Fred Tuckey, secretary of the chapel Trustees. (The HE listing credits 'Brookes of Broughton Astley', but no such person can be traced.) The principal stonemason was Dick Lane of Stoney Stanton. The builder was John Cook of Broughton Astley, 'builder, contractor and postmaster' – no other name is recorded of those who did the work. The stained-glass west window was donated in 1904 in memory of a daughter who died aged three: the donor, William Hincks, painter and decorator of Sapcote, painted it himself. The pine benches – and indeed, the east end furniture – all seem to have been made by local men. The detailing is delightfully naïve Art Nouveau.

Sapcote Methodist Church: gallery and east end

GOSBERTON CLOUGH, Lincs

SS Gilbert and Hugh | 1902–3
William Bucknall and Ninian Comper
PE11 4JR | By arrangement

What *is* it doing out here in the Fens? It would look more at home in Shropshire, Cheshire or even Norfolk. The roads here are flat and straight – yet the church tries its best to look coy and cute, as if enfolded by a copse in a Helen Allingham painting. It is half-timbered, with a rustic porch and vestry to match, and a roof that overhangs with an elegant curve. The chancel is rough-cast, as if from a different century entirely. In the bellcote, a single bell with a wheel and headstock, not just a rope. It is all very picturesque and faintly odd.

COLLIERS' CHURCHES

Emmanuel, Bestwood
S.S. Teulon | 1870, 1907 | NG5 9QP

St Mark, Bestwood
Medland Taylor | 1887 | NG6 8UU

St Mary, Jacksdale, Westwood
Percy Currey | 1899 | NG16 5QG

St Peter, Awsworth
Naylor & Sale; Frideswide Worthington
1902 | NG16 2QU

All by arrangement

None of these churches was designed by a member of the AWG, nor by someone who submitted work to the ACES, as far as is known. Nonetheless they express something else about the Arts & Crafts – that around 1880 there was a sense that craft skills (a) were dying out; (b) are a good thing, worth encouraging both for their moral quality and their usefulness – especially in places where employment was uncertain; (c) could be put to their highest purpose in a church; (d) could be *taught* in the context of the church, perhaps even and best by a clergyman at the head of his flock. It can perhaps be traced back to Morris's instincts about beauty and usefulness, and political worries about the dehumanising power of the machine. It might also be read, with 20/20 hindsight, as the last spasm of the end of church-going as a popular pastime.

In 2010 a Nottinghamshire Churches Mining Heritage Trail was initiated, with a useful leaflet guide: a by-product of the 1998 Southwell & Nottingham Diocese Church History Project. Their website shows more churches than these four – and all are worth visiting – but these are the most interesting through Arts & Crafts eyes. All but one are colliers' churches – with the air of Victorian missions. The furnishings, old-fashioned for their date, were made by the congregation, though we have no evidence that the men who made the lecterns and stalls ever set foot in the church otherwise.

The first and last have something extra – the work of artistic women, one an aristocrat, the other a vicar's sister-in-law. Both express another theme: that a church could be personal and decorated to satisfy one's aesthetic as much as religious sense – the two by this time perhaps much the same thing.

Emmanuel, Bestwood was built by the 10th Duke of St Albans. Enriched by the coal under his land, he had Samuel Sanders Teulon build him a monster new house, Bestwood Lodge. It had a chapel, deemed unsuitable to

accommodate the miners arriving in the area – the Duchess, Sybil (1848–1871), urged her husband to build them a church. She was an artist: she made, reportedly, the five windows in the original apse, embroidered the altar frontals and trained the choir. The western porch was erected in her memory in 1871: the bust is by Princess Louise, Queen Victoria's daughter. In 1907 the original apse was replaced by a more elaborate arrangement (why?) with new glass by Morris & Co., 1911, wall-painting and painted panels in a PRB taste (and with a Masonic flavour) and an apsidal ceiling painted with the *Benedicite*.

St Mark, Bestwood was the idea of an energetic priest, William Richard Cripps, and, again, the Duke of St

Albans. Services in the school were so well-attended, the colliery company decided a church would be desirable. The Duke and the company each provided half the money, plus £100 from Cripps. The church was built with sliding doors to close off the transepts, one of which was used outside services as a classroom for girls, with a cooking range and pantry. The other was for the choir. This practical, Nonconformist air is completed by mottoes over the fireplaces (in tiles), on the pulpit and lectern (painted), and on the beam over the sanctuary (incised in wood). Clearly there was no single guiding aesthetic hand. The furnishings were donated piecemeal – but who made them? Or the screen with its eccentric wooden 'chancel arch' – or the muscular altar rails? None of these is a shop-bought art manufacturer's piece. The free-standing reading stand was made by 'a Bulwell man' of Ronaldo's Wood Carvers of Bulwell, perhaps as late as 1963.

Left: Emmanuel, Bestwood: apse
Above: St Peter, Awsworth: choir stalls
Top right: St Mark, Bestwood: lectern

St Mary, Westwood, Jacksdale was Percy Currey's first church commission – a humble church for colliers, but with touches of unlooked-for charm and prettiness, especially in the porch. The feel at Stonebroom (p.186) is prefigured here – though much of the interior has been reordered, with new chairs (1999) and projector screens. Choir stalls were removed in 1995. Memorial stained-glass replaced the originally clear windows after 1915. What remains is highly suggestive – the rather pompous pulpit, with a Gothic triple arcade supporting the reading slope; faldstool and altar rails; sturdy panelling in the sanctuary; an extra lectern; an inexplicable further dwarf screen by the altar; rustic half-wheel light fittings projecting from the wall.

St Peter, Awsworth dates from 1746, but in 1902 it was enlarged with a new chancel to meet ever-growing numbers. There were new choir stalls and a pulpit, the work originally initiated by Henry Thornhill, the local undertaker, but completed by Frideswide Worthington, sister-in-law of the vicar. She also gave £800 to clear the church building debt – anonymous at the time. There is a bishop's chair, dated 1950 – but it must surely be earlier. It is said that Miss Worthington led a class for local men, teaching them carving – but that cannot be substantiated.

Does this all amount to anything? A reminder that craft, the hand-made, the felt not reasoned, existed beyond London and the AWG, and even now is little understood or appreciated. Mute inglorious Miltons people the land, Ruskinian chisel in hand.

There was money left over (!) in 1896 from the restoration of the parish church at Gosberton, SS Peter and Paul, several miles away. The vicar there, Edgar Torr Hudson, decided to build a chapel of ease for Gosberton Clough. In 1903 he wrote in the *Church Builder,* 'If these fen folk are to be won to the Church (and a great many of them are willing to be taught) it is by making it more possible for them to attend the Church services, as, with a dissenting chapel almost next door, it requires a great deal of courage and determination for many to start for a walk of four or six miles to attend church.' In the end, it seems the Hudson family footed most of the bill – the Hudson money was originally from soap, first made in West Bromwich. The church had Masonic connections – the foundation stone was laid by the Grand Chaplain of England, Canon Richard Bullock, Vicar of Spalding.

SS Gilbert and Hugh, Gosberton Clough from the southeast

The four wooden angels on sills – all that remains of an earlier English altar's riddell posts – were made in 1915, in memory of Hudson, by Belgian refugees from the Great War, sheltering in Spalding. Comper's hand is plain in the War Memorial east window, dated 1920. The church colour scheme is not quite his, though – the beams were black and the walls white until 1953.

LANGWORTH, Lincs

St Hugh's (ex-Walmsgate Hall chapel) | 1901
Henry Wilson (interior)
LN3 5DD | By arrangement

The building dates from 1962: it contains what survives of Henry Wilson's chapel at Walmsgate Hall, Louth, the seat of the Dallas-Yorke family: Winifred Dallas-Yorke married the 6th Duke of Portland, of Welbeck Abbey (see p.192). The chapel was a memorial to Haliburton Francis Dallas-Yorke, of the 10th Hussars, who died in 1899 aged 24. The Hall was demolished in the 1950s.

The contents of the chapel were offered to the diocese: the bishop selected elements to furnish the new church, built to accommodate them. There are three decorative Wilson beams in the nave, one painted with a golden vine, red and green chevrons and chequerwork. There is a painted wooden canopy over the altar. The sanctuary has Wilson grey marble floor and green marble wainscot. There are two hanging oil lamps, each with a Lethaby-ish globe in its chains (the lamps did not provide enough light in the chapel – too mysterious). There is a bronze font; sliding doors with Wilson bronze handles; silver altar cross and candlesticks. The memorial bronze bas-relief at the west end, painted pale green at some point for no known reason, seems not to be by Wilson. The window exterior stonework – mullions, drips, blind shields, quoins – and the sedilia inside came, it would seem, from the Chapel.

WALESBY, Lincs

St Mary | 1913–14
Temple Moore
LN8 3XL | Open

Temple Moore figures hardly at all in this book – he is so rarely 'Arts & Crafts'. But here in deepest Lincolnshire, for some reason, he was. The external stonework is playfully various, as if the accumulation of centuries – which it isn't. The wooden shutters (rather than louvres) of the bell chamber in the tower have rustic Voysey-ish heart-shaped holes. The panelling in the sanctuary has a crenelated top, and big plank panels with chunky wooden pegs. Door handles are in weathered iron. The aumbry door has strappy iron hinges. There is some eccentric glazing – 'crazy paving' leadwork, and two medieval traceried windows set inside and independent of the 1914 external frames. The double-lanceted squint must surely be unnecessary. The out-of-scale central arcade – this is a double-naved church – adds a fantastical note, seemingly stopping short at the chancel arch.

St Mary, Walesby: Voysey-esque bell-tower louvres

GRIMSBY, Lincs

St Augustine of Hippo | 1910–11
Charles Nicholson
DN32 0LA | By arrangement

Nicholson here seems half-way between the rollicking vernacular of Curbridge (p.70) and a more Comper-esque restraint. Over the west

St Augustine of Hippo, Grimsby:
Nicholson's electric-green congregation benches

door, a red cross on white plaster, with blue and black chequerwork. Inside, the green-painted pews have contrasting red fabric runners. The confessional is in a faded madder rose. The chancel screen was originally more brightly coloured – a painting hanging in the south chapel shows green chequerwork. Red and blue survive on the rood beam, with gold fleurons. The Stations of the Cross were reportedly designed by Nicholson. There is a jazzily multi-coloured paschal candle-stand. The chancel panelling is 1927. North aisle and chapel, also by Nicholson, 1935. There are two Comper windows. The vestry cupboards and choir stalls, and sacrament house atop the organ, are from other churches. The intended tower was not built.

Other Churches

Derbyshire

Baptist Church, Long Eaton | George Baines | 1903 | NG10 4LL
The Oasis Centre. Baines on top form, with heart-shaped ironwork, innovative glass, sculptured grotesques.

Christ Church Methodist Church, Long Eaton | Brewill & Baily | 1903–4 | NG10 4NE
Internally, heavily reordered.

St Andrew, Langley Mill | J.S. Brocklesby | 1911–13 | NG16 4BP
Bonier and more spare than his Burslem churches – a muted, pocket Roker perhaps?

Leicestershire

Barnabas Hall (was St Barnabas), Leicester | Goddard & Paget | 1884–6 | LE5 4BD
Robust vernacular shell – church stripped of its fittings to become a wedding venue in 2015.

Leicester Synagogue | Arthur Wakerley | 1898 | LE2 1AD
In the search for an 'Arts & Crafts synagogue', this is a contender at least.

St James the Greater, Leicester | Henry Goddard | 1899–1914 | LE2 1NE
Byzantine grandeur with Baroque details and Art Nouveau angels; frescoes by architect's daughter, 1935.

Robert Hall Memorial Baptist Church, Leicester | Walter Brand | 1900–1 | LE3 0PD
Sinuous ironwork; woodwork both rugged and chic; fashionable glass.

Elim Pentecostal, Narborough Road, Leicester | Charles Kempson | (?) 1901 | LE3 0BS
Built as Free Christian Church (Unitarian). Gertrude von Petzold, first woman minister in Britain, started here.

Loughborough Cong Church (now URC) | Barrowcliff & Allcock | 1907–8 | LE11 3BH

St Philip, Evington, Leicester | Everard & Pick | 1909–13 | LE2 1HN
Much altered following a fire.

Lincolnshire

St Paul, Morton by Gainsborough | J.T. Micklethwaite | 1890–1 | DN21 3AA
Morris glass, painted ceilings; rood screen.

St Peter & All Souls, Peterborough (RC) | Leonard Stokes | 1895–6 | PE1 2RS

John Robinson Memorial Chapel (URC), Gainsborough | R.C. & E. Sutton | 1896–7 | DN21 2JR

Welholme Congregational Church, Grimsby | Bell, Withers, Meredith | 1907 | near DN32 9JX
Closed after a chequered career.

St Hugh, Haycroft Ave., Grimsby | unknown | 1910 | DN31 2EA
Touchingly simple, bare mission church; green-stained benches.

St Thomas, Boston | Temple Moore | 1911–12 | PE21 7EJ
Artsy-craftsy treatment of bench ends; exuberant naïve chancel arch painting.

Beaconthorpe Methodist Church, Cleethorpes | Henry Harper | 1913–14 | DN35 7LB
Voysey-esque pulpit; glass; woodwork.

SS Peter & Paul, Glentham | medieval | LN8 2EW
George Jack pulpit, 1918; Whall window.

Northamptonshire

SS Peter & Paul, Chipping Warden, Banbury | medieval | OX17 1JY
East window by Christopher Whall; lectern and pulpit by Henry Wilson.

Congregational Church (now URC), London Rd, Kettering | Cooper & Williams | 1896–8 | NN16 0EE

Hope Methodist Church, Higham Ferrers | Thomas Dyer | 1902–3 | NN10 6DG
Abandoned in 2004, demolition planned in 2008, but now with a re-development scheme under way.

Carey Memorial Church (Baptist), Kettering | Cooper & Williams | 1911 | NN16 8QL

Nottinghamshire

St Columba (Presb), Mansfield Rd, Nottingham | Brewill & Baily | 1896 | NG3 4GG
Now Sikh: Sri Nabh Kanwal Raja Sahib Ji Gurdwara.

Friary Presb (now URC), Musters Road, West Bridgford | Brewill & Baily | 1898–1901 | NG2 7PR

Methodist Church, Musters Road, West Bridgford | Brewill & Baily | 1899 | NG2 7PQ

All Saints, Huthwaite | C. Ford Whitcombe | 1902–3 | NG17 2JT
The miners reportedly built it with stone removed from obstructing the coal seams they were working.

Rutland

St Andrew, Hambleton (chancel) | J.T. Lee | 1892 | LE15 8TL
Reredos by James Egan, who had worked for Morris & Co.; panels by Alfred Hemmings; glass.

PEACE

14

THE EAST OF ENGLAND

Cambridgeshire, Essex, Norfolk, Suffolk

No 'Arts & Crafts architect' of significance in the period settled in the East, though East Anglian architects were not immune to the influence: A. Winter Rose, who made the reredos at St Andrew, Bramfield, Suffolk; A.F. Scott, who built a church in Cambridge for the Primitive Methodists, and another in Norfolk for the Baptists. William Hayne was a busy architect in Essex – one of the two who built Frinton – but, though he imbibed some of the motifs of Artsy-Craftsy church design, he was perhaps something rather more pedestrian; Charles Spooner built one church in Suffolk and rebuilt another – his aunt and uncle were influential in the county, but he never lived there himself. John Coates Carter was born near Norwich, it is true, but he was in Hammersmith as a young man, and eventually practised in Cardiff and Gloucestershire – see Wales (pp 277–280). The most interesting architect of the era in the region was Revd Ernest Geldart, who arrived at something like Arts & Crafts ideals, but by a different and somewhat circuitous route: he was never a member of the AWG, but he cannot be ignored.

Nonetheless, East Anglia contains three churches worthy of a major detour, and a good number of appealing oddities, including a tiny Methodist church by Lutyens, the only church by Eric Gill, and a Moderne converted medieval barn. Most of the interesting work is on the coast, or near it. The most dramatic church of the period in the region, Walter Tapper's high and mighty St Erkenwald, Southend, 1905–10, was demolished in 1992 after a fire – not that it was especially Arts & Crafts: but Tapper was a careful and skilful user of craftsmen, as well as being a devout High Church man. His church of The Ascension at Malvern Link (p.176) shows he was perfectly capable of warmth and homely cosiness when working on a less orotund scale. Perhaps he was more Arts & Crafts at heart than he wanted to admit to himself.

St Mary the Virgin, Great Warley: chancel screen detail

GREAT WARLEY, Essex

St Mary the Virgin | 1902–4
Harrison Townsend and W. Reynolds-Stephens
CM13 3JP | Open Thurs and Sun pm

Great Warley tends to excite superlatives – which may have been the idea. It gives the lie to any idea that Arts & Crafts is about simplicity. It seems to have been commonly decided St Mary's is 'Art Nouveau': the church guidebook so describes it. Other commentators disagree. For Peter Davey it was 'a triumph of the Arts & Crafts spirit'. It was built for a stockbroker, Evelyn Heseltine (1850–1930), in memory of his younger brother. Heseltine chose the designer of the fittings – William Reynolds-Stephens (1862–1943, AWG 1888) – before he decided on the architect. The introduction to Reynolds-Stephens seems to have come about through Norman Shaw. In turn, Reynolds-Stephens introduced Harrison Townsend (1851–1928, AWG 1888) to Heseltine.

Heseltine's church-going conformed to social patterns of behaviour rather than religious commitment. He was keen to deflect accusations of self-glorification. The parish church was in a state of disrepair, inconvenient and inhospitable. But the new church was on the edge of the village, and no more convenient. However, the point of the church was essentially – and perhaps patronisingly – didactic: as Wendy Hitchmough suggests, the interior was designed as 'a carefully orchestrated sequence of symbols, colours and materials to evoke in its congregation an assurance of the promise of the Resurrection.' A printed booklet, *Explanatory Memorandum*, was issued to parishioners at the dedication service in 1904. (Heseltine was a friend of Mary Watts, whose Mortuary Chapel at Compton (p.92) also required a booklet to explain it.)

The rather humdrum exterior (based on Woodyer's church at Hascombe, Surrey), all simplicity and humility, gives little hint of the interior. Here is no restraint whatever. It is so decorative as to be almost more distracting than spiritual.

The apsidal ceiling is aluminium foil – as dear as silver in 1902. Oxidised aluminium ribs support the nave roof, with lilies rising from bulbs. Above are rose trees crowned with silver leaves, and painted white flowers. The brass chancel screen has more roses, with small silvered angels, each carrying a scroll bearing a Virtue – Long-Suffering, Gentleness, Goodness, Meekness, Temperance. The organ case has bas-relief panels of animals from the *Benedicite*. The chapel screen is in walnut and pewter.

The understated choir stalls are by Townsend. The painting over the vestry door may be by Louis Davis. The original stained-glass windows – 12 in the nave by Heywood Sumner, seven next to the font, by Louis Davis – were all destroyed in the Second World War. (The cartoons for Heywood Sumner's were published in *The Studio* in 1906.) The rose window is by Sumner, but restored. The seven replacement windows by the font are by James Humphries Hogan for Powells, 1946. There is a 1930 Morris & Co. window in the side chapel.

At the east end Christ stands above the altar in a robe of oxidised silver with a mother-of-pearl clasp, posed dramatically against a black marble vine. His heart is ruby

St Mary the Virgin, Great Warley: Christ in the reredos; aluminium foil in the apse

glass. This Christ is not in agony on the Cross, but benevolent – a sweet, approachable Saviour: Christ our friend, his blessing a cheery wave.

Great Warley is very much a church of the material world: the hand-made here is not so much honest, joyful and simple, as *expensive*. This church is brazenly dedicated to costly work – in 1973 John Malton wrote, 'its unorthodoxy made it expensive in time and labour, both in invention and execution … [yet] The thought of machine-made approximations to their work was abhorrent to [the craftsmen].' Having your cake and savouring it. This sort of manifestation of emotion in architecture disturbed traditionalists: William Butterfield nervously wrote, 'Creeds and definite principles are out of fashion. Our feelings take their place …'

GLANDFORD, Norfolk

St Martin | 1899–1906
Hicks and Charlewood
NR25 7QQ | By arrangement

St Martin's stands on a little knoll, up a narrow path next to The Shell Museum – the oldest purpose-built museum in Norfolk, 1905: the lord of the manor, Sir Alfred Jodrell (1847–1929), had an enthusiasm for collecting shells, and had it built to house his collection.

At St Martin's the spirit of the Arts & Crafts is surely present, but no one involved was much interested in the ideas, let alone the AWG. There was no smack of socialist politics in how the church was built. Sir Alfred – who paid for the church – was a man of liberal, even sentimental instincts, though a staunch Conservative in politics, but he chose a distinctly workaday architectural practice to do the job – Hicks and Charlewood of Newcastle, whilst admittedly experienced in church restoration, were not noted for artistic adventure.

The craftsmen who worked on the interior were certainly not members of the AWG, nor any other local Arts & Crafts society, but local men who made their living in this everyday way, and always had, without any special sense of its numinousness. Here was no sense of craft revival, or the reinvigoration of 'lost arts'. And no need for an AWG expert to arrive from London to work vernacular-seeming marvels.

Jodrell was a throwback to the country gentlemen of the 1850s who had their parish churches 'restored' by biddable architects. He was seemingly trying to re-create a great East Anglian church, but in miniature. Nonetheless, Jodrell recognised the contribution of his craftsmen by name: he had a tablet erected just inside the vestry door listing all the workers, from the architects and carpenters to the 'helpers' and labourers: quintessential Arts & Crafts.

Work began in 1899 and took seven years. It was, in reality, a complete rebuild, apart from the arcade and some of the masonry in the nave, chancel and tower.

There are several elements in the church which are direct copies of medieval work – not at all an Arts & Crafts approach: the outer door relates to St Margaret, Cley-next-the-Sea;

St Martin, Glandford: the profiles of Francis McGinnity and Walter Thompson, carvers, in the dado

the roof of the north chapel to Salle; the brass candelabra were brought from Italy by Jodrell. The font is a copy of the Walsoken font, which dates from the 15th century – but the 1897 Glandford copy was carved in Florence.

It is the woodwork in the church that peaks: a 20th-century version of a 15th-century East Anglian hammerbeam roof, screen and choir stalls, telescoped into a tiny space. It is all in local oak and cedar, and probably all from Jodrell's estate. All the wood-carving seems to have been done by Walter Thompson and Frank McGinnity, local men – rood, screen, bench-ends, choir stalls, frieze, ceilings, reredoses and altars.

In 1901 Francis McGinnity, wood sculptor, aged 22, was living in North Walsham, Norfolk, with wife, baby daughter and sister-in-law. He was born in Liverpool. His father was also a woodcarver from Liverpool; *his* father was a white-smith, born in Ireland. Walter Thompson has proved harder to track down: there were 51 Walter Thompsons in Norfolk in 1901. The two men worked together in harmony, it seems: so much so, they finished their work by carving a portrait of each other in the dado frieze. The odd thing is how very alike they look – the same bump on the bridge of the nose, the same liquid eyes with urgent ardency, and the same sensual mouth! And how very Bunthorne-ish they are – greenery-yallery aesthetical Green Men.

Jodrell's own pew had a bench-end with special significance. It was based on Landseer's painting 'The shepherd's chief mourner', but the dog depicted here was Jodrell's own dog, Nimble. Although the dog is shown with his head on his master's coffin, Nimble in reality pre-deceased Jodrell. There are monuments to 25 other of Jodrell's favourite dogs in the grounds of his house, Bayfield Hall. The church contains no other monument to its benefactor.

The impression one receives is that this church was the work of a band of brothers, with a kindly patron at their head: a benign Christian dictator.

HADLEIGH, Suffolk

The Row Chapel | 1892
Charles Spooner
IP7 5BT | By arrangement

The Row Chapel at Hadleigh, Suffolk, is a picture-postcard image of village England: a tiny, half-timbered, brick-nogged vernacular building, on a country lane, surrounded by cosy-looking almshouses. But what is it? A restored medieval chantry? An Elizabethan almshouse chapel? A 19th-century meeting house? In 1974 *Pevsner* called it a 'timber-framed C15 chapel (rebuilt)'.

Spooner was asked by his uncle, the Rector of Hadleigh, to restore a dilapidated building, at least 400 years old, in need of serious attention. He did so with caution, tact and care, his imagination tempered by a meticulous knowledge of joinery, and an obvious sympathy for medieval building methods. He didn't just invent. The result feels new and old all at once.

Pykenham's Almshouses were built under the terms of the 1497 will of William Pykenham, Archdeacon of Suffolk. The will makes no mention of a chapel. By 1891 the building, whatever its original purpose, had become associated with the almshouses,

which adjoin it. The almshouses were taken down and rebuilt. The chapel was left standing, though dilapidated.

Spooner recycled the essential fabric of bricks and beams where possible. He stripped the roof, inserted new rafters, and pieced in new wood elsewhere – a new oak sill in the north side, and the entire framing strengthened with iron ties, bolts and straps. It all seems authentically medieval, but closer examination on the ground suggests many of the bricks are modern. Some of the studs and braces appear to be original, but others have been moved and/or modified, and there are almost as many new. It would take a skilled surveyor to untangle the chronology.

The Row Chapel, Hadleigh: reredos painting, possibly by Minnie Dibdin Spooner

These careful repairs are a backdrop for a very different interior – an idiosyncratic 19th-century notion of how a pre-Reformation 'roadside mass chapel', as Spooner called it, might have looked. He reported, 'the window frames were quite rotten, so it was necessary to put in new ones': his replacements have imaginatively curvaceous tops, as does the doorcase. The overall effect is whimsical – something between romanticism and historicism, with a strong dash of nostalgia. A painting hanging in the chapel shows the interior as it was in 1936, revealing that the original scheme was more daring: a note in a 1914 parish newsletter refers to 'painting out the pattern on the chancel walls'. One exuberant note survives: a reredos, usually hidden behind a hanging cloth – greeny-yellow primroses and rather blue violets against a stylised rolling English countryside in apple green and gold, with sinuously Art Nouveau trees, possibly painted by Minnie Dibdin Spooner, the architect's wife.

IPSWICH, Suffolk

St Bartholomew | 1895
Charles Spooner
IP3 8HQ | Usually open

St Bartholomew, Ipswich was Spooner's first complete 'new-build' church. The client was Anna Frances Spooner (1830–1906), second wife of Spooner's uncle, the Rector of Hadleigh. She was born a Cobbold, of the wealthy Suffolk brewing family – a woman of some strength of character, and High Church views. St Bartholomew's was to be an Anglo-Catholic presence in a traditionally Protestant and Nonconformist town. The first vicar was another of her nephews, Fr George Cobbold, who had previously worked in a poor East End parish: he was 'High' enough to cause outrage. The main service was weekly Sung Mass; incense was used, and confessions heard. Fr Cobbold was pelted in the street with rotten tomatoes.

The part of Ipswich where the church stands was known as California, but not because of its climate or glamour. The 1848 Gold Rush coincided with the coming of the railway to Ipswich, and Rosehill, the proper name for the area where the company built houses for its employees, was as rough as a frontier town by the bucolic standards of Suffolk.

The first impression of the church is of bulk – it towers above the two-up-two-down terraces that surround it. It is stripped-down Gothic in conception and assertively brick: uncompromising, even harsh. Closer inspection, however, reveals surprising subtlety in the detail: thin 'Roman tiles' around the west window make a narrow string course from the dripstone stops. Over the west door, blue headers are set in diamond groups. The brickwork is set herringbone in the tympanum and stretcher-wise in the arch; in the doorway, a variation of Flemish bond rhythmically uses stretchers, headers and half-headers. The brickwork sets off a small but exciting flourish: a foliage and rope pattern on the gutter over the west door, a variation on Greek red and black vine ornamentation, here with mulberry leaves.

Between the double doors stands the dedicatory saint himself, genially presiding, flensing knife in hand. He and his supporting column are apparently carved from a single timber, and with a subtle twist ('wreath') to the column.

The east end's candidly simple barn-like gable is graced by an idiosyncratic window: not a rose but two vertical ellipsoids suggest the conjoined wings of an angel, or a butterfly in flight. The leading is restless and hypnotic.

Internally, the west end is dominated by the tall, painted chequerboard panel below the window – a baptistry 'reredos', simultaneously grand and informal. Each of the 35 panels is framed by thick, painted quarter-beading. The hand-made quality of the paintwork is ostentatiously explicit, with smudges here and there.

In this high, spacious interior, small-scale, intimate details have to be sought: the aisle

window glazing is a series of subtle rhythmic leading patterns and pale shades of clear glass; the metalwork and woodwork of the furniture is domestic – even rough and ready in the lectern.

The aunt was not pleased: she considered it 'too grand for its purpose of ministering to poor people.' The church was incomplete at her death in 1907. Spooner had planned a painted dado all round the church up to the sill of the windows. His drawing of the proposed interior also shows an elaborate Gothic rood screen, and a painted frieze above the arcades. None of these materialised, though a very simple rood on a high beam survives.

St Bartholomew, Ipswich:
the west doors with dedicatory saint

The ICBS made a grant in 1909 towards enlarging the church by adding a vestry and ambulatory, and completing the west end. The ambulatory corridor was in living memory still used for Easter and patronal processions. In 1926, under a new priest, the church was finally completed. An Ipswich architect, H. Munro Cautley (1875–1959) was to supervise

THE ROPES

There were three artistic Arts & Crafts Ropes. Two were cousins, and worked in glass: both were called Margaret – the elder, Margaret Agnes Rope (1882–1953), was known as Marga; the younger, Margaret Edith (Aldrich) Rope (1891–1988) was Tor. The third, Ellen Mary Rope (1855–1934), who was a sculptor, was their aunt.

They are important not only as exemplars of women in the Arts & Crafts – and working in an Arts & Crafts way by both designing and making – but as people whose work was not merely a series of church commissions, but was an expression of their religious commitment – art as a form of worship. They were not, what is more, mere gifted amateurs.

Marga was born in Shrewsbury. When she was a teenager her mother converted to Roman Catholicism. Marga (in 1923) and one of her sisters became nuns. One brother became a priest. Marga studied at BMSA, from 1901 under Henry Payne. She worked at Mary Lowndes's Fulham Glass House, 1911–23. Her principal works – she made about sixty windows – are the west window of Shrewsbury Catholic Cathedral and seven other windows there; Church of the Holy Name, Oxton, Birkenhead, Lancs; SS Peter and Paul (RC), Newport, Shropshire; St Mary, Lanark.

Tor (for 'Tortoise' – professionally usually 'M.E.A. Rope') – was born in Leiston, Suffolk, the niece of an RA, George Thomas Rope. She was taught at Chelsea School of Art, then Central School under Karl Parsons and Alfred Drury. She worked frequently with Marga, especially when they were both at Fulham from 1911. Her friendship with J. Harold Gibbons led to her first big commission: a Creation window for St Chad, Far Headingley, Leeds. Over a 50-year career she produced over 100 windows: All Saints, Hereford; St Saviour's Priory, Haggerston; St Peter, Clippesby, Norfolk; SS Peter & Paul, Bromley; St John, Coventry; St Peter, London Docks; St Barnabas, Northolt; St Paul, Chiswick.

Ellen Mary Rope ('Nell') was born on a farm in Blaxhall, Suffolk. She studied at Ipswich School of Art, then in 1877 went to the Slade, first to study drawing and painting, then from 1880 sculpture and modelling. She worked in London, sharing a studio with her niece, Dorothy Anne Aldrich Rope, also a sculptor. Nell specialised in bas-reliefs, using casting methods that allowed copies in metal or plaster – designed to be cheap to produce and repeated, 'so they could be used by others than the very rich'. She exhibited at the ACES exhibitions from 1889. She designed for Rathbone's Della Robbia Pottery in Birkenhead 1886–1906.

There are memorials to (and by) Ropes at All Saints, Kesgrave, Ipswich, Suffolk and St Peter, Blaxhall, Suffolk. More information and galleries of their works can be found at two expansive websites: www.arthur.rope.clara.net and, for Marga, margaretrope.wordpress.com

'The Creation', St Chad, Far Headingley, Leeds, by M.E.A. 'Tor' Rope, 1922
'Guardian Angel', St Peter, Blaxhall, Suffolk, by Ellen Mary Rope, *c.*1900

ERNEST GELDART

Ernest Geldart (1848–900) was not AWG or ACES. He was a priest rather than (though as well as) an architect. He was more a Victorian than an Edwardian. But he was interested in the way a church looked as much as in the way it worked – an aesthete as much as a liturgiologist. For him, the two were wholly interconnected. So there is something in him of Bodley and Burges and J.P. Seddon. But he was also hands-on – so there is something too of Gambier Parry and Henry Wilson. He was Arts & Crafts in mood, perhaps.

He was born into a religious family – his father was Secretary of the Manchester City Mission. Ernest was articled to Alfred Waterhouse in 1864, but in 1871 he left Waterhouse to go to King's College London to read theology: he was ordained priest in 1875. He was ardently Anglo-Catholic – a member of the Guild of St Alban, the Highest in the land; and founded the lay Brotherhood of St Dunstan. Brotherhood connections brought him commissions for church furnishings, and his first architectural work. In 1881 he was appointed Rector of Little Braxted.

His work is to be found in around 150 churches. In Essex, his clever, sensitive hand can be seen at some 40, of which five may stand for the many.

He rebuilt and added a north aisle and organ chamber to **St Nicholas, Rawreth**, 1880–2 (SS1 8SH), for which he designed all the fittings, exhibited at the Ecclesiastical Art Exhibition of 1882 – lectern, rood screen, altar, reredos, a chalice and paten, and frontals.

At **St Nicholas, Little Braxted** (CM8 3EU) he added organ, choir stalls, a piscina (which he carved), new windows, a new north aisle, low chancel screen, altar and reredos. He stencilled and painted the entire church: 'a mass of colour exquisitely blended and harmonised'. He made innovations in the ceremonial – coloured robes, multiple candles, robed choir, genuflections, etc. His biretta was mocked as 'fantastic babyish millinery'. He added a private chapel to the Rectory, 1896.

At **St Peter, Great Totham** (CM9 8NP) he designed the east window, 1882; added a vestry, clock and organ chamber, and a private pew for the de Crespigny family. At **All Saints, Great Braxted** (CM8 3EW) he rebuilt the west end, 1883; made a new east window, 1889; choir stalls, 1890, and reredos, 1919. At **St Mary, Ardleigh** (CO7 7LD) he painted the chancel, 1894–5, paid for by the English Church Union.

As well as decorative and furnishing schemes for churches, he was writing books – *The art of garnishing churches at Christmas and other times* (1882) and *Manual of church decoration and symbolism* (1899).

St Mary, Ardleigh: chancel painting by Ernest Geldart

the work, 'due to a strong desire to employ local talent'. It must have been galling to Spooner.

HUTTON, Essex

Hutton & Shenfield Union Church | 1913
William Hayne
CM13 2NA | By arrangement

Hutton & Shenfield Union Church stands on a large corner site in a leafy private estate, Hutton Mount, Brentwood. The houses around it are comfortable suburban villas: an Essex version of Betjeman's Home Counties, not quite achieving the grandeur of stockbroker-Tudor.

The church looks the part, described by James Bettley in the 2007 *Pevsner* as 'Domestic Arts and Crafts'. The tower is a scaled-down, toy-town version of a 'proper' tower, with battlements and miniature spire. At first it looks deliberately playful, but it is really just a small tower trying to look large – excessively battered to give a greater sense of height, with three 'storeys', though no bells or ringing chamber. The interplay of red and brown bricks, the triangular windows in the roof (dormers or a clerestory?) and the elaborate Edwardian bargeboard on the gable (not a transept, but a widening of the worship space at the liturgical east end) – all strive to give a sense of solidity and substance, yet light-heartedly. This is old England, but upbeat, bright and new. The chimney over the east end (where the organ is located) adds an almost comic domestic note. There is a rustic lych gate, with 'roses round the door'. This is a church at ease with itself, almost complacent. Arts & Crafts here is not a credo, but a look.

The Union Church was the practical act of a group of down-to-earth businessmen, who employed a local, Essex man to give them a useful, simple, uncluttered space that is as little about formal liturgy as possible. They chose William Hayne (1887–1941), whose domestic work dominates Frinton-on-Sea – his 1911 Free Church there is described in *Pevsner* as his *magnum opus*. Hayne was evoking the spirit in Hutton of an idealised 'English village', the church as the centre-piece of a suburban idyll – an enlightened, liberal paradise less than a mile from the railway station.

If Hayne was not Arts & Crafts, there was a flavour of egalitarian ideas among the church's founders. This is *possibly* the first 'union' church in the country – a church purposely built to be shared by two denominations: Baptists and Congregationalists; each succeeding minister is by turns Baptist or (now) URC. The inspiration and energetic leading light was Arthur Burns (1865–1943), an insurance broker and member of Lloyds. He kept a diary for 57 years. He saw making money as a way to provide opportunity for others.

Burns reported in his diary that there was a 'Proposal on behalf of our Wesleyan friends to erect a church at the corner of Priest's Lane…' (That came to nothing in the end.) The Secretary of Essex Congregational Union stated publicly that he should consider it a calamity if separate Congregational and Baptist Churches were started in a neighbourhood with such a small population. Burns, a Congregationalist, fretted about joining up with the Baptists – but felt 'to have opposed the new scheme, or given it the cold shoulder would have been to miss a great opportunity … of founding a strong Nonconformist church.'

A Provisional Committee was formed to explore the idea. A Declaration of Trust, 1906, gives their professions: Hosier and Outfitter, Railway Company Clerk, Wheelwright, Market Gardener, Fruit and Flower Grower, Hairdresser, Grocer, Commercial Traveller, Merchant. The land was given by Ernest Wood, JP, the developer of the estate, 'a magnificent and stimulating gift' according to the fund-raising leaflet. It was proposed the building should 'include in the first instance, the Church, Vestries for Minister and Deacons, Church Parlour, Class Rooms, Kitchen, etc, the Church to have seating accommodation for 324 persons … a credit to Nonconformity and an ornament to the district …'

There is no mention of ritual, of vestments, of history or precedent: 'no assent is required to any written or recited creed …. It is to be an association of Christian men and women whose aim is to secure helpfulness in worship, community in service, independence in character and moral integrity rather than uniformity of belief.' The four foundation stones were laid on 19 July 1913, and the church opened in the spring of 1914 with not one but three opening services.

Hayne laid his seating out in a curve, with no central aisle and narrow side aisles. There is a pronounced rake to the floor, so all can see and be seen. The benches are all numbered, and metal frames exist for name cards on each – pew rents were charged until as late as 1943. The dais was four steps raised above the floor,

Hutton & Shenfield Union Church from the south

with a fine set of elders' chairs and an altar rail. An organ was added in 1915.

The pulpit still dominates, though it is not the original of 1914. The altar rail has been removed. The elders' chairs have been demoted to the back of the dais. The gas lighting has been replaced by electric. Of late the original frosted glass windows in unstained frames have been replaced by double-glazed units which look rather less rustic.

Hayne was never a member of either the AWG or ACES. The evidence suggests he had no Clerk of Works here, and he seems to have had no assistant. But he had no pretensions to working in a particularly Arts & Crafts manner: he did not prefer local craftsmen, nor seek artistic makers. In appearance the church looks back to something solid, honest and English. But somehow this could not avoid, with a bourgeois taste for nostalgia, making it seem quaint to the point of arch. And anyway, inside, with its raked floor, unadorned doors, square-headed, clear-glazed windows and uncomplicated surfaces, this was a church to serve man and to bring him face to face with a democratic God who is equally down to earth, un-elaborated and every-day.

OVERSTRAND, Norfolk

Methodist Church | 1898
Edwin Landseer Lutyens
NR27 0AB | By arrangement

Lutyens was building a grand house at Overstrand, The Pleasaunce, for Lord and Lady Battersea – two seaside villas transformed into a rambling, eccentric holiday *bel esprit*. Lutyens had also designed nearby Overstrand House for Lord Hillingdon.

Lord Battersea acquired and gifted the land for the Methodist Church, either to satisfy the yearning of his Head Gardener for NC worship; to meet the needs of NC visitors to what was becoming a popular resort area; or following a fruitless decade of efforts by the Wesleyans in Overstrand to find a suitable site. Sources vary.

It has been said Lutyens based the design on a boat shed in Littlehampton. There is Rome in the pantiles and in the basilican design. Whatever its inspirations, it has the air of an

Methodist Church, Overstrand: west end

electricity sub-station, or a signal box on a forgotten Polish railway line.

There are no windows at ground-floor level. Instead, a clerestory of ten oversize semi-circular windows lights the interior. The protruding box that contains them is supported by thundering lead-encased beams on brick piers more like chimneys than buttresses. Pevsner called them 'aggressively functional' – they are as knowingly pugnacious as the green pipes at the Pompidou Centre: function exaggerated by form. The bricklayer was an Overstrand man, William 'Jockey' Reynolds.

The entrance has elaborate receding brick arches, as if to some far grander Byzantine shrine. And there are echoes too of Compton (p.92), and the same sense of something small pretending to be big as at Lutyens's later Anglican village church at Pixham, 1903 (p.89).

The interior is engagingly bare and simple – a good space for meeting and singing. Originally, it had chairs: they were replaced with benches from Happisburgh church in 1972, they in turn supplanted by new chairs in 1996.

GORLESTON, Great Yarmouth, Norfolk

St Peter (RC) | 1938–9
Eric Gill
NR31 6SQ | By arrangement

1939 seems rather late – but this is the only church by Eric Gill (1882–1940), and his idiosyncratic connection to Arts & Crafts ideas and practice insists St Peter be included.

Fr Thomas Walker had been priest at High Wycombe, where he had got to know Gill. So when Walker came to Gorleston, and wanted a new church, he asked his Bishop, Laurence Youens, if Gill could be involved. Gill had just completed the Stations of the Cross at Westminster Cathedral. Youens agreed.

Gill said he would work with another High Wycombe contact, Edmund Farrell, an architect 'well acquainted with the whole business of labour and materials of today'. Fiona MacCarthy writes that Gill 'seized on the project as a long-awaited opportunity to put into practice a multitude of related ideas about building, preaching, singing, church history, world politics, all burgeoning out from the elementary question: What is a church?'

St Peter, Gorleston: the crossing

The key idea – and perhaps a new one for 1939 – was that the altar should be central. Gill wrote, 'It is an interesting plan with crossed arches to make an octagonal central space … the church will be very plain and small – no ornaments except perhaps a figure of St Peter on the outside and a large crucifix hanging over the altar … It will be just a plain building done by bricklayers and carpenters.' He insisted that local craftsmen and methods be employed – he fretted that craft was being replaced by 'mechanical town methods'. The foundation stone was laid in February 1939, and the church opened in June.

The holy-water stoups, piscina, font and altars were made in Gill's workshops in High Wycombe. The foundation stone and altar have lettering by Gill. The tower fresco was painted to Gill's design by his son-in-law Denis Tegetmeier, who also painted the Stations, 1962. Gill designed the relief sculpture over the porch, carved by Anthony Foster.

SILVER END, Essex

St Francis | 1929–30
G.C. Holmes, W.F. Crittall
CM8 3SD | By arrangement

Silver End Garden Village was laid out in the 1920s for workers at the Crittall Windows works. In his autobiography, the factory owner, Francis H. Crittall, mused:

> I saw a pleasant village of a new order, planted amid fields and trees and streams; I saw its quiet thoroughfares, its fine open spaces, its modern dwellings with ample gardens; its playing fields, recreations and amusements; and above all I saw a contented community of Crittall families enjoying the amenities of town life in a lovely rural setting.

Plans included a Congregational chapel and an Anglican church. The Congregational church of 1930 stands nearby. St Francis is a thatched barn converted into an assertively plain church, half rustic, half Moderne. Why a barn conversion rather than new build is not clear.

The original barn dates from about 1700, though one wonders how much of the original survives: it was moved here from its original site in 1929, and converted that winter. Crittalls factory supplied the windows and doors. The original central wagon door was blocked, and new doors added at the west end. Mrs Crittall gave the window of St Francis, 1929, by Leonard Walker (1877–1964, AWG 1914). Mr Crittall gave the lych gate.

St Francis, Silver End

The interior mixes ancient and modern to interesting effect. The altar rails, lectern and pulpit – they would not look out of place in a Barbican flat – were made by Crittall workers to designs by Crittall's younger son Walter F. Crittall (known as Mr Pink) and the church's architect, G.C. Holmes. The chunky timber font was carved by the vicar from an oak reportedly planted in the 12th century. Svelte riddell posts survive from an English altar. The ceiling was originally darker than the current 1980s pale blue. The gold and silver stars are restorations, as presumably is the M (for Mary) monogram. The rough-hewn tie beams and their corbels were originally red – odd patches survive to show the impact this would have had.

Other Churches

Cambridgeshire

All Saints, Jesus Lane, Cambridge | G.F. Bodley | 1863–70 | CB5 8BW
Glass by Morris, Burne-Jones, Strachan; screen by John Morley, 1904; Bodley/Leach painting scheme; stalls.

Emmanuel URC, Cambridge | James Cubitt | 1872–4 | CB2 1RR
Morris & Co. windows in apse – Protestant heroes and martyrs.

Castle Street Primitive Methodist Chapel, Cambridge | Augustus F. Scott | 1914 | CB3 0AH
Interior retains complete, if rather austere, furnishing scheme, refurbished 2010.

Westminster College Chapel, Cambridge | Henry Hare | 1921 | CB3 0AA
Memorial Benedicite *windows by Douglas Strachan, 1921.*

Unitarian Church, Cambridge | R.P. Jones | 1928 | CB1 1JW
An unexpected essay in exuberant classicism by Liverpool's premier Unitarian architect.

Essex

St John the Evangelist, Twinstead | Charles Woodyer | 1859–60 | CO10 7NA
Bold polychromy in a humble church gives a glimmer of things to come.

St John, Stansted Mountfitchet | W.D. Caröe | 1889, 1895 | CM24 8JP
Liberated by client wealth, Caröe's first full church combines bricky Perp with lush metalwork.

St Nicholas, Kelvedon Hatch | John Newman | 1894–5 | CM14 5TJ
Straddles the boundary between Victorian and not-Victorian.

St Peter, Bocking | Micklethwaite, Somers Clarke | 1896–7 | CM7 5PY

Convent Chapel (RC), Bocking | J.F. Bentley | 1898–9 | CM7 9RS

St Alban, Westcliff-on-Sea | Charles Nicholson | 1898–1904 | SS0 7JY

SS Peter & Paul, Horndon-on-the-Hill | W.D. Caröe, C.R. Ashbee (repairs) | 1898–1904 | SS17 8NS
Cupboards, lectern, chest and possibly other interior furnishings by C.R. Ashbee and GoH; Whall glass.

Central Baptist Church, Chelmsford | William Hayne | 1908–9 | CM1 1LN

Frinton Free Church | William Hayne | 1911 | CO13 9PW

Christ Church, Southchurch, Southend | Charles Nicholson | 1921 | SS1 3BP
Began life as St Peter, Thorpe Bay. Masonic connections. Pulpit, lectern, English altar by Nicholson.

Norfolk

Sanatorium Chapel, High Kelling, Old Cromer | Randall Wells | 1903 | NR25 6QA
Simple indeed – clapboard, and inside plain to a fault. Hard to find. (Not All Saints, High Kelling, 1924.)

St Mary Magdalene, Silver Rd, Norwich | A.J. Lacey | 1902–3 | NR3 4TF

St Barnabas, Heigham, Norwich | A.J. Lacey | 1903–6 | NR2 4QT
Lacey was not adventurous, and his are conservative churches, and inexpensive: Gothic Lite.

Baptist Church, Dereham Rd, Norwich (Potters Church) | Augustus F. Scott | 1904 | NR2 4HS

St Joseph, Sheringham | Giles Gilbert Scott | 1908, 1934 | NR26 8RT
Externally, GGS in something of holiday mood – inside, severe and unbending.

Silver Road Baptist Church, Norwich | Norman Jewson | 1910 | NR3 4RS | **H**
Now a homeless shelter. Careful and craftsmanly brickwork.

Gresham's School Chapel, Holt | John Simpson and Maxwell Ayrton | 1914–16 | NR25 6EA

Suffolk

St Ethelbert, Herringswell | Arthur Blomfield (rebuild) | 1870 | IP28 6ST
Christopher Whall and Paul Woodroffe glass, 1902.

Our Lady & St John (RC), Sudbury | Leonard Stokes | 1893 | CO10 1HP
Re-ordered. As always with Stokes, hard to see quite what makes it Arts & Crafts, yet it somehow nonetheless is.

Our Lady Star of the Sea, Lowestoft (RC) (was Cong) | Baines and Richards | 1900–2 | NR33 0HS

St Andrew & St Patrick, Elveden | W.D. Caröe | 1904–6, 1922 | IP24 3TL
'Art Nouveau Gothic', says Pevsner. Brangwyn window.

Holy Family & St Michael (RC), Kesgrave, Ipswich | Brown and Burgess | 1931, 1950s | IP5 2QP
A gallery of work by the Ropes: glass, cartoons, memorials.

15

THE NORTH WEST OF ENGLAND

Lancashire, Cheshire, Manchester, Liverpool

Whilst the metropolitan self-assurance of London cradled the airy dreams of social democratic artists and young men in spats who could afford to be idealistic, the mercantile imperatives of Manchester and the wider world view of sea-fronted Liverpool subordinated those impulses to harder realities. There was much less consensus; less feeling of a 'movement'. Yes, there was the Northern Art Workers' Guild (1896), but it was small and did not draw in every artistic architect by any means – John Douglas and Medland Taylor, in their different ways, remained apart. Some architects seemed barely aware their churches were employing Arts & Crafts language – Richard Bassnett Preston, for one. The dramatic heart was Edgar Wood, whose flamboyant personality and intellectual grasp were as much European as English – a Middleton Rennie Mackintosh: he had connections in America and showed work at Turin and Brussels. The biggest Lancashire church architectural practice, Paley & Austin (in its various permutations), followed a different path – conservative and closer to a Bodleyan Gothic tradition, only occasionally venturing into something more fluid and adventurous. In 1909 Austin declined an invitation to join the ICBS Architects Committee because he was simply too far from London to attend easily: it did not seem worthwhile when there was so much to do in Lancashire. And, where Church of England and, in particular, Anglo-Catholic clients predominated in the south, artistic church architecture in the North West was driven by dynamic Nonconformists – the Unitarians of Liverpool in particular, but also Christian Scientists. Towards the end of the period, C.H. Reilly, Professor of Architecture at Liverpool University, set a brusquely Neo-Classicist/Modernist agenda, which tended to make Arts & Crafts sentiments look embarrassingly old hat by 1925.

First Church of Christ Scientist, Victoria Park, Manchester

SEFTON PARK, Liverpool

Ullet Road Unitarian Church | 1896–1902
Thomas Worthington & Son
L17 2AA | By arrangement

The robust red-brick bulk of Ullet Road Church is a muscular demonstration of urban wealth, independence of mind and municipal pride. This was (and is) no mere church, but a community centre, educational institute, with library, school room, meeting rooms and hall.

Its congregation began as a Puritan church near the Dingle, in the reign of James I – when Dingle was a village two miles from the port. As it grew, the congregation moved to bigger premises: by 1727 it was one of the most numerous and respectable Dissenter assemblies, including William Roscoe (1753–1831), the city's MP 1806–7, famous for publicly denouncing the slave trade in his home town, England's premier slaving port.

Ullet Road Unitarian Church, Sefton Park, Liverpool: west door by Richard Llewellyn Rathbone

At the opening of their new 1810 chapel in Renshaw Street, the preacher pronounced it to be a Unitarian Chapel, to the horror of many of the older members. In 1894 the Minute Book records it was decided 'the Chapel should be removed into a more residential neighbourhood.' Sefton Park was one of the most expensive and gracious parts of Liverpool – a 200-acre municipal park surrounded by a wide carriageway, with large detached villas around the perimeter, many on an heroic scale. Samuel Greg Rathbone (1823–1903) offered land for the new church next door to his Sefton Park mansion.

The older members warned against the allure of 'more impressive church architecture'. But Charles William Jones, Treasurer of the church Council, and George Holt, pressed ahead regardless – both were partners in the powerful shipowners Lamport & Holt. At the opening service in 1899, the *Daily Post* described a 'fashionable and crowded assembly'.

The interior of the church feels more Anglican than Nonconformist, and more self-consciously beautiful than a Nonconformist church need be: 'it is now certain when the building is completed, the congregation will possess one of the most beautiful churches in Liverpool' mused the Minute Book. The historian of Unitarianism in Liverpool, Anne Holt, writing in 1938, put it thus: 'these Dissenters … had at last been able to lay the bogey of idolatry, and could see in beautiful surroundings influences which could lead to greater awe and reverence.'

Though the exterior was scarlet Ruabon brick, the inside – reputedly at the suggestion of Anne Holt as a very young girl, to her father – was lined in Runcorn warm pinky-purple sandstone. It was expansively equipped – choir stalls with elaborate neo-Gothic architectural niches on a cathedral scale. The local paper said, 'Critically speaking, every hinge and handle, every bit of tracery and carving, is pleasing to the artistic eye, and in every branch work has been accomplished of the highest quality ….'

The architects, Thomas Worthington & Son (they won a competition for the work) were established in Manchester as *the* Unitarian architectural practice. Thomas (1826–1909) was active in voluntary societies promoting reform. By 1895 the bulk of their work was being carried out by his son Percy (1864–1939), a partner from 1891. He was instrumental in the creation of a school of architecture in the university. 'The architects … have evidently spent the most loving care in securing harmony and beauty throughout this important work.'

In 1900 two more merchant princes funded an expansion. John Brunner (1842–1919) founded Mond & Co in 1874 – which became ICI. Henry Tate (1819–99) made his fortune from West Indies sugar and the invention of the sugar cube. They funded a Church Hall, library, school room, meeting rooms, all designed by Percy Worthington, and, importantly, a cloister passage in which tablets commemorating leading members of the congregation could be displayed – a sort of Unitarian Valhalla.

The artist-craftsmen who worked on Ullet Road were clearly in sympathy with Arts & Crafts ideas. Richard Llewellyn Benson Rathbone (*c.*1864–1939, AWG 1892) designed memorial plaques at the church, and made the massive bronze doors to the north, west and south of the lobby to the church, praised in the press: 'particularly worthy of examination, not only because of the beauty in design, but by the perfect workmanship'. The light fittings were made by the Artificers' Guild. In 1900 Gerald Moira (1867–1959, AWG 1898) was commissioned to decorate the new library. His first major public work had been friezes for the Trocadero restaurant in London, 1896. His are the motifs over the stage at the Wigmore Hall.

In 1906 the most 'Arts & Crafts object' appeared: the movable font by Ronald Potter

Ullet Road Unitarian Church: the movable font by R. P. Jones

Jones (1876–1965, AWG 1909), a member of the Century Guild. He became perhaps the leading Unitarian architect of the early 20th century. He wrote *Nonconformist Church Architecture* (1914), and designed two Unitarian churches, at West Kirby and Cambridge, both 1928. In 1957 Jones wrote a detailed eye-witness account of the building of Ullet Road.

The church is at once old-fashioned – big, rather ungainly, full of stained glass and enormous stone and woodwork – and new: Arts & Crafts overlays an excessively dignified church, lending a touch of youthful light-heartedness and egalitarianism to the serious intent of its grandly philanthropic congregation. Neither quite city munificence, nor yet suburban comfort.

WALLASEY

Unitarian Church, Liscard | 1898–9
Ware and Rathbone
CH44 1DA | By arrangement (HCT)

Unitarianism started on the Wirral in 1888; there was an 'iron church' at Liscard from 1892. The Chairman of the Church Committee died in 1896: his widow, Martha Elam, gave money for the building of the new church. She appointed Edmund Ware (1852–1934) and Edmund Rathbone (1863–1924) as her architects in 1897, before she had selected a Building Committee, possibly because they had recently designed the nearby school hall at Egremont Baptist

Unitarian Church, Liscard, Wallasey: communion table painting by Bernard Sleigh, detail

Church, Wallasey (1896). Ware and Rathbone were committed Unitarians – the connection was close and strong. *The Studio* approved: 'There is something very fresh, unconventional and fitting in the design …'

Edmund Rathbone was the Liverpool representative of the Century Guild. He ran The City Beautiful Wayside Café, a meeting place for Liverpool's artistic elite. He was also a poet: in 1907 he wrote, 'let me make pretence, however small | Humanity to serve, and citizen to be!' His brother, Harold (1858–1929) founded the Della Robbia pottery company in Birkenhead; his cousin, Richard Llewelyn Rathbone, made the doors at Ullet Road. The Rathbone family were patrons of Ullet Road: it is hard to disentangle now, but the younger generation, at Wallasey, was possibly at variance with the older at Ullet Road, and more forward-looking.

The decorative ironwork on the street is by Walter Gilbert, who co-founded the Bromsgrove Guild (see p.165). Benjamin Creswick (1853–1946) of Birmingham, also of the Guild, made the figures sculpted in the porch – not the four Evangelists, but – as befits a more artistic worldview, perhaps – Meditation, Eloquence, Devotion and Music. He also carved the figures on the choir stalls. The coppered bronze hanging light fittings are by Gilbert, 1899, as is the sinuously foliaged lectern.

Unitarian Church, Liscard, Wallasey: pulpit stair painted by Bernard Sleigh

The bench ends, pulpit and communion table were painted by Bernard Sleigh (also of the Guild). It may seem odd to have his PRB 'stunners' on pew ends, but it was not intended to shock, rather to reflect an acceptable view of connections between heaven and earth. (Sleigh's religious inclinations are not known – but he did believe in fairies.) The panels on the pulpit show Intellectual Truth, Moral Goodness and Spiritual Beauty; on the choir stalls, the Four Elements; on the table, Christ in Majesty, and Faith and Charity on either side. The panel above the altar, fulfilling in part the office of a reredos, is from the Della Robbia Pottery – the largest piece they ever made. The congregational seating was originally stained green – another Arts & Crafts motif.

The contrast with Ullet Road is striking – there gravitas, here levity; there hints of conventional Anglicanism, here purposeful unorthodoxy. Employing the Bromsgrove Guild, in particular Sleigh and Gilbert, to decorate the interior, expressed not only the new generation of Unitarians' awareness of European artistic ideas, but a commitment to liberal, even humanist values.

MIDDLETON

Methodist Church, Long Street | 1899–1901
Edgar Wood
M24 6UN | By arrangement

In 2014 the supporters of Edgar Wood's Middleton church registered their website as artsandcraftschurch.org – they go so far as to call their church 'The Arts & Crafts Church' on their website's opening page. As if it is and was the only one. Good for them. Their determination, enthusiasm and enterprise has not so much saved the church (which it has – there is a vigorous continuing programme of restoration, redecoration and re-presentation) as given Middleton a focal point for civic pride, separated it from the mass of towns subsumed into Greater Manchester (whose dominance it resists), and reminded those who bother about these things that there is more to 'Arts & Crafts church' than Sloane Street, Roker and Brockhampton.

Edgar Wood (1860–1935) is the sort of local hero every town needs. He rarely worked

Methodist Church, Long Street, Middleton: pulpit

beyond Middleton's boundaries, and then principally in towns around Manchester; everything he designed has interest and flair; he was himself a flamboyant character, theatrically extravert in cape, floppy tie and wide-brimmed hat – the very image of the architect as artist – though in manner oddly shy and disinclined to lead. He was the first Secretary of the Northern AWG, founded by Walter Crane in 1896, though not formally affiliated to its London predecessor, the AWG, of which Wood was not a member (though the NAWG included some members who were AWG). In the Arts & Crafts way, he was an architect who also designed jewellery, stained glass, plasterwork and furniture, though he did not make any of these.

His father was in cotton, and Edgar was intended to go into the family business. But he was instinctively repelled by what he called 'the solemnity of commerce.' He wanted to be an artist. Architecture was, it seems, the compromise.

Methodism was a force in Middleton from the 1760s. A procession of 1400 Methodists round the town in 1890 to celebrate the centenary of the first chapel led to fund-raising for something bigger and better. The church (rather than the rest of the complex, perhaps) reminds many of Art Nouveau in its details. It is stylistically close to the sorts of devices Mackintosh employed at the Glasgow School of Art – if less exaggerated. Wood was far too grounded to be a 'Spook', but there are direct similarities with Mackintosh's Queen's Cross Church. Being out of London had advantages for risk-taking minds.

The several foundation stones are carved, as is often the case in NC churches, with benefactors' initials – but where else are they so stylishly stylised? Inside, the bronze figure on the font is by Thomas Stirling Lee (1857–1916, AWG 1889, and NAWG). The pulpit figure is reported to be his also. The metalwork in copper, including a commemorative plaque to the Rector, Robert Catterall, 1911, is by James Smithies (NAWG) who showed work with the ACES; the woodwork by James Lenagan, who taught at Middleton Technical Classes; the painting probably by Frederick Jackson (NAWG), a friend of Wood's, who painted the original mural in Wood's first Unitarian commission, the Middleton Unitarian Church (1892). (Wood was a life-long Unitarian.) The glass in the doors is Mackintosh in spirit if not in fact – Glasgow roses. The congregational benches

Methodist Church, Long Street, Middleton: glass in internal door

were originally stained green, to contrast with the orangey-red walls.

Wood's other churches demonstrate a wide range of approaches and a readiness to address any spiritual agenda: **Temple Street Baptist Church, Middleton**, 1889 (M24 2HL), now a nursery, and private; Old Road Unitarian Church, Middleton (1892), demolished in 1965; **Silver Street Chapel, Rochdale**, 1893 (OL12 6QG), at the time of writing closed and for sale; St Aidan's Mission church, Marland, Rochdale (1897), demolished in 1960; and **The First Church of Christ Scientist, Victoria Park**, 1903–7, whose history has been chequered (p.231). Wood also provided the furnishings for the Wesleyan Methodist church, Lindley, Huddersfield, Yorkshire, 1894–5.

His spiritual stance can best be summed up by the inscription on the steps leading to Jubilee Park, Middleton: 'Who works not for his fellows starves his soul. His thoughts grow poor and dwindle, and his heart grudges each beat, as misers do the dole.'

LOW MARPLE, Cheshire

St Martin | 1868–70, 1895, 1909
John Dando Sedding and Henry Wilson
SK6 5DT | By arrangement

The client was Ann Hudson, a wealthy Anglo-Catholic who did not approve of the low worship at the parish church, All Saints. She gave the site: her daughter Maria Anne paid for the building. The commission was won by Edmund Sedding, but he died after making initial proposals, and his brother John Dando took over, building chancel and nave – the church sat just 224. Sedding also designed the screen, 1888 (but not the rood above it: and the small Christ is clearly from another source); the gilded alabaster reredos; pulpit with bronze panels by Richard Arthur Ledward (1857–1890, AWG 1888); the font; and, outside, the lych gate and the Hudson family memorial cross to the north of the church.

After Sedding's death in 1891, Henry Wilson took over. In 1895 he added the north aisle and Lady Chapel, with a gesso ceiling of swallows (why not martins?), golden trees and owls, by Christopher Whall. Whall also painted the reredos, which shows Mary (reportedly a portrait of Miss Hudson) greeted by Gabriel on the banks of the (nearby) River Goyt. Wilson designed the altar, altar rails, inlaid gates (made by Trasks) and candlesticks (Longden & Co.). Foliate panels – some suave, some rugged. The nearby reliquary (containing

St Martin, Low Marple: sanctuary panel, seemingly designed by John Dando Sedding

no relic) is also by Wilson: Christ crucified atop a fortified hill, with four blue-green rivers.

In 1900 Wilson designed the elaborate font cover in ebony and white fruit wood with a border of lively fish. It is suspended from a complex openwork orb and circling dove.

In 1909 the St Christopher Chapel was added, with its huge, David-like figure of the saint, designed and modelled by Wilson, opposite the south door – the church wall had to be pushed out to accommodate it. The heavy marble frame, with chequerwork panels, though Wilsonian in taste, seems to not quite fit the figure. The door to the north aisle – the west end is now the vestry – has a dark,

St Martin, Low Marple: Lady Chapel ceiling

convoluted Wilson handle outside. Then Wilson's sombre War Memorial plaque, 1924.

The east window has figures variously by Morris, Burne-Jones, Rossetti and Madox Brown – conservation is being discussed. The west window is by Whall, 1892; and also his in the south aisle, 1899.

In the sanctuary, on the wall, a panel of three angels, as if one wing of a triptych, the outlines in raised mastic. It looks like the work of Heywood Sumner, but was seemingly designed by Sedding, all that survives of a more ambitious scheme – but for where? And why? And who made it?

The St Martin's Heritage Trust is steadily and knowledgeably cleaning, conserving and restoring the interior.

FOUR DEBATABLE ARCHITECTS

Between 1880 and 1920 the North West was as full of church and chapel building as anywhere – fuller. But, apart from the churches of Edgar Wood, and the two Unitarian churches on Merseyside (pp 220 and 222), few individuals or practices can unquestionably be understood as Arts & Crafts. And, for the purposes of this study, architects ought to belong to the AWG – but, so far from London, they tended not to; or exhibit with the ACES – which, on the whole, as they were not makers, they did not.

What remains discernible is a response, conscious or unconscious, by architects to what was in the air – to the new churches published in journals, to new fashions in ornament and materials, and to the notion that a church was not now only a machine for worshipping in, but an expression of an individual or a congregation's (and architect's) interest in spirituality, religious sentiment, feelings, beauty, and the desire to articulate those intangibles in new visual languages.

It is no good trying to maintain hard borders when there is so much cultural osmosis about.

JOHN DOUGLAS

John Douglas (1830–1911) was prodigiously prolific: he designed around 500 buildings, and upwards of 40 churches. At first, 1860–84, he worked alone, then went into partnership, 1884–98, first with Daniel Porter Fordham (1846–99), then, 1898–1909, with Charles Howard Minshull (1858–1934), before reverting to sole practice for his last years. His principal client was Hugh Lupus Grosvenor (1825–99), Duke of Westminster, for whom he carried out many estate projects – the Duke's lands included much of North Wales, and Douglas churches are to be found, therefore, on pp 280 and 284 as well as here.

Douglas's biographer Edward Hubbard identified 1870 as Douglas's watershed: 'On the one hand was a more solemn age, with Gothic of strongly religious affinity pursued as a crusade by its serious-minded proponents. On the other was an age more redolent of the social graces … whose moral earnestness was that of William Morris ... rather than that of the ecclesiologists.' Douglas's Vernacular Revival and 'Old English' manner – to use Hubbard's stylistic analysis – could best be observed at **St Paul, Boughton, Chester**, 1876; new aisle 1902 (CH3 5UL), alas closed in 2016, but most endearingly at the sweet, half-timbered **St Michael, Altcar**, 1878–9 (L37 5AA), 'a complete historical pastiche' where, Hubbard suggests, 'one can wallow in the sheer beauty of the wood.' This, had Douglas been working in the south, might have foreshadowed an Arts & Crafts career – as, for example, with Nicholson at Curbridge (p.70).

Douglas's next churches are altogether more circumspect and conventional: **St Mary, Pulford**, 1881–4 (CH4 9EY); **St Werburgh, Warburton**, 1882–5 (WA13 9SS); and, in more expansive vein – and now in partnership with Fordham – **St Andrew, West Kirby, Wirral**, 1889–91; east end 1907 (CH48 5DW), with its imposing reredos, and Biblical texts carved in Gothic ribbons on the outside walls. Douglas revisited the vernacular at **St James, Haydock**, 1889–91 (WA11 0NJ) with its curious combination of brick-nogged walls and inset wooden tracery windows, and an open-work pulpit reminiscent of Woolmer Green (p.130). Experience seemed to generate greater invention. At **St Wenefrede, Bickley**, 1892 (SY13 4EB) there is a beam carved and painted with a minatory quotation from the Book of Habbakuk; and picturesque rood beam and reredos survive at the now evangelical **Christ Church, Chester**, 1893–1904 (CH1 3JD). **St John the Evangelist, Weston, Runcorn**, 1895–8 (WA7 4LY), perched above

St Paul, Boughton, Chester: reredos, detail

ring road and chemical works, exerts great toy-town charm – a country church despite it all. **St John the Evangelist, Sandiway**, 1902 (CW8 2JU), in Douglas's natal village, is a 'dear little toy church in the better than Caröe manner one expected from *happy* Douglas', according to Goodhart-Rendel. **Hope Church, Hoylake**, 1905–6 (CH47 4AA) (was Congregational; reordered), has windows by Henry Gustave Hiller (1922), and A.J. Davies (1977–1953) of the Bromsgrove Guild.

Left: St Michael, Altcar
Right: St Katherine, Blackrod: reredos

RICHARD BASSNETT PRESTON

Richard Bassnett Preston ARIBA (1855–1934) was not a member of any Arts & Crafts body, nor was he necessarily 'Arts & Crafts' in instincts or outlook. He is thought of – if thought of at all – as 'merely' a Lancashire provincial architect, with offices in Diocesan Chambers, Manchester. Some of his churches are pedestrian, but some, seen by the light of Arts & Crafts aesthetics, have an engaging, albeit muffled, artistic liveliness, and very often contain good craft skills with thoughtful detailing. Yes, they can seem to be pale imitations of Bodley (often in harsh brick), but often there is more. He loved mosaic pavements in the sanctuary, and intricate reredoses.

Emmanuel, Southport, 1895–8 (PR9 9PR) is ponderous, but has a dashing Great War Memorial screen and bookstand with carved service-men and women by W.E. Vernon Crompton (AWG 1916). **St Alban, Offerton, Stockport**, 1896–1900 (SK2 5AG) has a handsome pulpit and dwarf screen. **St Michael, Foulridge**, 1903–5 (BB8 7NP) has green-stained benches, an elaborate gesso reredos and a font in the manner of Laurence Turner. The font at **St Cuthbert, Burnley**, 1906 (BB10 1UL) is similar, but in marble. There is fine glass at **St John the Evangelist, Old Trafford**, 1907–8 (M16 7GX); an intriguing *faux naif* gesso reredos with Burne-Jones angels and altar at **St Katharine, Blackrod**, 1910–11 (BL6 5EN); intense woodwork at **Holy Trinity, Colne**, 1910–12 (BB8 8JE). At **St Anne, Lydgate**, 1910–11 (OL4 4JJ), Preston made an earnest attempt at something classical. At **St John, Furness Vale**, 1912 (SK23 7PX), near Stockport, there is inventive tracery, and sensitive wood carving in the pulpit and choir stalls – it is also the church of his that *looks* most Arts & Crafts from the road.

Surely the most fully realised – and now the saddest – is **St Thomas, Leigh, Wigan**, 1902–9 (WN7 2DB), with naturalistic squirrels, a lion and seabirds on the choir stalls, a powerful carved and painted reredos, a big-boned pulpit – all now derelict and relentlessly vandalised.

JAMES MEDLAND TAYLOR

James Medland Taylor (1834–1909), who had worked with S.S. Teulon, practised with his brother Henry (1837–1916), from an office in St Ann's Churchyard, Manchester. Medland's son, Isaac (1871–1948) joined the practice, and there were architect cousins, uncles and nephews. An aunt wrote 'Twinkle, twinkle little star'. The brothers' practice was essentially ecclesiastical: they built about fifty churches, of which perhaps half have been demolished. They are, on the whole, cheap and cheerful in no-nonsense Ruabon brick, often with the bustling air of a Victorian railway station or small factory. Pevsner identified a 'quirky inventiveness, a love of oddity and an element of risk-taking and willingness to experiment'.

St Mary, Haughton Green, 1874–6 (M34 7GD) has the raw energy of a mission church, but with the bonus of vigorous and original woodwork

and glass. (The brothers had added transepts to medieval St Laurence, Denton in similar vein in 1872.) Nearby, the thrillingly hectic **St Anne, Haughton, Denton**, 1881 (M34 3EF) was built for a mill-owning chemist with an interest in botany, Edward Joseph Sidebotham, and is full of flower imagery in mosaic, glass and stone, and marguerite daisies (symbol of St Anne) in memory of his late wife.

With one eye, this all looks over-wrought Victorian – with another, craftsmanship, perhaps over-zealous, sacrificing restraint to delight. Why not? At **St James, Gatley**, 1881 (SK8 4NF) – reportedly built, and perhaps furnished, by the villagers – restraint is not much in evidence. There is even more *joie de vivre* at **All Saints, Great Saughall**, 1895–6 and 1909–11 (CH1 6EW). (See also St Mark, Bestwood, Notts, p.195.) Flamboyance is no crime. One of the principal mourners at Medland Taylor's funeral was Edgar Wood.

PALEY & AUSTIN: AUSTIN & PALEY

By far the busiest church architectural practice of the period in Lancashire was the practice started by Edmund Sharpe (1809–77) in 1835. By 1868 it was Paley & Austin; from 1886 Paley Austin & Paley; in 1895 Austin & Paley; briefly in 1914 Austin Paley & Austin; and finally, from 1915 Austin & Paley again, disappearing by 1944. They did far more than churches, and they worked further afield than Lancashire – but this was their heartland. (However, see Hertford, p.139.)

Between 1886 and 1915 they built or rebuilt 52 churches and four school chapels. The practice was not associated with the AWG, nor NAWG. They made no great point about working on equal footing with craftsmen. Do any of their churches show signs of Arts & Crafts influence – foregrounded craftsmanship, conscious but unnecessary beauty, self-conscious Olde Worlde charm? Only the most indulgent observer would see it. There is a regularity, discipline, even severity, all of which sits ill with Arts & Crafts adventure and individuality. It is all a bit regimented – but, with so many churches to choose from, there are gladsome glimmers here and there.

The prettiest churches tend to be the smallest – **St Mark, Dolphinholme**, 1897–8 (LA2 9AJ) is made to look cute by its position, and its squat, fat tower, and, internally, its barn-like timber roof can be interpreted as in Arts & Crafts taste. At **Good Shepherd, Tatham Fells**, 1888–9 (LA2 8PU) they built a church for Arthur Foster, whose wife was later to ask Lethaby to build them All Saints, Brockhampton. **St John, Flookburgh**, 1897–1900 (LA11 7JY) is honest and unfussy, almost delightful. In the 1920s, practising on his own, Harry Paley (1859–1946) showed all sorts of sparks of invention – **St Hilda, Bilsborrow**, 1926–8 (PR3 0RP) stands out. But it remained all very proper.

St Anne, Haughton, Denton
St Hilda, Bilsborrow: pulpit and chancel

VICTORIA PARK, Manchester

First Church of Christ Scientist | 1903–7
Edgar Wood
M14 5GH | Wedding and events venue

The culminating ecclesiastical building in Edgar Wood's career was for a very rich Christian Scientist in South Manchester, Lady Victoria Alexandrina Murry, daughter of the Earl of Dunmore, and a godchild of Queen Victoria. As at Middleton – which Wood had just completed – it is a grouping of worship space and ancillary buildings, most importantly, a Reading Room. Originally Wood planned a quadrangle with one side open, as at Middleton, but in the end, it was laid out in a modified butterfly, or Y-plan.

First Church of Christ Scientist, Daisy Bank, Victoria Park, Manchester: main-door doorplates

Its life has been difficult. In 1971 the church closed suddenly, and thieves swiftly looted all the valuable and portable metals. After a long period of casual vandalism, it was restored by Manchester City Council by 1975, and then variously an annexe to the Manchester School of Domestic Economy ('Domski'); around 1980, the Edgar Wood Centre, a drama and music department of Manchester College of Higher Education; and offices for Manchester City Council. In the 21st century it became the Manchester branch of the United Churches of the Kingdom of God, an evangelical church of Brazilian origin. Since they left in 2015, it has been lavishly developed as a wedding and events venue, and is once again 'The Edgar Wood Centre'.

The interior was, bit by bit, stripped of all its furnishings: what remained were the Arabian screen (*mushrabiyyah*) at the 'west' end, and elements of the marble-lined apse at the 'east'. The worship space in Christian Science is essentially an auditorium – there are no processions or liturgical set pieces. But there is much reading aloud, so an elevated 'east' end: Wood designed chairs for it, some of which are now in the Whitworth, along with a lectern. The stained-glass windows were designed by Benjamin Nelson (who trained at Central School), saved from destruction. Outside, the steep front gable has windows in a cruciform; the main entrance has double doors and exotic doorplates. To the side, a port-cochere with 'God is Love' in plasterwork over the door, and remnants of abstract motifs in the stonework and rainwater goods.

HALE, Cheshire

St Peter | 1890–2
Tate & Popplewell
WA15 9SS | By arrangement

The buff and pink church has no great Arts & Crafts feel from outside. Inside, things are very different – warm, glowing and intimate.

St Peter, Hale:
Great War Memorial plaque by Walter J. Pearce

The huge clerestory windows are a magical array by Heaton, Butler & Bayne of 1910, reportedly designed by Walter J. Pearce (1856–1942), who certainly painted the figurative panels in the glass mosaic and marble walls either side of the War Memorial baptistry. Pearce was a founder member, 1896, and later Master of the NAWG, and until 1917 Head of the Painting and Decorating Department at Manchester Municipal School of Art. He co-authored *Stencils and Stencilling* (1895) and wrote *Painting and Decorating* (1898). (There is a complete scheme by Pearce at St Mary, Martlesham, Suffolk; and a set of elaborate flower windows at Didsbury URC church.)

The altar has Aesthetic panels of lilies. The lectern is not an eagle, but a lissom angel. There are massy Edwardian chandeliers and crisp artistic choir stalls.

EARBY

All Saints | 1909–12
Bromet and Thorman
BB18 6JL | By arrangement

Earby is only just (and recently) in Lancashire – it was in Yorkshire until 1974. This may explain why a Tadcaster architect practice built this church, rather than Austin & Paley, whose rather mundane proposal did not succeed.

The present church is hardly revolutionary, but its character and detail blossom as you climb the hill and look inside. Communion rails, reredos, 1923, by Ralph Hedley (1848–1913) (p.265). On the stone pulpit, a devil with pointed tail clings tenaciously. Simple vernacular light fittings.

All Saints has an unusually large architectural archive: presentation drawings, coloured sections and plans, and many working drawings, for example for the door latches by George Wragge. The drawings – there are about 100 – were found in a wet cellar, and carefully and lovingly dried out by a conscientious member of the congregation. They need conserving – and writing up (there is a PhD to be had). This is not a rich church – they do not want to be inundated by antiquarians or rubber-neckers … but it would be wonderful if someone reading this were to write the PCC a big fat cheque.

BRIGGS, WOLSTENHOLME & THORNELY

Frank Gatley Briggs (1862–1921) and Henry Vernon Wolstenholme (1863–1936) both started in Blackburn, and were well-established in Liverpool when Arnold Thornely (1870–1953) joined the practice in 1906. Before then, Briggs and Wolstenholme had designed police courts, fire stations, a library and town hall; then, alongside Thornely (BWT) and another partner F.B. Hobbs, the Mersey Docks and Harbour Building (1903–7), one of the 'Three Graces'.

BWT's strong suit was the municipal, but in their early days, three churches.

Liverpool Bluecoat School, Wavertree is stolid, muted Edwardian Baroque. The chapel is to match, rather with the character of a Carnegie Library, but with a dome, and internally rather coolly classical.

At **Egremont** BWT's Arts & Crafts associations are clearest, though the church closed in 2011, and it is currently to let. The windows survive at the time of writing, and are a primer of 1900s Arts & Crafts glass: designs by Burne-Jones, Gilbert P. Gamon of Chester, the Percy Bacon brothers, Wilhelmina Geddes, John Houghton Bonnor of the Artificers' Guild, Edward Woore, who had worked with Whall, Henry Gustave Hiller, who had studied under Walter Crane, and William Aikman, who had been with Powells, and latterly taught at Camberwell. It is one of those churches crying out for rescue – far too big, but heart-rendingly beautiful. As recently as 2008 it drew attention to itself as a *vade mecum* of Arts & Crafts glass for the North-west. Now it is dark and forlorn, its future uncertain.

The White Church, Fairhaven – which the practice won in a four-way competition – was a dramatic departure. Did Thornely's increasing importance in the practice bring new verve? The church is dazzling Byzantine (seemingly influenced by Westminster Cathedral's success) in white Ceramo tiles (by Middleton Fireclay, Leeds), for the Congregationalists (UFC since 1972). It was unapologetically to be a distinctive architectural feature of the district. The rationale for the tiles was their being proof against sea, sand and salt.

Inside, in an altogether calmer mood, the pulpit – originally placed centrally – has beaten brass War Memorial panels by Walter Marsden (1882–1969, AWG 1930). The narrative windows – key moments in scripture and church history – were made by Abbott & Co. of Lancaster to designs by their designer Charles Elliot, from a scheme conceived, through much prayer, and supervised, by local *éminence grise*, Luke Slater Walmsley (1841–1922), retired carver and gilder and art dealer, the driving force behind the church, and an admirer of Ruskin: in 1985 his son left Ruskin's bookcase to the National Trust.

BWT also designed the unremarkable Hollins Road Congregational Church, Darwen, 1907. Thornely earlier, with W.G. Fraser, designed the Presbyterian church at Blundellsands, 1898–1905.

The Chapel at Liverpool Bluecoat School
Wavertree | 1903–6
L15 9EE | Private

Egremont URC
Wallasey | 1907–10
nr CH44 0EE | Closed

The White Church
Fairhaven | 1911–12
FY8 1AX | By arrangement

Top: The White Church, Fairhaven; *Left:* Egremont United Reformed Church, Wallasey from the west

Other Churches

Cheshire

St John, High Legh, Knutsford | Edmund Kirby | 1893 | WA16 6ND
The Arts & Crafts spirit, if not the practice. Kirby was assistant to John Douglas, and master to W.D. Caröe.

Our Lady & the Apostles (RC), Stockport | Edmund Kirby | 1903–5 | SK3 8BQ
In an immense expanse of brick, inventive and well-intentioned wood carving.

Christ Church, Port Sunlight, Wirral | William and Segar Owen | 1904 | CH62 5EF

St Oswald, Bollington | Frank Oakley | 1907–8 | SK10 5EG

St Paul, Over Tabley | Anthony Salvin | 1853–5 | near WA16 0PP
Screen by Fred Crossley 1908, tester 1915, altar rails?; windows by Whall; Eric Gill monument in churchyard.

St John Bosco Chapel, Shrigley | Philip Tilden | 1933 | SK10 5SB
Now the spa at Shrigley Hall wedding venue: some stonework detail survives. Private.

Lancashire

Emmanuel (FCE), Morecambe | Architect not known | 1886 | LA4 6HJ
Mission church with big ideas and carpentry – some fine, some primitive.

Holy Trinity, Southport | Huon Matear | 1895, 1903–1913 | PR9 9DX
Furnishings by the Bromsgrove Guild.

St Paul (FCE), Fleetwood | Stephen Frost Johnson | 1908 | FY7 7AP
A congregation member acquired a block-making machine: and the congregation then built the church themselves.

St Mary & All Saints, Whalley | medieval | 1909 | BB7 9SY
'Done up' in SPAB spirit: work by George Jack, Christopher Whall.

St Leonard, Downham, Bowland | Mervyn Macartney | 1909–10 | BB7 4BJ
'No surprises', says Pevsner, rightly. But Macartney did co-found the AWG.

Blackpool Reform Synagogue | R.B. Mather | 1914–16 | FY1 4EX
Abandoned and for sale – by date it might have been Arts & Crafts (The last service, 2012, is on YouTube).

All Saints, Wallasey (Jubilee Church) | Giles Gilbert Scott | 1915, 1927 | CH45 0LB
Drastically re-ordered. Stencilled roof and glass may survive.

Unitarian Church, West Kirby | R.P. Jones | 1928 | CH48 4EL
Now Arts Centre.

Isle of Man

Our Lady Star of the Sea, Ramsey | Giles Gilbert Scott | 1909–12 | IM8 1BH
Full of Arts & Crafts-y ideas – font, painted beams, reredos, stonework.

St Ninian, Douglas | W.D. Caröe | 1914 | IM2 5BT

Greater Manchester

St Paul, Heaton Moor | Frank Oakley (extension) | 1896 | SK4 4RY
Merely Edwardian meets Victorian? But look at those choir stalls. Reredos by R. Bassnett Preston.

Christ Church, Moss Side | W. Cecil Hardisty | 1899–1904 | M14 4GP
A heavy-handed rapture: reredos, font cover, exterior stonework. Font from Tapper's demolished St Erkenwald.

St Mark, Levenshulme | C.T. Taylor | 1900 | M19 3NF
As if Baines in understated, modest, artistic mood – Art Nouveau detailing on piers; homely screen.

St Hilda, Prestwich | Frank Oakley | 1904 | M25 1HA
Struggles not to be Victorian, with mixed success.

St Matthew, Crumpsall | Isaac Taylor | 1910 | M8 4QU
After Medland Taylor's vigour, his son reveals a fragile sensitivity: label stops, font, organ case, glass.

Synagogue, Wilbraham Rd, Fallowfield | Joseph Sunlight | 1913 | M14 6JS
Closed. Plans exist to turn it into student accommodation. Online images of the interior are suggestive.

St Joseph (RC), Longsight | Lowther & Rigby | 1915 | M13 0BU
Sinuous stonework, Deco-ish glazing, rustic light fittings – the details are right, even if the whole is not quite it.

Liverpool and Merseyside

Gustav Adolfus Kyrka | W. D. Caröe | 1883–4 | L1 8HG
His first commission – otherwise, only tangentially relevant.

St Clare (RC), Sefton Park | Leonard Stokes | 1889–90 | L17 2AU
As ever, the 'RC Arts & Crafts architect' fails to quite persuade. Reredos by Anning Bell and George Frampton.

St Andrew, Stanley Rd, Litherland | Willink & Thicknesse | 1903–4 | L20 5AE
Closed and for sale.

Liverpool Cathedral Lady Chapel | Giles Gilbert Scott | 1904–6 | L1 7AZ
The last of Gothic? Start here to understand the transition. Noble Women windows; reredos; carvings. Stupendous.

Emmanuel Church, Fazakerley | W.H. Ward & W.G. St J. Cogswell | 1908 | L9 9DJ
Ward was pupil to Arthur Blomfield, improver with Ernest George, assistant to Lutyens. Vigorous and unfussy.

St Nathanael, Walton-on-the-Hill | Frank Rimmington | 1909 | L9 2AJ

St Paul, Stoneycroft | Giles Gilbert Scott | 1913–16 | L13 3DJ
Now St Mary & St Cyril Coptic Orthodox church. Brobdingnagian. Re-ordered.

St Pius X (RC), Upper Parliament St | W. H. Ansell | 1914 | L8 7LA
Built as Temple of Humanity; subsequently 3rd Church of Christ Scientist. For sale.

16

YORKSHIRE

In Yorkshire, the Arts & Crafts lack any local exponent, save perhaps the woodcarver Robert 'Mouseman' Thompson of Kilburn (1876–1955), who came slightly later, as part of a resurgence of craft in the 1920s, and whose craft, thanks to his whimsical device, can look like a pose, which it wasn't. The only Yorkshire architect with 'Arts & Crafts' to be found against his name with any frequency in modern assessments, is Walter Henry Brierley of York (1862–1926). Nonetheless, there were architects following a path very similar in love and respect for craftsmanship – Robert James Johnson (1832–92), for one.

And there were those who, either from an instinct towards the modern, or the fashionable, or because it was commercially expedient to *look* like it, were a *bit* Arts & Crafts – W. J. Hale of Sheffield, Garside & Pennington of Pontefract, Chorley & Connon of Leeds, for example, knew what was happening in the wider aesthetic world and responded to it with varying degrees of warmth.

In the landscape of the Dales or the Wolds the fripperies of the Arts & Crafts might have looked mere affectations. Even David Hockney becomes matter-of-fact when painting Yorkshire landscapes. And there is, perhaps, a taste in the county for low-cost solutions. Meanwhile incomers, and those trying to make a splash, brought in the latest ideas to impress the locals – as with Norman Shaw at Ilkley. And there is a long tail of Arts & Crafts-looking buildings well into the 1930s, which could be explained by a tendency for fashion to take time to catch on.

Against this backdrop, the opportunity arises to foreground some churches that might slip under the radar elsewhere, which, if they may not quite 'be' Arts & Crafts, indicate there is something novel, anti-Victorian and original in the architectural air. Or perhaps it is plain Yorkshire cussedness.

St Clement, Barkerend, Bradford: sanctuary ceiling

BARKEREND, Bradford

St Clement | 1892–4
E.P. Warren
BD3 9DF | By arrangement

On its cover, the church guidebook modestly proclaims it 'An Arts & Crafts church'. Its slightly dour exterior conceals a heart of gold.

This was the first commission of Edward Prioleau Warren (1856–1937, AWG 1892). He designed seven churches in all, and altered or added to a handful more. He was more a house man, and schools and hospitals – and his brother was President of Magdalen College, Oxford, so he had work there. He trained under Bodley, and was on the ICBS Architects Committee (along with – in 1909 – John Oldrid Scott, Temple Moore, C.H. Mileham, Fellowes Prynne, Caröe, Prior, Hodgson Fowler, Bidlake, Charles Spooner and Aston Webb).

The client was Frances Sarah Whittuck, née Butler (1845–1916), daughter of the Lord of the Manor, Viscount Mountgarret. It was built as a memorial to her mother, Frances Penelope (d.1886). There is a memorial plaque (by whom?) in which Sarah, as donor, holds the church devoutly in her hands. Sarah married Edward Arthur Whittuck of Claverton Manor, Bath, so there may have been a West Country connection: Warren was born in Bristol. Whittuck had been a law tutor at Oriel College, so there may have been an Oxford connection too. The Whittucks seem to have lived a rather swish, moneyed London life. The church was extravagantly costly: £23,000, when churches were being built elsewhere for £5,000. This was as fashionable and showy as could be.

The gesso ceiling was designed by Burne-Jones and executed by Morris & Co. Comparisons have been made with Morris's work for Pugin on the ceiling at Jesus College, Cambridge: but that was executed in 1867, 25 years earlier. Barkerend is richer and denser, and has something of the air of Mary Watts at

St Clement, Barkerend, Bradford: spandrel angel

Compton (p.92) or of Bodley's church interiors at Jesus Lane, Cambridge, where Kempe had a hand. The rather solemn angels in the spandrels are also to Burne-Jones designs, 1900–01, but executed in an altogether more homespun manner, suggesting local hands.

The pulpit was 'inspired' by Morris, but its designer and maker are not recorded. It has a robust Jacobethan air, on jaunty wooden legs, like a Toby jug. The wall paintings in the sanctuary, 1898–1900, are by William Mainwaring Palin (1862–1947), who had been apprenticed at Wedgwoods in Stoke, then established himself as a decorator with an ambitious allegorical scheme at Rowand Anderson's opulent McEwan Hall, Edinburgh University, 1894–7. His Crucifixion has, it seems, only women mourning Christ. The reredos is by Salviati. The windows are by Kempe – why not Morris & Co.?

CROSS GREEN, The Bank, Leeds

St Hilda | 1876–82
John Thomas Micklethwaite
LS9 0DG | Often open

There are Micklethwaite (and Somers Clarke) churches all over the country. If you only see one, see this. That it is more or less unchanged makes it all the more worthy of study and appreciation.

St Hilda was built before the founding of the AWG, so it might best be considered as a 'pre-cursor' (p.316). However, whilst almost all the interior furnishings are to Micklethwaite designs, they were largely made and installed in the 1920s. The church is thus a loving, scholarly version of itself – conceived before there was any Arts & Crafts, but fulfilled in its aftermath.

The outside is frowning red brick, slightly daunting, 'in Gothic Revival style' according to the HE listing. Inside, the impression is wholly different – pale, almost watery, high and spacious, and with woodwork painted in a variety of interpretations of medieval styles.

John Thomas Micklethwaite (1843–1906, AWG 1884) represents the first turnings-away from Gilbert Scott and the High Gothic Revival. In his *Modern Parish Churches* (1874) he was vigorously antipathetic to 'over-pedantic antiquarianism and vulgar professionalism'.

The new church for 'a congregation of colliers living without God' was the initiative of Dr Edward Bouverie Pusey, who had founded the nearby St Saviour's. Pusey hoped to appoint Butterfield as architect, but it was not to be. In 1873 there was an 'Iron Church' (recycled from another parish) on donated land. In 1874 the Vicar of St Saviour's, Richard Collins, met Micklethwaite by chance, and interested him in the new church project. (It was to be only Micklethwaite's second new-build church.) Building did not start until 1876. Then Collins suddenly died, and intestate – his £10,000 estate went to his brother rather than, as perhaps he had intended, to pay for the church. A succession of sickly and temporary priests, arguments about liturgy, and lack of funds, meant completion took six years. In the end the *Church Times* called it 'plain, but large, lofty and dignified with … no stint of space in any direction'.

Its glories are in its furnishings. The font and pulpit, 1882, are by Micklethwaite. He had plans for a high screen with a singing gallery over it, which could not be undertaken for lack of means. However, there was a rood beam and cross by 1904, to Micklethwaite's design, made

ILKLEY

St Margaret, Ilkley | 1878–9
R. Norman Shaw | LS29 9QL

St John, Ben Rhydding | 1903–4
Chorley & Connon | LS29 8PN

Ben Rhydding Methodist Church
1909
Garside & Pennington | LS29 8PP

Ilkley was known for its waters by the 1780s: by the 1840s it was becoming a spa town. The Ben Rhydding Hydropathic Establishment opened in nearby Wheatley in 1844 – Britain's first purpose-built hydro, with its own railway station by 1865. Wheatley went so far as to change its name to Ben Rhydding – supposedly the ancient name for the hill on which the Hydro stood. (The Hydro was demolished in 1955.) The town was fashionable, and soon booming. It is a happy hunting ground for Arts & Crafts church-fanciers. All Saints, the parish church, was enlarged and heftily overhauled in 1860. Then came Christ Church Congregational (now URC) in assertively Decorated style by J.P. Pritchett, 1868–9, and the Friends Meeting House, 1869.

Norman Shaw's **St Margaret's** was built in the grounds of the Hydro. Shaw wanted to do something simple: 'I am sure it is mass that tells and not mouldings.' The sloping site gave him the opportunity for drama – the vestries are under the chancel. And Shaw introduced wide windows – ten lights wide – at east and west, something new. But there was no tower, for fear of the 'spongy sort of ground'. Shaw designed the pulpit, 1880–1, and the font cover (in partnership with Harry Sutton), 1910–11. The font itself may have been designed by E.S. Prior, who had been despatched to Ilkley by Shaw to superintend the building work – here Prior learnt, as he wrote in *The Builder*, 'there is no science of construction, but there was an experience of construction to be gained by the man who worked with his own hands'. The glass is largely Powells and some late Morris – though Shaw was not a fan: 'Morris is no good. His work is sometimes splendid (not always) but he is so full of cranks and general stubbornness …' The screens round the choir, organ and Lady Chapel are by James Elwell of Beverley (1836–1926).

Next came the RC church, Sacred Heart (Edward Simpson of Bradford, 1878–9; rebuilt and unrecognisable, 1979), and the Baptist Chapel (1902), pretty but bare.

St John's is Arts & Crafts in taste without necessarily having anything to do with the AWG. Charles Roberts Chorley (*c.*1830–1914) and John Wreghitt Connon (1849–1921) were partners in Leeds from 1885. Chorley's son Harry Sutton Chorley (1869–1939) was articled in 1891, and partner 1897. Chorley senior retired in 1904, so by 1903 it is probable that Harry was taking the lead – he was Diocesan Surveyor to both Ripon and Bradford Dioceses. He was practising alone by 1921.

The church is full of restrained craftsmanly wood-carving – a vigorous frieze of vines with grapes round the baptistry, overlooking a brusque, chunky font; naturalistic flower carving on the pulpit and priest's stall; more vines – a different hand – round the sanctuary; altar rails with twisted foliage; panelling. Some of the window exteriors have playful scalloped heads.

Other Chorley (and Connon) churches worth visiting include **St Aidan, Hellifield**, near Gargrave, 1905–6 (BD23 4HY), which has been slightly re-ordered, but retains a strikingly Art Deco-ish pulpit and lectern, and other wood-carving, some of it clearly local; **St James, Manston**, Leeds, 1913 (LS15 8JB), whose stern stone whalebone arches across the nave are each wider from west to east, giving a theatrical sense of arrival, and unnerving perspective distortion; and **St Cuthbert & St Oswald, Winksley**, 1917 (HG4 3NR), a more sumptuous

St John, Ben Rhydding from the north-east

and conventional affair, built in memory of Baron Furness (d.1912), by his widow.

Ben Rhydding Methodist Church comes rather at the end of the town's fashionableness: it is modishly Arts & Crafts rather than politically so. It mixes ancient and modern: a very non-Nonconformist niche over the door, awaiting a saint who will never come; gargoyles on the tower, and wooden angels in the ceiling, albeit with wings primly folded.

George Pennington (1872–1961), son of a Wesleyan minister, was a Sunday School teacher, and Circuit Steward from 1902. He built 22 churches – he never called them 'chapels'. Samson Howard Garside (1860–1948) was more political: Pontefract Town Councillor and a founder of the Pontefract Co-operative Society.

There is a full complement of 'Arts & Crafts' features: a squat, square tower, crenelated; chunky buttresses, battered; and an intriguingly complex roofline. Inside, the pulpit is tactfully to one side, with 'chaste ornamentation of grapes, vine leaves and cherubs' as *The Ilkley Gazette* put it. The communion rail is on sinuous supports. By 1908 the language of church building was so Arts & Crafts-influenced the church was received as appropriately contemporary: the *Gazette* again – 'a most picturesque building, calling to mind many quaint old country churches of rustic England, and when time has mellowed its outward appearance it will be hard to recognise in it a twentieth century structure.'

Pennington always used craftsmen for his furniture: surviving accounts name T. Hirst & Sons of Castleford for the interior oak work; Walter Hudson, painter; A. Halliday, iron work, 'hand-hammered'. The church has gradually filled with other craft furnishings: a cross by 'Mouseman' Thompson, 1930; memorial window in the north-west aisle designed by Harry Stammer, who worked freelance, in the kiln at York Minster, from the 1950s.

A selective list of other, if less suave Garside and Pennington NC churches of the period, in and around Yorkshire, that survive – most are altered: **Wakefield,** 1902 (WF1 2PN), **Hensall,** 1902–3 (DN14 0RY), **Saltburn,** 1905 (TS12 1DJ), **Healing,** 1906 (DN41 7LY), **South Ossett,** 1908 (WF5 0EF), **Pateley Bridge,** 1909 (HG3 5NL), **Bowers Allerton** (Great Preston), 1927 (LS26 8DF), **Airedale,** 1929 (WF10 3TG).

Left: Ben Rhydding Methodist Church: pulpit
Right: St Margaret, Ilkley: east end

by William Horsman Reynard of nearby St Hilda's Road, described in the 1911 census as a 'Printer's Joiner'. Reynard also made the small screens across the north and south aisles, 1915.

After Micklethwaite's death in 1906, the driving force was the fourth vicar, John Starky Willimott, who arrived in 1908. His intentions were very High indeed. The Reynard rood was replaced in 1921 by a new screen and loft to a design, based on Micklethwaite's, by William Henry Wood (1861–1941), the Durham diocesan architect, who had taken over the practice of C. Hodgson Fowler in 1911. It was made by local craftsmen Chadwick and Ibbotson, and painted by seven members of the congregation. The carved figures are by Alfred Southwick (1875–1944, AWG 1934). The bas-relief panels in the screen, 1924, are by James Taylor Ogleby (1884–1925), 'wood and stone carver' of Newcastle on Tyne, and painted by Stanley Watkins (1853–1928). The reredos, designed by Wood, came in 1927. The figures on the font cover, 1938, are also by Alfred Southwick.

St Hilda, Cross Green, Leeds: rood loft

HAREHILLS, Leeds

St Aidan | 1889–94
R.J. Johnson and A. Crawford Hick
LS8 5QD | Often open

Robert James Johnson (1832-–92) (see also p.25) was in Gilbert Scott's office 1849–58. He had various partners in London and Newcastle, including, most fruitfully, 1875–1882, William Searle Hicks (1849–1902), great-nephew of Sir Charles Barry. But in the 1890s, in failing health, Johnson took into partnership A.B. Gibson and A. Crawford Hick. The huge church – its wide-open basilican plan intended to encourage congregational worship – was utterly bare when completed: 'nobbut a factory' according to one early worshipper.

Gradually adornments arrived, most thrillingly the mosaics by Frank Brangwyn (1867–1956), 1910–16. The second vicar, Arthur Swayne, arrived in 1897. He married well – Eva Kitson, niece of the city's leading Liberal politician. Her brother, Sydney Kitson, was an architect, and he seems to have designed new fittings and managed repairs. But it was her nephew, Robert Hawthorne Kitson (1873–1947), friend of Wilson Steer and George Clausen, who brought in Brangwyn, who had designed rooms for Kitson's house in Sicily.

Brangwyn – a devout Roman Catholic – had been introduced to William Morris by A.H. Mackmurdo of the Century Guild, and worked with Morris for two years. He saw himself primarily as a painter. In 1895 he was commissioned to decorate the Paris house of Samuel Bing, owner of the *Art Nouveau* shop. He was invited to join the Vienna Secession in 1897. His great mural scheme in the Skinners'

Livery Hall in London (1902) established his reputation as something rather greater than an interior designer – which remains (see also p.81).

The first proposal was for tempera frescoes. Brangwyn started on the designs in 1909, but in 1913, having seen Leeds in the sun, when 'no shadows were cast upon the ground', he decided 'no painting could exist in such an atmosphere', and decided to switch to mosaic. A cheaper synthetic compound – Rust's Vitreous Enamel – was proposed instead of costly Venetian glass: the work was executed under Sylvester Sparrow, a glass painter who had worked for the Rust company in Battersea. He selected and trained 40 women and girls to cut the tesserae and mount them on paper sheets, which were then transported to Leeds. The scheme is the life of St Aidan, who appears as a dignified, if idealised, labourer – just as Ruskin/Morris saw the past. It was cleaned in 2002. Also worth noting are the exalted west-end baptistry; the pulpit with lavish marbles and alabaster; and the rood screen. The confessional and lectern are by Mouseman Thompson. The rood is by Ralph Hedley, 1898.

LEEDS

St Anne's RC Cathedral | 1901–4
Eastwood and Greenslade
LS2 8BE | Open

When Betjeman proclaimed Holy Trinity, Sloane Street 'the Cathedral of the Arts & Crafts' he seems rather to have overlooked St Anne's – which *is*, after all, unlike Holy Trinity, a cathedral. And if the collection of objects by

St Aidan, Harehills, Leeds: apse by Frank Brangwyn

WALTER HENRY BRIERLEY

Goathland, St Mary | 1894–6
YO22 5LX | Open

Rufforth, All Saints | 1894–5
YO26 6QG | By arrangement

York, St Luke | 1900–12
YO30 6DG | By arrangement

Brierley was York Diocesan Surveyor 1908–21, and in 1909 one of three names suggested to join the ICBS Architects Committee (the others were Charles Spooner and H. J. Austin of Paley & Austin). He was influenced by the Arts & Crafts, but cautious in using untraditional forms. The *Builders' Journal* identified him as 'an ardent advocate of "local style"'. He admired Walter Tapper, W.H. Bidlake and Giles Gilbert Scott.

He seems to have been something of a despot in his office. He sketched out first thoughts on squared paper, to be worked up by his assistants: but he was not an artist, and he relied heavily on his Clerk of Works, John Vause. He hated mass-produced church fittings on principle: he respected traditional work too much. He wanted craftsmen to work to his instruction, not to have their own ideas – he did not get on with Eric Gill. But he did work with George Bankart, and Gertrude Jekyll designed gardens for three of his houses.

He was in partnership with James Demaine (1842–1911) until the latter's retirement in 1899. The first two churches were in London: St Philip, Buckingham Palace Road, 1887, and St Thomas, Kensal Green, 1888.

St Mary, Goathland promises much: the stumpy tower, snecked stone in the porch, battered plinth, scalloped louvres in the belfry, and lamps in the churchyard suggest Arts & Crafts inclinations – the interior comes up a little short. The choir fittings are Brierley's, and there is a Mouseman Thompson reredos.

All Saints, Rufforth expresses 'a note of stern, four-square strength, a sparing use of enrichment' (*Builders' Journal*). But it is really a rather jolly affair, with singing birds in the frieze over the porch, and a bold cornice band extolling George Middlewood, whose widow paid for the church. Inside there are pretty carvings on doors inside and out, and a painted reredos of 1898, at once simple and intense (Shrigley and Hunt?). The woodcarving is all by George Walter Milburn of York (1844–1941), who also worked in stone – there are statues in York by him of William Etty and Queen Victoria.

St Luke, York is in workaday brick – the interior feels more like Charles Nicholson, or Caröe at his most restrained: painted chancel ceiling, rough-hewn processional cross, dainty altar rails. In 1909 Brierley decorated the interior of **St Stephen, Snainton** with stencilling in green and blue, bands of ornament in Indian red, monograms and crowns in red and gold in the window reveals – all subsequently obliterated!

Left: All Saints, Rufforth: reredos frieze
Right: St Mary, Goathland

members of the AWG in Sloane Street underlines the multivalence of Arts & Crafts practice, the building itself is Sedding in, albeit frolicsome, Gothic mode, with the initial glass and interior scheme by Burne-Jones and Morris & Co. – all rather *avant la lettre*.

St Anne's, by contrast, coming 15 years later, had absorbed the spirit. Eastwood 'determined that it should not be a dead work but a living work of the present day, although to some extent it might be based on something which had gone before'.

John Henry Eastwood (1843–1913) was never AWG, though his partner, Sidney Kyffin Greenslade (1867–1955), was, in 1915. Neither was ever at the heart of things – though Greenslade later knew Nelson Dawson, Harold Stabler and Curtis Green. The building seems therefore somehow peripheral. Added to which, the church has been altered as liturgical fashions have changed – also a consequence of its city centre and diocesan importance. Substantial cosmetic changes were made to the interior in 1954, and there was re-ordering in 1962–3, in perhaps precipitate anticipation of Vatican II – the sanctuary wholly changed, a dwarf screen and canons' stalls removed, congregational chairs replaced by benches.

A renovation scheme in 2005–6 restored some of the original colour scheme, while adding a number of new features, and reconfiguring the choir. The great reredos has survived. To see the church as it was intended, one has to look through, back and beyond what is in front of us now.

When the original 1878 Cathedral was demolished by the council to straighten a curve on the city's tramway, the present cramped and awkward site was offered in compensation. Bishop William Gordon wanted a Catholic architect, and chose Eastwood who, though working in London, was born in Yorkshire (Leeds usually claims him, but birth records suggest Hull). In his office was Sidney Greenslade, an erstwhile assistant to W.D. Caröe. Of the surviving 554 drawings (of 749 prepared), 180 have been credited to Greenslade and 59 to Eastwood. It was Eastwood who corresponded with the Bishop: Greenslade's work was mainly on details, and the decorative nuances are perhaps more his than Eastwood's. The 'Arts & Crafts-ness' of the building lies in the minutiae – where is the evidence of designer and craftsman working on companionable, equal footing? On the contrary, the drawings indicate all the stone-carving was worked out minutely on paper, giving scant opportunity for personal expression by craftsmen.

Some of the later furnishings *are* by a man of the AWG: the Stations of the Cross, 1912; War Memorial, 1920; Sacred Heart statue, 1922; and mosaics in the sanctuary, 1928 are by Cesare Formilli of Rome (1860–1942, AWG 1908). He had moved to London in 1896, and later worked on the interior of Brompton Oratory, 1927–32. And there was at least one local hand: the benches in the Lady Chapel were made, 1915, by a Leeds cabinet-maker, Arthur Walker, who also made the cross in the Pieta chapel, some confessionals, and furniture for the sacristy.

Elsewhere there is high-quality 'commercial' work: the Pieta, 1913, by Boulton & Son of Cheltenham; the Chapel of St Joseph, 1904, by H.H. Martyn & Co. of Cheltenham, to Eastwood's design. The Chapel of the Sacred Heart, 1904, executed by Nathaniel Hitch (who often worked with Caröe) to a design by Greenslade. The main reredos, 1904, is by

Flint Brothers of Clapham, to a design by Greenslade. Eastwood designed the Shrine to Our Lady of Perpetual Succour, 1913, and the St Urban reliquary, 1904. The reredos in the Lady Chapel by A.W.N. Pugin, 1842, is from the earlier church: it was restored in 2007. Recent renovations have revealed murals in the spandrels (1937, and 'not good' according to *Pevsner*), seemingly painted over in the 1950s. There is an 1897 pulpit by J.F. Bentley, put into storage in 2005, and perhaps to be reinstated.

The built surfaces seem bare, with little to distract in colouring or materials. But closer attention finds surprises – almost playful paired openings (not windows) below the clerestory; shafts with idiosyncratic tops running up the main nave piers; the dentils in the frieze below the ceiling in broken rhythm, and the spaces between painted dark blue; statues in the niches on the chancel arch; and fleurons including the Evangelists' symbols in the frieze above.

There are two forces at work here, and to some extent in opposition – the devout, rather ascetic piety of Eastwood, and the somewhat buttoned-down aesthetic extraversion of Greenslade. Two footnotes illuminate the difference. In 1880 Eastwood expressed commitment to ecclesiastical architecture by joining the Guild of St Gregory and St Luke, established by Catholic laymen in 1879 for the Puginesque goal of 'promoting the study of Christian antiquities and of propagating the true principles of Christian art': other members included J.F. Bentley and Leonard Stokes. Greenslade's interests lay elsewhere: he was an enthusiastic supporter and collector of Martinware, the eccentric pottery produced by the Martin brothers of Fulham and Southall; and in 1918 he was appointed Consulting Curator to the University of Wales's Arts & Crafts Museum at Aberystwyth – a rather touching metaphor of the Arts & Crafts, of which he had been part, being now, officially, in the past, but worth remembering, and on another, this time geographical, periphery.

CLAYTON, Bradford

St John the Baptist | 1920s
Marbles and mosaics by Gaetano Meo
BD14 6AX | By arrangement

The rather unspectacular church dates from 1849–50, by Mallinson & Healey: no matter – this is an instance where an interior 'qualifies' a church, though no doubt some will argue

St Anne's Cathedral, Leeds: looking east

WILLIAM JOHN HALE

St Luke's Wesleyan church
Crookes, Sheffield | 1899–1900
S10 1QS | (Now flats: Hale Court)

Crookes Congregational Church
Sheffield | 1906
S10 1LP | (Now offices)

Wesley Hall, Crookes, Sheffield
1908 (re-ordered)
S10 1UD | By arrangement

Rawmarsh Methodist Church
Rotherham | 1907–8
S62 6NJ | By arrangement

Posterity has not been kind to the churches of W.J. Hale – 'sane, if unheroic' as he described himself. Almost none of his work remains as built. Like George Pennington and Harry Chorley, Hale was not an Arts & Crafts man in attitude or practice – he was dismissive of the 'no art school… simplicity approaching barbarity'. But he nonetheless responded to the aesthetics, and applied them with tact and imagination. He was a Methodist Trustee, Circuit Steward and Sunday School Secretary. He believed in service, and that 'living architecture [can never] be produced so long as mere monetary gain [is] the main object of the designer'.

St Luke's and its adjacent Sunday School (now flats) can only be admired from the street. It has Art Nouveau railings, crisp carving round the rather municipal porch and a Tree of Life on the gable, both by Frank Tory (1848–1938), Sheffield's leading stone-carver; twin flat-capped buttress spirelets, and a prettily traceried west window.

All was paid for by the Chairman of Bassett's Liquorice Allsorts.

Crookes Congregational Church, offices since 1989, towers magnificently over its steep street. The worship space was an enormous octagon, far too big for the congregation, but wonderful for the acoustics. Again, intense stone-carving on the exterior, including a Tree of Life and pomegranates; and flat-capped buttresses.

Crookes Wesley Hall is another octagon. What survives of the interior detail is a surprising collection of putti on the capitals, a severely flat-fronted gallery enlivened by panels of pomegranates assembled in cruciform, and some green and white glass which gives a hint of how Hale adorned his other two Crookes buildings, if less expressive.

Rawmarsh is big and muscular, with yet more putti – this time on the porch – and more green and white glass, some with Art Nouveau leading. The benches survive – the insertion of a floor means the worship space is now what was the gallery.

After 1909, there was something of a halt in Hale's architectural work until 1924 – the Sheffield churches that follow set off in a new direction. **Banner Cross** (1929) suggests an Arts and Crafts mindset beginning to pursue Modernism. Similarly **Southey** (1929) and **Bents Green** (1932). Attercliffe (1926) was demolished.

Sheffield's Victoria Hall was completed by Hale in 1908, after the death of its original architect – Hale added a wealth of Glasgow School detail in glass and tiles.

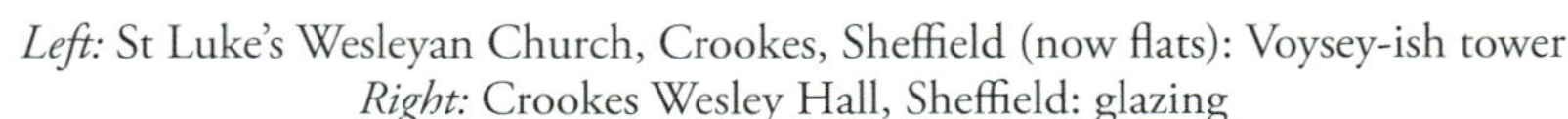

Left: St Luke's Wesleyan Church, Crookes, Sheffield (now flats): Voysey-ish tower
Right: Crookes Wesley Hall, Sheffield: glazing

that Gaetano Meo (1849–1925) is 'not Arts & Crafts'. But craftsmanship, painstaking and artistic, by a designer who was also a maker, is foregrounded, even revered.

The floor and walls are in costly marbles – 43 marbles in all, from ten countries. Meo's mosaic panels show Ruth; an angel cradling Christ; and Britannia, as a memorial to Colonel Buchanan-Dunlop, killed at Vermelles, 1915. Two further War Memorial panels in the tower are probably by Meo too. There are two mosaics by Salviati: the reredos (which Meo appears to have acquired); and a Last Supper, no longer wanted in the new Charterhouse School chapel, and installed here in 1948.

Meo's story is far-fetched and Romantic: he walked to London from his home in southern Italy 'with only his harp and asses' skin cloak' according to family tradition; he was discovered busking in the street by Simeon Solomon (or was sent by his barber to meet Dante Gabriel Rossetti); he became a model for the PRB; met Henry Holiday, who taught him to paint; he was sent back to Italy to learn about mosaic and *opus sectile*; returned, married a Belfast girl, had five children; in 1886 was naturalised as a British citizen – the celebratory party guest list included Burne-Jones and William Richmond; he worked for Halsey Ricardo at Debenham House; by 1913 he was working at Westminster Cathedral. From then until 1921, he was also working at Clayton – now, perhaps for the first time, working to his own ideas and designs. Where Salviati's mosaic method meant most of the work could be done by semi-skilled workers using the designer's cartoon, Meo's mosaics appear to have been assembled by Meo himself.

The benefactor was Harrison Benn (1852–1921), head of Joseph Benn, Ltd, of Great Horton, worsted manufacturers, a leading light of the Conservative party, who in 1903 was developing worsted manufacture at Greystone, Rhode Island.

St John the Baptist, Clayton, Bradford: looking east

STALLING BUSK, Wensleydale

St Matthew | 1908–9
Thomas Gerard Davidson
DL8 3DH | Open

Davidson (1878–1956) had been in practice in distant Bloomsbury since 1902 when Frederick Morris Symonds Squibb, Vicar of Askrigg, commissioned this tiny new church – perhaps there was a family connection. Davidson was not a prolific architect, nor eminent – his later work appears to have been houses, including his own in Walberswick. In 1905 he published a design for a church in Grantham with shades of Caröe, and for a bank in the Hague in *Building News* (11 May 1906), in a distinctly Norman Shaw Scotland Yard vein. Stalling Busk is an altogether less ambitious work – cosy and nest-like, but with spiky angular details. The bellcote over a lean-to baptistry suggests a bulldozer. The triangular buttresses are as sharp as icebreakers' prows. Inside, everything is much quieter – quaint and informal.

St Matthew, Stalling Busk

SCARBOROUGH

St Martin | 1862–3, 1879, 1890, 1902
G.F. Bodley
YO11 2BT | Open

Bodley was a hero to Arts & Crafts church architects. 1911's *Recent English Ecclesiastical Architecture*, probably under the editorship of Mervyn Macartney, was an anxious, reflective 'state of the nation' in church architecture following Bodley's death in 1907. St Martin's throws a little light on the way in which Bodleyan clarity commingled with Pre-Raphaelite indulgence – the church guidebook proclaims it 'A Pre-Raphaelite Church' – and eventually relaxed into Arts & Crafts nostalgia.

The chancel ceiling is by William Morris and Philip Webb – Bodley was an early champion of their work (see Selsley p.152). Webb painted the canopy over the altar. There is much Morris glass of various dates and hands

St Martin's Lodge, Scarborough: reredos detail

– the east window has a Crucifixion by Madox Brown and surrounding panels by Rossetti. (For a full breakdown of who designed which window, see www.friendsofstmartins.co.uk.) The south aisle windows are to designs by Burne-Jones, as is The Adoration of the Magi in the elaborate Bodley-designed east wall. The painted panels on the north side of the pulpit are by Rossetti; the other panels designed by Madox Brown and Morris, and painted by Morris's foreman, George Campfield.

The Baptistry was added in 1879. The reredos, by Farmer & Brindley to Bodley's design, was added in 1890. The rood-screen came in 1894, with panels painted by Charles Edgar Buckeridge (1864–98), who, as a result, was employed later by Norman Shaw at Richards Castle (p.147). Bodley himself had painted the wall above in 1862. The alluring paintings on the Bodley organ case are by Spencer Stanhope (1829–1908), around 1890. The Lady Chapel was added by Bodley in 1902: its reredos is by Laurence Turner, who worked often with Bodley in plasterwork. The Cross at the west end, a war memorial rescued from Low church wrath in 1921, is set against an Artsy-Craftsy text, whose painter is not, it seems, recorded.

Intriguingly, in a street nearby, is **St Martin's Lodge**, with a tiny chapel whose reredos was painted (in 1888?) either by Spencer Stanhope, or someone with a Burne-Jones eye if not quite hand, perhaps some of the resident convalescents – 'gifted amateurs'.

TOLLER LANE, Manningham, Bradford

St Chad | 1912–13
Nicol & Nicol
BD8 9DE | By arrangement

It is a surprise, perhaps, to find a 'Birmingham' Byzantine church in Bradford – less so when the architects are from Birmingham: what were they doing in Bradford?

John Couldson Nicol (1848–1933), born in Aberdeen, and his son George Salway Nicol (1878–1930) practised together in Birmingham – Acocks Green and Colmore Row – from about 1904 until perhaps 1926. They rarely ventured far from the West Midlands – their other church of note is St Benedict, Bordesley, 1905–9 (B10 9AY) (p.164), with walls painted by Henry Holiday.

The land for St Chad's was given in memory of George and Elizabeth Ackroyd by their children in 1909. Ackroyd was an orphan who obtained a junior clerkship in Bradford Bank and worked his way up to be Managing Director.

The windows in the apse, and the *opus sectile* mosaics in gilded glass are by James Powell & Son, designed by their chief designer Charles Hardgrave (1848–1920), who, coincidentally, came from York. The mosaics are Great War memorials, finished in 1919 – possibly Hardgrave's last work. There are also geometric windows in the double wooden doors, with striking flashes of red glass. Fragments of 14th-century glass are incorporated in some of the round-headed windows in the Lady Chapel, possibly from St Augustine's,

St Chad, Toller Lane, Manningham, Bradford: east end

A Ω
EST·DE·SPIRITU·SANCTO·EX·MARIA·VIRGINE·ET·HOMO

Canterbury, excavated in 1913, and brought to St Chad's by a curate from Canterbury. The choir stalls have idiosyncratic geometric carved detail. The church is more or less as built.

EAST MOORS

St Mary Magdalene | 1879–82
Temple Lushington Moore
near YO62 5HJ | Open

The drawings were made by Moore's then master, George Gilbert Scott ('Middle Scott') in 1879. By the time the building started in 1881, Moore was superintending the project. In this remote (and hard to find) location, Moore was flexing his young muscles – this is arguably his first church. He had not yet quite grown sensible. This feels like fun.

The church is tiny. On paper, the elements are merely Victorian – painted wagon roof, tall east window and carved and painted reredos. In the flesh, the painting is almost careless (joy in labour?), and there is comical ironwork – a crenelated rainwater spout serving the office of a gargoyle, and matching crenulations on wall lights. The reredos, 1908, is to a design by Moore. The baptistry doubled as a Sunday school, with a squint – the hinges on its doors (!) are quite unnecessarily playful.

CASTLETON

St Michael & St George | 1924–6
Leslie Moore
YO21 2EL | Open

Leslie Moore (1883–1957) was Temple Moore's son-in-law – their surnames are the same by coincidence. Temple died in 1920 and Leslie carried the practice on, partly in the same spirit as Temple, for whom he had respect and an almost reverent regard, but with less devotional ardour, and rather more Arts & Crafts sympathy.

His first new-build church (from Temple Moore's 1919 design) at Shiregreen, Sheffield, was demolished in 2014. His church at Drypool, Hull (1924–5) was destroyed in 1941. Other churches from the 1930s survive.

Castleton stands not only as an example of how Moore expressed a late diminuendo of Arts & Crafts in architecture, but contains a robust furnishing scheme by Mouseman Thompson which indicates how the spirit of Gimson's 'good citizens' furniture' lived on. The chancel screen is a Great War memorial, though it was not installed until 1938. The reredos was designed by Mary Moore, Leslie's wife (and Temple's daughter). The building process was almost

St Michael & St George, Castleton: looking west

self-consciously Arts & Crafts – Moore specified a traditional goats' hair recipe for the plaster, and 'finest grown English oak' finished with an adze.

WHITBY, West Cliff

St Hilda | 1884–8
Robert James Johnson
near YO21 3EG | By arrangement

Johnson (1832–92) has passed below the horizon. He trained under Gilbert Scott, who thought him 'an able and original man'. G.E. Street, asked to sign off a drawing by Johnson, said, 'Anything Johnson has done I will pass without examination'. Mervyn Macartney's view, in *REEA*, was that 'the works that have been erected from his designs mark him out as a man of rare and even extraordinary ability'. *The Builder* noted he was 'one of the very few men standing in the front rank of the profession who continued to practise in the country instead of being absorbed in the great vortex of London.' He was Diocesan Architect for Durham (1871) and Newcastle (1882). And so – damningly in England – provincial.

Besides, he was self-effacing and religious: his obituarist recorded that he 'prayed over his designs and had a single eye on *ad majorem Dei gloriam*.' And he was conscientious: he

St Hilda, Whitby:
reredos detail

worked too hard and suffered a stroke shortly after opening a new office in York.

St Hilda is High Victorian Gothic with knobs on. At the time it was admired, even reverenced: the *Newcastle Daily Journal* called it 'a prayer in stone.' W.S. Hicks said Johnson's churches were 'a witness for his earnest-minded search for whatsoever things are honest and lovely', which sounds rather more artistic than architectural: 'the greatest pains were taken with this church and with all its details'. But does this make St Hilda Arts & Crafts? The quality of the craftsmanship and the way in which it is integrated so seamlessly and sympathetically with the architecture suggest Johnson, a keen and scholarly antiquarian, was somehow, like Bodley, seeing the future. That J.T. Micklethwaite wrote one of his obituaries suggests an AWG sympathy. See also 'The Big Lamp' (p.270).

Other Churches

St James, Warter (now Yorkshire Wolds Heritage Centre) | Habershon and Pite | 1862 | YO42 1XW
Monument by Frampton, 1905; glass by Anning Bell; war memorial; other monuments.

St Martin, Potternewton, Leeds | Adams and Kelly | 1879–81 | LS7 3LB
Murals by Hemming & Co., 1912–13 – late flowering Victorian.

St Andrew, Netherton | J.D. Sedding | 1880–1 | WF4 4HE
Sedding's first – humble, cheap and otherwise unremarkable: strictly for completists.

St Lawrence, East Rounton, Northallerton | R.J. Johnson 'restoration' | 1884 | DL6 2LB
Strachan glass. Lych gate and gallery by Philip Webb. One of Johnson's last jobs – tactful, self-effacing.

St John, Kirk Hammerton | C. Hodgson Fowler | 1890–1 | YO26 8DL
Dazzling murals 1895–8 by George Ostrehan (1865–1903).

St Magnus, Bessingby, Bridlington | Temple Moore | 1893–4 | YO16 4UH
Still feeling his way, and, while serious and intent, not yet unrelentingly stern.

Wesleyan Methodist church, Lindley, Huddersfield | Edgar Wood (additions) | 1894–5 | HD3 3ND
Chancel, vestry, transept added by Wood; also communion table and choir stall fronts.

All Saints, Helmsley | medieval | 19th-century rebuild | YO62 5AD
North aisle mural designed by Revd C.N. Gray, 1909; ceiling painting designed by Temple Moore; further murals.

Giggleswick School Chapel | T.G. Jackson | 1897–1901 | BD24 0DR
The concept is Imperial Classical – the detail is heartfelt craftsmanship in wood, glass and especially mosaic. Private.

St Columba, Middlesbrough | Temple Moore | 1900–3 | TS1 1SH
Big-boned, confusing, unsatisfactory, magnificent – as if he is about to lose his way.

St Saviour, Scarborough | J.T. Micklethwaite | 1901–2 | YO12 7BJ
Modest, unfinished – with some touches of Arts & Crafts taste.

Central Methodist Church, Brighouse | John Wills, Percy Jackson | 1905–7 | HD6 1AQ
If only for its rakish profile, and a truly original pier, velodrome-shaped in section.

St Mary, Bolton-upon-Swale | DL10 6AQ
Carpenter chapel: plasterwork by E.M. Rope, 1905.

St Joseph, Potter Hill, Pickering (RC) | Leonard Stokes | 1907–11 | YO18 8AD
Eric Gill font. Stokes's detailing here is freer and livelier than anywhere else.

St Andrew, Kirkby Malzeard | J. Oldrid Scott (rebuild) | 1908 | HG4 3RT
After a fire. New fittings by Bowman & Son 1909, 1910, 1925, 1926. Mouseman Thompson chapel.

St Oswald King and Martyr, Guiseley | Charles Nicholson (extended) | 1909–10 | LS20 9BB
Ravishing gilded woodwork for Revd Hugh Lothian Bell; rood, reredos, doors either side of altar, organ screen.

St Mary, South Elmsall | J. Nicholson Johnston | 1910 | WF9 2JA
If only for the six naïve painted lady angels on the altar, with 1920s hairstyles.

St Oswald, Lythe | Walter Tapper | 1910–11 | YO21 3RW
Tapper 'restored' the church with an Arts & Crafts eye, if not heart – worth going for the screen alone.

St Aelred (RC), Harrogate | W.H.H. Marten | 1912 | HG2 7BE

St John, Brighouse | Charles Nicholson | 1913–14 | HD6 1HL
Nicholson severe in stone, but inside, Artsy-Craftsy organ case. Mouseman choir stalls and pulpit. Altar rails.

St John & St Mary Magdalene, Goldthorpe, Barnsley | A.Y. Nutt | 1914–16 | S63 9JY
All-concrete church, fitted in the Highest liturgical style. Circling angels on Lady Chapel altar front.

St Andrew, Psalter Lane, Sheffield | J. Armory Teather | 1915–30 | S11 8YL
Was Methodist. Flashes of unexpected colour in small lights in the glass; Instruments of Passion on corbels.

St Philip & St James, New Bentley | Captain F.N. Masters | 1915 | DN5 0EZ
Paid for by the miners. Everything squared off in military manner – and a balcony from which to review the laity.

All Saints, Totley, Sheffield | Currey and Thompson | 1924 | S17 4AA
Currey chancel screen; light fittings, door furniture, glazing. 'Anglo-Saxon Revival'? (And see p.187)

Our Lady & English Martyrs (RC), Addingham | W.H.H. Marten | 1928 | LS29 0NJ
Rustic, with some unexpected 'Art Deco' glass in doors and panels.

St Mary, Hawksworth Wood, Leeds | W.D. Caröe | 1932–3 | LS5 3PT
Caröe pulls out all available stops at a rather late date.

St Matthew, Owthorne, Withernsea | Milner and Craze | 1934–35 | HU19 2DY
Lively tussle between Arts & Crafts (external brickwork, benches) and Modern (font, altar, interior brickwork).

St Wilfrid, Halton, Leeds | Randall Wells | 1937–9 | LS15 7JA
Just to see where the architect of Kempley ended up. An obsession with spindles. Kindred to Gill's Gorleston (p.214).

17

THE NORTH OF ENGLAND

Cumbria, Northumberland, Durham, Tyne & Wear

The North is rather indifferent to London and the South. It brings out original thinking – one-offs and innovations, and things ahead of their time. The pre-eminent 'pre-cursor' church is here, at Wreay, 1842 – wholly fresh, against the grain, idiosyncratic and exotic, and by a woman architect. There's a slightly later 'pre-cursor' too – the only complete church by William Morris's architect friend, Philip Webb, revered by Lethaby and his circle: St Martin, Brampton. St George, Jesmond is another tantalising one-off, by an architect who saw himself as a painter. And St Andrew, Roker is yet another candidate for 'Arts & Crafts Cathedral' – according to its website – though there is much more to it than mere size. Alas, on Lindisfarne, Lutyens was not asked to build a chapel.

Without the untrammelled aristocratic Howards and the North's gilded industrialists and shipping magnates, such buildings would not exist. But it is not the whole story, as Gunnerton and Lucker tell: there is grassroots craftsmanship here, and ordinary working men doing wonderful things. There was a Northumberland Handicrafts Guild, a Newcastle Arts & Crafts Guild, the (Newcastle) Handicrafts Company, and the KSIA, but there was never any sense of a 'movement', apart from a reaching towards education.

St Andrew, Roker, Sunderland, Tyne & Wear: altar cross

Flames of creativity flash up, unhindered by circumspection or caution. And there are important glass and woodwork designers and makers here, though no 'native' Arts & Crafts architect, apart from R.J. Johnson of Newcastle, perhaps, whose most thrilling church is in Yorkshire (see p.253), though it is not *quite* Arts & Crafts – rather, something finer. Hicks and Charlewood, who followed in his wake, were essentially restorers and adders.

A surprise is that the Lake District harbours no Arts & Crafts church – here Voysey, Baillie Scott and others built spacious houses for merchant princes at play. But no new church. Perhaps the rich were too busy having fun, and the farmers and shepherds too busy toiling in Wordsworthian obscurity. The Nonconformists built at the coast – but many of their chapels, in Barrow, notably, have perished. There was no great Revival here as in Wales, and no critical mass of miners or ship-workers to build their own chapel, or even start a brass band.

The county boundaries have wandered to some extent – Westmorland is no more, and Cleveland is a more recent not-quite-effaced memory. Away from the coast and outside the towns and cities, the landscape is big and sparse – churches don't make much of an impact against such competition. The aura of the Ruthwell and Bewcastle Crosses, of Hadrian's Wall, and the fells of the Lake District cut architectural ambitions down to size.

WREAY

St Mary | 1840–2
Sara(h) Losh
CA4 0SA | Open daily

St Mary's keeps on being discovered. Its terms of reference are wholly unfamiliar. Clearly it cannot be an 'Arts & Crafts church' by date: it is 50 years too early. Sara Losh (1786–1853) – she spelled it Sarah in later life – built St Mary's as a memorial to her sister Katherine, and added hints, some would have it, of a lost lover, killed on the North West Frontier. Sara provided the land and the funds to build the new village church on condition 'that I should be left unrestricted as to the mode of building it'. Gavin Stamp describes it as 'proto-Arts & Crafts'. Simon Jenkins suggests, 'The Arts and Crafts Movement took half a century to catch up with her.' It is the only church in this book to have its own biography: Jenny Uglow's *The Pinecone* (Faber, 2012).

In plan it is, as many later 'proper' Arts & Crafts churches were to be, without transepts, and apsidal. The woodwork can be seen as either naïvely vernacular, or wildly overwrought: the pulpit is a single bog oak tree-trunk carved to look even more gnarly; there are two reading desks – a pelican and an eagle, both in chestnut. There are naturalistic animal reliefs on the pew ends – compare the suave animal carvings at Henry Wilson's Brithdir (p.276). The font was carved from alabaster by Sara and her cousin William Septimus Losh: on its cover water lilies 'float' on a mirror – gauche, or romantic?

The design details seem to have no antecedents: high windows overlaid with alabaster cut-outs of fossils; a vision of heaven as a wooden row of angels and palm trees; the marble altar rests on two giant bronze eagles. Stone-carving on the exterior – still sharp in local stone – includes butterflies, beetles and birds among evergreen fir, coral and ammonites in the window openings; and grotesque oversize animals and monsters in the eaves (some are part of the ventilation system). Other motifs in the church include pinecones, arrows, vines, lotus flowers. Also to be found are bats, an owl, a cock, a snake, a lizard. The symbolism is more natural history or pantheist than Christian – some see it as proto-scientific – life, death and resurrection. There is no suggestion that religion and science are at odds – they are not. But not much evidence of Christ the Redeemer. There is no crucifix in the church.

Sara was highly educated, numerate, multilingual and travelled widely in Europe (well before Ruskin). Whatever she had in mind, its expression suggests a new spirit of individuality in religious observance. Far away from critical Ecclesiological eyes, she constructed a church to reflect her own notions of theology, using an alternative iconography. Her inclination to please herself, to do something different and personal, in an effort to encounter, express or celebrate God, was original.

After her father's death – he was a successful chemical manufacturer – and her brother seemingly with learning difficulties, Sara was rich, and effectively lord of the manor. The work was all carried out by local men under her eye and to her instruction: the stonework by William Hindson, Master Carpenter (1809–1908) and his son (both living 30 miles away in Dufton in 1861); and wood-carving (the west door) by Robert Donald, her

gardener; much of the glass is by Geoffrey Rowell of Carlisle. The Agnus Dei and emblems of the Apostles seem to have been added in the 1880s. In 1869 Rossetti thought Sara Losh, 'must have been really a great genius and should be better known.' He wanted Philip Webb to see the church. There is no evidence he did.

The churchyard contains a mausoleum to Katherine, and a collection of potent gravestones, designed by Sara. The nearby Chapel of Rest (1835), also by her, is now the Sarah Losh Heritage Centre. In 2005 all this was unknown and unloved: now it is garlanded to an almost excessive degree, in danger of becoming a version of itself. It *is* still a church.

St Mary, Wreay: east end

BRAMPTON

St Martin | 1877–8
Philip Webb
CA8 1SH | Usually open

Philip Webb (1831–1915) was revered – W.R. Lethaby wrote a hagiography in a series of articles in *The Builder* as early as 1925. Webb embodied so much the AWG admired – single-mindedness, commitment, originality, insistence on his own ideas – and he was also, inspiringly, disinclined to take on more than one job, nor to take on work (or clients) of which he did not approve. He was allergic to publicity, ascetic, acerbic and morally scrupulous. Lethaby wrote, 'He thought the worst rot of the age was greed.' He was not interested in money, and lived and died poor.

And he did not trust to craftsmen – he designed every detail himself.

Webb was a defining intelligence in the gestation of Arts & Crafts. Lethaby saw him, firmly, as 'the architect of the Pre-Raphaelite group'. Famously, he was the architect of William Morris's Red House, 1859. He was a partner with Morris, Burne-Jones and Rossetti in Morris, Marshall, Faulkner & Co. He and Morris founded the SPAB, to which Webb devoted much of his energies, and whose Manifesto he co-wrote. Webb was Treasurer of Morris's Socialist League. And he was agnostic – which adds to his interest as a church architect, and partly explains why he built only this one parish church (though he designed one for Thurstaston, Cheshire, 1871, never built; and a chapel in Clapham for Morris's sister and her Rochester Diocesan Deaconess Institution, now stripped).

The client was George Howard, 9th Earl of Carlisle (1843–1911), for whom Webb had already built houses, including his London house, 1 Palace Green, 1868–70. Howard was artistic as well as rich, and a patron of the PRB, whose members overlap with and intertwine with Morris and his younger circle. Howard was also an early member of the SPAB.

The church attracted opprobrium and admiration in equal measure. Some in the town objected to having a fashionable London architect parachuted in by a local aristocrat to build a church more expensive and bigger than they required: a 'precious warehouse of a place'. Some felt the town had more need of a tramway. Webb and Howard were far more interested in the building as art than in liturgy: they thought it 'poetical' and Webb always saw it as a 'composition'. But its plan, with the chancel hardly expressed as a separate space, reflected the Broad Church views of the new vicar, Henry Whitehead (who had been installed at Howard's suggestion).

The main attraction is the Morris & Co. glass, which is everywhere – and, in the east window, in colours which are Morris at his richest, definingly PRB, and with comfortable, womanly angels by Burne-Jones. It was Whitehead who insisted on Morris glass, and foresaw its reputation: 'The time will come when strangers will seek Brampton … for the windows in St Martin's church.' There is no Crucifixion or Judgement, but Virtues, Biblical heroes, the Good Shepherd and Paradise. (It is voluminously online.)

The space is wide and open, emphasised by the white-painted ceiling. The two aisle roofs are wholly different – why? – and with no clerestory but instead tiny dormers. The tower was not completed until 1904–6, by George Jack, who had been Webb's assistant.

St Martin, Brampton:
the south aisle roof

The terracotta relief of St Martin is by Ellen Mary Rope, 1906. The reredos, 1928, is by Hicks and Charlewood, incorporating a gesso panel from the original Morris scheme. The font cover is by the Keswick School of Industrial Arts (KSIA). Otherwise all is pretty much as Howard, Whitehead and Webb intended: Arts & Crafts in embryo.

ROKER, Sunderland, Tyne & Wear

St Andrew | 1905–7
E.S. Prior, Randall Wells
SR6 9PT | Usually open

Roker is officially a masterpiece: it is so celebrated in the sumptuous *Arts & Crafts Masterpieces* (Phaidon, 1999).

The Sunderland suburbs of Roker and Fulwell boomed in the 1890s. Charles Prior, the architect's brother, was Chaplain to the Bishop of Durham 1895–7, and must surely have had a hand in helping Prior to the commission. The money did not come until 1903, when John Priestman (1885–1941), shipbuilder ('first-class builders of steamers of the "tramp" and small passenger classes') moved to a grand house overlooking Roker. He wanted the church built in memory of his mother – and for his £6000 he wanted the patronage of the living, approval of the plans, and choice of dedication. A further £3000 was to be raised from other sources, and the church to be built by the end of 1905.

Prior worked with Randall Wells (see p.145): during the building. Wells lived in Roker as resident architect, according to the *Newcastle Daily Journal*, in charge of 'the building work and construction, the details, and the finishings and furnishings'. Prior was

St Andrew, Roker, Sunderland, Tyne & Wear

consultant architect, and devised the plan and 'general scheme.' Wells said, 'we try as far as possible ... to use local materials – in any case good material, that is, material durable and pleasant to the eye – and what traditional workmanship has survived the "contractor"'. Prior put it thus: 'The aim had been the ordinary one of the artist, to do the best with the materials and conditions of his work in view of what interests him most.' Some of the

carpentry and all of the ironwork were carried out in Priestman's shipbuilding yard.

Prior found dressed stone was going to be an expensive luxury, so Roker is essentially a reinforced concrete building faced with stone: the material determined the shape of the nave arches, based on ellipses to simplify pouring the concrete. Rough-hewn oak rafters 'cheerfully co-exist' with the concrete. The glass for the windows, except the east window, and the Lady Chapel (by Henry Payne of Birmingham), are 'Prior's Early English Glass' – to a formula devised by Prior, reviving medieval glass's unevenness and variable thicknesses. The first vicar noted 'the size of panes suggested the size of the windows, and the measurements of the windows determined the length of the bays, and the number of bays give character to the church.'

The chancel is lined in English oak panelling, designed by Ernest Gimson, who also designed the altar rails, altar, Bishop's chair, pulpit, lectern (all made at Sapperton, Glos.), choir stalls; candlesticks, altar cross and processional crosses (made by Gimson's Gloucestershire blacksmith, Alfred Bucknell). The tapestry behind the altar is from cartoons by Burne-Jones, made by Morris & Co. Louise Powell (1865–1956) designed and executed (with Francis Channer) the festival frontal. The beaten silver alms dishes were made by the Newcastle Arts and Crafts Guild. The foundation stones were carved by Eric Gill; in 1927 his brother, MacDonald Gill, painted the chancel ceiling, based on a scheme by Prior, by then old and ill.

St Andrew, Roker, Sunderland, Tyne & Wear: lectern by Ernest Gimson

WYNYARD HALL, County Durham

Chapel | 1903–5
Henry Wilson
TS22 5NF | Private

Wynyard Hall – originally Wynyard Park – is now a country house hotel and wedding venue. It was built 1822–8 in the classical taste to designs by Benjamin Wyatt, later revised by his brother Philip, intended as a grateful nation's gift to the Duke of Wellington, to replace his house at Stratfield Saye, Berks. The Duke did not care for the scheme: the plans were bought by his former lieutenant, Lord Stewart, to replace his own Georgian mansion, now that he had married substantial Durham coal money. Much of the new house was gutted by fire in 1841, and the owner – now the 3rd Marquess of Londonderry – had the original rooms replicated with materials lavish enough to make Disraeli, staying as a guest, feel overwhelmed. When the Marquess died in 1854, his widow commemorated him with a catafalque aggrandised with numerous battle-honours in a Monument Room adjoining the chapel.

In 1888, another fire gutted the chapel. In 1903 the 6th Marquess approached Henry Wilson to restore it, yet more richly, and to update the Monument Room. The sumptuous work in the chapel includes glass by Louis Davis, and wood-carving by Sedding's favoured firm – now also Wilson's – Trasks. The robust west cedarwood screen with round-headed *faux* masonry windows, has squirrels, an owl, a hedgehog, frogs, fish, a stoat, and birds among throbbing foliage. The dwarf screen has diamond marble panels: columns to the adjoining Monument Room

CRAFT SKILLS

Christ Church, Hepple
Hodgson Fowler | 1897
NE65 7LH | Open

St Hilda, Lucker
rebuilt 1874
NE70 7JJ | By arrangement

St Andrew, Stanley
J G Holt | 1876–7
DH9 0PA | By arrangement

Away from the cities, rural and mining communities (as in Nottinghamshire) needed new sources of work and/or entertainment. Often it was the vicar who took the initiative, as pastoral care extended into informal adult education – the Arts & Crafts had swiftly interested itself in fostering skills.

The Keswick School of Industrial Arts (KSIA) was founded by Canon Rawnsley and his wife in 1884 in response to a perceived shortage of local employment. By 1888 around seventy men were enrolled in metalwork and wood-carving classes. Apart from some work in Rawnsley's own Crosthwaite Church (1889), and some memorial plaques, the Keswick School, oddly, seems not to have produced any significant church interior. It is on the east of the country that the most complete schemes are to be found of work produced to high, even exhibition, quality by local people – three examples must suffice. If it were not patronising, they might be classified as 'gifted amateurs' (see also pp 133 and 138).

At **Christ Church, Hepple** the hands were not workmen's. The lectern was carved by William Proud, the village schoolmaster (1894–1900); the altarpiece was painted by Cecilia Boothley, 'a distinguished amateur artist and a frequent visitor to Hepple'; there is stained glass by Herbert Bryans (1855–1925), an associate of Kempe. The wooden panels in the choir were carved by (unnamed) members of the Hepple Carving Class, 1907 and 1925. The painting of the screen, reredos frame and chancel ceiling were 'executed as a part of a scheme of decoration carried out under the direction of Major Hubert Adderley of the Coldstream Guards', 1922–5, although, again, who actually did the work is not recorded.

The Northumberland Handicrafts Guild, founded in 1900, set up craft classes with the County Council. The Guild's first exhibition was in 1901: the class at **St Hilda, Lucker** took first prize. It was organised by the vicar, and initially taught by Florence Hedley, daughter of Ralph Hedley. Hedley's workshop produced the figures of saints for the pulpit in 1904, but the class made the surrounding panels. The names of the carvers are recorded: James Bruce, a tailor who eventually became a teacher of carving; Ralph Gatty, a shoemaker in nearby Adderstone; Charles Grieve, a platelayer on the railway; Joseph Punton, a gardener; Arthur Ryott, a farmer. These men – together with Gertrude Jane Ryott and two unidentified persons (JD and WDG) – also carved panels for the front of the choir stalls. The pulpit, 1904, was designed by

Christ Church, Hepple: altar and reredos
St Hilda, Lucker: pulpit figure

Charles Septimus Errington (1869–1935), who went on to be architect of Tilley's Tearooms, Newcastle, 1909.

At **St Andrew, Stanley**, an unremarkable mid-Victorian church, a woodcarving class was established, the object being to carve an oak pulpit for the church to replace a stone one. 'The instructor, Mr J W Masson, prepared the design – 15th century pattern – the parishioners carved it, and it was assembled by Mr J W Henderson, Prudhoe Street, Newcastle …Later [1909] a carved oak Litany Desk, carved by parishioners, was added.' It is all recorded in a calligraphed History Album in the vestry. There is also a credence table carved by another member of the congregation in 1912.

There are many other examples of committed 'amateurs'. At **St Hilda, Jesmond** (NE2 3ET), fittings were made by craft students working as The Newcastle Handicraft Company, and the three Davies sisters, Louise, Elizabeth and Barbara, who lived locally, and also taught crafts. At **St Helen, Amotherby**, North Yorkshire (YO17 6TN), a 'craftsman vicar', Charles Peach, designed and made the pew ends, pulpit and font, 1886.

St Hilda, Jesmond: War memorial by Fra Newbery, detail

RALPH HEDLEY (1848–1913)

Ralph Hedley managed to be both artist and craftsman. He was born in Yorkshire, but grew up in Newcastle, where he was apprenticed to Thomas Hall Tweedy (1816–92), an outstanding woodcarver. Hedley set up on his own account in 1869 with fellow apprentice James Wishart, who died suddenly two years later. Hedley's woodwork had a distinctive finish – precise, yet clearly hand-carved. In 1883 he made the choir stalls for the newly promoted Newcastle Cathedral, to designs by R.J. Johnson. In 1887 he was making a choir screen to designs by T.R. Spence for St George, Jesmond. The Hedley workshop was allowed considerable latitude in how it treated details, even for architect-designed items. However, for Gothic work, the detailing was derived from standard pattern books. Hedley exhibited furniture at ACES exhibitions, jointly with Spence. By 1900 he espoused a ruggedly radical Arts & Crafts stance: he wrote in the foreword to the first exhibition catalogue (1901) of the Northumberland Handicrafts Guild: 'You might learn to plough a furrow or wield a flail, or throw a shuttle, or thatch a roof…But the machine is doing all that for us …then blow up the machine.'

JAMES EADIE REID (1868–1928)

Reid painted portraits and murals on canvas, designed in glass and mosaic, and worked as an illustrator. He started as a commercial artist in Dundee, then studied fine art in Edinburgh. He joined C.R. Ashbee's Guild of Handicraft in London 1890–1, painting furniture and illustrating pamphlets; he resigned and became assistant to William Richmond, working on the mosaics in St Paul's Cathedral. He worked with Richmond at Christ Church, Cheltenham, 1893–4. He painted *The Dream of Fair Women*, 1902, a mural in the Princess Hall at Cheltenham Ladies' College, where he was a visiting art teacher.

Richmond recommended Reid for the fresco commission at St Columba, Southwick, Sunderland, 1898, his first introduction to the North East. He spent time in Paris around 1900, producing both stained-glass designs and easel paintings. He worked with Ralph Hedley on murals, painted altar and reredos panels. From about 1900 to 1926 Reid was both principal share-holder and chief artist of The Gateshead Stained Glass Company (formerly the stained-glass department of the Sowerby glassworks).

are in white and green Cipollino from Italy, and Pavonazza ('peacock') from Turkey. The lattice-work ceiling has panels of vines picked out in silver and gold. The impact is dense and palatial – like being in First Class on an Edwardian luxury liner. The towering Italianate baldachino is inscribed with part of the opening of Psalm 8: 'Out of the mouth of babes and sucklings thou hast perfected praise'. The Monument Room was never upgraded to Wilson's design, though a typically suffocating Wilson drawing of fevered over-ornamentation survives (online at RIBA 12464).

The Chapel, Wynyard Hall, Durham: west screen

JESMOND, Newcastle, Tyne & Wear

St George | 1887–9
Thomas Ralph Spence
NE2 2TF | Open a.m.

Designs and fittings from the church were shown at the Second ACES Exhibition (1889) and the Third (1890) – but there was not quite the intimate contact between designer and maker that the AWG aimed for: here the '&' in Arts & Crafts was still rather a class divider.

Spence (1845–1918, AWG 1886) was born in Yorkshire and, after a short time as an architect, went off to London to paint: he exhibited at the RA in 1890, and had a solo show at the Fine Art Society in 1910. Meanwhile he was Secretary of the Arts Association of Newcastle (AAN), from which Newcastle industrialists bought their art. The client for Jesmond, Charles Mitchell (1820–95), an Aberdeen-born shipbuilder, underwrote seven AAN exhibitions, at least partly because his son, Charles William Mitchell (1854–1903, AWG 1886), was an exhibitor. Spence had recently enlarged the father's house, Jesmond Towers (now demolished). Mitchell said, 'I have learned that the House of Prayer and God's House should be exceedingly magnifical ... it is not what it costs but what is best. I am building one house for God and I shall put the best material into it from east to west.' He was conscious the church was breaking new ground: he told the *Newcastle Daily Journal*, 'the elements in St George's Church were treated considerably different to what was seen in everyday churches.' Spence had never designed a church.

There is more than a whiff of ego here: on Mitchell's elaborate memorial (1898), by George Frampton (1860–1928, AWG 1887), his shipbuilding wealth is signified by two angels standing aboard ships – one holds a model of the church, the other a model of the Graduation Hall at Aberdeen University, largely funded by Mitchell. Bas-relief figures present Mitchell as industrialist, inventor, aesthete and philanthropist. There is another memorial, to

St George, Jesmond, Newcastle:
Left: Mitchell Memorial detail
Right: north-east corner

his son, also by Frampton, in the south aisle, less laudatory. The Morning Chapel was reserved for the exclusive use of the Mitchell family, accessed through a private door.

The craftwork is foregrounded, either by local firms or AWG craftsmen. It does not so much bring one to one's knees, as crane one's neck to see the magnificence.

The east end dazzles – glass mosaics to outshine Ravenna. The three figures in the reredos and the 12 apostles high on the walls were designed by Mitchell junior, and executed by Rust & Co. of Battersea (see p.243). The tiles with abstract twirling leaf patterns were

St George, Jesmond, Newcastle: baptistry mosaic

painted by George Wooliscroft Rhead (1855–1920, AWG 1890), who also painted the roundels of the Evangelists. The altar – a single block of marble – and reredos are by Emley & Sons of Newcastle. The tesserae in the chancel floor were reputedly laid by Mitchell's house servants. The carved pulpit, on a base of alabaster, and jasper columns, is by Ralph Hedley (p.265), as are the side screens, some of the poppy heads, pew ends and, presumably, the fleurons in the dado. The font is a single block of Mexican onyx. The bronze of St George, cast by Moore & Co. of Thames Ditton, was designed by Spence. The group of figures in oil in panels in the east corner of the north aisle are also by Spence. The Nativity and west window are by John William Brown (1842–1928, AWG 1890). The other windows were designed by Spence and largely made by John George Sowerby of Gateshead. Spence designed the entrance gates, made by Alfred James Shirley (*c.*1848–1912, AWG 1889), all that remains of an elaborate ironwork scheme that ran round the churchyard. Among many other craftsmen named in the archives are Robert Beall, sculptor of Tyneside (1861–1909), and Heywood Sumner (1853–1940, AWG 1884) for gilded gesso work – perhaps the last two panels in the east corner of the north aisle.

GUNNERTON, Northumberland

St Christopher | 1899–1901
Revd John Hawes
NE48 3ET | By arrangement

The building had its origins in a meeting between John Hawes (1876–1956) and the vicar of the parish's mother church, Wilfrid Bird Hornby, retired Bishop of Nyasaland, who asked him to visit local farms as lay minister, and design and supervise a new church.

Hawes's life was on two parallel tracks – architecture and devotion. He attended evening classes at the RIBA and the Architectural Association, and also classes at Central School in wood- and stone-carving. In 1897 he began in practice as an architect. In 1898 he submitted a model for an imaginary church 'set amongst the mountainous

St Christopher, Gunnerton: south door

Cumberland fells' to the RA exhibition. It was noted by Hornby, who contacted him.

The same year Hawes offered himself as a missionary to the Universities Mission to Central Africa, but was rejected on health grounds. In 1901 he began to train for the priesthood, and was ordained in 1903. In 1906 he was with the Benedictines on Caldey Island, where, as Brother Jerome, he made the first attempts at the designs for the new Monastery, subsequently taken over by John Coates Carter (p.278). He hoped to found a Franciscan Order, and seems to have worn a Franciscan habit – a 'homespun brown suit' – as his normal dress. He became RC in 1910, and was ordained a Catholic priest in 1915. He was sent to Western Australia, where he was not only priest, but architect of 15 churches. (He also designed ten in the West Indies.) He ended his religio-architectural career as a hermit in a Hermitage he designed and built at the top of a mountain on Cat Island, in the Bahamas.

Gunnerton is self-consciously pretty. The interior is High Church on a pocket scale: both austere and homely. The chancel was repainted in 2005 to Hawes' original scheme – Indian red and blue-green. There is a rather severe chancel screen and an exuberant canopy over the altar cross. There are carved oak panels at the west end, where Hawes put a gallery for the choir (now removed): an odd mixture of sophistication and naïvety – the *Benedicite*, but with dancing whales, elephants and a dodo, carved by Montague Baker, retired from the Indian civil service, and church organist at Humshaugh, five miles away. The *British*

Architect reported: 'All the work, including practically all the fittings, is of local craftsmanship, being carried out from beginning to end under the personal supervision, on the spot, of Mr John Hawes, the architect, as clerk of works.' The builder, William Smith, and the stonemason, Edward Welton, were both from Gunnerton.

The *British Architect* added tantalisingly, 'The "inventory" of church furniture is to be enriched by a chalice and paten from the hand of Mr H[enry] Wilson.' What became of it?

BENSHAM, Gateshead

St Chad | 1900–3
William Searle Hicks
NE8 4QU | By arrangement

The church was built to serve a predominantly working-class area, over which it massively towers. Hicks (1849–1902) was a dominant figure in Newcastle church architecture, with his partner Henry Clement Charlewood (1857–1943), who completed the church after Hicks's sudden death.

The furnishing and fittings unite antiquarian scholarship with 'modern' design. The wood-carving is by the Newcastle workshop of Ralph Hedley: richly carved roofs and rood beam, screens, stall fronts, desks and reredos. James Eadie Reid designed chancel murals and reredos panel paintings (both since painted over), and designed many of the figurative panels in Hedley's woodwork. London Arts & Crafts specialists supplied other fittings: stained glass in the Chapel of All Saints, 1911, by Caroline Townshend (1878–1944), who had been a pupil of Christopher Whall; further glass by Leonard Walker (1877–1964, AWG 1914), and the Percy Bacon Brothers. The altar plate is by William Bainbridge Reynolds (1855–1935, AWG 1888). Altar, pulpit and litany desk by James Taylor Ogleby (see p.242)

The metalwork was supplied by The (Newcastle) Handicrafts Company (established July 1899) – light fittings (now lost), and the richly enamelled processional crosses. St Chad's was amongst the first commissions for the Company, which specialised in metalwork and embroidery for churches.

SUMMERHILL, Newcastle

St Matthew – 'The Big Lamp' | 1877–1905
R.J. Johnson, W.S. Hicks
NE4 6EJ | By arrangement

St Matthew was to be 'a beacon of Anglo-Catholicism set amidst artisan housing'. It was reportedly its architect's favourite work. It proceeded in fits and starts – the first part was begun in 1877 and consecrated in 1880. After St Nicholas Newcastle became the new diocese's cathedral, Johnson, as Cathedral architect, was busy adapting it to its new dignity. And funds ran low. Johnson died in 1892: the reredos in St Matthew is a memorial to him, designed by W.S. Hicks, Johnson's surviving partner in Austin, Johnson & Hicks. It has been suggested it is based on a design by Johnson himself, discovered after his death. Hicks went on to complete the building and its tower – positioned differently from Johnson's original design – 1895–1905. The sanctuary cupboards seem to pinpoint the fulcrum between the romantic medievalism of Philip Webb's Red House and the later version, the

theatrical braggadocio detectable in the metalwork of Bainbridge Reynolds and the interior design of Reynolds-Stephens.

FENHAM, Newcastle

St James and St Basil | 1927–32
Eric Edward Lofting
NE4 9XP | Open

Sir James Knott (1855–1934) had the church built as a memorial to two of his sons killed in the Great War. He owned the Prince Line: 45 steamships in 1914, mainly working to Mexico and New Orleans. He sold up in 1916, and devoted his life to good works. The complex – church, parish hall, vicarage and public garden of remembrance – were all paid for by him.

St Matthew, Summerhill: sanctuary cupboards

Lofting (1888–1950, AWG 1923) had served in the war with the Kent Fortress Royal Engineers, who fought at the Somme. He was, at the time, Assistant Surveyor to Westminster Abbey, working with (and recommended by) Lethaby, then the Surveyor. Lofting had trained under Temple Moore.

The fixtures and fittings are a different matter. Five of the 13 large windows are by Edward Woore (1880–1960, AWG 1919), who had been a pupil of Christopher Whall. The rest are by George Jack (1855–1931, AWG 1906), seemingly his only designs for stained glass, in which his unfamiliarity was remedied by Woore. There are condors, whales, storks and mountain goats; and a black cat curled up on Christ's lap. Jack also designed the original crystal electroliers, and seems to have been responsible for much of the detailing in the external stonework, and the enormous clock.

The presiding genius in all this was Lethaby, who advised and suggested, and drew together the team of artist-craftsmen. The carved woodwork, including the inlaid altar table (and matching credence?), designed by Jack, was made by Laurence Turner. The pierced organ screen has the unintended air of the seraglio – even more so, the screen at the east end of the south aisle. The silver altar plate was by John Paul Cooper (1869–1933, AWG 1908). Graily Hewitt (1864–1952, AWG 1903) lettered the Ten Commandments on the north aisle panelling.

St James and St Basil, Fenham, Newcastle: screen over memorial chapel

Other Churches

Cumbria

St Kentigern, Crosthwaite | medieval | CA12 5QG
Furnishing elements by KSIA, 1880s: reredos, lights, mosaic, pulpit.

Holy Trinity, Casterton | George Webster | 1831–3 | LA6 2SG
Wall paintings and glass by Henry Holiday, 1893–9; and James Clark (1858–1943), 1905–12.

St Oswald, Burneside | C.J. Ferguson | 1880–1 | LA9 6QT
Reredos by 16 members of an evening class under Arthur Simpson, 1890.

St Philip, Eaglesfield | C.J. Ferguson | 1890–1 | CA13 0RX
Plain and simple. Pulpit given and possibly carved by Mrs Sewell of Brandling Hall, Gosforth. Reredos.

St Bartholomew, Barbon | Paley, Austin & Paley | 1892–3 | LA6 2LJ
Woodwork by Joseph Kilbride of Windermere.

St Columba, Broughton Moor | W.D. Caröe | 1904–5 | near CA15 7SS
Caröe in rugged mood. Built by the men from the local colliery. Both mine and church now closed.

St John, Plumpton Wall | Robert Lorimer | 1907–8 | CA11 9PA
His only parish church in England. Restrained and spare. Woodwork. Reredos from an Edinburgh church.

St Mary & St Michael, Urswick | medieval | LA12 0TA
Woodwork scheme by Alec Miller of GoH, 1909–12, in a rather Renaissance taste.

Northumberland

Hexham Community Church (was Prim) | Cackett & Burns Dick | 1909 | NE46 3LS

St Mary, Stannington | R.J. Johnson | 1871 | NE61 6HW
The Ridley Chapel by Detmar Blow and Reynolds-Stephens, 1914.

Whitley Bay Crematorium (was cemetery) chapel | Edward Cratney | 1913 | NE26 4NH
Plasterwork by George Bankart – oversize angels and tondos.

Durham

St Oswald, Hartlepool | Hicks & Charlewood | 1897–1904 | TS24 8EY
Hedley woodwork, figures by Eadie Reid; font by Robert Beall; screen by J.R. Crimson of Gateshead.

St John, Rookhope | Caröe and Passmore | 1905 | DL13 2AE
Built by the villagers. Closed and for sale; possibly to become a house. **H**

St Luke, Hartlepool | E. Priestly Cooper | 1914–16 | TS26 8NF

Tyne & Wear

St Gabriel, Heaton | Frank W. Rich | 1898–1905 | NE6 5QN
Woodwork, reredos.

Westgate Hall (Wesleyan), Newcastle | Crouch & Butler of Birmingham | 1902 | NE4 5QD
Methodists in good-time, dance-hall vein: angel corbels and big glass roof. Now heavily modified.

St Gabriel, Sunderland | C.A. Clayton Greene | 1910–11 | SR4 7TF
A more restrained, smaller-scale Roker.

All Saints, Gosforth | R.J. Johnson | 1885–7 | NE3 4ES
Ralph Hedley wood; chancel gates.

Holy Trinity, Jesmond | Hicks & Charlewood | 1908, 1920–2 | NE2 1HB
Nicholson glass; fittings. Re-ordered for Evangelical worship.

18

WALES

Some of the most evocative Arts & Crafts churches are in Wales – all designed, and almost all paid for, by outsiders. The great exception ought to be Herbert Luck North (1871–1941) – but, much as he is identified with Wales now, North was born in Leicester, and his connection to and affection for Llanfairfechan were sparked by boyhood holidays there. In time, he became more Welsh than the Welsh. He built two churches and two chapels: in Wales one chapel survives as an inaccessible college store-room.

John Coates Carter (1859–1927), whose architectural career ended in a crescendo of church interiors in Pembrokeshire, especially reredoses (if such intimate objects can be a crescendo), was born in Norfolk, and came to Wales almost by accident.

John Douglas, essentially the architect of the Duke of Westminster and his Chester estates, designed a number of churches in North Wales and one in mid-Wales: they each express widely differing takes on craftsmanship and beauty, and therein lies their interest – but none of them is 'Welsh'.

So, is there a Welsh architect, building Welsh churches or chapels, who embodied the ideals, the spirit, of the Arts & Crafts? Surely, there must be one. But benevolent attitudes towards craft and working men, and an interest in beautiful things for their own sake, were not characteristics of Welsh churchmanship. Chapel architects tended to be chosen because of their adherence to the denomination that commissioned them, for then they could be trusted to do the right thing: respectability, seriousness, Godliness were the qualities sought, not artistic invention. There was competition too – not for numbers, but for supremacy. Street frontages were declamatory and imposing rather than enticing.

One possible candidate might be William Beddoe Rees (1877–1931) who built 29 chapels, many of which show signs he was aware of what was in fashion (p.287).

The abiding sense now, and especially in South Wales, is of buildings closed, abandoned, ruined, ignored. Partly there were simply too many of them – too many denominations, and, at the coast, sometimes doubled up to cater for both Welsh-speaking locals and English-speaking visitors. Partly it is simply a matter of economics – Wales has experienced steep industrial decline. Partly it is cultural: the turning away of Wales from chapel-going has been sharp – from the peak of the Great Revival of 1904–5, when attendances soared, followed by a rapid decline by the 1930s, until today all denominations are in retreat amounting to a rout. The Church in Wales is equally embattled. Congregations have simply walked away.

Look now, before it is all too late.

St Mark, Brithdir looking east

BRITHDIR, Gwynedd

St Mark | 1895–8
Henry Wilson
LL40 2RN | Open (FoFC)

St Mark's is an exotic intruder embodying ideas which have little to do with Wales. It was built by Louisa Tooth (1841–99), returned from Florence, wealthy and widowed, in memory of her second husband. She died not long after it was completed. The relationship between the client and her architect, Henry Wilson (1864–1934, AWG 1892), was conducted entirely through a dense exchange of letters: she kept all of his to her, and drafts also survive of some of hers to him.

Mrs Tooth's husband was Chaplain of St Mark's English church, Florence. His last wish was that 'his worldly possessions should be sold, and further the cause of Christ's Church, to which he had devoted his life.' Louisa wrote to the Ecclesiastical Commissioners: 'I am anxious to build a small church at Brithdir, as all the district … is so far from a church, and the people are simply given to dissent.' Hardly a surprise in Wales.

Louisa had firm views: she wanted the altar 7 feet wide; and 'either there must be a connection between an organ in the gallery and manuals below, or the player must sit in the gallery, and I disapprove of both.' Despite its modest size – it seats no more than 120 – St Mark's has a processional way from vestry to altar. The altar incorporates a 'mensa', a box containing a saint's relic, whose presence was essential for the Catholic mass to be consecrated. The pulpit and altar both bear inscriptions from the *Vulgate* – a Roman Catholic text. The first vicar was expected to conduct three services every day, plus a fourth on the first and third Sundays.

Wilson's idea was Italian: 'I have constantly in mind one or two of those delightfully simple churches just south of the Alps where all the effect comes from the management of the light and the proportions of the roof and walls …' 'While probably no detail will be exactly like any Italian [church] I know …'

Henry Wilson was, in 1906, to Hermann Muthesius, a 'well-known and brilliant architect'. Alastair Service called him a 'genius of Arts & Crafts free design'. In 1895 he was much less celebrated. He became Assistant to John Dando Sedding (1838–91) in 1888: when Sedding died suddenly, Wilson took over the practice.

St Mark, Brithdir: bench-end carving

As a good Arts & Crafts man Wilson wanted to use local materials and skills, despite their obvious limitations: 'the essential condition of real architecture is … that the building shall be formed of materials gathered in the neighbourhood … In order that the work may be done locally, I have omitted everything like carving or elaborate masonry …' At one level this worked: 'The masonry is wonderful and it all looks as if it had sprung out of the soil instead of being planted down on it.' But getting the result was not easy. Wilson visited the site only a dozen times in three years. Day-to-day the project was in the hands of Mrs Tooth's bailiff, William Williams, who, according to Wilson, 'knows no more of building than a cat'. Wilson worked through assistants he sent to the site: Herbert Luck North and C.H.B. Quennell.

Wilson relied on Trasks for the detailed carving on pew ends and altar rails; they were also involved with the making of the altar and pulpit. The font was made to a design by Wilson, modelled by Arthur Grove, and cast at the Central School by William Dodds, a master plumber. The altar frontal, the figures modelled and the whole chased by Wilson himself, dominates the east end. The pulpit, with its copper panels, perturbed Mrs Tooth, who feared it would look like a flower pot. It doesn't. The doors are to a design by Wilson.

Wilson impressed himself: 'the chief merit of Brithdir is that it is *personal* … I have no hesitation in saying that what is done at Brithdir must live, because it has come out of my own life.'

And besides, 'if I had done the ordinary thing everybody would have accepted it …'

LLANDELOY, Pembrokeshire

St Eloi (Teilo, Teilaw) | 1924–6
John Coates Carter
SA62 6LJ | Open

St Eloi hunkers down against the elements – it seems to have almost no windows. The interior has, according to Phil Thomas, the Coates Carter expert, 'something of the intense, sheltering stillness and mystery of a cave or rock-cut shrine'. Coates Carter gave 'his thoughts and works free, neither does he demand pay for the time that he has spent in preparing the plans'. He found 'the great interest of this work more than repaid him'.

The original church was probably ruinous from the 1840s. Photographs from the 1920s show the surviving west wall and bellcote (precariously leaning), chancel arch and screen wall, and a good deal of a 16th-century rood stair. Coates Carter suggested 'the original church would appear to be … perhaps twelfth century… but it is difficult to assign dates in a building that has no architectural details.' He thought the surviving squint might be Celtic.

His approach was ultra-careful and conservative, out-SPABbing SPAB: 'care being taken to preserve every vestige of old work in its original position; and while building the new in harmony, to make it clear where the old

St Eloi, Llandeloy: rood screen

ends and the new begins.' His intention was to re-set the church in its 16th-century prime – a pre-Reformation Catholic vision.

The rood loft and screen in fumed English oak, are by Pearce, Bunclark of Prestbury, Glos., the village to which Coates Carter and his family moved in 1908 from Penarth. It is in memory of a local farmer's son, killed in the Great War, but also a homage to the surviving screens and lofts in Welsh churches such as Llananno and Llangwm Uchaf.

The altar is surmounted by a gesso-work reredos, almost certainly painted and perhaps also carved by Coates Carter himself. The doll-like figure of Christ, and other motifs here – rainbow, sun and moon, figures in the landscape – appear in other reredoses in Pembrokeshire by Coates Carter (see opposite), all of them worth visiting.

CALDEY, Dyfed

Abbey | 1907–13
John Coates Carter
SA70 7UJ | By arrangement

There was a monastery on the island from the 6th century, and Benedictines from 1136 until the Dissolution. The *Anglican* Benedictines 'returned' to the island – gifted to them – in 1906. Their charismatic, headstrong leader, Aelred Carlyle, dreamed of a vast monastic complex, and plans were drawn up by one of the monks, Brother Jerome – who later, as Revd John Hawes, designed the church at Gunnerton (p.268). His first efforts at Caldey were over-ambitious. Carlyle called in help from Coates Carter, who was at that date the leading ecclesiastical architect in South Wales, based in Cardiff. It was by far his biggest job.

There were constant setbacks, compromises, disappointments and disasters. This account considers only the two worship spaces – the Chapel and the Abbot's Chapel.

The Chapel was part of the original, and intended-to-be-temporary 'cottage monastery', 1907. The permanent version was to come later – but never did. In 1940 the space was gutted by fire. All the elaborate furnishings by Coates Carter – lectern, stalls, abbot's throne, hanging lamps, screen, gallery – were destroyed, as was a reredos by F.C. Eden. A hanging pyx by Ninian Comper had been removed in 1913, and is now in Truro Cathedral. The chapel was re-built in the 1950s, but the only sign of Coates Carter's work is the hinges of his doors, which were re-used.

The Abbot's Chapel, 1911–13, is part of what was the palatial Abbot's house, and private. The fabric survives – piscina, holy water stoups and a silver-fronted tabernacle designed by Coates Carter – as well as some atmospheric glass. The movable furnishings – chair, litany desk, floor candlesticks – were taken to Prinknash when the monks, who

Caldey Abbey

COATES CARTER'S REREDOSES

John Coates Carter (1859–1927) has been called 'the leading Welsh Arts & Crafts architect'. But he wasn't Welsh: he was from Norfolk.

He was articled to a Norwich architect in the 1870s, and attracted the notice of John Pollard Seddon (1827–1906), Surveyor to the Archdeaconry of Monmouth *ca.* 1863–1904, in Great Yarmouth supervising a new church. Though based in London, Seddon had an established ecclesiastical practice in South Wales: Carter became its manager, and was in practice on his own account in Cardiff from 1904. He designed exciting houses and public buildings in Penarth. He is best known for Caldey monastery, where he started work in 1906. In 1908 he moved to Prestbury, Glos., for reasons that remain unclear.

His architectural life in Gloucestershire was unexciting – houses, church furnishings. But, towards the end of his career, Coates Carter produced a number of handmade, naïve, intense reredoses in painted gesso, for small country churches in Pembrokeshire. In many cases he painted them himself, and he also seems to have carved the Christs that appear on some.

At **St Mary, Carew Cheriton**, 1923 (SA70 8SR), he seems to be channelling the Italian renaissance, or a medieval book illuminator. At **St James the Great, Walwyns Castle**, 1925 (SA62 3EA) Christ presides over a starburst of gold and a triptych of worshipping angels. At the out-of-the-way **Fisherman's Chapel** at **Angle**, 1926 (SA71 5AP) there is a golden ship, fishermen, reapers and a milk-maid. At **St Andrew, Narberth**, 1927 (SA67 7BH), the geometric reredos is a setting for something yet higher: a crowning adornment like a celestial tiara.

There are powerful, but more conventional carved oak, unpainted Coates Carter reredoses at **St John, Pembroke Dock**, 1919–20 (SA72 6AR); **St Mary, Haverfordwest**, 1920 (SA61 2DA), originally in St Thomas, Haverfordwest; **St Mary, Herbrandston**, 1922 (SA73 3SJ) – a doubly thankful village (all its men returned from both World Wars); and **St Katherine, Milford Haven**, 1925 (SA73 3JU).

Even more elaborate and larger versions are to be found elsewhere: at **St Gabriel, Cricklewood**, 1912? (NW2 4RX); **St Mary, Nolton, Bridgend**, 1921 (CF31 3NL); **Ascension, Portsmouth**, 1921 (PO2 0JG); **SS Andrew and Teilo, Cathays, Cardiff**, 1924 (CF24 4DX).

St James the Great, Walwyns Castle: reredos

converted to Roman Catholicism in 1913, moved there in 1928. They also seem to have taken a sanctuary lamp by Henry Wilson.

Elsewhere in the complex, one sees some of the careful Arts & Crafts aesthetics of Coates Carter: the elaborately vernacular timber roof of the refectory; the hand-crafted staircase, cupboards and metalwork in the Abbot's House; some fireplaces with quirky detailing; a sundial and birdbath, 1913. The island's small church, St David's, restored by Coates Carter, has his ironwork, and a date stone by Eric Gill.

The monks here now are Trappists. The island is visitable by boat from Tenby, but access to the Chapel is restricted, and to the Abbot's Chapel difficult to arrange.

BARMOUTH, Gwynedd

St John the Divine | 1889–95
John Douglas
LL42 1AG | By arrangement

The arrival of the railway (Barmouth Junction, 1865) brought visitors, which strained church provision in the town. The far-sighted vicar, Edward Hughes, was not only keen to provide for visitors, he also founded Barmouth Sailors' Institute (1890) as 'a haven for men of all creeds'.

In 1887 a rocky precipice above the town was donated for an Anglican church: *The Builder* suggested the site was 'rendered somewhat difficult to treat owing to the, in parts, almost precipitous nature of the rocks'. The work was largely funded by a moneyed widow with a holiday home in the town, Sarah Dyson Perrins, branches of whose family founded variously the Dyson-Perrins Laboratory and Worcester Sauce. The chancel, tower, north-east chapel, organ chamber and vestries were a memorial to her late husband, James. Following a major structural collapse (unexplained) during building in September 1891, she seems to have paid most of the cost of

entirely rebuilding this part of the church. Douglas himself contributed £1550. This monster church – it was designed to sit 967 plus a choir of 36 – demonstrates how a rich, self-possessed client could make a statement of both public piety and conspicuous consumption.

John Douglas was not a member of the AWG, nor the NAWG; nor did he exhibit with the ACES; nor was he FRIBA (see p.228). He was working at the same time as the Arts & Crafts, but only tangentially part of it. He was self-contained: he never seems to have wanted the company of other architects. St John's exemplifies how, by the 1890s, an established provincial architect could design in a way

St John the Divine, Barmouth: lectern detail

comparable with AWG flair and mannerisms, even if he was not part of the inner circle.

Barmouth is garnished inside with unexpected things: the font – a marble kneeling angel bearing a huge scallop shell – is a copy by Andrew Davidson, Monumental Mason and Sculptor of Inverness (1841–1925), of one in Copenhagen cathedral by Bertel Thorvaldsen; the copper and wrought-iron lectern is by Singers of Frome, founded by John Webb Singer, silversmith, as Frome Art Metal Works. A bronze foundry was added in 1888. Singer's sons Herbert (AWG 1889) and Edgar ran the company from 1899.

St Mary, Llanfair Kilgeddin: sgraffito panel by Heywood Sumner

LLANFAIR KILGEDDIN, Mon.

St Mary | 1873–6
John Dando Sedding, Heywood Sumner
NP7 9BG | By arrangement (FoFC)

To gain access, you must telephone Friends of Friendless Churches, who own it, in advance, to be put in contact with the keyholder: 020 7236 3934.

The medieval church was largely rebuilt by Sedding, and tactfully. He seems to have brought in the screen, whose source is unclear – some say Somerset. But it is not the screen we come for.

The interior is glorified by a dazzling series of sgraffito panels, 1887–8, on all the walls, of

HERBERT LUCK NORTH

North 'was' Arts & Crafts in a number of ways. He buried himself in the country. He worked in an honest, simple way. He used local materials. He was painstakingly passionate about the details of his buildings. He was sensitive and difficult; shy and diffident. He was interested in liturgy and ceremonial – and he loved dressing up, and pageants, which he often organised.

He would have liked to build mainly churches, but the opportunity did not arise – partly because he worked in Wales, where Nonconformist chapels abounded. North did not have a wealthy patron, nor a reputation as the coming man. His life was one of quiet frustration, and he channelled his energies into the building of idiosyncratic houses, including a development, on his own land, of cottages at Llanfairfechan, worth exploring.

In his early career he furnished and decorated existing churches. Notable are the screen and painted ceiling (possibly painted by North's wife) at **All Saints, Cellan, Ceredigion**, 1908 (SA48 8HX), and the later screen at **St Mary, Llanfairfechan**, 1925 (LL33 0HS). As to new churches, in all he built just two, and two school chapels. One of the chapels survives, the **Bangor Church Hostel chapel**, 1933, (LL57 2BD) now demoted to an inaccessible university store-room. The other, for St Winifred's School, Llanfairfechan, 1929–30, was bulldozed in the 1970s.

His surviving church is **St Catherine, Blackwell, Worcestershire**, 1939–41 (B60 1BN): it displays some of the characteristic chaste severity of his structural treatment, and typical motifs like narrow lancet windows and steep roofs, and with one ceiling to remind of how he loved to colour his roofs and walls. His other surviving church, Holy Spirit, Harlescott, Shrewsbury (SY1 4LP), now seems closed.

Thus North figures less in this account than he might. Partly because of his geographical isolation, partly through temperament. North had few followers, and very little discernible influence beyond North Wales. His intense, personal churches are a sad loss – idiosyncratic, heartfelt and wholly original. Wales could do with them.

Bangor Church Hostel chapel (closed)

verses from the *Benedicite*, illustrated with figures and the local landscape in blue, red, purple, green and orange. The work is a memorial to the wife of Revd William John Coussmaker Lindsay, second cousin to Sir Coutts Lindsay, founder of the (greenery-yallery) Grosvenor Gallery, where Burne-Jones and his circle exhibited. This may be how he came to meet Heywood Sumner (1853–1940, AWG 1884), whose work the sgraffito is. Sedding and Sumner were AWG friends.

Sumner adopted and developed the Roman sgraffito technique, revived by F.W. Moody at South Kensington in the 1870s. It is laborious and unpredictable. Working from holes pricked through a full-size cartoon drawing, sections of plaster in five colours are applied to the walls. Next morning, a top layer of plain plaster is applied. Then, using the cartoon, the prick holes are used to show which bits of the top layer of plaster are to be removed, to reveal the desired colours beneath. The cutting away has to be done by lunchtime, or else the plaster is too hard to work – if the cuts are in the wrong place, it all has to be chiselled off. Sometimes it didn't *quite* work, and 'cheats' can be found, where the colour was painted in afterwards.

The scheme includes walruses, dolphins, a whale, a boy with a hoop, and Abergavenny's local mountains, slightly rearranged for effect. The authors of the *Benedicite* – Ananais, Azarias, Misael (a.k.a. Shadrach, Meshach and Abednego; a.k.a. The Three Holy Children) – are shown, as are Adam and Eve and the Evangelists, among much else.

ABERCARN, Monmouthshire

St Luke | 1923–6
John Coates Carter
NP11 5NX | Derelict and dangerous

This is a problem building in every way. It is abandoned and dangerous – a favourite with intrepid urban explorers, who have in the past negotiated the broken fencing and clambered up the steep hillside to take often dramatised photographs which they publish on the web. There has been a planning application for housing on the site since 2007, stalled in 2016.

In 1921 the *Western Mail* reported the Archbishop of Wales, visiting the town, 'was surprised there was not a large church at Abercarn, but he would be more surprised if there were not one next time he came'. Five years later, at the consecration, the preacher praised 'this perfectly magnificent church'. How it came to be commissioned and paid

St Luke, Abercarn from the east

for is unclear. In 1958 it was reported to be suffering from severe subsidence. Flat concrete roofs were installed, but seemingly to no avail. It closed in 1980.

It is a striking sight: sheer walls of local sandstone; a spookily cavernous central entrance. The interior – now inaccessible – 'a forest of concrete arcades as dense as a Welsh oak wood', is wholly stripped: all furnishings, font and pulpit long since removed. Coates Carter's glass has all gone. Yet something of its majesty remains even after 30 years of vandalism, and destruction of everything that could be broken or burned.

BUCKLEY, Flint.

St Matthew | 1898–1905
John Douglas
CH7 3JN | By arrangement

An 1821–2 church (by John Oates) – the only Commissioners' church in Wales – was first enlarged, then more or less wholly rebuilt by Douglas with Charles Howard Minshull (1858–1934), who was advanced from assistant to partner in 1898, after it was discovered the walls were unsafe: new vestries, remodelled chancel and tower, new porch (in memory of John Ruskin), re-constructed nave. They added the lych gate in 1901.

It is the most Arts-&-Crafts-looking interior of Douglas's career, largely because of the extravagantly painted walls, and some beautiful wood- and copper-work. The baptistry was stencilled and painted by William Frank Lodge (1849–1905), to a design by Douglas, 1903: Lodge later worked with J.L. Davenport, art director of Watts & Co. The timber-framed panels below the clerestory windows represent the Beatitudes, to a design by Minshull, 1910, painted by Robert John Ellis (1863–1925) and his brother Henry (*c.*1867–1912), in partnership in Chester. There are windows by Henry Holiday (1939–1927, AWG 1884) 1901, 1902 and 1910; and C. Ford Whitcombe (1872–1930), 1908–9; as well as more recent work by Trena Cox, 1948, Harry Stammers, 1953, and others.

The font cover is by Herbert Read (1860–1950, AWG 1926), who also made the altar rail, credence table, litany desk, bishop's chair and prayer desk, and possibly the choir stalls and pulpit. The reredos, altar furniture (cross, candlesticks), large candlesticks (in oak with repoussé copper), altar desk, hymn board and prayer board, were designed and made by Robert Hilton (1852–1939), later director of the Keswick School of Industrial Arts.

St Matthew, Buckley:
north aisle decoration

Harry Drew, the incumbent from 1897, was Gladstone's son-in-law: much of the work was paid for by the Gladstones. Douglas and Minshull had added a porch at St Deiniol, Hawarden (1896), the Gladstone family church. After Gladstone's death, Douglas designed the Gladstone memorial Library at Hawarden, 1902 (St Deiniol's).

DOLANOG, Powys

Ann Griffiths Memorial Chapel | 1903–4
G.E. Dickens-Lewis
SY21 0LH | Open

Ann Griffiths (1776–1805) was a poet and hymnographer who lived all her life in Dolanog. She was born an Anglican, but in the 1790s her family became Calvinistic Methodists. The Chapel is built on the site of Salem Methodist Chapel (1830), in a poor state by 1900. The Presbyterians decided to build anew.

Their architect was George Edward Dickens-Lewis (1876–1919) of Shrewsbury, the son of the Divisional Secretary for Wales & Shropshire of the British and Foreign Bible Society, and great-grandson of Thomas Charles, founder of the Welsh Presbyterian Church.

Nonconformist distaste for show vies with a yearning for the pretty – a playful ogee over the entrance, with a semi-circular lobby; flat-capped corner buttresses; extravagant stays

Ann Griffiths Memorial Chapel, Dolanog: *set fawr*

for the gutters. Inside there are more flat tops, this time on newels, and curvy bench ends; stick balusters linked by horseshoe arches and with a flattened ogee. The eye-catcher is an embroidered angel – not quite Ann Macbeth, Walter Crane or Bernard Sleigh – in a panel below the reading desk in the *set fawr*. Unexpectedly, the corbels supporting the hammerbeam roof are portraits of leading Nonconformists, including Ann – the only image of her that exists.

BORTH-Y-GEST, Porthmadog, Gwynedd

St Cyngar | 1911–13
Henry Harold Hughes
LL49 9TU | By arrangement

Hughes (1864–1940) was a friend of Herbert Luck North – they compiled *The Old Churches of Snowdonia* together (1908). Hughes has won even less renown than North. He was appointed Diocesan Surveyor to Bangor in 1900, and carefully repaired many churches – he was a member of the SPAB. His first love seems to have been archaeology. St Cyngar is his only new church.

It is a holiday church, built, according to the petition to the Bishop, 'in consequence of the increasing popularity of the village … as a place of summer resort'. The site and 'a donation' were given by Lord Harlech; Lady Harlech laid the foundation stone. The funds seem to have not quite been enough, as the west end remains 'temporary' – the porch was added in 1964.

It couldn't be simpler – almost not worth noticing. But the exterior repays scrutiny – the chevron indentations in the mortar; the catslide roofs of the meeting room (beneath the east end); the jovial rhythm of 'crazy-paving' stonework and single-stone mullions. There are Instruments of the Passion as corbels in the nave.

It is hard for a church to be jolly in dark local stone – even when the sun shines. And it is all very understated – but this is how vernacular revival looks, perhaps, in a place where it never went away.

St Cyngar, Borth-y-Gest, Porthmadog: studied quaintness

CYMDU, Powys

Hermon Calvinistic Methodist Chapel | 1908
Unknown architect
near SY10 0EF | Open

Hard to find. It is three miles north of Llanrhaeadr-ym-Mochnant, on the lane – Cymdu – to Llanarmon Dyffryn Ceiriog – its location is given as both these villages in different sources! (Not to be confused with Llanarmon Mynydd Mawr.)

WILLIAM BEDDOE REES

Born of English Baptist stock in Maesteg, Rees (1877–1931) was an established architect in Cardiff by 1900. Unusually for an architect by then, he focused on chapels – and published *Chapel Building: Hints and Suggestions* (1903). In 1914 he was Managing Director of Welsh Garden Cities Ltd, which was responsible for developments in Wrexham, Aberaman, Hengoed, Pengam and Barry. During the war he worked for the Ministry of Munitions, and was knighted. In the 1920s he became a successful businessman, in shipping and coal, was an MP by 1922 – and bankrupt in 1930.

He designed 29 chapels, of which 13 survive. One – his most ambitious – is heroically under restoration: **Capel Bethania, Maesteg**, 1908 (CF34 9EJ) in a 'Beaux Arts' mode. He was architect to four other chapels in Maesteg: the Wesleyan, Hope English Baptists, Bethel English Baptists and Tabor Welsh Calvinistic Methodists. Beddoe Rees was flexible as to styles, and very capable of neo-Baroque.

The other survivors which speak most strongly of an Arts & Crafts eye or sensibility are these: **Van Road Congregational, Caerphilly**, 1903–4 (CF83 1JZ) with chunky tower, exotically coloured interior pillars (original?) and unexpectedly classical decoration in the secular hallway; **English Presbyterian Church, Ithon Road, Llandrindod Wells**, 1904–5 (LD1 6AG), with his characteristic 'giant anthemion' gallery frontage, and sinuous ironwork on the set fawr and in the street railings; the tiny **Pentyrch Street English Baptist, Cardiff**, 1905 (CF24 4JW) with a Voysey-ish pulpit; **Trinity English Presbyterian Church, Wrexham**,

1908, looking a bit like a Baines church (LL11 1LE); **Mount Calvary English Baptist Church, Manselton, Swansea**, 1909 (SA5 8QF); **Rhydybont Independent, Llanybydder**, 1911 (near SA40 9RP) with inventive west window tracery bordering on the exuberant; **New Saron Baptist Chapel, Llandybie, Ammanford**, 1913 (SA18 3LN), stripped back and rather austere; **Ararat Baptist church, Whitchurch**, 1914–5 (CF14 1PT) with a friendly little tower. Most have jolly 'pub' glass in cheerfully garish colours, especially in internal doors.

Top: Van Road Congregational Church, Caerphilly
Bottom left: Pentyrch Street English Baptist Chapel, Cardiff: pulpit stair
Bottom right: Mount Calvary Baptist Church, Manselton

A chapel of 1827 was re-built to commemorate the Revival of 1904–5 – according to the three foundation stones in Welsh. What actually seems to have happened was the addition of an entirely new, fashionable façade, and modifications to the school room, including a new fireplace. It has been suggested it may be by Shayler & Ridge (of Shrewsbury, Oswestry and Welshpool), who built other chapels in the area, including **Capel Seion, Llanrhaeadr** (SY10 0JR), but nothing with this swagger and exoticism.

Inside hangs a copy of a poem (a complex metre and alliteration pattern called Englyn) by Arwel Emlyn Jones of Ruthin, commemorating the chapel's centenary in 2009: 'From the beginning, here, once – in some meeting | singing in full sail with gusto and joy, | and surviving from the start of the journey | to sing that a hundred times – a spirited crew in their worship – verses | signifying centenary, | the singing in its glory, | the Welsh of Cymdu celebrating the century. | Verse, and chapter, and faith – sharing | this which is everlasting, | a fine old home for belief, | Cymdu Chapel celebrating the day.' (Translation by Mari Prichard.)

Hermon Calvinistic Methodist Chapel, Cymdu

AMMANFORD, Carmarthenshire

All Saints | 1911–15, 1924–6
W.D. Jenkins
SA18 2NR | By arrangement

The church closed in 2010, but local activists had it re-opened: it was re-dedicated in 2016. Hurrah.

From the outside, All Saints is solid, worthy, interesting, but a little predictable, and not especially 'Arts & Crafts' – though there are hints, such as the way the buttresses slope out towards the bottom rather than go straight

All Saints, Ammanford: Wilson-esque corbel

down ('battered'). But 'looks like' doesn't mean 'is': the architect, William David Jenkins of Llandeilo (1847–?1907), did not belong to the AWG or ACES. The tower, massive and squat, was built, as a War Memorial, by a different hand, Charles Wilfrid Mercer of Swansea.

Inside, the story is rather different. The angel head on the corbel/stop supporting the chancel arch reminds of images on memorial plaques by Henry Wilson. The woodwork is refined, elegant, especially the chancel desks and choir stalls: they were made by Haughton of Worcester, who also did the woodwork for the Church of the Good Shepherd, Upper Colwall, Worcs (1909–10), whose HE listing mentions a possible link to Voysey.

There is something rough-hewn and vivid about the eagle lectern, 1914 – but who made it? The hanging lamps have the air of local blacksmith. The fleurons in the stonework above the tower door, with their date of 1915, are self-consciously medievalistic, but modern with it: Arts & Crafts all over. The reredos is 1936.

So, is it Arts & Crafts? Or simply that, in the context of Wales, with so few 'Arts & Crafts churches', All Saints' faint echoes of the spirit ring loud: uncluttered, direct, with a touch of prettiness, the occasional unnecessary beauty, and an air of unaffected simplicity? It is the most important work of art in Ammanford: a landmark such as many a Welsh town will one day wish it had retained.

LLANGAMMARCH WELLS, Powys

St Cadmarch | 1915–16
W.D. Caröe
near LD4 4BY | By arrangement

Caröe's one and only new church in Wales. The detailing of the doors – horizontal boards and sinuous ironwork – look 'right'. Reredos, 1918 and lectern in sympathy: 'a paean of praise to traditional Welsh craftsmanship' according to Caröe's biographer. The oak pews are simple, but studiedly so. Here one can best assess the ambiguity of Caröe's engagement with Arts & Crafts – was he honest, did he love and trust his craftsmen (none of whom is named), or is it all a bit mechanical, heartless and superficial? The tower is 1927.

St Cadmarch, Llangammarch Wells: porch

LAMPETER

College Chapel | 1877–80
T.G. Jackson
SA48 7ED | Private

The chapel was rebuilt to mark the golden jubilee of the College. Thomas Graham 'Anglo' Jackson (1835–1924, AWG 1889) brought the woodwork for the stalls from New College, Oxford, and designed the painted ceiling. W.D. Caröe was commissioned to design a new Chapel in 1906, but only the organ was renovated, 1908, and later his War Memorial tablet, 1922; pulpit, 1928; and reredos, 1934. There was a substantial reordering 2005–6: pulpit removed, new altar and lectern; pews replaced by chairs.

The College Chapel, Lampeter, looking west

Other Churches

North

John Douglas: from High Victorian to something homelier – vernacular-feeling woodwork; fonts, reredoses

—**St Mary the Virgin**, Halkyn, Flintshire | 1877–8 | CH8 7TX

—**Bryn-y-maen**, Clwyd | 1897–9 | LL28 5EN

—**All Saints**, Deganwy, Llandudno, Gwynedd | 1897–9 | LL31 9DZ

—**St Ethelwold**, Shotton, Queensferry, Flintshire | 1898–1902 | CH5 1QX
Reredos by Nathaniel Westlake.

Peniel, Trefriw, Gwynedd | George Dickens-Lewis | 1907–10 | LL27 0JL
Woodwork; portraits of great preachers in windows. In danger of closure – access difficult.

Lighthouse Community (Baptist), Llandudno | Richard Beckett | 1911–12 | LL30 2BY
In a competition, judged by W.D. Caröe, H.L. North's design came second. Lewis Carroll font.

Tabernacl, Holyhead, Anglesey | Owen & Thomas | 1913 | LL65 1RT
Art Nouveau/Deco-ish exterior, classical interior.

Mid

St Paul, Bryncoedifor, Gwynedd | Henry Kennedy (?) | 1846 | near LL40 2AN
20th-century pulpit, rood screen; swashbuckling lych gate – by whom?

St Philip, Caerdeon, Gwynedd | Revd John Lewis Petit | 1861–2 | near LL42 1TL
Rugged, eclectic. Built for the architect's brother-in-law, outrageously teaching undergraduates in English!

St Wddyn, Llanwddyn, Powys | F.W. Holme | 1887–8 | SY10 0LX

Capel Seion, Llanrhaeadr-ym-Mochnant, Powys | Shayler & Ridge | 1904 | SY10 0JR

South

John Coates Carter: two fortresses; one tiny mission church; the fourth posh – all almost Arts & Crafts in spirit:
—**St John, Wainfelin**, Pontypool, Mon. | 1912–4 | NP4 6DY
—**SS Julian & Aaron**, Newport, Mon. | 1923–6 | NP19 7JT
—**St Philip**, Newport, Mon. | 1924–5 | NP19 0GR
—**St Peter**, Dinas Powys, Glamorgan | 1929–30 | CF64 4BY

George Halliday: flirted with Arts & Crafts, but, fanciful metalwork apart, could not quite shake off Gothic:
—**St James**, Llwydcoed, Glamorgan | 1895 | CF44 0UW
—**St George**, Cwmparc, Treorchy, Glamorgan | 1895–6 | CF42 6LY
—**SS Andrew & Teilo**, Cathays, Cardiff | 1893–1901 | CF24 4DX

Heol-y-Crwys Calvinistic Methodist, Roath, Cardiff | John Henry Phillips | 1899–1900 | CF24 4NJ
Exterior as exotic as a seaside theatre. Now soberly converted to Shah Jalal Mosque.

Hanbury Rd Baptist Chapel, Bargoed, Glamorgan | James & Morgan | 1906–7 | CF81 8QR
Now a library – interior still very well worth visiting. Set fawr *survives in the worship space at rear.*

Whitefield Presbyterian, Abergavenny, Mon. | Edwin A. Johnson | 1907–10 | NP7 5UD

St Bridget, Skenfrith, Mon | medieval | NP7 8UG
Interior by William Weir, 1909–10; lectern by George Jack, 1910.

Barry: A short walk to see Artsy-Craftsy responses to the Great 1904 Revival in then-booming Barry:
—**Porthkerry Methodist Church**, Barry (now flats) | Jones, Richards & Budgen | 1897 | CF62 7BA | **H**
—**Bethel English Baptist Church**, Barry | George Morgan | 1902–3 | CF62 5SA
—**Windsor Road Cong** (URC), Barry (now flats) | W.E. Knapman | 1904 | CF62 7AY | **H**
—**All Saints**, Barry | Col. E.M. Bruce Vaughan | 1908, 1915 | CF62 6NU

West

Tabernacl, Milford Haven, Pembrokeshire | Owain Thomas (of D.E. Thomas) | 1909–10 | SA73 3JP
Now the Pembrokeshire Masjid and Islamic Centre.

Capel y Drewen, Cwm Cou, Ceredigion | J. Howard Morgan | 1921 | SA38 9PB
Laboriously playful.

19
SCOTLAND

Scotland is different. Here there was no AWG to draw men and ideas together, and no ACES to promulgate and exhibit the results. Yes, there was the Scottish Society of Art Workers, exclusive and artistic (and open to women), but it was very much Glasgow based, and only lasted from 1898 to 1901. And, besides, in Scotland there was less money.

Was Arts & Crafts ever even the same here as in England? There were great figures – dashing, enigmatic (nowadays mythic) Charles Rennie Mackintosh (CRM), not that he was terribly important at the time, and wasn't he really 'European'? On the other hand, there was Sir Robert Lorimer to keep things dignified – architecture as lucid Scottish nationalism, always carefully informed by tradition. But not terribly playful. There were, besides, any number of original idiosyncratics – Sydney Mitchell, Archibald Macpherson. And two enigmatic figures at either end of the period – R. Rowand Anderson, who trained some of the architects, but was not *of* them; and P. MacGregor Chalmers, who was prolifically capable both of Romantic nostalgia and stern Modernism.

There *was* ecclesiology too – at the very moment its power was waning in England – through the correct-minded Aberdeen Ecclesiological Society (1886), later the Scottish Ecclesiological Society, though its High-Church-inclined writ by no means ran everywhere.

In Scotland religion was serious, its adherences and disruptions deep and political. There was much less call for exuberance, and less inclination amongst clients to commission exciting, new, personal churches. Much of the work in the period was careful restoration and re-fittings, with a sense of propriety, historical responsibility and restraint. Besides, (pp 32–34) Scotland had already been more than filled with churches.

Overall the impression is of Scotland's architects around 1900 drawn to Arts & Crafts aesthetics; using vernacular motifs and diligent craftsmanship as expressions of something approaching patriotism; with no architect or client single-mindedly intent on their own individuality. The result is a collection of churches even more miscellaneous and heterogeneous than in any English region – and more sober. And each even more arguably *not* Arts & Crafts. As a visitor, the churches are intriguing and powerful, but they are so frank and unadorned, one finds oneself casting round for evidence of Arts & Crafts attitudes, and usually being mildly disappointed.

St Matthew, Queen's Cross, Glasgow:
perspective drawing by Charles Rennie Mackintosh

PORT SETON, East Lothian

Chalmers Memorial (CofS) | 1904
A.G. Sydney Mitchell
EH32 0HG | By arrangement

The impact of Chalmers Memorial Church's tower and spirelet (liturgical west: geographical north) is bold and uncompromising, but the body of the Kirk is modest, crouching in a tidy garden, with welcoming parish rooms beyond.

It was built for (and by) the fishermen of the newly formed United Free Church (UFC), and in anticipation of an influx of workers to the area's mines. The principal funder was Mrs William Wood (1823–1902), born Margaret Parker Chalmers, daughter of Revd Thomas Chalmers (1780–1847), a prime mover in the 1843 Disruption. Her husband was connected to the Cadells, Lairds of Cockenzie – and thus also to F.C.B. Cadell, the Scottish Colourist.

Sydney Mitchell (1856–1930) was by 1902 a well-established Edinburgh architect. He was well connected – his father was a Director of the Commercial Bank of Scotland, and prominent in the Scottish Mental Health Association. Thus much of Mitchell's early work was the design of asylums and banks. In the 1890s he came under the spell of Norman Shaw, but he was never AWG nor exhibited at the ACES. In 1902 he built himself a house, The Pleasance, at Gullane, right by Muirfield golf course: Mitchell was a keen golfer. At Gullane he designed the Free Church Hall and Manse, 1891, and later Gullane UFC church, 1908, now a house (St Peter's).

The exterior of Chalmers Memorial Church is both rough-hewn and sophisticated: it exhibits Arts & Crafts qualities of modesty, simplicity, honesty. But its large dormers have a faintly whimsical air – a French farmhouse, perhaps; its buttresses seem unnecessarily and picturesquely bulky; it has interestingly placed small windows; and the flush-pointed masonry is artfully various. In short, a building to meet the humble station of a fishing community, but in a style to delight the artistic eyes of the benevolent grandees who supervise and manage it.

The interior woodwork includes a pulpit perhaps by the Edinburgh makers Whytock & Reid, or Scott Morton; the carvings on the pulpit stairs seem to be by brothers William and Alexander Clow of Edinburgh. (All these makers were regularly used by Lorimer: the Clows carved the figures in the Thistle Chapel at St Giles Cathedral, 1910–11, and St Michael in the Scottish National War Memorial, from 1924, for Lorimer.) The panelling behind the font was likely made by local Cockenzie joiners.

It is not so much the woodwork that draws the eye, as the mass of painted stencilling on the roof timbers. Blue fish, gulls, waves and stylised foliage riot and cluster on the ceiling.

Chalmers Memorial Church, Port Seton: painted ceiling

In the chancel, its higher status reflected in rich reds and gold, a scarlet 'dossal' emphasises the east end behind the elders' chairs. The effect is unnervingly 'High'.

Who carried out this colourful artistic outpouring on walls and ceiling? It may have been the Edinburgh firm of Moxon & Carfrae, though there is no evidence to connect them to the work. Another possibility is this: the lady who laid the foundation stone had two great-nieces, Agnes 'Aggy' Morison Cadell (1873–1958) and her sister Florence 'Flo' St John Cadell (1877–1966), both respected, albeit minor, painters. They lived in Edinburgh, and, according to a member of the family, 'went everywhere in a pony and trap – and bred dogs and goats'. On the assumption the stencilling and painting was done around 1905, Aggy and Flo would have been 32 and 28 respectively – just the age to be shinning up scaffolding and wielding brushes. There is an anecdote regarding the stencilled paintwork, told in the church's listing: 'The congregation, who largely funded the work, were mostly of the fishing community, and when the building reached the stage of final decoration, the elders were away for the season fishing out of Yarmouth. The designers were left with a free hand and, on the return of the fishermen, there was an outcry from many over the perceived irreverence of the work, to the extent that the decoration was nearly painted over!' Perhaps an association of the church with bohemian *women* artists would have been even more shocking for the Kirk Session, despite the Biblical probity of the Galilee imagery of fishes, and gulls impersonating doves.

PAISLEY

St Matthew's Church of the Nazarene | 1905–7
William Daniel McLennan
PA1 1XD | By arrangement

Superficially, this is Mackintosh-ish without being *by* Mackintosh. The execution is muscular, rather than effete. In taste, Art Nouveau, but with less sinuosity. Were it in England, it would be famous.

It was built as St George's for the UFC. McLennan (1872–1940) was a member of the congregation: he was just 33 when he received the brief for a church 'in the Gothic Cathedral style' to seat 800. He had by that date built

St Matthew's Church of the Nazarene, Paisley: elders' bench

WILLIAM GARDNER ROWAN

GLASGOW, Tollcross Park
St Margaret (CofS) | 1900–1
G32 8PJ | By arrangement

GLASGOW, Shettleston
Eastbank Church (CofS) | 1901–4
G32 7JG | By arrangement

Rowan (1846–1924) was the son of a steam hammersmith, and seems first to have been apprenticed to a civil engineer, then worked for a railway engineer.

He built schools and churches, mainly in Glasgow, with his partner John McKissack in the 1870s. His first church on his own seems to have been **Girvan North Parish Church**, 1883 (KA26 9HE), utterly conventional in red sandstone, but inside with a spectacularly stencilled ceiling, representing 'the seabed with scallop shells and seaweed, the surface of the sea with undulating lines, and the good earth with flowers of the field.' Then Charing Cross, Grangemouth, 1884, 'expressionist and Nordic … in brown ashlar', demolished in the 1980s; the tiny and unremarkable New Church at Scone, 1885; the conventional St Ninian's, Gorbals, Glasgow, 1888, demolished; the Wynd Free Church, Gorbals, 1889, also demolished; and Trinity Church (Glencairn) Pollokshields, 1891, in rather laboured Gothick, destroyed by fire in 1988.

Happy survivals, then, are two humbler buildings in the East End of Glasgow.

St Margaret, Tollcross Park was built to a tight budget – £2203 'exclusive of fees, but inclusive of all else.' Rowan wrote in *Building News*, 'The details of screens and stalls are exceedingly simple, and the pulpit is merely composed of two or three courses of ashlar enriched by a text. At a small outlay I tried to touch up the gas fittings and make them look interesting. That, with a few texts on the greenish stained woodwork in white, is all the decoration I had money for.' The church has been rather radically re-ordered – the original chairs replaced by pews, and those in turn removed. The chancel retains carved panelling and sober built-in elders' chairs.

At **Eastbank Church** (built for the UPC), 'Art Nouveau creeps into the tracery and the Glasgow style into the charming furnishings' according to the 1990 *Pevsner*. The interior has been little altered, and the chancel/east end is a complete survival, with a muscular imposing communion table with pegged joints. The pulpit has crisply carved panels, as has the gallery – less demonstrative than CRM's, but more restful. The *Te Deum* is elaborately lettered across the panelled ceiling, and there is more of Rowan's distinctive and characteristic gold stencilling on the aisle ceilings, under the galleries.

Rowan did not enjoy good health, and this meant 'he never attacked big subjects.' Nor did he travel, apart from one or two trips to England, instead relying on books and journals. He admired Bodley, Gilbert Scott and J.F. Bentley. He was meticulous to a fault: 'For a bit of carving, precious because of the compelling economy elsewhere, he would cheerfully give time and trouble, while ordinary painter work became decoration by his labouring over quaint lettering or ornamental device that cost little but effected much.'

Eastbank Church, Shettleston:
dedicatory stones; stencilled aisle ceiling

two small local churches, Ralston and East Church Elderslie; enlarged a third, Renfrew Trinity; and designed furniture for a fourth, Erskine Parish Church. He registered as probationer with RIBA, 1891, but never sought membership. McLennan was productive – all of his 50 or so works are in the Paisley area.

The principal donor was probably Lady Smiley, wife of Sir Hugh Smiley, a newly created Ulster baronet with a large new house in Paisley: she laid the foundation stone. No building committee minutes survive, so the relationship between architect and client is unknown, nor anything of the craftsmen, though McLennan elsewhere employed Paisley cabinet-makers.

Dark-stained woodwork with small square windows in doors; stylised tulip motif in the gallery front and the larger windows. East window by Robert Anning Bell (1862–1933, AWG 1891) as a Great War memorial. The intended spire was never built. It became CofS at reunification in 1929; St Matthew's Church of the Nazarene since 1988.

BLACKFORD, Edinburgh

Reid Memorial Church (CofS) | 1929–33
Leslie Grahame Thomson
EH9 3HY | By arrangement

The listing (1974) calls it 'Arts and Crafts Gothic' – 'a free and modern rendering of Gothic' in the church's own leaflet. The overwhelming impression is of soaring vertical grandeur enlivened with somewhat buttoned-up beauty. There are all sorts of creatures in the woodwork – a snail, rabbits, two different pelicans in her piety, a lion, a lamb caught in a thicket – but none quite breaks free of the sculpture to breathe: a circumspect Creation.

The carving is by Lorimer associates Scott Morton & Tynecastle Co. There is sinuous metalwork too, by Thomas Hadden (1871–1940), another of Lorimer's regulars, but not much of it, and kept well within bounds. The exterior stonework carving is by Alexander Carrick RSA (1882–1966); stained glass by James Ballantine II FSAScot (1878–1940); reredos painting by William Lawson (1894–1950). All in all, craftsmanship of the very highest quality – but 'was the carver happy while he was about it?'

QUEEN'S CROSS, Glasgow

St Matthew | 1896–9
Charles Rennie Mackintosh
G20 7EL | Museum: admission charge

'A must-see for Mackintosh fans – kids go free!' trumpets a 2010 leaflet: 'The only church built to Charles Rennie Mackintosh's design.' Alas,

Reid Memorial Church, Blackford, Edinburgh: sanctuary carving

it is no longer a church, and thus somewhat lacking in spiritual power: one needs to see beyond the appropriation of the building as a secular shrine to CRM.

The commission was won by the well-established practice of Honeyman & Keppie: their young trainee CRM was entrusted with the job. It is contemporary with his Glasgow School of Art. Like all of CRM's buildings, its spirit is communicated best in his drawings: his perspective (p.292) was exhibited at the Royal Glasgow Institute of the Fine Arts in 1898. The *Glasgow Herald* wrote, 'The design … is obscured by the singular character of the drawing, which arrests and holds attention.'

St Matthew, Queen's Cross, Glasgow: porch

What remains of the interior feels somewhat fragmentary. No choir stalls, no organ; the rood beam (though it has no rood), removed in the 1950s, is a replica, 1990. But the pulpit survives, with birds' heads looking down lovingly on gardens of new seedlings (p.44). And in the wall panelling, Glasgow School stylised foliage and birds. There are similar devices – even more stylised – in the stonework. The 'Blue Heart' east window vibrates with pent-up emotion. CRM's communion table has been returned, and there are chairs from a private collection.

The stone-carving above the double-height porch door seems to fuse the Burning Bush, emblem of the Free Church of Scotland, with the dove and olive branch of the UPC. The two churches were in discussion about a merger in 1897, and achieved union in 1900 as the UFC.

The full list of craftsmen and tradesmen, as well as an extensive gallery of images, is at www.mackintosh-architecture.gla.ac.uk/catalogue/pdf/M125.pdf

GRETNA, Dumfries and Galloway

St Andrew (CofS) | 1917–8
Courtenay Melville Crickmer
DG16 5AS | By arrangement

As the Great War dragged on there was a constant and growing demand for munitions. The materials were inherently dangerous, especially cordite, manufactured using nitro-glycerine. A factory – nine miles long – was built between Gretna and Eastriggs on the Solway – remote enough for the safety of the public, yet near good railway communications. Twenty thousand workers

were recruited, mainly women, from all over the country. They were provided with housing, shops, a cinema, and churches – still regarded as an essential amenity. Provision was made for all the main denominations, English as well as Scots.

Raymond Unwin, architect of Letchworth Garden City, was in overall charge: he appointed Crickmer (1879–1971), a Garden City colleague, as resident architect. Money and time were short, so there was little embellishment.

St Andrew's looks both back and forward, a tangible transition from the Byzantine/Italianate strain in Arts & Crafts churches to something like Modernism. The *Annandale Observer* called it 'very simply designed as a war building, depending for its effect on a broad dignified treatment'. It was used by both CofS and UFC.

The Episcopalians had **All Saints**, designed by Geoffry Lucas, 1917 (DG16 5DH), with wood-carving by Laurence Turner; the RCs **St Ninian**, now the Anvil Hall wedding venue, by C. Evelyn Simmons, 1918 (DG16 5AB); Unwin and Crickmer's **St John Eastriggs**, 1917, also survives (DG12 6QE). There is scarcely a trace of the factory.

St Andrew, Gretna looking east

CHARLESTOWN of ABERLOUR, Moray

Sacred Heart (RC) | 1909
Archibald Macpherson
AB38 9LL | By arrangement

Archibald Macpherson (1851–1927) was Rowand Anderson's chief assistant (1873–6), in practice on his own account from 1877. He was far travelled and an accomplished linguist, 'equally at home in Italian, Spanish and French … Few …. possessed his encyclopaedic knowledge of the ecclesiology of the middle ages …. His scholarly understated style appealed to converts and to the old Catholic gentry' (*DSA*). He was known for his draughtsmanship: 'finished drawings were rare, details being redrawn and altered many times over, and often a set of working drawings being ruthlessly scrapped and begun again.' His practice was largely confined to the archdiocese of Edinburgh, the dioceses of St Andrews and Dunkeld, and Aberdeen. He was FRIBA in 1906.

Aberlour is humble: 'built to serve the Catholic population … as a mission station…' The furnishings are by Hughes & Watt of Edinburgh.

There is care, discretion and self-effacement in the work, coupled with devotional intensity and richness of treatment – gold stencilling on dark wood and an intense rood and reredos – and light-hearted optimism.

Sacred Heart, Charlestown of Aberlour: looking east

PHOEBE ANNA TRAQUAIR

As Charles Rennie Mackintosh has become to Glasgow, Phoebe Anna Traquair might be to Edinburgh – revered, put on a pedestal, pummelled into a brand. She has the additional appeal of feminist icon. She was not an architect, but, though she was expert in illustration, enamels and textiles, her principal works – and especially in the context of this book – are architectural decoration.

Mortuary Chapel
Royal Hospital for Sick Children, Morningside | 1885–6
EH9 1LF | Access problematic

Song School
St Mary's Episcopal Cathedral, Edinburgh | 1888–92
EH12 5AW | Tours available

Mansfield Traquair Centre,
Edinburgh | 1893–1901
EH3 6BB | Usually open

In 1885 she was commissioned by the Edinburgh Social Union (ESU) to decorate the tiny **Mortuary Chapel** of the Royal Hospital for Sick Children. The chapel was demolished in 1894, but parts of her work were moved under her direction, and reworked to fit a new building (George Washington Browne, 1891–2), 1896–8. The Chapel – currently in the hands of developers, and with access uncertain – sets her earlier saccharine Victorian Sunday School prize illustration alongside a later, freer, lighter, more joyous combination of naturalistic and symbolist images.

The decorative scheme in **St Mary's Cathedral Song School** (designed by John Oldrid Scott, 1885, executed by Rowand Anderson) is a festal elaboration on the *Benedicite*. The choristers process around the walls, encouraged by angels strewing flowers, and Cathedral clergy of the day, reportedly accurate portraits. Tennyson, Browning, Rossetti, Carlyle, Watts, Blake, Dante, General Gordon and Cardinal Newman also figure. Sparrows, wagtails, chaffinches, blackbirds and hawks crowd a flower-filled landscape. A fish is introduced to the water by a divine hand.

The Catholic Apostolic Church (now the **Mansfield Traquair Centre**) was built to an enormous budget to the designs of Rowand Anderson in 1873–84. The ESU suggested Traquair should decorate it. The apocryphal story, told in *The Studio* in 1905, has it that she wandered into the church, heard the music and prayers, and said to one of the Deacons, 'I want to paint these walls.' It captures her confidence, determination and impish bravado. The murals are her response to the richness of the Catholic Apostolic ritual and music – reportedly executed without preliminary sketches, and 'following the promptings of her instinct and mood'.

Traquair's church decorative work in England is at **Thorney Hill** (p.72) and at St Peter, Clayworth, Notts (DN22 9AB). In 1910 she designed and made enamel plaques for the Knights of the Thistle stalls in Lorimer's **Thistle Chapel**. In 1920 she designed a triptych for **All Saints' Church, Jordanhill, Glasgow**.

Song School, St Mary's Episcopal Cathedral, Edinburgh: window embrasure

BRECHIN, Angus

Gardner Memorial (CofS) | 1897–1900
John James Burnet
DD9 6AW | By arrangement

Revd Alexander Gardner died in 1893 and left £7000 for the building of a church in memory of his lawyer son, who had committed suicide. A further £7000 was donated by Gardner's friends, local landowners Mrs and Miss Agnes Milne. The churches of J.J. Burnet (1857–1938) are less strait-laced than others', more fun and more approachable – he built around twenty 'long, low, friendly churches'.

Gardner Memorial Church, Brechin: stonework grotesque

It teeters on the boundary between stern Gothic and something less dogmatic. The red sandstone helps: comic grotesques in the exterior stonework frieze, including a grinning devil coyly covering his ears, a sharp-elbowed elder, a man seemingly draped only in a towel, and a chubby gryphon (?) in what looks like a lawyer's wig. Empty niches do not suggest statues to come, but recollect, perhaps, images that would have been swept away. An open cloister adds a frankly quaint note – and is useful in Scotland's occasional rain.

Inside, on the pulpit, a bear, and an angel who seems about to take off. And an even greater example of teetering, this time liturgical: for here is a rood beam not only without a rood, but without any figures at all – 'to avoid the worship of man's workmanship rather than his creator'. The figures were not removed – they were never there.

MELSETTER, Hoy, Orkney

Chapel of SS Colm and Margaret | 1899–1900
W.R. Lethaby
KW16 3NQ | Private
At the time of writing, it is not possible to visit this chapel.

Melsetter was Lethaby's only house in Scotland, and his only country house other than Avon Tyrrell (1892). It was built for Thomas Middlemore of Edgbaston, whose family made their money supplying saddles and harness to the Army. Thomas sold the business in 1896, and wished to do the gentlemanly thing and acquire a grouse moor – he had to content himself with the Melsetter estate: 40,000 acres including four islands. His wife, Theodosia – a Scot born in Kinlochbervie, Sutherland – was artistic: she showed embroidery at the ACES. Her friend May Morris visited Melsetter a number of times.

Lethaby's interests were deeper and wider than mere Christianity: it is not clear how religiously committed either of the Middlemores was. The chapel – which from the outside seems no more than a converted beast house (it isn't) – is humble and rather cave-like. Over the door is a keystone with a stylised sun (a simple circle), crescent moon and cross. (There is a comparable moon and star on the south gable of the east front of the house.) Over the altar is a star-shaped window, and on the north side, an assertively rustic aumbry.

The chapel roof is an unreinforced concrete vault, the prototype for the vault at Brockhampton (p.142). It springs from low on the walls, with a robust stone arch in the office of a screen. The sandstone font, like an enlarged egg cup, employs a Lethaby motif of incised waves. The window embrasures have free-standing columns, elongated quatrefoil in section – Lethaby later did something similar at Brockhampton. Two small windows by Christopher Whall; and a window each to designs by Burne-Jones and Madox Brown. The chapel was designed to seat 39 people – it would be a squash.

COLINTON, Edinburgh

Parish Church | 1907–8
A.C. Sydney Mitchell (rebuild and interior)
EH13 0JR | Usually open

Where at Port Seton (p.294) Mitchell was ruggedly vernacular on the outside and primitively exuberant on the inside, his rebuild of Colinton is sophisticated and

Colinton Parish Church looking east

ROBERT LORIMER

Edinburgh, Murrayfield
Good Shepherd (Episc) | 1897–9
EH12 6AX

Edinburgh, Morningside
St Peter (RC) | 1906–7, 1928–9
EH10 4AN

Edinburgh, St Giles Cathedral
Thistle Chapel | 1909–11
EH1 1RE

Edinburgh Castle
National War Memorial | 1919–27
EH1 2YT

Glasgow, Knightswood Cross
St Margaret (CofS) | 1928–32
G13 2HA

Access to the churches, by arrangement. The Thistle Chapel and National War Memorial are usually open.

Lorimer (1864–1929) is such a colossus he almost defies inclusion in this book. It has been debated whether he is the Scottish Lutyens, or Lutyens the English Lorimer. Both men had their beginnings in Arts & Crafts, had Arts & Crafts instincts, and enjoyed working that way – but their later reputation and status as articulators of national spirit, and in particular, national grief, and the architectural expectations placed upon them – not least by themselves – have tended to obscure their Arts & Crafts hearts.

Lorimer differs from Lutyens in this important respect – he was devoted not only to fine craftsmanship, but to a group of men, especially wood workers and a favourite metalworker, whom he used again and again. Were they personal friends and equals? Or was Lorimer always the deferred-to great man? He had a reputation for being dictatorial, especially as he grew older.

He was the son of a Law Professor at Edinburgh University, so there was always intellectual heft. He is said to have been drawn to architecture when his father rented Kellie Castle, Fife as a holiday home, possibly on a repairing lease – there was grandeur from the start.

He started in the office of Rowand Anderson in 1885 – their relationship was always difficult. Lorimer was prickly and could be tactless. He went to London in 1889, and worked for Bodley – he met Norman Shaw and Walter Tapper. He was elected to the ACES in 1897, and was a regular exhibitor at ACES shows. But he was not AWG until 1922, by special invitation.

Back in Scotland, he was in the office of Dunn & Watson, who took over James MacLaren's practice after his death in 1890 – Lorimer had earlier worked with MacLaren too. After he set up in practice on his own, he kept the office small. Among his many assistants and apprentices were Ramsay Traquair, 1897–9, and Reginald Fairlie, 1901–6.

His practice was primarily houses: churches were of no great significance. Taken out of the context of his wider domestic and national oeuvre, the churches seem a motley collection.

His first was **Good Shepherd, Murrayfield** which remains unfinished – proposed statues on the porch are blank blocks yet. There is a pretty reredos, and light-hearted stone carving on the sedilia – a cheeky squirrel, and birds. The screen has small smiling angels, and there are more above the chancel arch – Honour and Glory. Lorimer designed the lectern.

At **St Peter, Morningside** there are objects to ravish the eye – but the church itself lacks coherence: partly due to the cataclysmic reordering of the chancel following Vatican II. Nonetheless the eye is drawn to the hefty lead font (by Bankart), the marble floor in the sanctuary with its inset fish (shades of Weir Schultz at Westminster), the radiator grilles (more fish), the light fittings, a huge canvas by Frank Brangwyn; and, externally, bas-relief sculptures, lion gargoyles, ironwork with Parisian swagger, and a sense of something oddly Italian – despite the replacement of the original red roof pantiles. It was a radical experiment which led nowhere.

St Peter, Morningside: railings

Lorimer took over the **Thistle Chapel** at St Giles Cathedral from the failing, elderly Thomas Ross. This is craftsmanship writ large: wood-carving by the Clow Brothers (see p.292), glass by Louis Davis and Douglas Strachan. But it is, in Arts & Crafts terms, copyist: the spirit is St George's Chapel, Windsor – looking back to a golden age with undisguised grandiloquence. (The over-reaching went even farther at Dunblane Cathedral, where Lorimer overwhelmed the surviving medieval stalls with something grander yet.)

The Great War took him beyond the Scottish context to the War Graves Commission, and war memorials. And then the **Scottish National War Memorial** – not a church, but very nearly one: it borrows ecclesiastical aesthetic language to express a disciplined commingling of grief and pride, of remembrance that is never celebration, but dignified reflection. Glass, bas-relief panels, sculpture, by over 200 artists, including eminent sculptors Alexander Carrick and Charles Pilkington Jackson (1887–1973), the glass designer Morris Meredith Williams (1881–1973) and his maker wife Alice (1877–1934). Lorimer encouraged young female artists, notably the sculptor Phyllis Bone (1894–1972); and here too his coterie of favourite makers, including the metalworker Thomas Hadden, and the woodcarving Clow brothers. All the glass is by Douglas Strachan.

Lorimer's last, **St Margaret, Knightswood Cross** has the austere simplicity which, but for national prominence, might have been Lorimer's metier. There are echoes in the interior of Fortingall church, especially in the woodwork (Clow brothers). The building was executed by his partner, John Fraser Matthew.

There are examples of Lorimer's church work in England – at St John, Plumpton Wall, Cumbria, 1907 (CA11 9PA); the reticent garrison church of St Andrew, Aldershot, Hants, 1927 (GU11 2BY); and the overwhelmingly classical chapel of Stowe School, 1927–9, completed after Lorimer's death (MK18 5EH).

St Peter, Morningside:
font; organ case; from the south

somewhat mysterious – was Byzantine really wanted in this douce suburb?

The semi-circular apse – often dramatically lit – is embellished with a tenuous oak screen, and, across its top, in modish lettering, 'O worship the Lord in the beauty of holiness'. On either side are panels with yet different lettering, signed off with entwined hearts. The apse is lined with dado panels of pale blue stencilled stylised trees, 1929, and the timber entablature above is decorated with flat white silhouetted Instruments of the Passion. The rather attenuated font is surmounted by a muscular cover with cheerful putti, and an Ark resting on Mount Ararat, counterbalanced by a descending dove. The capitals of the columns in the nave also have putti heads, and there are low relief plaster angels in the spandrels.

The windows in the apse are by James Ballantine II – angels of Love, Joy, Peace, Long-Suffering, Gentleness, Goodness and Faith. (Self-Control and Kindness have been boarded over.) The pulpit has dramatic saints. The communion table has a chunky St Andrew's cross.

The whole feels quite unlike what an Edinburgh parish church ought to be – far from chilly, but embracing and dumbfounding.

FORTINGALL, Perth

Parish Church | 1900–2
Dunn & Watson
PH15 2NQ | Usually open

Donald Currie (1825–1909) was a rags-to-riches Scot in the grand Carnegie tradition – from shipping clerk to head of the Union-Castle steamship line, and MP for Perthshire. He bought his first Perthshire estate – the Garth – in 1880, and Glenlyon, which includes Fortingall village, in 1885. He engaged James Marjoribanks MacLaren (1853–90) to transform the straggle of dilapidated cottages into a model estate village. MacLaren's sympathies lay in the past, and his ideal was Scots medieval – harling, corbelling and crow-stepped gables. His early death, aged 37, meant he did not live to restore the parish church – instead, his successor colleagues William Dunn (1859–1934) and Robert Watson (1865–1916) were commissioned by Currie in 1899 to build

Fortingall Parish Church from the west

an entirely new church on the ancient site of the previous church. It is possible they used a MacLaren design.

The building – as so often in Scotland – is a reticent celebration of direct, unelaborated reverence. Outside, a sundial with the dour reminder, 'The Night Cometh'. Dunn & Watson's five high-canopied elders' stalls, 1913, unequivocally face the congregation, asserting hierarchy and authority. The Lord's Prayer and Ten Commandments are on boards to right and left, in a typeface that is both medieval and modern – as if to remind us of their eternal verity. All very correct.

Yet in the windows, gentle leading includes hearts (or tear-drops?); the pulpit is modestly low, and plainly embellished with linen-fold; the barrel vault in Hungarian oak has daintily carved bosses.

RAVELSTON, Edinburgh

St Andrew (RC) | 1902
Unknown architect
EH4 3DS | By arrangement

A remarkable survival – a 'temporary' wooden church which has lasted over 100 years, and with Arts & Crafts furnishing and decorative detailing. Seemingly not bought from a

St Andrew, Ravelston, Edinburgh looking east

catalogue, nor made to a catalogue design – but who *was* its designer? It was built (by the parishioners?) in six months, for £850. Local tradition has it that it came from Austria – but there is no evidence.

The *Catholic Directory* (1902) was charmed: 'It occupies a very picturesque site, designed in a style of Old English architecture, with quaint crossbeams and diamond paned windows and a practical miniature belfry. Seated with chairs, the interior presents a pretty if somewhat rustic appearance.'

The open timber roof rests on slender timber pillars, with almost Century Guild flat-topped capitals. There are robust and patriotic hanging lights and sconces, rather old-fashioned for their date. Wooden child angels kneel meekly on either side of the altar steps. There is unexpectedly rich carving in a side chapel, and attention to detail everywhere.

It did not, perhaps, *intend* to be Arts & Crafts, but it stands yet to reflect the ubiquity of the taste by 1902.

FORFAR, Angus

Lowson Memorial Church (CoS) | 1912–14
A. Marshall Mackenzie
DD8 2HY | Usually open

John 'Jock' Lowson (1813–1903) was a linen baron – in the 1860s he built Forfar's Victoria Works ('Jock's Works') to capitalise on the

Lowson Memorial Church, Forfar: Douglas Strachan glass

new steam looms. He told his wife that money was coming in from the business 'in barrowfu's'. When he died, he left £200,000 – more than enough to build a new church, even though there were already two CofS churches in the town. Lowson's daughter, Mrs Steele, was the driving force to add the third, which some argued (for several years) was quite unnecessary.

'Ample funds' were placed at the architect's disposal, and 'his talents were not hampered by narrow-minded restrictions'. Marshall Mackenzie did not strike out on new ground – he rarely did. Here he drew on ideas found in Elgin Cathedral (he was born in Elgin) and King's College Chapel, Aberdeen (his practice was in Aberdeen); and the font was based on one at Restenneth Priory, of about AD 700.

The principal draw is the huge scheme of dazzling glass by Douglas Strachan (1875–1950), dedicated in 1914.

ST ANDREWS, Fife

All Saints (Episc) | KY16 9BQ
John Douglas (chancel) 1905–9
Paul Waterhouse (rest) 1920–4
Open

The chancel, in memory of Episcopalian champion T.T. Oliphant (also co-editor of a book of golf stories, 1894), was designed by John Douglas of Chester. The rest was funded (£25,000) from 1920, by Annie Younger, wife of a brewery heir and herself a scion of the Paton yarn-spinning dynasty. Her money paid for nave, chapel, baptistry, rectory, church hall, gymnasium, club rooms, library and billiard room, as well as vestments, pulpit, font and other furniture.

This was the last work, and one of only three church jobs, by Paul Waterhouse (1861–1924) (p.112) – he had built a house for the Youngers (as had his father), and Paul married a Younger. The squat pillars – a Waterhouse enthusiasm – and the theatrical baptistry metalwork move, somewhat lugubriously, towards Art Deco. There are Frenchified chancel gates; an Italian-looking pulpit; Henry Wilson-style angels. The hanging crucifix, and spirelet over the reredos were carved by Nathaniel Hitch to Waterhouse's brief. (Did he make the gleaming

All Saints, St Andrews

ROBERT ROWAND ANDERSON

St Sophia (RC)
Galston, Kilmarnock | 1884–6
KA4 8HT
By arrangement

St Cuthbert (Episcopal)
Colinton, Edinburgh
1888–93 | EH13 0BD
Often open

Rowand Anderson (1834–1921) is the Bodley of Scottish Arts & Crafts: an inspiration to the young architects who came after him – many had trained under him – and, though he did not quite subscribe to their nationalist vision, had he been 30 years younger, he might have. In Anderson's office at different times from 1869 were Archibald Macpherson (p.298), Robert Weir Schultz (pp 106, 130), Sydney Mitchell (p.292), Robert Lorimer (p.302) and twenty or more others.

His inclusion here is primarily for that influence. He trained under Gilbert Scott 1857–9: his early churches show it. His RIBA proposers included John Belcher, William Burges, Gilbert Scott and Aston Webb. He was startlingly prolific for 60 years. However, he completed no new-build church after St Paul, Greenock, 1890.

St Sophia, Galston is a Scottish Byzantine vision of Hagia Sophia, built for the third Marquess of Bute, who having been to Istanbul, wanted a dome. Bute's favourite architect, and friend, William Burges, died in 1881. Anderson had meanwhile been awarded the job of the palatial new home for the Butes, Mount Stuart 1878–96. The first designs for a Byzantine church (for Troon – not built) were drawn up by Anderson in 1882: Weir Schultz was with Anderson 1876–81, so he may have had a hand, perhaps.

St Cuthbert, Colinton shows a more typical Anderson – he was a parishioner and partly funded the church. The decoration, at one time thought to have involved Phoebe Traquair (not now), is rich and extensive, in a Bodley mode – the walls were whitewashed over in 1939. Anderson was also the designer of Edinburgh's Catholic Apostolic Church (now Mansfield Traquair Centre, p.301).

Left: St Sophia, Galston
Right: St Cuthbert, Colinton: gargoyle

font cover too?) Windows by Louis Davis, 1913 and 1923; also by Karl Parsons and Strachan.

The intensity and immanent gloom of a Henry Wilson chapel – arches, shadows and mass – with, for once, exhilarating objects coalescing into something articulate and coherent: 'a church in keeping with modern ideas', according to the local paper at the time.

KIRRIEMUIR, Angus

St Mary (Episc) | 1903
Ninian Comper
DD8 4HX | Key at rectory

It rather surprises Sassenachs to learn that Comper (1864–1960) was a Scot. The churches of his maturity at Wellingborough and St Cyprian, Clarence Gate, London seem so utterly English in their courteous clarity and etiolated dignity.

He was born and bred in Aberdeen, a son of the manse. After a year at Aberdeen School of Art, he was briefly at the Ruskin School in Oxford, then started architectural training in London, first with Kempe, then Bodley. He was in partnership in London with another Scot, William Bucknall, from 1888 (see Gosberton Clough, p.191). He married Bucknall's sister.

Kirriemuir, replacement for a predecessor destroyed by fire, demonstrates his feeling for assertively Scottish ideas. Externally, it is 'Scots Revival', with crow-stepped gables and a Baronial turret. Inside all the furnishings are by Comper, including much of the glass: mild, full of thoughtful detail. Perhaps the church's connection with his late father – one of the windows is a memorial to him – explains the plangent note of the past.

Comper did a good deal of other work in Scottish churches, including a lot of furnishings. His first church buildings are

St Mary, Kirriemuir

very much Bodleyan. The churches that most strike an Arts & Crafts note are perhaps these. **St Margaret, Braemar**, Aberdeenshire (Episc), 1898–1907 (AB35 5YP) is now a music venue and usually open. It retains the bare bones of Comper's 'English altar', a delicate screen and a rood beam. His work at **St Michael, Inverness** (Episc) (IV3 8HH) – a series of alterations from 1904 to 1928, of the 1903 reconstruction of Alexander Ross's 1886 church – almost qualifies it as 'his': and it is surprisingly dramatic. His final Scottish note is one of backward-looking romance at the self-consciously simple **St John, Rothiemurchus,** Aviemore, Cairngorm (Episc) (PH22 1QH), where the foundation stone was laid in 1913, but the building not completed until 1929–30. The rose damask baldachino captures a calm pre-Reformation world.

MIDSTOCKET, Aberdeen

was St Ninian (CofS) | 1897–1900
William Kelly
AB15 5NZ | By arrangement

William Kelly (1861–1944) was Aberdeen's busiest architect in the period – granite offices for banks, and houses for the burgeoning bourgeoisie, as well as asylums, schools, hospitals and a handful of churches. He was in London 1883–6 accumulating experience – he was an exceptional draughtsman – before returning to Aberdeen.

St Ninian's was won in a competition – J.J. Burnet was the adjudicator: 'A new and striking addition to the ecclesiastical architecture of the city'. Grey granite makes for a fiercely stripped-back exterior – the playful 1902 sundial ('Now or when') strives to lighten the tone. Inside – it has been reordered – there is a sense of control: nothing to detract from the serious matter of the service. Closer inspection reveals glories. Pulpit and communion table are inlaid with neat and canny contrasting woods; there is a densely sculpted Minister's chair; and, in the side aisle, a moving and beautiful lectern, 1902, to the memory of two infant children – designed by Kelly and made under the supervision of David Graham, master wood-carver. Chancel window by Strachan, 1903.

Midstocket Church, Aberdeen: sundial

PETER MACGREGOR CHALMERS

MacGregor Chalmers (PMC) (1859–1922) was essentially, and prolifically, a church architect – some 130 church projects in all, though by no means all new-builds. But 'is' he Arts & Crafts? In any sense? Insofar as it is a meaningful question – the more doubtful in independent-minded Scotland – the answer remains equivocal. This article tries to pick out those of his churches most likely to reward a seeker after Arts & Crafts vibrations.

Carriden Parish Church, Bo'ness, West Lothian, 1907–9 (EH51 9LU) stands hard by its predecessor of 1766, now a ruin. The need was for something bigger. The exterior is imposing, rugged, uncompromising, with clever stonework in the west door archway. Just above, an inscription in an oddly jazzy typeface – 'The Lord loveth the Gates of Zion.' There are more of these lively Bible tags – carved by David Aitken (of Bo'ness?) – in stone panels to be found inside. (They occur often in PMC churches.) The work was all carried out by local men – Jimmy Mann in charge of the masons, the Turnbull family undertaking the woodwork. The highlight is perhaps the unexpected painted (gesso?) Christ in Majesty in the half-dome baptistry ceiling, with a gilded Pelican in her Piety – but who painted it? There is a boldly Anglo-Norman (?) communion table, and, high in the capitals round the apsidal chancel, detailed scenes from the life of Christ.

A rather less oppressive version of the same ideas is **St Cuthbert, Saltcoats**, 1907–8 (KA21 5AF); and a variation in red sandstone at **St Nicholas, Prestwick**, 1908 (KA9 1NW), with a lively range of elders' stalls. At **St Columba, Blackhall**, Edinburgh, 1903 (EH4 3QU) the motifs are more refined, and the carving less cumbersome. **St Anne's, Corstorphine**, Edinburgh, 1912 (EH12 6JR) shows something of Italian influence. **Kirn Parish Church**, Dunoon, 1906 (PA23 8HQ) is more modest. At **St Margaret's, Newlands**, Glasgow, 1910–35 (G43 2DS), these same well-worn ideas seem altogether more committed and heartfelt – the confident communion table is stone, the pulpit is elaborated and potent, there is more of the Celtic in the stone motifs, and the apsidal ceiling is in vivid mosaic. **Holy Trinity, St Andrews**, 1907–9 (KY16 9NL) is a shrewd and careful re-imagination of the church to its assumed medieval appearance – theatrical as much as historicist. Nonetheless, the furnishings smack very much of the Arts & Crafts. Not proven.

Above: St Columba, Blackhall
Top right: St Anne, Corstorphine
Bottom right: St Margaret, Newlands

Other Churches

Borders and South

St John (RC), Cumnock, Ayrshire | William Burges and J.F. Bentley | 1882 | KA18 1HB
Too good to exclude. Apse ceiling a Burges extravaganza. Side altar by Bentley and N.J. Westlake.

Crichton Royal (Memorial), Dumfries | Sydney Mitchell | 1890–7 | DG1 4UQ
Lavish.

Clark Memorial Church (UFC), Largs | William Kerr | 1892 | KA30 8BL
Glass from Glasgow, 1892: Stephen Adam (1848–1910).

Skelmorlie Church | John Honeyman | 1893 | PA17 5DY
CRM-designed lamp over entrance. Glass by Honeyman, Stephen Adam, Douglas Strachan, etc.

All Saints (Episc), Lockerbie | John Douglas | 1903 | DG11 2BQ
Douglas's only Scottish church. Picturesque. Comper reredos, 1925.

St Andrew's (Episc), Innerleithen | C.E. Howse | 1904 | EH44 3JA
East end mural in the style of Phoebe Traquair by William Blacklock of Edinburgh.

Kirkandrews Kirk, Dumfries & Galloway | G.H. Higginbottom | (?)1906 | DG6 4UB
For James Brown of Knockbrex, fond of Celtic motifs and castles.
Craftsmen included Cheshire cabinet-maker Frank Hallows, coppersmith James Smithies, and pewterer W.J. Englefield of London.

Our Lady & St Meddan (RC), Troon, Ayrshire | Reginald Fairlie | 1911 | KA10 6NJ
15th-century hommage. Angels with Instruments of the Passion on hammerbeams; rood beam.

St Ninian Episcopal, Troon, Ayrshire | James Archibald Morris | 1913–21 | KA10 6HZ
Cosy. Idiosyncratic hammerbeam roof; stone-carving; lots of wood-carving by Mouseman Thompson.

Portland Church, Troon (was UFC, now CofS) | Clifford & Lunan | 1914 | KA10 6EF

St Adrian, Gullane, East Lothian | Reginald Fairlie | 1926 | EH31 2AE
Chancel window by Douglas Strachan, 1934.

Glasgow and Edinburgh

Archbishop of Edinburgh's Chapel (RC) | R. Weir Schultz | 1904–7 | EH10 4BJ | **H**
Weir Schultz setting for 1889 House of Falkland furnishings by William Frame. Private.

St Andrew in the East, Alexandra Parade, Glasgow | James Miller | 1903–4 | G31 3LN | **H**
Now flats. Smaller church next door by James Salmon Jr, 1899.

First Church of Christ Scientist, Edinburgh | Ramsay Traquair | 1910 | EH3 5NS
Now an advertising agency. Exuberant woodwork – elders' bench, panelling, naturalistic animal carving.

Glasgow University Chapel | John James Burnet | 1914; 23–29 | G12 8QQ
A marginal case. Sombre grandeur; Strachan windows; meticulous woodwork by Archibald Dawson.

St John Renfield, Kelvindale, Glasgow | James Taylor Thomson | 1927–31 | G12 0NY
Original fittings, lights. Douglas Strachan glass.

North and Highlands

St Conan's Kirk, Loch Awe | Walter and Helen Campbell | 1881–1930 | PA33 1AQ
Sui generis. 'Outsider Art'? Self-built, with woodwork by Campbell. Open daily and entry is free.

Dunblane Cathedral | Rowand Anderson ('restoration'), 1889; Robert Lorimer, 1889, 1914 | FK15 0AQ
Douglas Strachan glass scheme.

St Mary (Episcopal) Church, Aberfoyle | James Miller | 1893–4 | FK8 3UJ

Crathie Kirk (CofS), Braemar, Aberdeenshire | A. Marshall Mackenzie | 1893–5 | AB35 5UL
High Victorian excess, but worth visiting for the reredos of 1910.

Chapel, House of Falkland, Fife | R. Weir Schultz | 1895–7 | KY15 7AF
No-expense-spared Jacobethan. Now inaccessible – part of school for boys with behavioural problems.

Our Lady (RC), Chapeltown, Glenlivet | John Kinross | 1896–7 | AB37 9JS
Lush decorative colour, heightened by clear glass windows. May have involved Archibald Macpherson.

Chapel Royal (RC), Falkland Palace, Fife | John Kinross ('restored') | 1896 | KY15 7BU
Altar, retable by Weir Schultz, 1909. Paid entry as part of tour of Palace.

St Ninian's Chapel, Mar Lodge, Braemar | A. Marshall Mackenzie | 1898 | AB35 5YJ
Intimate. Reredos with painted panels of angels.

Fyvie Church, Aberdeenshire | A. Marshall Mackenzie (chancel) | 1903 | AB53 8QD
Breath-taking Tiffany east window. Jacobethan pastiche Laird's Pew with fanciful woodwork.

St James (RC), St Andrews, Fife | Reginald Fairlie | 1910 | KY16 9AR

Memorial Chapel, House of Falkland (unfinished) | Reginald Fairlie | 1912–16 | KY15 7AF

Findochty Methodist Church, Moray | William Hendry of Buckie | 1914–16 | AB56 4QJ
An exterior flash of the Arts & Crafts dialect – built for fishermen who had been to England.

Kippen Parish Church | Reginald Fairlie (redesign) | 1924–6 | FK8 3DT
Includes work by Henry Wilson, Alfred Gilbert, James Woodford, et.al.

Islands

Corrie Parish Church (CofS), Arran | John James Burnet | 1887 | KA27 8JB

St Molios, Shiskine, Arran | John James Burnet | 1889 | KA27 8EP
Vigorous carving of figures on elders' seats; carving of sandstone capitals; imposing east end.

St John, Port Ellen, Islay | Sydney Mitchell | 1897–8 | PA42 7DH
Complex and off-beat externally, sternly austere inside.

St Colman (Episc), Burravoe, Yell, Shetland | R.T.N. Spier | 1900 | ZE2 9AY
Folding Gothic chair by Morris & Co. Painted altar front – by whom?

Kilmore Church, Dervaig, Mull | P. MacGregor Chalmers | 1905 | PA75 6QJ
PMC in Scots vernacular vein – white harled and pencil tower. Painted apse. Stephen Adam glass.

Canna Rhu Church, Canna | P. MacGregor Chalmers | 1912–14 | PH44 4RS
One for the hardiest of completists only. Tiny. 'The Rocket Church', because of its tower.

EXCEPTIONS AND EXCLUSIONS

1 PRE-CURSOR CHURCHES

There are a number of churches built before 1884, which, either in method, ethos or in some cases appearance, might be considered 'proto-Arts & Crafts'.

Sara Losh at St Mary, Wreay, Cumbria in 1842 (p.258) seems to be well ahead of the field.

Other churches from the 1870s are almost as interesting in what they foreshadow. Some of these churches appear in the main body of the text, usually because they form part of another story – of a town or an architect. There are numerous others, of which this is a selection of the most thought-provoking.

NORMAN SHAW

St Matthew | Meerbrook, Staffs | 1868, 1873

St Michael | Bournemouth, Dorset | 1872–83

St Swithun | Bournemouth, Dorset | 1875–92

St Thomas | Groombridge, East Sussex | 1883–4

Harrow School Mission | Latimer Rd, Hammersmith, London | 1883

St Augustine | Armoury Road, Highgate, London | J.D. Sedding, Henry Wilson | 1880–1916

St Paul | Truro, Cornwall | J.D. Sedding | 1882–4

St Peter | Hornblotton, Somerset | T.G. Jackson | 1872–4
Sgraffito scheme executed by E Wormleighton and Owen Gibbons, long before Heywood Sumner 'revived' the art

St Pancras | Rousdon, Devon | Ernest George | 1872 | **H**

Cowper Memorial (URC) | Olney, Bucks. | John Sulman | 1879–80

St John | Charfield, Glos. | W. Wood Bethell | 1881–2
Frenchified Gothic restlessly trying to be something else.

St John (RC) | Cumnock, Ayrshire | William Burges with J.F. Bentley and R. Weir Schultz | 1882

2 DEMOLISHED OR THREATENED CHURCHES

Good Shepherd | Lee, Lewisham | Ernest Newton | 1881 | Blitzed; rebuilt

St Paul | Truro, Cornwall (chancel) | J.D. Sedding | 1882–4 | closed 2007 | demolition threat

Richmond Presbyterian Church | London | William Flockhart | 1883–5 | demolished

St James the Less | Plymouth, Devon (chancel) | T.R. Kitsell | 1884 | Blitzed 1941

St Dyfrig | Cardiff, Glamorgan | J.D. Sedding, Arthur Grove | 1889 | demolished 1970

St Frideswide | Poplar (Christ Church mission) | W. Clarkson | 1889–92 | Blitzed | demolished 1947

St John | Farley Hill, Bucks. | George Truefitt | 1890–2 | closed

Unitarian Church | Middleton, Greater Manchester | Edgar Wood | 1892 | demolished 1965

Chapel at St John's Lodge | Regent's Park, London | R. Weir Schultz | 1892 | demolished 1950s

Methodist Chapel | Storey Sq., Barrow-in-Furness, Cumbria | not known | 1894 | demolished

Douglas Castle Chapel | Lanarkshire | Henry Wilson | 1894 | demolished

St Anselm | Davies Street, Mayfair, London | Balfour & Turner | 1894–6 | demolished

Doddridge Memorial church | Northants | Mosley & Anderson | 1895 | demolished 1998

Hindhead Cong Chapel | Surrey | W.R. Lethaby (furniture) | 1896 | closed

Chapel of St Philip | Begbroke, Oxon | Leonard Stokes | 1896–99 | stripped

St Michael and All Angels | Little Ilford, Essex | Charles Spooner | 1897 | demolished

St Aidan's Mission Church | Marland, Rochdale, Lancs | Edgar Wood | 1897 | demolished 1960

Kirby Muxloe Free Church | Leics | J Tait | 1897 | Blitzed 1940

Garden Chapel at St John's Lodge | London | R. Weir Schultz | 1899–1900 | demolished 1916

Chapel at Dumfries House | Ayrshire | R. Weir Schultz | 1899 | effaced 1930s

SS Andrew & Michael | Greenwich | Basil Champneys | 1900–2 | demolished 1986

All Saints Mission Chapel | Pentonville, London | R A Briggs | 1901–2 | demolished

Hope Methodist Church | Higham Ferrers, Northants. | Thomas Dyer | 1902–3 | closed

New Buckingham Baptist Chapel | Hotwells, Bristol | George Oatley | 1903 | demolished

Royal Masonic School Chapel | Bushey, Herts. | Gordon & Gunton | 1903 | abandoned

St Luke, Bristol Street | Birmingham | Mansell & Mansell | 1903 | demolished

St Andrew | Stanley Rd, Litherland, Liverpool | Willink & Thicknesse | 1903–4 | closed

Wesleyan Methodists | Upper Tooting, London | James Gibson | 1904 | demolished

St Columba | Broughton Moor, Cumbria | W.D. Caröe | 1904–5 | closed

Marylebone Presbyterian Church | London | William Flockhart (extension) | 1905 | demolished

Vickerstown Methodist Church | Walney, Barrow, Cumbria | not known | 1905 | abandoned

St Erkenwald | Southend, Essex | Walter Tapper | 1905–10 | demolished

UMFC Ashley Road | Leeds, Yorks | H. Ascough Chapman | 1906 | demolished 1984

Prescot Methodist Church | Merseyside | not known | 1909 | for sale

Presbyterian Church | Finchley Road, Golders Green, London | T. Figgis | 1910–11 | demolished

Mellish Road Methodist Church | Walsall | Hickton & Farmer | 1909 | demolished
Waterloo Baptist Church (now UFC) | Crosby | George Baines | 1910 | closed
St Gregory | Horfield, Bristol | A.R. Gough | 1911 | replaced 1936
St Stephen | Grimsby, Lincs. | Walter Tapper | 1911 | demolished 1973
St Luke | Heneage Road, Grimsby | Charles Nicholson | 1912 | demolished 1970
St Nicholas, Hull (memorial to Edward VII) | John Bilson | 1915 | demolished 1960
St Winifred's school chapel | Llanfairfechan, Conwy | H.L. North | 1920s | demolished 1960s
Quaker Meeting House | Cambridge | Fred Rowntree | 1926 | demolished
St Peter | Lowestoft, Suffolk (chancel) | E.P. Warren | 1920s | demolished

RICHARD BASSNETT PRESTON

St Stephen, Harpurhey
St Anne, Belfield | 1911–13
St Augustine, Stockport | 1890–3 | demolished 1974
St Ambrose, Pendleton | 1910–11 | burnt out in WW2.

WILLIAM BEDDOE REES

Windsor Place English Congregational, Cardiff | 1900–01
Hope English Baptist, Caerau | 1905 | abandoned
Tabernacl Welsh Calvinistic Methodist, Resolven | 1904
Nebo Welsh Independent, Glyncorrwg | 1904 | ruin
Mount Zion English Baptist, Blaengarw | 1904 | ruin

3 OTHER ARCHITECTS

Churches by a number of architects who did not identify (or identify strongly) with the Arts & Crafts are nonetheless included. Others are not included. This section attempts to explain why.

The midwife of the AWG, **Richard Norman Shaw** (1831–1912, AWG 1897) – who designed 16 churches – predates the phenomenon (see p.316), but his All Saints, Leek (p.162) is a bellwether of Arts & Crafts ideas to come; and St Michael and All Angels, Bedford Park (p.111) exemplifies the spirit of original individuality, overlaid by the same ideas later morphing into a self-conscious version of themselves. His grandiloquent All Saints, Richards Castle (p.147) adds a valedictory note.

The equally kindly inspirer of adventure in young architects, **John Dando Sedding** (1838–1891, AWG 1884) is seen as a rather more significant figure, with his pronouncements against conventional church architecture. Though most of his churches fall before our period, the fact that **Henry Wilson** finished them means most are considered alongside his.

One would have liked to include work by **C.F.A. Voysey** – but he never built a church, though he designed one private chapel, now stripped of its fittings, and, as part of a private hospice, impossible to visit. Others who built no church include **Halsey Ricardo**, **Baillie Scott** and **F.W. Troup** (though he was one of the group involved in the great unbuilt 'Arts & Crafts cathedral', the Liverpool Cathedral competition entry, under the aegis of Lethaby and invloving also Henry Wilson, Halsey Ricardo, Stirling Lee, Weir Schultz and Christopher Whall).

Some architects never participated, yet the spirit sometimes shows through.

W.D. Caröe's early work sits comfortably in the genre, even though he was rather dismissive of Arts & Crafts preciousness, and did not identify with the politics: but he could not escape the aesthetic influence, and St Michael, Colehill (p.51) and St Hugh, Charterhouse-on-Mendip (p.57) in particular are discussed at length. (See also p.115.)

John Douglas never belonged to any guild or society, not even the NAWG, but at many of his churches he could dip into Arts & Crafts motifs, and shy away from Gothic orthodoxy: pp 228, 280 and 284.

Giles Gilbert Scott is a puzzle: his artistic intensity might suggest Arts & Crafts – The Annunciation, Bournemouth clearly imbibes some of those heady fumes, as does St Joseph, Sheringham and Our Lady, Ramsey, Isle of Man. Yet very different, and aesthetically distant from Arts & Crafts are his churches after 1913: The Assumption, Northfleet, Kent; St Paul, Stoneycroft, Liverpool; and Charterhouse School Chapel. Nonetheless, Our Lady Star of the Sea, Broadstairs, 1925, and Our Lady and St Alphege Church (RC) Bath, Somerset, as late as 1927–9, seem to approach Arts & Crafts ideas with a new and original vigour.

In Birmingham, **Holland Hobbiss**, even though his churches date from the 1920s and 30s, seems to perhaps think in an Arts & Crafts way at St Giles, Rowley Regis, and Queen's College chapel, Edgbaston.

It would have been hard to exclude **Greenaway & Newberry**: though they made no pretensions to great artistic heights, St Hilda, Crofton Park is included – though some of their later churches seem to march to a different, more Modernist drummer.

John Oldrid Scott, not widely regarded as Arts & Crafts, also contrives to have one of his churches considered.

There are several figures whose *early* work 'fits' but who later moved in other directions: of the 38 parish churches by **Charles Nicholson**, the 16 designed before 1920 are suggestive, especially St John the Baptist, Curbridge (p.70). **Lutyens** goes on to far greater things.

Then there are those who do not fit at all, much as one might like them to.

Paley & Austin (p.230) built around twenty churches in the period, mainly in Lancashire. They were carrying on in the Gothic vein, and no matter how hard one tries, Arts & Crafts never really shows its face, even at the magical St Mark, Dolphinholme.

The claims of two 'Bodleyites' have been pressed upon me: of **C. Hodgson Fowler**, only Christ Church, Hepple, Northumberland, 1897, rings any bells, and not for its architecture (p.264). Of the other, **H.P. Burke Downing**, I could find no connection with Arts & Crafts ethos or sensibility. **Fellowes Prynne** I take to be Edwardian rather than Arts & Crafts. He is never naughty, but always scrupulously correct, for example, St Paul, Westham, Weymouth, Dorset. The same applies to **F.A. Walters**.

Ernest Shearman is idiosyncratic and interesting, but his language is foreign to Arts & Crafts, even at St Barnabas, North Ealing, and the astounding St Silas, Kentish Town. Yet at St Francis of Assisi, Osterley something like the authentic note is sounded, albeit stridently.

There are numbers of less distinguished architects whose work, generally speaking, never seems to rise above the everyday, rather pale Victorian – bland and unexciting. To name but a few: **William Bassett Smith, James Brooks, B.J. Capell, J.E.K and J.P. Cutts** (thought there is much to admire at All Saints, East Finchley), **Hemsoll & Paterson, J.D. and S.D. Mould, Smee Menge & Houchin**. I have drawn the line at **George and R.P. Baines** (on the whole).

I have been ruthless in excluding (apart from two churches, pp 152, 249) the architect so many Arts & Crafts men hero-worshipped, **G.F. Bodley** – Arts & Crafts is very much 'after' him, lesser than, 'not worthy of' even. And his story is told eloquently in Michael Hall's book. I also found it easy not to include any church by **J.L. Pearson, G.E. Street, Ewan Christian, William White** or **Walter Tower.**

Which rather leaves two conundrums: **Temple Moore** and **Ninian Comper.** It is almost as if by looking at these two one can discern most clearly what is *not* Arts & Crafts. **Comper** was distinctly anti-Arts & Crafts in his public utterances. And yet, and yet… his Kirriemuir (p.309) is so very Arts & Crafts in spirit! **Temple Moore**'s St Mary, Walesby, Lincs. (p.197) seems entirely Arts & Crafts in flavour; St Magnus, Bessingby – close, but no cigar. This is not an exact science. It is not a science at all.

ENDNOTES

Chapter 1
Introduction: What is an 'Arts & Crafts Church'?

1 Peter Davey, *Arts & Crafts Architecture* (Architectural Press, 1980; enlarged edition, Phaidon, 1995).

2 There has been a seminal article: Alan Crawford, 'Arts and Crafts Churches', in Andrew Saint and Teresa Sladen (eds.), *Churches 1870–1914* (Victorian Society, 2011), pp 62–79, which discusses eight churches: Sloane Street, Brithdir, Brighton, Brockhampton, Kempley, Great Warley, Dodford and Roker.

3 Thomas Hardy, 'A Tragedy of Two Ambitions' in *Life's Little Ironies* (1894) (Alan Sutton, Pocket Classics, 1990), p.67.

4 Quoted in J.S.L.[loyd], *W Curtis Green, RA: Architect and Draughtsman 1875–1960,* catalogue of exhibition at RIBA Heinz Gallery, January 1978 (Green, Lloyd and Adams), p.5.

5 Anon, 'Influence of the War on Architecture', *British Architect,* 18 June 1915, p.303.

6 Gavin Stamp, 'The Arts and Crafts church', lecture at Rewley House, Oxford, 15 May 2005, as part of a study weekend, 'The Architecture of the Arts & Crafts Movement', 13–15 May 2005 (unpublished).

7 John Betjeman, 'There and back AD 1851 to AD 1933. A History of the Revival of Good Craftsmanship', *Architectural Review* 74, July–December 1933, pp 4–8: p.8.

8 Alan Crawford, 'Pevsner and the Arts & Crafts Movement', lecture to The Victorian Society, 29 October 2011 (unpublished).

Chapter 2
Arts & Crafts Churches in Context: Architecture as Art

9 Linda Parry, *Textiles of the Arts & Crafts Movement* (London: Thames & Hudson, 1988, revised 2005), pp 9–15.

10 Peter Stansky, *Redesigning the World: William Morris, the 1880s and the Arts and Crafts* (Princeton: Princeton University Press, 1985).

11 Mary Greensted, *The Arts and Crafts Movement in Britain* (Osprey/Shire, 2010).

12 *Of the Decorative Illustration of Books Old and New,* (London: George Bell, 1896), p 242. And in *Arts and Crafts Essays by Members of the Arts and Crafts Exhibition Society:* 'The movement… towards a revival of design and handicraft…has been growing and gathering force for some time…represents…a revolt against the hard mechanical, conventional life.' (London: Rivington, Percival & Co., 1893; William Morris Library reprint, 1996) pp 11 and 12. Crane used the word again – this time capitalized – in 'Of the Arts and Crafts Movement: its general tendency and possible outcome' in *Ideals in the Art of the Arts and Crafts Movement* (London: George Bell, 1905), pp 1–34.

13 C R Ashbee, in a note in his typewritten autobiography, 'The Ashbee Memoirs', Vol. 1, p.125, undated, but, from its position in the typescript, after August 1899. (NAL: MSL/1959/2168–2173). He uses the phrase again in a 1902 Guild of Handicraft pamphlet, p.8. In 1908 he wrote of 'the Arts and Crafts movement' (lower case m) in *Craftsmanship in Competitive Industry* (Chipping Campden: Essex House, 1908). ('Movement' is capitalized in the Contents.)

14 A H Mackmurdo, *A History of the Arts and Crafts Movement* (unpublished, undated MS at William Morris Gallery, Walthamstow).

15 T J Cobden-Sanderson, *The Arts & Crafts Movement* (Hammersmith: Hammersmith Publishing Society, 1905).

16 Alan Crawford, 'Supper at Gatti's: the SPAB and the Arts and Crafts Movement' in Chris Miele (ed.), *From William Morris: Building Conservation and the Arts and Crafts cult of Authenticity 1877–1939* (Yale, 2005), pp 101–127

17 Walter Crane, letter to W A S Benson, February 1887 (ACES papers in the V&A archives: AAD1/8).

18 Nikolaus Pevsner discusses the genesis of 'Decorative Art' as separate from Art, under the influence of William Morris in 'Art Furniture of the 1870s', *Studies in Art, Architecture and Design: Victorian and After* (Princeton: Princeton University Press, 1968), pp 119–130.

19 Davey, *Arts and Crafts Architecture,* op cit, p.7.

20 Personal communication in an e-mail to the author, 20 September 2011.

21 Davey, p.10.

22 Andrew Saint, personal comment, August 2009.

23 John Betjeman, *Collins Guide to English Parish Churches* (1958), p.255

24 See Peter Cormack, *Arts & Crafts Glass* (Yale University Press, 2015).

25 Alan Powers, 'A Movement of the Mind', *Crafts* 166, September/October 2000, pp 40–43.

Chapter 3
Arts & Crafts Churches in Context: Religion

26 James Obelkevich, 'Religion', in F M L Thompson (ed.), *Cambridge Social History of Britain 1750–1950*, vol. 3, (Cambridge: Cambridge University Press, 1990) pp 311–356; p.328.

27 Nigel Yates, *Anglican Ritualism in Victorian Britain* (Oxford: Oxford University Press, 1999), p.170.

28 Quoted in Yates, *Anglican Ritualism,* p.330.

29 W H Frere, *The Principles of Religious Ceremonial* (London: Longman, 1906), p.25.

30 G K A Bell, *Randall Davidson* (Oxford: Oxford University Press, 1935; 2nd edition 1938), p.1325.

31 Peter Anson, *Fashions in Church Furnishings 1840–1940* (London: Studio Vista, 2nd edn, 1965), p.303.

32 Yates, *Anglican Ritualism*, op. cit. p.336.

33 Percy Dearmer, *The Parson's Handbook* (London: Grant Richards, 1899; 4th edition 1903), pp 4 and 6; then 52.

34 Gerald Parsons (ed), *Religion in Victorian Britain* (Manchester: Manchester University Press, 1988), IV *Interpretations*, p.203.

35 *The Freeman,* 7 March 1890, quoted in Nigel Scotland, *Squires in the Slums: Settlements and Missions in Late Victorian England* (London: I B Tauris, 2007), p.175.

36 Circular promoting the settlement, 1890, quoted in Scotland, op cit, p.178.

37 Charles Lee, 'From a Letchworth Diary', *Town and Country Planning,* 21, 113, Sept 1953, pp 435–6. Quoted in Mark Swenarton, *Artisans and Architects: the Ruskinian Tradition in Architectural Thought* (New York: St Martin's Press, 1989), p.152.

38 F B Smith, 'The Atheist Mission' in Robert Robson (ed.) *Ideas and Institutions of Victorian Britain: Essays in Honour of George Kitson Clark* (London: G Bell & Sons, 1967), pp 205–235.

39 Parliamentary Papers, lxxxi, 761, 775, cited in Owen Chadwick, *The Victorian Church* (volume 1) (London: A and C Black, 2nd edn, 1970), p.407.

40 Chadwick, *The Victorian Church,* p.421.

41 'In 1800 there were seventeen places of worship representing eight nonconformist denominations in Birmingham. By the end of the century (1892) there were 220 places representing 21 denominations': J Dunning, *St Philip's in the Victorian Era* (Birmingham: Provost and Chapter of Birmingham Cathedral, 1985), p.F1. The quotation is cited as 'Local Guide Book 1819'. The total for CofE churches in the period was about 60.

42 Properly, Methodists are not NC – they only broke from the CofE in 1791. Figures on the Methodists here derive principally from 'Extracts from the *Report of the Census of Religious Worship,*

1851' (House of Commons, 1852–3), in David M Thompson, *Nonconformity in the Nineteenth Century* (London: Routledge and Kegan Paul, 1972), pp 147–155.

43 Thompson, op cit, p.13.

44 H B Kendall, *History of the Primitive Methodist Connexion* (1888), p.32 at North Staffordshire Methodist Heritage website, https://archive.org/stream/historyofprimitioounknuoft#page/n5/mode/2up [accessed 13 March 2020].

45 Ibid, Chapter VI (n.p.) [accessed 5 January 2016].

46 Robert Tudur Jones, *Congregationalism in England 1662–1962* (London: Independent Press, 1962), p.319.

47 Ibid, p.302.

48 Ibid, p.295.

49 Ibid, p.317.

50 Jose Harris, *Private Lives, Public Spirit: a Social History of Britain, 1870–1914* (Oxford: Oxford University Press, 1993), p.173.

51 'The people of Lambeth thought of themselves as Christians, but insisted upon defining their own religious beliefs rather than taking them from the clergymen.' Jeffrey Cox, *The English Churches in a Secular Society: Lambeth 1870–1930* (Oxford: Oxford University Press, 1982), p.92.

52 Obelkevich, 'Religion', op cit, p.340.

53 Cox, op cit, p.95.

54 Obelkevich, 'Religion', p.349.

55 Figures on Scotland are from Andrew Drummond and James Bulloch, *The Church in Late Victorian Scotland 1874–1900* (Edinburgh: St Andrew Press, 1978), p.167; p.144; p.139; p.159 (FC numbers extrapolated from their figures for East Lothian) and p.153 (Duirnish).

56 Quoted in Drummond and Bulloch, p.207.

57 J Burleigh, *A Church History of Scotland* (Edinburgh: Hope Trust, 1983), p.377.

58 Drummond and Bulloch, p.146.

59 Robert Tudur Jones, *Faith and the Crisis of a Nation: Wales 1890–1914* (Cardiff: University of Wales 1981–2; in English 2004), p.4.

60 Ieuan Gwynedd Jones, *Explorations and Explanations: Essays in the Social History of Victorian Wales* (Llandysul: Gwasg Gomer, 1981), p.229.

61 Tudur Jones, *Faith and Crisis…*, p.46.

62 Ibid, p.41.

63 T M Bassett, *The Welsh Baptists* (Swansea: Ilston House, 1977), p.242.

64 Tudur Jones, *Faith and Crisis…*, p.10.

65 Frances Knight, '1850–1920' (Chapters 12–14) in Glanmor Williams, William Jacob et al, *The Welsh Church from Reformation to Disestablishment 1603–1920* (Cardiff: University of Wales, 2009), pp 309–398; p.358: 'Between 1851 and 1910, 347 new [CofW] churches were built in Wales, and almost all the old churches, nearly 1,000 of them, were renovated or rebuilt.' (quoting John Davies, *History of Wales* (Harmondsworth: Penguin, 1993), p.435.)

66 This figure is for churches only: the 1851 figure is 'gathered churches (640) and chapels (700)'.

67 Anthony Jones, *Welsh Chapels* (Cardiff: National Museum of Wales, 1984; reprinted Stroud: Alan Sutton, 1996), p.49, gives the figure for 1895 as 2,794.

68 This figure includes Particular (854) and all others (901). Jones gives the figure (1902) as 896.

69 Julian Orbach, in a lecture to The Victorian Society, 'Later Welsh Chapels', 17 October 2006, stated the situation in Aberystwyth thus: in 1864 there were 4 NC churches in the town (Baptist, Independent, Calvinistic Methodist, Welsh Methodist). Following the arrival of the railway that year, the three main NC denominations built English-language churches (Baptist, Congregationalist and 'Welsh Methodist'), and a [English] Presbyterian church was also built. The Anglicans meanwhile built three further churches in the town.

70 D Gareth Evans, *A History of Wales 1815–1906* (Cardiff: University of Wales, 1989), p.242.

71 Orbach, 'Later Welsh Chapels', op cit.

72 Powys Digital History Project at http://history.powys.org.uk/history/common/church8.html [accessed 2 February 2010].

73 Frances Knight, '1850–1920', op cit, p.319.

74 Anthony Jones, *Welsh Chapels*, p.120, quoting T M Bassett, *The Welsh Baptists*, op cit (n.p.).

75 Knight, '1850–1920', p.319.

Chapter 4

Arts & Crafts Churches in Context: Society

76 Keith Francis, William Gibson, et al (eds.), *The Oxford Handbook of the British Sermon 1689–1901* (Oxford: Oxford University Press, 2012).

77 Obelkevich, 'Religion', op cit, p.347.

78 William Lawrence, Bishop of Massachusetts 1893–1927, quoted in L Ziff, *Introduction* to Theodore Dreiser, *The Financier* (New York: A L Burt, 1912), (London: Penguin, 2008).

79 Cox, op cit, p.273.

80 Jonathan Rose, *The Edwardian Temperament 1895–1919* (Athens, OH: Ohio University Press, 1986).

81 George Gissing, *The Private Papers of Henry Ryecroft* (London: Constable & Co, 1903), pp 159–160.

82 C F G Masterman, *The Condition of England* (London: Methuen, 1909), p.2.

83 George Peel, *The Future of England* (London: Macmillan, 1912), p.29, quoted in Roger Lloyd, *Church of England in the Twentieth Century* (London: Longman, 1946, 1950); vol. 1, p.39.

84 C Maurice Davies, 'Father Stanton at St Alban's' in his (ed.), *Orthodox London: or Phases of Religious Life in the Metropolis* (London: Tinsley Bros, 1876), pp 267, 271–8; reproduced in James Moore, (ed.), *Religion in Victorian Britain* vol. III (Manchester: Manchester University Press, 1988), p.271.

85 Walter Arnstein, review of John R Orens, *Stewart Headlam's Radical Anglicanism: The Mass, the Masses, and the Music Hall* (Urbana-Chicago: University of Illinois Press, 2003) in *Catholic Historical Review*, vol. 90, no 3, July 2004, pp 559–560.

86 'The Guild of Saint Matthew has been referred to as the 'shock troops' of Christian Socialism in the 1880s and 90s. The guild, under Stewart Headlam's influence, more than made up for its smallness in number by the militancy of its tactics and the audacity with which it expressed its … convictions,' www.anglocatholicsocialism.org/matthew.html [accessed 1 February 2010].

87 Arnstein, review, op cit, p.560.

88 B G Worrall, *The Making of the Modern Church: Christianity in England since 1800* (London: SPCK, 1988), p.59.

89 Andrew Mearns, *The Bitter Cry of Outcast London: An Inquiry into the Condition of the Abject Poor* (London: James Clark, 1883), quoted in Scotland, *Squires in the Slums*, op cit, p.6.

90 Scotland, *Squires in the Slums*, pp 10–11.

91 Ibid, p.15.

92 Ibid, p.13.

93 *Leaves of Grass* was begun (1855) before the *Sesame and Lilies* lectures were delivered (1864). However, Egremont, who was then in America, presumably posted Mrs Ormonde the latest, 1881, 6th edition.

94 Walt Whitman, 'The base of all metaphysics'.

95 Circular promoting the settlement, 1890, quoted in Scotland, *Squires*, p.178.

96 'L[ecturer]: 'The self-sacrifice of a human being is not a lovely, thing, Violet. It is often a necessary and a noble thing.' *Of Queen's Gardens,* in *Sesame and Lilies* (E T Cook and Alexander Wedderburn, *Library Edition of the Works of John Ruskin* (London: Allen, 1903–12) Vol. 18, p.283). See also Ruskin, *Lectures on Architecture and Painting*, Addenda to Lectures 1 and 2: 'Gothic ornamentation is nobler than Greek construction.'

97 Jose Harris, op cit, p.174.

98 Undated cutting in a bound collection of newspaper cuttings at Haslemere Educational Museum, gathered by a local early 20th century journalist, W A Sillick.

99 *Farnham, Haslemere and Hindhead Herald* n.p., n.d. (but 1937), in the Sillick cuttings collection.

100 Virginia Woolf, 'Mr Bennett and Mrs Brown' (1924).

101 Raymond Williams, *Culture and Society 1780–1950* (Harmondsworth: Penguin, 1961), p.165, quoted in Alan Powers, '1884 and the Arts and Crafts movement', *Apollo*, 1 April 2005, p.60.

FURTHER READING

This highly selective bibliography is split into three parts.

Section 1 lists the **principal books and articles on the Arts & Crafts**.

Section 2 (p.327) gives further reading for the **architects and artists** who figure largest in this book, listed alphabetically by their surname. (In many cases, there is no good academic source.)

Section 3 (p.334) gives additional resources for **individual churches**, listed alphabetically by location (the word in capital letters at the head of the description in the main text). However, since many individual churches are only discussed in books about their architects, check Section 2 as well, and perhaps first. If there is no entry for a church in this section, it means there is no worthwhile source known to the author, apart from the church's own guide booklet (if one exists): these are not listed separately here, unless of exceptional interest.

Also not included are histories of religious denominations, social histories, biographies of divines, histories of socialism, or general surveys of liturgiology or Victorian church architecture.

Place of publication is London, unless otherwise stated, or clear from the name of the publisher.

GENERAL

The most recent 'Pevsner' *Buildings of England, Buildings of Scotland* and *Buildings of Wales* give definitive analytical descriptions of almost all of the churches.

The Victorian Web is well worth consulting: churches and information on architects are being added all the time, though many of the churches in this book are not to be found there (yet): www.victorianweb.org

Many of the modern journal articles are available online at J-Stor, accessible for a monthly fee.

Other useful sites your search engine will take you to include the *Dictionary of Scottish Architects* (DSA) at www.scottisharchitects.org.uk; artsandcraftsmovementinsurrey.org.uk; *Mapping the Profession and Practice of Sculpture* at sculpture.gla.ac.uk. *Victoria County Histories* (VCH) for some counties are online as British History Online www.british-history.ac.uk

The most useful journals of the period – some of which are online, and more being added – are: *Academy Architecture, The Architect, Architects' and Builders' Journal, The Architects' Journal (*founded as *The Builders' Journal), Architectural Review, The Art Workers Quarterly* (1902–6), *The British Architect, The Builder, Builders Journal and Architectural Record, Building News, The Church Builder, Country Life, The Studio.* Try archive.org

Nonconformists published Yearbooks in the period, which often give detailed descriptions of new churches: *The Congregational Yearbook, The Baptist Handbook.*

1. THE ARTS & CRAFTS

Churches

Alan Crawford, 'Arts and Crafts Churches', in Andrew Saint and Teresa Sladen (eds.), *Churches 1870–1914* (Victorian Society, 2011), pp 62–79. Includes discussions of eight churches: Sloane Street, Brithdir, Brighton, Brockhampton, Kempley, Great Warley, Dodford, Roker.

Alec Hamilton, 'The Arts & Crafts in church-building in Britain 1884–1918', DPhil thesis, University of Oxford, 2016. Discusses 35 churches. Online at Oxford Research Archive (ORA) from December 2022.

Hermann Muthesius, *Die neuere kirchliche Baukunst in England* (Berlin: Wilhelm Ernst & Sohn, 1901)

Architecture

Peter Burman (ed.), *Architecture 1900* (Shaftesbury: Donhead, 1998)

Peter Davey, *Arts and Crafts Architecture* (Architectural Press, 1980; Phaidon, 1995)

T. Raffles Davison (ed.), *The Arts connected with Building: Lectures on Craftsmanship and Design* (Batsford, 1909)

A. Stuart Gray, *Edwardian Architecture: a Biographical Dictionary* (Wordsworth, 1988)

Margaret Richardson, *Architects of the Arts & Crafts Movement* (Trefoil, 1983)

Alastair Service (ed.), *Edwardian Architecture and its Origins* (Architectural Press, 1975)

R. Norman Shaw and T. Graham Jackson (eds.), *Architecture: a Profession or an art? Thirteen short essays on the qualifications and training of architects* (Murray, 1892)

Objects

The Arts & Crafts Exhibition Society (ACES) catalogues (15 volumes, 1888–1931): online and keyword searchable at archive.org

Alan Crawford, 'Ideas and Objects: the Arts & Crafts Movement in Britain', *Design Issues,* vol.13, no.1, Spring 1997, pp 15–26

History and overviews

Isabel Anscombe and Charlotte Gere, *Arts & Crafts in Britain and America* (Academy, 1978)

Rosalind Blakesley, *The Arts and Crafts Movement* (Phaidon, 2006)

Anthea Callen, *The Angel in the Studio: woman artists of the Arts & Crafts movement 1870–1914* (Astragal, 1979)

Annette Carruthers, *The Arts & Crafts Movement in Scotland* (Yale, 2013)

T.J. Cobden-Sanderson, *The Arts and Crafts Movement* (Hammersmith Publishing Society, 1905)

Peter Cormack, *Arts & Crafts Stained Glass* (Yale, 2015)

Alan Crawford, *By Hammer and Hand: the Arts and Crafts Movement in Birmingham* (Birmingham Museums and Art Galleries, 1984)

Elizabeth Cumming, *Hand, Heart and Soul: The Arts and Crafts Movement in Scotland* (Edinburgh: Birlinn, 2006)

Elizabeth Cumming and Wendy Kaplan, *The Arts & Crafts Movement* (Thames & Hudson, 2002)

Peter Faulkner (ed.), *Arts and Crafts Essays by Members of the Arts and Crafts Exhibition Society, with a preface by William Morris* (1893; facsimile Bristol: Thoemmes, 1996)

Mary Greensted, *The Arts and Crafts Movement in Britain* (Osprey/Shire, 2010)

Wendy Kaplan, *The Arts & Crafts Movement in Europe & America: Design for the Modern World* (Thames & Hudson, 2004)

Karen Livingstone and Linda Parry (eds.), *International Arts and Crafts* (V&A, 2005)

A.H. Mackmurdo, *History of the Arts and Crafts Movement* (typescript in the William Morris Gallery, Walthamstow)

H.J.L.J. Massé (ed.), *The Art Workers' Guild 1884–1934* (Oxford: Shakespeare's Head, 1935)

Gillian Naylor, *The Arts & Crafts Movement: a study of its sources, ideals and influence on design theory* (Trefoil, 1990; originally Studio Vista, 1971)

Linda Parry, *Textiles of the Arts & Crafts Movement* (Thames & Hudson, 1988; revised 2005)

Alan Powers, 'A Movement of the Mind', *Crafts* 166, September/October 2000, pp 40–43

Alan Powers, '1884 and the Arts and Crafts Movement', *Apollo*, vol.161, April 2005, pp 60–65

Peter Stansky, *Redesigning the world: William Morris, the 1880s and the Arts and Crafts* (Princeton University Press, 1985)

Mark Swenarton, *Artisans and Architects: the Ruskinian Tradition in Architectural Thought* (New York: St Martin's, 1989)

Gazetteers

Barrie and Wendy Armstrong, *The Arts and Crafts Movement in the North West of England* (Wetherby: Oblong, 2005); *The Arts and Crafts Movement in the North East of England* (Oblong, 2013); *The Arts and Crafts Movement in Yorkshire* (Oblong, 2013)

2. ARCHITECTS AND ARTISTS

There are monographs for most of the principal, more famous architects, and for some of the artist/makers. But for many of the lesser figures there is either nothing at all, or only an article or chapter, or an MA dissertation – these last are not online as yet: you have to go to the institution and read the document in their library. PhD theses are increasingly online, via EThOS, ORA, or similar.

A very few individuals have a good online source devoted to them – a website run by an enthusiast, often a descendant.

There is an increasing number of useful pages on Wikipedia – for example, a thorough list of the works of Christopher Whall, and the buildings of John Douglas. Wikipedia often gives its own brief bibliography. But treat 'factual' information on Wikipedia (and all blogs) with caution.

Online searches will reveal obituaries, especially at the British Newspaper Archive: www.britishnewspaperarchive.co.uk. The *Oxford Dictionary of National Biography* (ODNB) is available online through your local library: your card number gives you access at home.

This list identifies either the only sources, or, where there are many, the most useful. There are sure to be unintended omissions – apologies.

Rowand Anderson

Sam McKinstry, *Rowand Anderson: 'The Premier Architect of Scotland'* (Edinburgh University Press, 1991)

George Faulkner Armitage

Rosamond Allwood, 'George Faulkner Armitage 1849–1937', *Furniture History*, vol.23, 1987, pp 67–87

Gill Fitzpatrick, 'Portrait of a Studio: George Faulkner Armitage and his apprentices', *Journal of the Decorative Arts Society*, 31, 2007, pp 36–45

C.R. Ashbee

Alan Crawford, *C R Ashbee: Architect, Designer and Romantic Socialist* (Yale University Press, 1985; 2nd edition, 2005)

J.L. Ball

Phillada Ballard (ed.), *Birmingham's Victorian and Edwardian Architects* (Wetherby: Oblong Press, 2009), pp 401–22

Herbert Baker

Nicolette Duckham, 'The evolution of Herbert Baker's domestic style, 1892–1926', PhD thesis, Open University, 2007, on EThOS

Sidney Barnsley

See Ernest Gimson

W.A.S. Benson

Alan Crawford, 'W A S Benson: Machinery and the Arts & Crafts Movement in Britain', *Journal of the Decorative and Propaganda Arts*, 24, 2002, pp 94–117

Ian Hamerton (ed.), *W A S Benson, Arts and Crafts Luminary …* (Antique Collectors Club, 2005)

W.H. Bidlake

Ballard (see J.L. Ball), pp 369–400

T.G. Mitchell, 'W H Bidlake, architect, 1861–1938', MPhil thesis, Manchester University, 1994

Detmar Blow

Michael Drury, *Wandering Architects: in Pursuit of an Arts and Crafts Ideal* (Stamford: Shaun Tyas, 2000; revised 2016) – on Blow and his contemporaries: Philip Tilden, Randall Wells, Herbert North and others.

W.H. Brierley

Anon., 'Men who build. No 60: Messrs Demaine and Brierley', *Builders' Journal*, 25 July 1900, p.455

Charles Carus, 'Walter Henry Brierley, Architect, 1862–1926', thesis for Diploma in Architectural Studies, University of York, 1973

Patrick Nuttgens, *Brierley in Yorkshire: the Architecture of the turn of the century* (York Georgian Society, 1984)

J.S. Brocklesby

Christopher Spencer, *Elbow Room: the story of John Sydney Brocklesby, Arts and Crafts Architect* (Ainsworth and Nelson, 1984)

Bromsgrove Guild

Quintin Watt, *The Bromsgrove Guild, an Illustrated History* (Bromsgrove Society, 1999)

Charles Buckeridge

Andrew Saint, 'Charles Buckeridge and his family', *Oxoniensia,* vol.XXXVIII, 1973, pp 357–72

W.D. Caröe

Jennifer Freeman, *W D Caröe: his architectural achievement* (Manchester University Press, 1990)

W D Caröe, 'Church Furniture', *JRIBA* 1894, pp 423–9

John Coates Carter

Phil Thomas, 'John Coates Carter: Building a Sense of Place', *Buildings Conservation Directory: Special Report on Historic Churches,* 17th edition, 2010, pp 34–9

Walter Cave

Judith Patrick, *Walter Cave: Arts and Crafts to Edwardian Splendour* (Andover: Phillimore, 2012)

Century Guild

Stuart Evans, 'Arthur Heygate Mackmurdo 1851–1942 and the Century Guild of Artists', MA thesis, Manchester University, 1986. Also his article at Grove Art Online, 2003

Basil Champneys

David Watkin, *The Architecture of Basil Champneys* (Newnham College Cambridge, 1989)

Chorley & Connon

Christopher Webster (ed.), *Building a Great Victorian City: Leeds Architects and Architecture 1790–1914* (Northern Heritage, 2011), pp 197–218

Ninian Comper

Anthony Symondson and Stephen Bucknall, *Sir Ninian Comper* (Reading: Spire Books and The Ecclesiological Society, 2006)

John Betjeman, 'Ninian Comper', *Architectural Review*, February 1939, pp 79–82

Walter Crane

Isobel Spencer, *Walter Crane* (Studio Vista, 1975)

www.waltercrane.com

Percy Heylyn Currey

Andrew Polkey, Little Eaton Local History Society website: lelhs.org.uk/percy-currey/4594147549

Andrew Polkey, *Percy Heylyn Currey - Architect of Derby School* at www.oldderbeians.co.uk/wp-content/uploads/2018/05/currey-bio.pdf

Louis Davis

Nigel Hammond, 'Louis Davis, 1860–1941…' *Oxfordshire Local History Journal*, vol.7, no.5, January 2006

Guy Dawber

Anon, 'Men who Build', No.63, Guy Dawber', *Builder's Journal,* 3 April 1901, pp 148–9, 153 and supplement

Laurie Kinney, 'Guy Dawber', in Malcolm Airs (ed.), *The Edwardian Great House* (Oxford: OUDCE, 2000), pp 133–43

C.H. Reilly, 'Guy Dawber' in *Representative British Architects of the Present Day* (Batsford, 1931), pp 80–87

John Douglas

Edward Hubbard, *The Work of John Douglas* (Victorian Society, 1991)

Dunn & Watson

jmmaclaren.org/people/dunn-and-watson

Eastwood and Greenslade

David Chappell, 'John Henry Eastwood and St Anne's Cathedral, Leeds', in G.T. Bradley (ed.), *Yorkshire Catholics* (Leeds Diocesan Archives, 1985), pp 56–65

F.C. Eden

W.I. Croome, 'Frederick Charles Eden FSA FRIBA', *Journal of the British Society of Master Glass Painters* vol.XIII, no.4, 1962–3, pp 554–557

Garside and Pennington

L.J. Turner, 'Garside and Pennington: architects of Castleford and Pontefract', *Journal of the Wesley Historical Society (Yorkshire Branch),* vol.82a, Spring 2003, pp 2–10

L.J. Turner, 'Garside and Pennington's Churches', *Victorian Society, West Yorkshire Group Journal,* 1979, pp 19–25

The Gaskins

Anon. (but George Breeze), *Arthur & Georgie Gaskin* (Fine Art Society, 1981)

Ernest Geldart

James Bettley, 'The Reverend Ernest Geldart (1848–1929) and Late Nineteenth Century Church Decoration', PhD thesis, Courtauld Institute, 1999

James Bettley, 'The Master of Little Braxted in his prime: Ernest Geldart and Essex, 1873–1900', *Essex Archaeology and History,* 31, 2000, pp 169–94

Eric Gill

Fiona MacCarthy, *Eric Gill* (Faber & Faber, 1989)

MacDonald Gill

www.macdonaldgill.com

Ernest Gimson

Annette Carruthers, Mary Greensted and Barley Roscoe, *Ernest Gimson: Arts & Crafts Designer and Architect* (Yale, 2019)

Mary Comino, *Gimson and the Barnsleys* (Cheltenham Art Gallery and Museum, 1980) (republished as Mary Greensted, *Gimson and the Barnsleys* (Stroud: Alan Sutton, 1991))

W. Curtis Green

Anon., *W Curtis Green RA: architect and draughtsman 1875–1960* (Green Lloyd and Adams, 1978)

C.H. Reilly, 'W. Curtis Green' in *Representative British Architects of the Present Day* (Batsford,1931), pp 99–112

Greenaway and Newberry

Kenneth Richardson, *The 'Twenty-Five' churches of the Southwark Diocese* (Ecclesiological Society, 2002)

W.J. Hale

N.D. Wilson, '"Sane, if unheroic": the work of William John Hale (1862–1929), Wesleyan Methodist and Architect' in Clyde Binfield (ed.), *The Chapels Society Miscellany I,* 1998, pp 51–73

W.A. Harvey

Ballard (see J.L. Ball), pp 527–54

John Hawes

Peter Anson, *The Hermit of Cat Island* (New York: P.J. Kenedy, 1957), online at archive.org

John Taylor, *Between devotion and design: the architecture of John Cyril Hawes 1876—1956* (University of Western Australia Press, 2000)

Ralph Hedley

Clodagh Brown, ralphhedleyarchive.com

Tony Peart, 'The Lost Art Workers of Tyneside', *Decorative Arts Society Journal* 17 (1993), pp 13–22

Henry Holiday

Dennis and Joan Hadley, 'Henry Holiday, 1839–1927', *Journal of Stained Glass,* vol.XIX, no.1, 1989, pp 48–75

George Jack

Amy Clarke, 'George Jack, Master Woodcarver of the Arts & Crafts Movement', *Journal of the Decorative Arts Society 1850 - the Present,* 2004, pp 82–107

Thomas Graham Jackson

William Whyte, *Oxford Jackson: Architecture, Education, Status and Style 1835–1924* (Oxford University Press, 2006)

R.J. Johnson

George Austen, 'The late R J Johnson', *Architectural Review,* vol.17, 1905, p.222

Thomas E. Faulkner, 'Robert James Johnson, Architect and Antiquary', *Durham University Journal,* January 1995, pp 3–10

W.S. Hicks, 'Remarks on the late Mr Robert Johnson FSA', *Proceedings of the Northern Architectural Association,* 1892

Arthur Keen

Only his obituaries: *Baptist Times,* 5 January 1900; *JRIBA,* 9 January 1939, pp 255–6 and 20 March 1939, p.523; *The Builder,* 23 December 1938, p.1201 and 13 Jan 1939, p.116; *The Times,* 17 December 1938, p.16

W.R. Lethaby

Godfrey Rubens, *William Richard Lethaby: His Life and Work 1857–1931* (Architectural Press, 1986)

Robert Lorimer

Peter Savage, *Lorimer and the Edinburgh Craft Designers* (self-published, 1980)

Sara Losh

J.B. Bullen, 'Sarah Losh: architect, romantic, mythologist', *Burlington Magazine,* vol.143, 1184, November 2001, pp 676–84

Rosemary Hill, 'Romantic Affinities', *Crafts,* vol.166, 2000, pp 34–9

Jenny Uglow, *The Pinecone: The Story of Sarah Losh, Forgotten Romantic Heroine – Antiquarian, Architect and Visionary* (Faber, 2012)

Mary Lowndes

Ann O'Donoghue, 'Mary Lowndes – a brief overview of her life and work', *Journal of Stained Glass* XXIV, 2000, pp 38–52

Edwin Landseer Lutyens

Jane Brown, *Lutyens and the Edwardians: an English Architect and his Clients* (Penguin, 1997)

Christopher Hussey, *The Life of Sir Edwin Lutyens* (Country Life, 1953, republished AAC Art Books, 1984)

Mary Lutyens, *Edwin Lutyens: A Memoir* (John Murray, 1980)

Robert Lutyens, *Sir Edwin Lutyens: An Appreciation in Perspective* (Country Life, 1942)

Jane Ridley, *The Architect and his Wife: a Life of Edwin Lutyens* (Chatto, 2002)

Chris Skidmore, 'Chapel beginnings of a secular architect: the case of Edwin Lutyens', *Chapel Society Newsletter,* 50, 2012, pp 10–12

Mervyn Macartney

Jan Ward, *Mervyn Edmund Macartney, Architect 1853–1932* (self-published, 1998)

Charles Rennie Mackintosh

Alan Crawford, *Charles Rennie Mackintosh* (Thames & Hudson, 1995)

Wendy Kaplan (ed.), *Charles Rennie Mackintosh* (Abbeville Press, 1996)

James Macaulay, *Charles Rennie Mackintosh: A Biography* (W.W. Norton, 2010)

John McKean, *Charles Rennie Mackintosh, Architect, Artist, Icon* (Lomond, 2000; 2nd edition 2001)

Arthur Heygate Mackmurdo

See Century Guild

James MacLaren

Alan Calder, *James MacLaren: Arts and Crafts Pioneer* (Donington: Shaun Tyas, 2003)

W.D. McLennan

Gillian Sinclair, 'The work of Paisley architect W D McLennan', dissertation, Glasgow School of Art, 1987

Frank Walker, 'Art Nouveau Patterns in Paisley: the architecture of W D McLennan', *Country Life,* 10 August 1978, n.p.

Frank Walker, 'William Daniel McLennan of Paisley', *Bulletin of the Scottish Georgian History Society,* no.6, 1979, pp 17–25

H.H. Martyn & Co.

John Whitaker, *The Best: H H Martyn & Co* (Cheltenham: Promenade Publications, 1998)

J.T. Micklethwaite

Peter Howell, '"A man at once strong in the present and reverent of the past"– John Thomas Micklethwaite (1843–1906)' in Christopher Webster (ed.), *Episodes in the Gothic Revival: six church architects* (Spire, 2011), pp 199–229

J.T. Micklethwaite, *Modern Parish Churches* (Henry S. King, 1874)

Alec Miller

Graham Peel, *Alec Miller, Carver Guildsman Sculptor* (self-published, 2014)

Sydney Mitchell

D.C. McDowell, 'Scottish Assets: the commercial architecture of A G Sydney Mitchell', *Architectural Heritage,* vol.14, no.1, pp 45–66

Gerald Moira

Harold Watkins, *The Art of Gerald Moira* (E.W. Dickens, 1923)

Leslie Moore

Tim Ellis, 'The Ecclesiastical Work of Leslie Moore' in Geoffrey Brandwood (ed.), *Temple Moore, an Architect of the Late Gothic Revival* (Paul Watkins, 1997), pp 184–211.

Temple Moore

Geoffrey Brandwood, *The Architecture of Temple Moore*, (Shaun Tyas, 2019)

Charles Nicholson

Edward Bundock, *Sir Charles Nicholson: Architect of Noble Simplicity* (West Raynham: JewelTree, 2012)

Michael Drury, 'Sir Charles Nicholson: Portsmouth's First Cathedral Architect' in Sarah Quail and Alan Wilkinson (eds.), *Forever Building…* (Portsmouth Cathedral, 1995), pp 121–142

Charles Nicholson and Hubert Corlette, *Modern Church Building* (RIBA, 1907)

Herbert Luck North

Ian B. Allan, 'The life and work of Herbert Luck North 1871–1941', PhD thesis, University of Liverpool, 1988, online at EThOS

Adam Voelcker, *Herbert Luck North: Arts and Crafts Architecture for Wales* (Aberystwyth: RCAHMW, 2011)

Paley & Austin

Geoff Brandwood, *The Architecture of Sharpe, Paley and Austin* (English Heritage, 2012)

Joseph Phillips

F. Hamilton Jackson, 'Wood Carving of Mr J Phillips', *Magazine of Art,* 25, 1900–1, pp 515–8

Godfrey Pinkerton

Only his obituaries: *The Builder,* 16 July 1937, *JRIBA* vol.44, 26 June 1937

The Pinwills

Helen Wilson, 'The Emergence of the Pinwill Sisters', *Devon Buildings Group Newsletter* 34, 2016

Helen Wilson, www.pinwillwoodcarving.org.uk

Charles Ponting

Anthony Nicholson, 'Charles Edwin Ponting FSA 1849–1932, Architect', BA dissertation, University of Exeter, 2007

E.S. Prior

Lynne Walker, 'E S Prior, 1852–1932', PhD thesis, Birkbeck College, University of London, 1978, available online at EThOS, 285017

George Fellowes Prynne

Ruth Sharville, www.gfp.sharville.org.uk/work.htm

C.H.B. Quennell

Nicholas Collins, 'C H B Quennell - A Legacy Protected?', MSc dissertation, Oxford Brookes University, 2002

Elizabeth McKellar, 'C H B Quennell', *Architectural History* 50, 2007, pp 213–4

The Rathbones

Colin Simpson, 'The Della Robbia Pottery: from Renaissance to Regent Street', *William Morris Society Magazine*, Summer 2016, pp 3–5

W. Beddoe Rees

Capel (Chapels Heritage Society) 9, Autumn 1989, pp 1–3

W. Reynolds-Stephens

Caroline Sherlock, *William Reynolds-Stephens: a life's work* (private, 2002)

C.C. Rolfe

Andrew Saint, 'Three Oxford Architects', *Oxoniensia* vol.XXXV, 1970, pp 53–107

The Ropes

Arthur Rope, *Margaret Rope of Shrewsbury* (Aylsham: Pangapilot Press, 2016)

www.arthur.rope.clara.net
margaretrope.wordpress.com

Fred Rowntree

Peter Robson, *Fred Rowntree, Architect* (Easingwold: Newby Books, 2014)

George Gilbert Scott ('Middle Scott')

Gavin Stamp, *An Architect of Promise: George Gilbert Scott Junior (1839–1897) and the Late Gothic Revival* (Donington: Shaun Tyas, 2002)

Giles Gilbert Scott

David Lewis, 'Modernising tradition: the architectural thought of Giles Gilbert Scott (1880–1960)', DPhil thesis, University of Oxford, 2014, online at ORA

E.H. Sedding

Helen Wilson, 'The Architect Edmund H Sedding and his Devon Churches', *Devonshire Association Report and Transactions*, 148, June 2016, pp 255–92

John Dando Sedding

John Paul Cooper and Henry Wilson, 'The Work of John Sedding, Architect' *Architectural Review*, 1897 III, pp 35–41, 60–77, 125–133, 188–194, 235–237 and IV November 1898 pp 33–34

Paul Snell, "The Priest of Form': John Dando Sedding (1838–91) and the Languages of Late Victorian Architecture', PhD thesis, Manchester University, 2006, available online at EThOS, 497489

Paul Snell, 'John Dando Sedding and Sculpture in Architecture' in Rebecca Daniels and Geoff Brandwood (eds.), *Ruskin and Architecture* (Spire, 2003), pp 320–353

William Seth-Smith

Helena Seth-Smith, www.seth-smith.org.uk

Richard Norman Shaw

Reginald Blomfield, *Richard Norman Shaw R A* (Batsford, 1940)

Andrew Saint, *Richard Norman Shaw* (Yale University Press, 1976; revised edition, 2013)

Charles Spooner

Alec Hamilton, *Charles Spooner, Arts & Crafts Architect* (Donington: Shaun Tyas, 2012)

Leonard Stokes

Rory Spence, 'Leonard Aloysius Scott Stokes (1858–1928)', PhD thesis, Sheffield University, 1970

Jan Ward, *The Leonard Stokes Directory* (private, 2009)

Douglas Strachan

Peter Cormack, *Arts & Crafts Stained Glass* (Yale, 2015) pp 135–146, 296–300

Juliette MacDonald, 'Aspects of Identity in the works of Douglas Strachan', PhD thesis, Universtiy of St. Andrews, 2003

Heywood Sumner

Jane Barbour, 'Heywood Sumner – a Very Private Person', *Hatcher Review*, 1990, vol.3, no 29, pp 438–48

M. Coatts and E. Lewis (eds.), *Heywood Sumner, Artist and Archaeologist 1853–1940* (Winchester City Museum, 1986)

Gleeson White, 'The Work of Heywood Sumner', *Studio International*, vol.13, 61, April 1898, pp 153–163 online at digi.ub.uni-heidelberg.de/diglit/studio1898a

Walter Tapper

John Whitworth, www.sir-walter-tapper-churches.co.uk includes

David Dolan and Leigh O'Brien, 'Life and Work of Sir Walter Tapper' in *Sir Walter Tapper and the Guildford Grammar School Chapel* (n.d., n.p.)

Charles Harrison Townsend

Sarah Sullivan, www.charlesharrisontownsend.org.uk

Phoebe Anna Traquair

Elizabeth Cumming, *Phoebe Anna Traquair 1852–1936* (National Galleries of Scotland, 2005)

Elizabeth Cumming, 'Phoebe Anna Traquair and the decoration of the Mansfield Place church' in Susan Herzmark and Kennedy Wilson (eds.), *Phoebe Anna Traquair* (exhibition catalogue: Edinburgh, Mansfield Traquair Trust, 1993)

(Charles) Trask & Co.
No academic source known

Laurence Turner
Jane Wight, 'England's other Turner', *The Spectator*, 21 August 1976, pp 10–12

Mary Seton Watts
Melanie Unwin, 'Art and Craft in the Career and Marriage of Mary Watts', *Journal of Design History*, vol.17, no.3, 2004, pp 237–50

Philip Webb
Peter Burman, '"A Stern Thinker and Most Able Constructor": Philip Webb, Architect' *Architectural History* 42, 1999, pp 1–23

W.R. Lethaby, *Philip Webb and his Work* (Oxford University Press, 1935)

Sheila Kirk, *Philip Webb* (Chichester: Wiley/Academy, 2005)

William Weir
Anon., 'Mr William Weir and his Work', *SPAB Annual Review*, 1926, pp 20–26

Robert Weir Schultz
Gavin Stamp, *Robert Weir Schultz, Architect, and his work for the Marquesses of Bute* (Curwen Press, 1981)

David Ottewill, 'Robert Weir Schultz (1860–1951): An Arts and Crafts Architect', *Architectural History* 22, 1979, pp 87–115

Randall Wells
Charles Keighley, 'Randall Wells and the Ruskinian Tradition', MA dissertation, Royal Holloway College, 1994, revised 1995

Nikolaus Pevsner and Enid Radcliffe, 'Randall Wells', *Architectural Review* 136, November 1964, pp 366–8

Christopher Whall
Peter Cormack, *Christopher Whall 1849–1924, Arts & Crafts Stained Glass Worker*, exhibition catalogue (William Morris Gallery, 1979)

Peter Cormack, *Aglow with Brave Resplendent Colour: the Stained Glass Work of Christopher Whall 1849–1924* (Boston: Boston Public Library, 1999)

Walter Shaw Sparrow, 'Christopher Whall and his Influence' *Studio* 90, 1925, pp 365–8

Henry Wilson
Cyndy Manton, *Henry Wilson: Practical Idealist* (Cambridge: Lutterworth Press, 2009)

Henry Wilson, 'Art and Religion', *Architectural Review* 6, June–December 1899, pp 276–8

Edgar Wood
John Archer, *Partnership in Style: Edgar Wood & J Henry Sellers* (Manchester City Art Gallery, 1975)

John Archer, *Edgar Wood (1860–1935) a Manchester 'Art Nouveau' Architect* (Lancashire and Cheshire Antiquarian Society, 1996)

David Morris, '"Here, by experiment": Edgar Wood in Middleton', *John Rylands Library Bulletin*, 89, 2012/13, pp 127–69

Jill Seddon, 'The Furniture Design of Edgar Wood (1860–1935)', *Burlington Magazine* 17, 873, December 1975, pp 857–61 manchesterhistory.net/edgarwood/home.html

Thomas Worthington
Anthony Pass, *Thomas Worthington: Victorian Architecture and Social Purpose* (Manchester Literary and Philosophical Publications, 1988)

3. CHURCHES

Consult the entry for the church's architect and/or artists in Section 2 first – that is where you are most likely to find out more about any church. Online, find the HE listing.

Most of the churches in this book celebrated their centenary in recent years – or will do so soon. In many cases, a centenary history has been produced to mark the event. Since these tend only to be available at the church, they are not included in this bibliography. Nor are other church guidebooks – it would simply take too much space to include them.

However, where the church guidebook goes further than a mere account of the building, it is included here.

Parish newsletters are not included, even when – as in rare cases – those from the period survive. If runs of newsletters do survive, they are most likely to be found at county Records Offices or Archives.

NB Primary sources – drawings, correspondence, diaries – are not included. If you want to know more about primary sources for any church, and you have not been able to find where they are, if they exist, via Google, contact me for help: alechamiltonchurches@outlook.com

Where a church is not listed here it means no satisfactory other publication is known to this author (although there may well be primary sources in archives).

Barkerend

Dale Barton, *St Clements: an Arts & Crafts Church* (HLF, 2016)

Barrow Hill

Ann Pickard, *The Parish Church of Saint Andrew Barrow Hill with Hollingwood: the Parker and Unwin church* (ALD Print, 2010)

Bedford Park

Andrew Saint, *Bedford Park, Radical Suburb* (Bedford Park Society, 2016)

Michael Broom, *The Birth of a parish* (St Michael's, 2000)

Blackheath

Olive Maggs, *Anna Lea Merritt's Murals: wall paintings in a Surrey church* (Society for the Arts & Crafts Movement in Surrey, 2011)

Bothenhampton

Architectural Association Notes, November 1896, vol.II, p.120

Brampton

Arthur Penn, *St Martin's Church: the making of a masterpiece* (David Penn, 2008)

Brighton

Nicholas Taylor, 'Byzantium in Brighton', *Architectural Review* 139, April 1966

Anthony Dale, *Brighton Churches* (Routledge, 1989)

Brithdir

Ian Allan (ed.), 'Henry Wilson's Brithdir letters', *Journal of the Merioneth Historical and Record Society,* vol. VIII (1977–80), pp 277–302 and 409–43 (The 71 letters from Wilson to his client, Mrs Louisa Tooth, transcribed with commentary. The originals are at Dolgellau Area Records Office.)

Cyndy Manton, 'Henry Wilson's Welsh Church' in *Design History: Fad or Function?* (Design Council, 1978), pp 79–86.

Brockhampton

Peter Blundell Jones, 'All Saints Brockhampton', *Architects' Journal*, vol.192, 15 August 1990, pp 24–43

E.S. Goodstein, 'Portrait of a 'Modern' Victorian Church: W R Lethaby's All Saints' Church, Brockhampton', *Victorian Institute Journal*, Virginia Commonwealth University, Richmond VA, vol.23, 1995, pp 84–107

Hugo Mason, *All Saints' Church, Brockhampton, Herefordshire* (Brockhampton PCC, 2002, 2011)

Nikolaus Pevsner, 'Lethaby's Last', *Architectural Review* vol.130, 1961, pp 354–7

L[awrence] W[eaver], 'Brockhampton Church, Herefordshire, designed by Professor W R Lethaby', *Country Life,* 15 May 1915, supplement pp 2–3.

Charterhouse-on-Mendip

There is a brief reminiscence, 1981, by Alban Caröe in an information sheet in the church

Cheltenham College Chapel

Nicholas Lowton, *Cheltenham College Chapel* (The Cheltonian Society, 1996)

A.S. Owen, *Cheltenham College Chapel* (Cheltenham: Darter, 1928)

Clayton

Malcolm Greenwood, 'Inspired creator of Romantic dream: Gaetano Meo's Mosaics at Clayton Parish Church', *Andamento* 2, 2008, pp 12–17

Margaret Dalgety, *Clayton Then and Now* (Countryside, 1985)

Colehill

George Sadler, *Village on the Hill: the story of Colehill in Dorset* (Dorset Publishing Company, 1992)

J. Spatchet, 'Some of St Michael's Finer Details' in *St Michael and All Angels Church, Colehill: The Building of the Church* (PCC, n.d. but 2005)

Dorset Rootsweb at southernlife.org.uk

Compton

Mark Bills, *Watts Chapel: a Guide to the Symbols of Mary Watts's Arts and Crafts Masterpiece* (Philip Wilson, 2010).

Louise Boreham, 'Compton Chapel', *The Victorian* 3, March 2000, pp 10–13

Veronica Franklin Gould, *The Watts Chapel* (Watts Gallery, 1994)

Edwin Heathcote, 'Restoration of the Watts Chapel, Compton, Surrey', *Church Building* 48, November–December 1997, pp 24–6

Mrs George Frederick Watts (Mary Seton Watts), *The Word in the Pattern* (Astolat Press, 1904)

Cricklewood

L. Malpas, *Cricklewood Baptist Church: a concise history* (n.d., but 2008)

Crofton Park

Kenneth Richardson, *The twenty-five Churches of the Southwark Diocese: An Inter-war Campaign of Church Building* (Ecclesiological Society, 2002)

Cross Green

Stephen Savage, *The story of St Hilda's, Cross Green, Leeds* (self-published, 2003)

J.S. Willimott, *The Story of St Hilda's, Leeds, 1845–1932* (Private, 1932)

Curbridge

Tim Partridge, *Anglican Churches in Curbridge: a brief history written for the Centenary of the present church in 2006* (self-published, 2006)

C. Smith, *Two Men's Ministries: based on the diary of two Victorian Rectors of Witney* (Witney: Trustees of St Mary's Preservation Appeal, 1983)

Dodford

Diana Poole, *The Last Chartist Land Settlement: Great Dodford 1849* (Dodford Society, amended edition 2003), p.17

Dolanog

www.living-stones.info/downloads/guides/13_Ann_Griffiths_web.pdf

Ealing (St Peter's)

R. Hayes, *New & Old: A History of St Peter's Mount Park Road, Ealing* (St Peter's, 1985)

Ealing Common (Spencer Perceval)

Kenneth Bryant, *The Spencer Perceval Memorial Church* (self-published, 2005)

Fairhaven

Clyde Binfield, 'The White Church, Fairhaven: an Artist Trader's Protestant Byzantium', *Transactions of the Historic Society of Lancashire and Cheshire* vol.142, 1992, pp 155–77

Forfar

A.B. Whyte, *In the beginning: the Lowson Memorial Parish Church, Forfar* (Forfar and District Historical Society, 2004)

Galston

Rosemary Hannah, 'St Sophia's Church, Galston: 'The Vast Space of the Interior'', *Architectural History*, vol.46, 2003, pp 255–268

Glandford

Jenefer James and Peter Stone, *Sir Alfred Jodrell, Philanthropist* (Fakenham: Larks Press, 1996 and 2011)

Gloucester Cathedral

David Welander, *The Stained Glass of Gloucester Cathedral* (Gloucester Cathedral, 1985)

Gorleston

Anon., *The Catholic Church of St Peter the Apostle, Gorleston-on-Sea: a brief history of the parish and church 1888–2007* (n.p., n.d., but 2008)

Great Warley

John Malton, 'Art Nouveaux in Essex' (1973) in J. Richards, N. Pevsner and D. Sharp (eds.), *The Anti-Rationalists and Rationalists* (London: Architectural Press, 2000), pp 159–69

Wendy Hitchmough, 'Studies in the symbolism and spirituality of the Arts and Crafts Movement', PhD thesis, University of Sussex, 2001

H.R. Wilkins and A.W. Wellings, *The Church of St Mary the Virgin, Great Warley, Essex: History and Guide* (self-published, 1976)

Gretna

Gordon Routledge, *Gretna's Secret War* (Bookcase, 1999)

Harehills

Janet Douglas, 'Patronage and Politics in a Leeds Parish – the story of the Brangwyn Mosaics in St Aidan's Church, Harehills', *Journal of the Tiles & Architectural Ceramics Society* 6, 1996, pp 23–8

Haslemere

Catherine Eyre, peasant-arts.blogspot.com

Alec Hamilton, 'The Lure of 'The Arts & Crafts church': a prodigious priest and his saintly architect at St Christopher's, Haslemere, Surrey (1900–1903)', *Ecclesiology Today*, 46, July 2012, pp 3–22.

Luther Hooper, 'Art of To-day. Fine and Otherwise: Art in the Church', *Art Journal* (London),February 1911, pp 47–52 and March 1911, pp 83–87

W.A. Sillick, Collection of newspaper cuttings in several albums at Haslemere Educational Museum

W.R. Trotter, *The Hilltop Writers: a Victorian Colony among the Surrey Hills* (Book Guild, 1996)

Hatch End

Pamela Davies, *The Parish Church of St Anselm, Hatch End* (G & P Davies, 1998)

Hoarwithy

Philip Anderson, *The Beautification of Hoarwithy church* (Pink Publication no.13, Ross on Wye & District Civic Society, 2002)

Anon (almost certainly Philip Anderson), 'Prebendary Poole – a Victorian Benefactor and Eccentric', *Ross on Wye and District Civic Society newsletter*, Spring 2001, no 76

Madeline Hopton, *Records of Hentland Parish, Herefordshire, AD 500–1915.* Typescript transcription in the possession of Philip Anderson. Whereabouts of the original is not known

Hutton

N. Bitton, *A Tribute to Arthur Burns: a Good Life* (Malvern: Priory Press, n.d. but probably 1945 or 1946)

Ilkley

Kathleen Pinder, *Ben Rhydding Methodist Church 1909–2009* (Ben Rhydding: BRMC, 2009)

Inkpen

Anon. (but Richard Griffiths) w-woodhay-and-kintbury-benefices.org.uk/html/1409__history_of_inkpen_church.html (1999)

E.A. Martin, *Inkpen Yesterday* (St Columb, Cornwall: Edyvean Printers, 1993)

F.J. Driscoll, *Inkpen and its Church* (private, 1945)

Ipswich

J. Burrows, *St Bartholomew, Ipswich: One Hundred Years 1895–1995* (self-published, 1995)

Jesmond

D.F. McGuire, *Charles Mitchell 1820–1895, Victorian Shipbuilder* (Newcastle City Libraries, 1988)

Neil Moat, "A Theatre for the Soul': St. George's Church, Jesmond: the Building and cultural reception of a Late-Victorian church', PhD thesis, Newcastle University, 2011

Michael Johnson, 'Architectural taste and patronage in Newcastle upon Tyne, 1870–1914', PhD thesis, Northumbria University, 2009

Kempley

Anon. (but probably Randall Wells), 'New Church, Kempley', *Architectural Review* 16, July–Dec 1904, pp 181–5

Lawrence Weaver, 'Kempley New Church, Gloucestershire, designed by Mr Randall Wells', *Country Life,* 19 August 1916, supplement pp 2–3

Randall Wells, 'Kempley Church', *British Architect,* 5 March 1909, pp 165–6

Landport

Roger Bryant, *Don't touch the holy Joe: Father Dolling's battle for Landport and St Agatha's church* (Hampshire: Ragged Right, 1995)

Robert Dolling, *Ten years in a Portsmouth slum* (London: Brown Langham, 1903)

Charles Osborne, *The Life of Father Dolling* (London: Edward Arnold, 1903)

Leeds

David Chappell, 'The Cathedral of St Anne, Leeds', *Yorkshire Architect* 45, Nov/Dec 1975, pp 26–7

Robert Finnigan, *The Cathedral Church of St Anne, Leeds* (The Universe, 1988)

Leek

Michael Fisher, *All Saints Church Leek: History and Guide* (Landmark, 2008)

Llandeloy

Phil Thomas, 'Invention, tradition and a sense of place – John Coates Carter and the church of St Eloi, Llandeloy', *Ancient Monuments Society Transactions*, vol.45, 2001, pp 29–44

Lower Kingswood

Martin Brandon, 'The Lost Jewel in the Arts & Crafts Crown: The Church of the Wisdom of God', BA dissertation, Southampton Institute, 2001

James O'Connor, *A History of the Church of the Wisdom of God, Lower Kingswood* ('limited edition', 2001)

Mary Greensted, 'The Arts and Crafts Movement: exchanges between Greece and Britain (1876–1930)', MPhil thesis, University of Birmingham, 2010

Low Marple

Mark Whittaker, www.marple-uk.com/stmartins.htm

Madresfield Court

Clive Aslet, 'Madresfield Court', *Country Life,* 1980, pp 1461–1553

John de la Cour, *Madresfield Court* (n.d.) at www.elmley.org.uk/pdf/guidebook.pdf

Jane Mulvagh, *Madresfield: The Real Brideshead* (Random House, 2009)

Matlock Dale

Anon., 'Private Chapel, Matlock, Derbyshire', *The Builder,* 29 October 1898, p.386

Julie Bunting, 'A Hidden Gem (St John the Baptist's Chapel, Matlock)', *Peak Advertiser,* June 1994

Melsetter

Trevor Garnham, 'William Lethaby's Chapel of SS Colm and Margaret', *Church Building*, May-June 2000, pp 61–65

Midhurst

Anon., 'The King's Sanatorium and its Chapel', *The Studio*, January 1907

H. Percy Adams, 'The King Edward VII Sanatorium, Midhurst, Sussex', *Architectural Review*, June 1906, pp 277–312

North Cerney

Alec Hamilton, 'Re-constructing the pre-Reformation church: Will Croome and F C Eden's antiquarian ecclesiology at North Cerney, Gloucestershire', *Ecclesiology Today* 55 & 56, 2017, pp 123–48

Jonathan MacKechnie Jarvis, 'W I Croome', *Cirencester Miscellany* 3, (Cirencester Archaeological and Historical Society, 1996), pp 13–31

Will Croome, Photographic log book, showing the 'repair, discovery and decoration of the fabric' of the church, 1900–1952. Gloucestershire Archives, P70 CW 3/48

Will Croome, *Notes on William Smith, carver, and his work in the church, and details of other craftsmen concerned with the church 1900–1950.* Gloucestershire Archives, P70 CW 3/12

James Turner, *History of North Cerney and its church* (n.d., ca 1981): Gloucestershire Archives, P70 IN 4/17

Overstrand

Monica Sykes, *Overstrand Methodist Church Centenary 1898–1998* (n.p., 1998)

Oxford

Elain Harwood and Otto Saumarez Smith (eds.), *Oxford and Cambridge* (Twentieth Century Society, 2013), pp 53–65

Alan Middleton, *A Pre-Raphaelite Jewel: the Chapel of Harris Manchester College, Oxford* (Harris Manchester, 2006)

Geoffrey Tyack, 'Baker and Lutyens in Oxford: The Building of Rhodes House and Campion Hall, *Oxoniensia,* LXII, 1997, pp 287–308

Geoffrey Tyack, *Oxford: An Architectural Guide* (Oxford University Press, 1998)

Pamphill

Geoffrey Brown, *To Partake of Tea: The Last Ladies of Kingston Lacy* (Salisbury: Hobnob Press, 2006)

Joanna and Simon Heptinstall, *Kingston Lacy* (National Trust, 2012)

D. McGillivray, 'Distant Voices, Gay Lives 4: William Bankes, Country House Rescue', *QX Magazine*, 30 March 2011

A. Sebba, *The Exiled Collector: William Bankes and the Making of an English Country House* (Dovecote Press, 2004)

Pamela Watkin, *A Kingston Lacy Childhood: Reminiscences of Viola Bankes* (Dovecote Press, 1986)

Philbeach Gardens

Donald Findlay, 'All Glorious Within: an appreciation of St Cuthbert's Philbeach Gardens', *Annual of the Victorian Society*, 1991

Pixham

Patricia Bennett, *The Living Stream: Pixham and its People* (Dorking Local History Group, 1994)

Mary Mayo, *Pixham 1862–1912* (Chiswick Press, 1912)

Lynn Parnell, 'Pixham Church' in Alexandra Wedgwood (ed.), *A History of St Martin's Dorking* (Dorking: Friends of St Martin's, 1990)

Port Seton

Anon., *Chalmers Memorial Church Port Seton: Brief History and Key to interior decoration and symbolism* booklet (self-published, 1993)

J.R. Hume, 'A Fisherman's Church', *Life and Work*, November 2011, p.35

Queen's Cross

www.mackintosh-architecture.gla.ac.uk/catalogue/pdf/M125.pdf

Richards Castle

Andrew Saint, 'Norman's Shaw's letters: A Selection', *Architectural History*, vol.18, 1975, pp 60–85

Rosemary Harral, *All Saints Church Richards Castle, The First Hundred Years: 1892–1992* (Richards Castle Local History Group, 1992)

Roker

Trevor Garnham, *Arts and Crafts Masterpieces … St. Andrew's Church, Roker* (Phaidon, 1999)

Michael A. Johnson, 'Cathedral of the Arts and Crafts Movement: St Andrew's Church, Roker,' BA dissertation, Northumbria University, 2002

Dennis Marsh, *Description and Notes Concerning the Church of St Andrew, Roker* (1914)

Settlements

Nigel Scotland, *Squires in the Slums: Settlements and Missions in Late Victorian England* (I.B. Tauris, 2007)

Shaldon

See E.H. Sedding

Shefford Woodlands

Notes of the 82nd General Meeting (July–August 1935), *The Wiltshire Archaeological & Natural History Magazine* , vol.XLVII, nos.162–6, June 1935–June 1937, p.319

Silver End

Anon., *Welcome to St Mary and All Saints the Parish Church of Rivenhall and to St Francis Church in the Garden Village of Silver End* (Rivenhall PCC, n.d. but after 2005)

Slindon

Jane Benton, *St Chad's, Slindon: the first fifty years* (Slindon: St Chad's, 1993)

Sloane Street

Peyton Skipwith, *Holy Trinity Sloane Street* (Trinity Arts & Crafts Guild, 2002)

Small Heath

G.L. Loasby, *The Story of St Aidan's Mission, Small Heath* (St Aidan's Church Council, 1921)

Stonebroom

Sally Mason, *A brief history of St Peter's Church* (1995), 'Parish Project' ring-binder in her possession

Alan Randle, *Stonebroom: St Peters' Church and the Village: a Hundred Years 1900–2000* (Alan Randle, 2000)

Tavistock Square

J. Sutherland, *Mrs Humphry Ward: Eminent Victorian, Pre-eminent Edwardian* (Oxford University Press, 1990)

Ullet Road

Anne Holt, *Walking Together: a study in Liverpool Nonconformity 1688–1938* (George Allen and Unwin, 1938)

L. de B. K[lein], *Ullet Road Church, Sefton Park, Liverpool: Mr Gerald Moira's Paintings in the Vestry and Library*, Liverpool Archives: 288 ULL 7/12/25(i)

Len Mooney, *A Guide to Ullet Road Unitarian Church* (Liverpool, 1996)

Wallasey

Jacqueline Bailey, 'In what way was the Memorial church, Manor Road, Liscard, of 1899 influenced by the Arts & Crafts Movement?', Open University Course A305 project, 1982

Watford

R. Bennett and J.E. Wright, *Church of The Holy Rood, Watford: A History and Description of the Church* (self-published, 1989)

Westminster Cathedral

John Browne and Timothy Dean, *Westminster Cathedral: Building of Faith* (Booth-Clibborn, 1995)

Peter Doyle, *Westminster Cathedral, 1895–1995* (Geoffrey Chapman, 1995)

W. Curtis Green, 'Recent Decoration at the Roman Catholic Cathedral Westminster', *Architectural Review,* July 1916, pp 7–12

Rene Kollar, *Westminster Cathedral: from dream to reality* (Edinburgh: Faith & Life, 1987)

Patrick Rogers, *Westminster Cathedral: from Darkness to Light* (Burns & Oates, 2003)

West Woodhay

M.H. McClintock, *The Queen Thanks Sir Howard: the Life of Major-General Sir Howard Elphinstone, VC, KCB, CMG, by his daughter* (John Murray, 1945) and *Portrait of a House: A Period Piece* (Carroll and Nicholson, 1948)

Wreay

Stephen Matthews, *Sarah Losh and Wreay Church* (Bookcase, 2007)

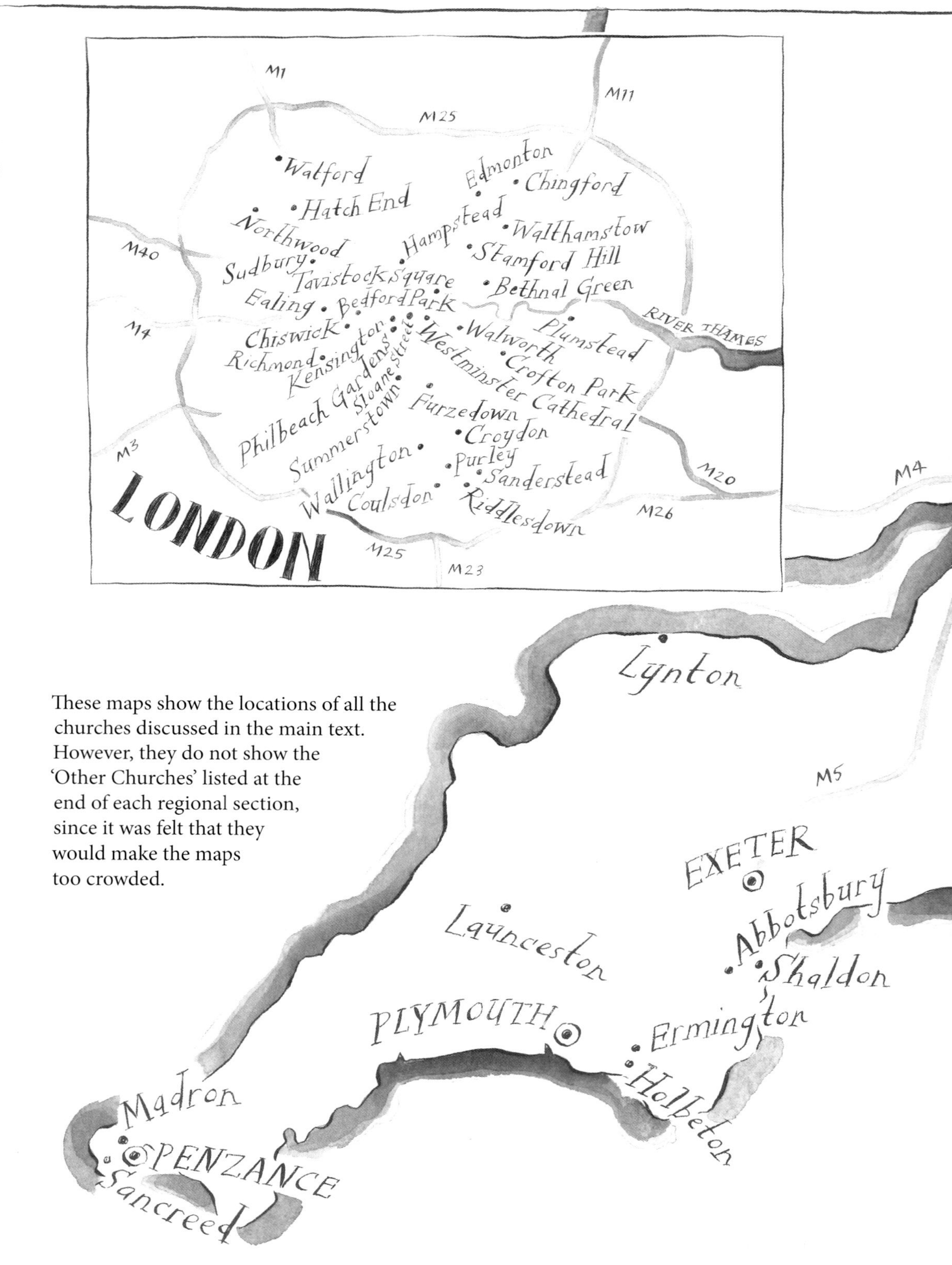

These maps show the locations of all the churches discussed in the main text. However, they do not show the 'Other Churches' listed at the end of each regional section, since it was felt that they would make the maps too crowded.

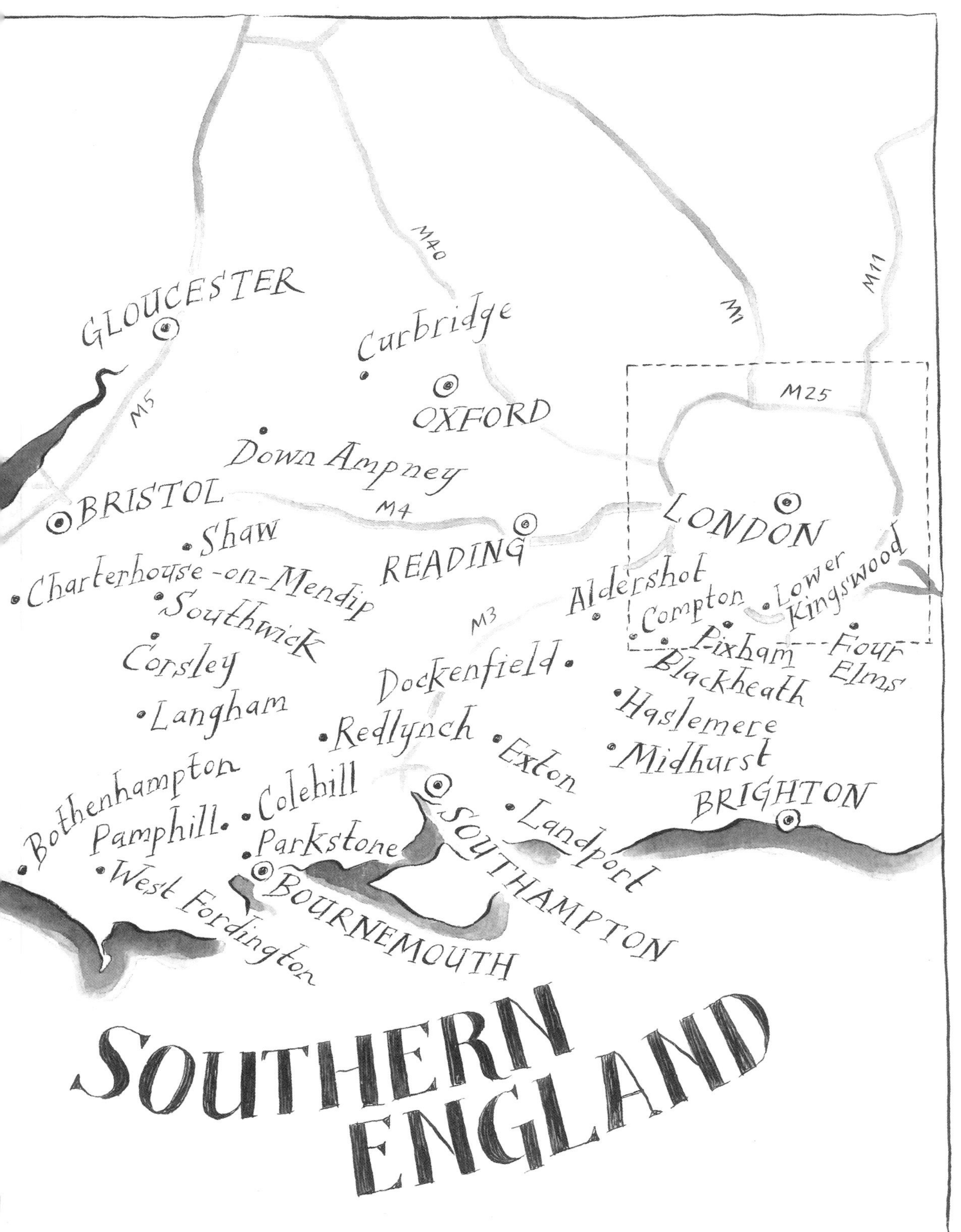
GLOUCESTER
M5
BRISTOL
M40
Curbridge
OXFORD
Down Ampney
M4
READING
M1
M11
M25
LONDON
Shaw
Charterhouse-on-Mendip
Southwick
Corsley
Langham
Bothenhampton
Pamphill
Colehill
Parkstone
West Fordington
BOURNEMOUTH
M3
Dockenfield
Redlynch
Exton
SOUTHAMPTON
Landport
Aldershot
Compton
Lower Kingswood
Pixham
Blackheath
Four Elms
Haslemere
Midhurst
BRIGHTON
SOUTHERN ENGLAND

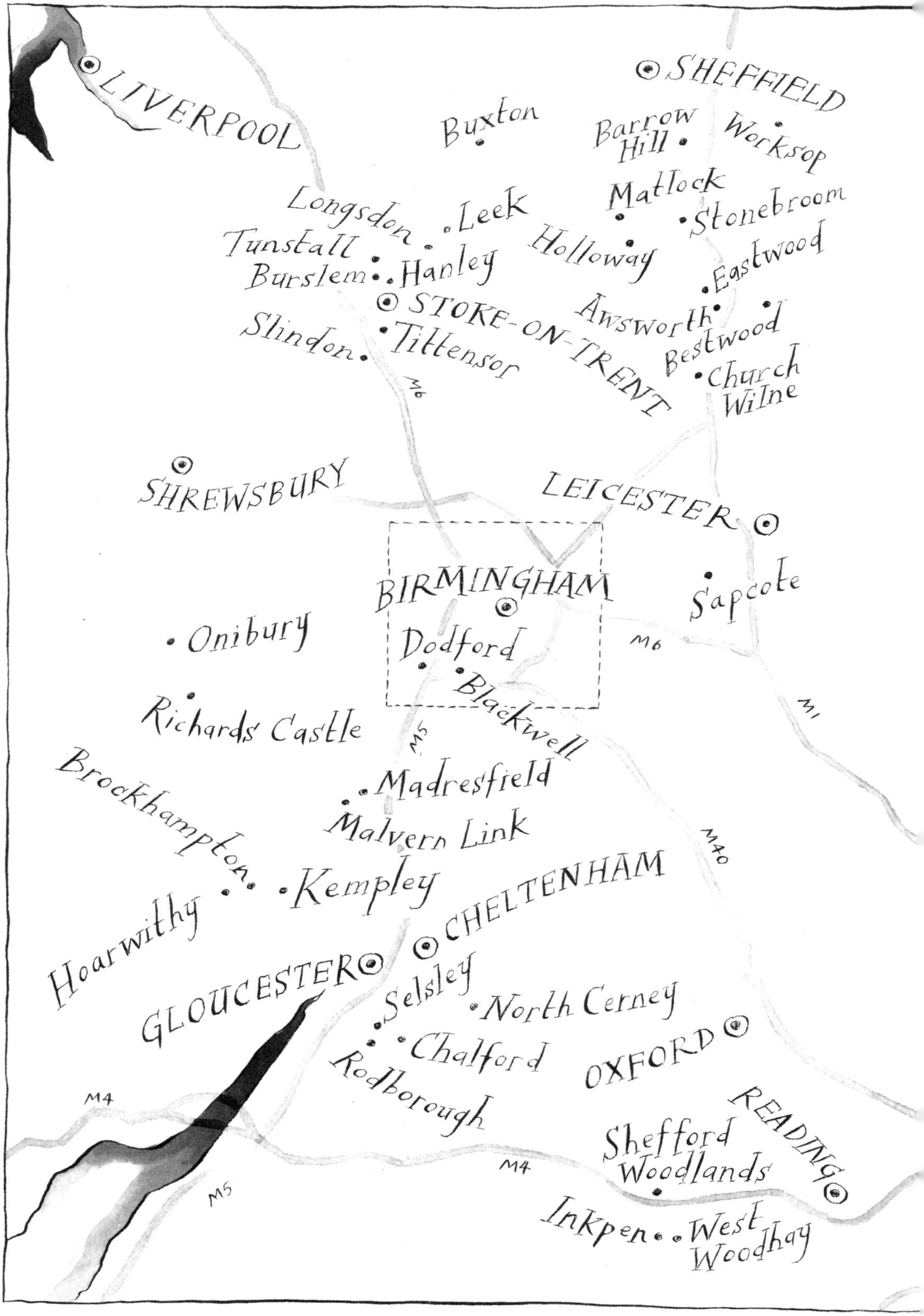

LIVERPOOL
SHEFFIELD
Buxton
Barrow Hill
Worksop
Longsdon
Leek
Matlock
Stonebroom
Tunstall
Holloway
Burslem
Hanley
Eastwood
STOKE-ON-TRENT
Awsworth
Bestwood
Slindon
Tittensor
Church Wilne
M6
SHREWSBURY
LEICESTER
BIRMINGHAM
Sapcote
Onibury
Dodford
M6
Blackwell
M1
Richards' Castle
M5
Brockhampton
Madresfield
Malvern Link
M40
Hoarwithy
Kempley
CHELTENHAM
GLOUCESTER
Selsley
North Cerney
Chalford
OXFORD
Rodborough
M4
READING
Shefford Woodlands
M4
M5
Inkpen
West Woodhay

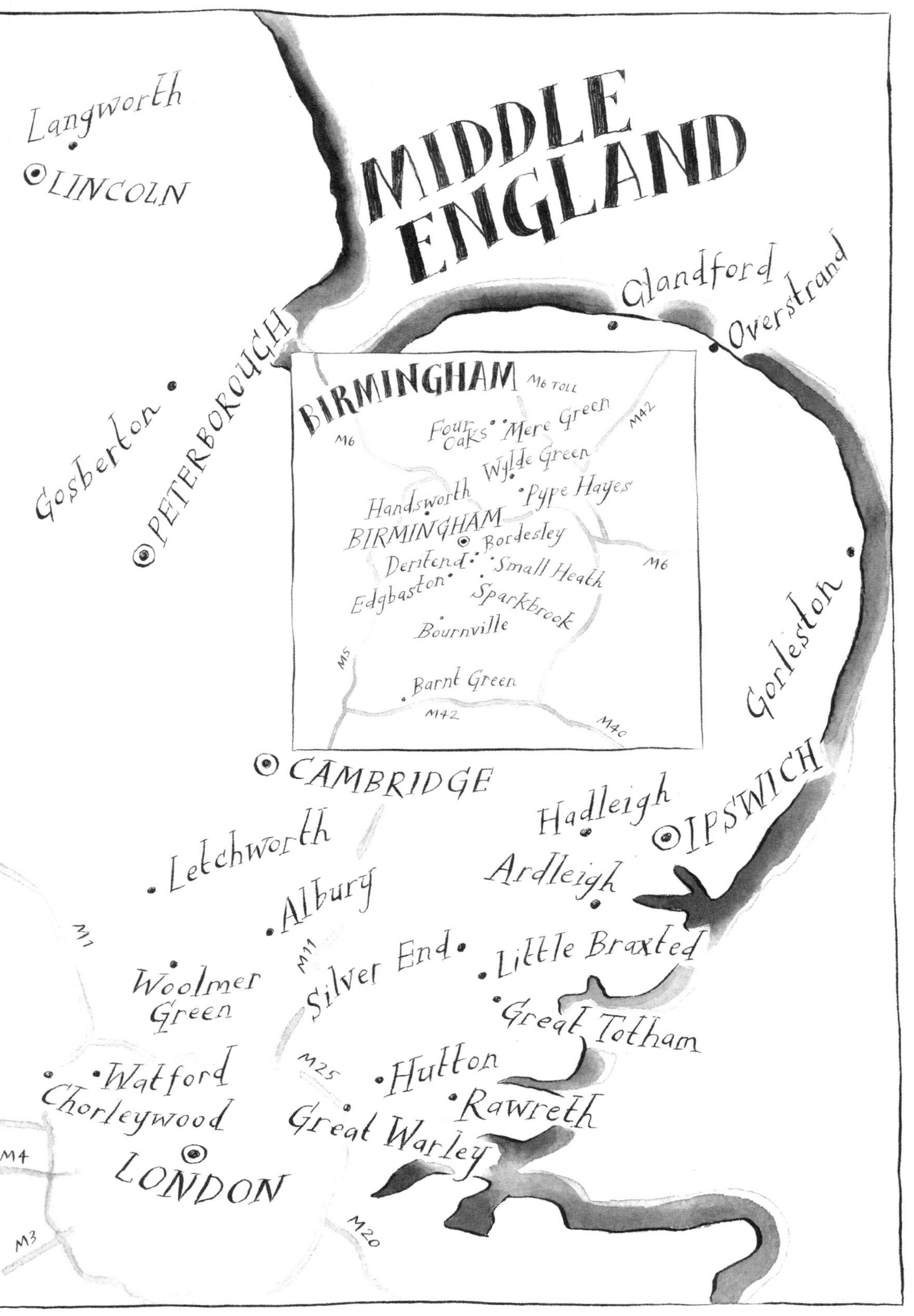
MIDDLE ENGLAND
Langworth
LINCOLN
Glandford
Overstrand
Gosberton
PETERBOROUGH
BIRMINGHAM
M6 TOLL
Four Oaks
Mere Green
M42
M6
Wylde Green
Handsworth
Pype Hayes
BIRMINGHAM
Bordesley
Deritend
Small Heath
M6
Edgbaston
Sparkbrook
Bournville
M5
Barnt Green
M42
M40
Gorleston
CAMBRIDGE
IPSWICH
Hadleigh
Letchworth
Ardleigh
Albury
M1
M11
Silver End
Little Braxted
Woolmer Green
Great Totham
M25
Watford
Hutton
Chorleywood
Rawreth
Great Warley
M4
LONDON
M3
M20

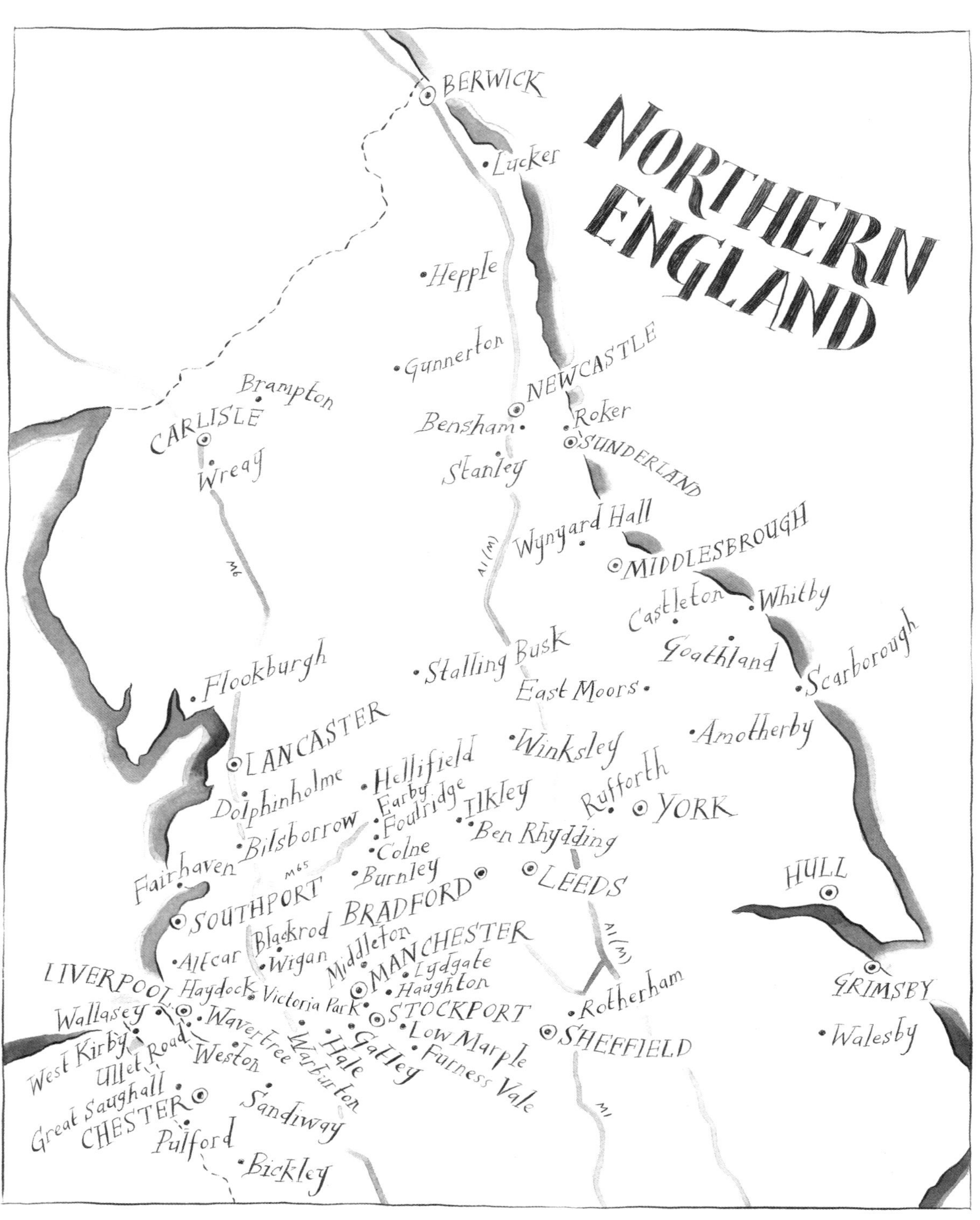
NORTHERN ENGLAND
BERWICK
Lucker
Hepple
Gunnerton
NEWCASTLE
Brampton
CARLISLE
Wreay
Bensham
Roker
SUNDERLAND
Stanley
Wynyard Hall
MIDDLESBROUGH
A1(M)
M6
Castleton
Whitby
Goathland
Flookburgh
Stalling Busk
East Moors
Scarborough
LANCASTER
Winksley
Amotherby
Dolphinholme
Hellifield
Earby
Foulridge
Ilkley
Rufforth
YORK
Bilsborrow
Ben Rhydding
Colne
M65
Fairhaven
Burnley
BRADFORD
LEEDS
HULL
SOUTHPORT
Blackrod
Altcar
Wigan
Middleton
MANCHESTER
Lydgate
Haughton
LIVERPOOL
Haydock
Victoria Park
STOCKPORT
Rotherham
GRIMSBY
Wallasey
Wavertree
Low Marple
SHEFFIELD
Walesby
West Kirby
Ullet Road
Weston
Warburton
Hale
Gatley
Furness Vale
Great Saughall
CHESTER
Sandiway
M1
Pulford
Bickley

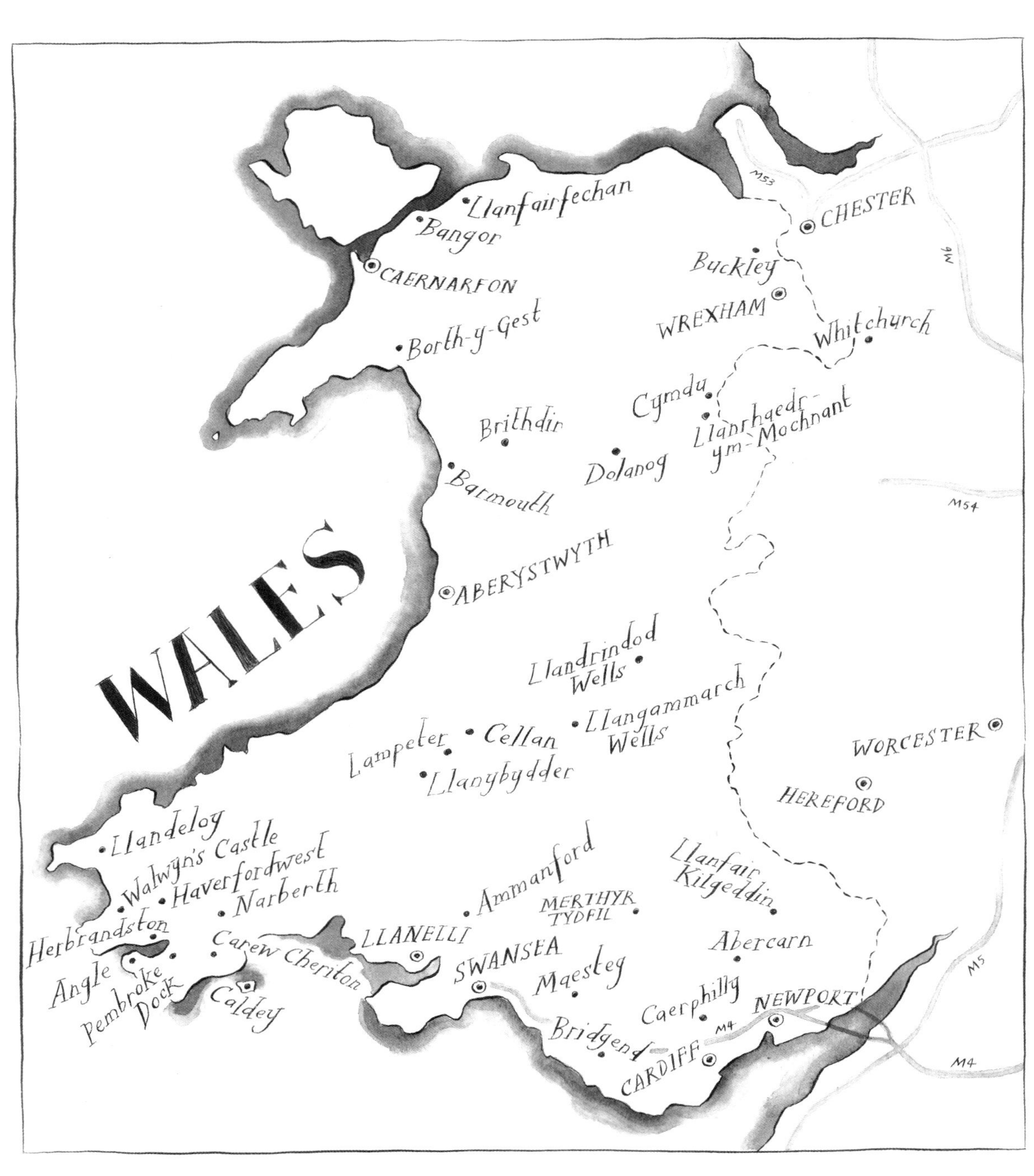
WALES
Llanfairfechan
Bangor
CAERNARFON
Borth-y-Gest
CHESTER
Buckley
WREXHAM
Whitchurch
Cymdu
Llanrhaedr-ym-Mochnant
Brithdir
Dolanog
Barmouth
ABERYSTWYTH
Llandrindod Wells
Llangammarch Wells
Lampeter
Cellan
Llanybydder
WORCESTER
HEREFORD
Llandeloy
Walwyn's Castle
Haverfordwest
Narberth
Herbrandston
Angle
Pembroke Dock
Carew Cheriton
Caldey
Ammanford
LLANELLI
SWANSEA
MERTHYR TYDFIL
Llanfair Kilgeddin
Abercarn
Maesteg
Caerphilly
NEWPORT
Bridgend
CARDIFF
M53
M6
M54
M5
M4

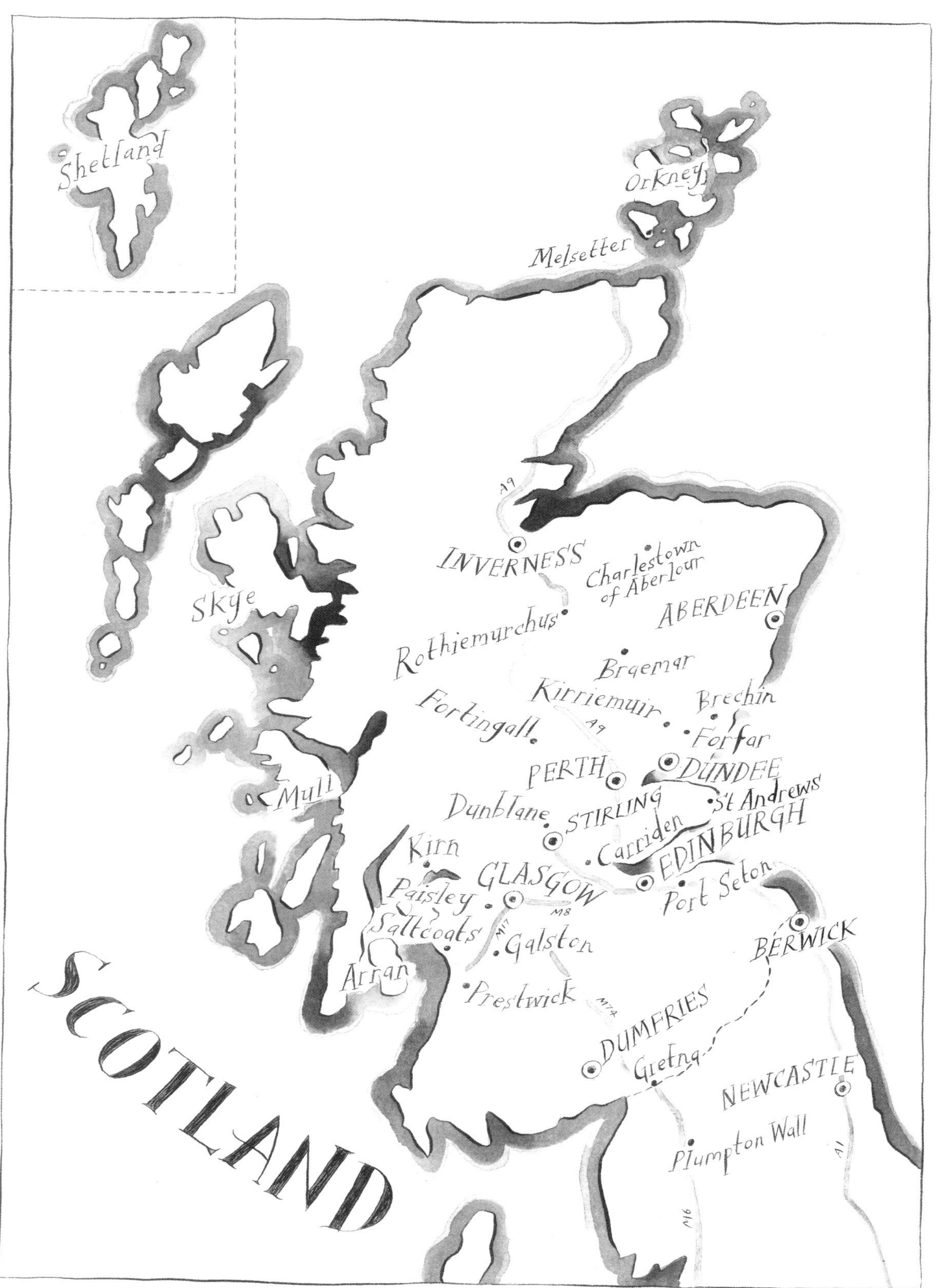
Shetland
Orkney
Melsetter
INVERNESS
Charlestown of Aberlour
Skye
ABERDEEN
Rothiemurchus
Braemar
Kirriemuir
Brechin
Fortingall
Forfar
PERTH
DUNDEE
Mull
Dunblane
STIRLING
St Andrews
Carriden
EDINBURGH
Kirn
GLASGOW
Paisley
Port Seton
Saltcoats
Galston
BERWICK
Arran
Prestwick
SCOTLAND
DUMFRIES
Gretna
NEWCASTLE
Plumpton Wall

INDEX

Some terms are too ubiquitous to index – ACES, AWG, God, Gothic Revival. Also not indexed: 'Other Churches', the Endnotes, 'Demolished or Threatened Churches' and 'Further Reading'. Page numbers in **bold** indicate fullest entries.